Praise for Charlene Spretnak's new framing of comparative religion:

"Charlene Spretnak has fashioned a web of meaning. . . . Her interdisciplinary approach makes manifest the subversive nature of the core teaching of the wisdom traditions and the power of even the simplest spiritual practice. She has created a unitive network of intelligence designed to flare across our political darkness, illuminating both the wreckage and new possibilities for communion and resistance to further ecological and cultural destruction. . . . I treasure this work; it is potent alchemy."

—*Whole Earth Review*

"Charlene Spretnak's *States of Grace* is a passionate, convincing, important, and responsible work. . . . On every page, Spretnak writes with clarity and prophetic energy."

—*National Catholic Reporter*

"This extraordinary book—insightful, comprehensive, and incisive—goes a long way toward restoring harmony and balance to the intellectual arena of the American scene. Few works evince the clarity, sanity, and boldness of Spretnak's *States of Grace*. It is a profoundly revolutionary volume, useful to feminists, Green people, literati, and philosophers. Brava!, Ms. Spretnak."

—Paula Gunn Allen, author of *The Sacred Hoop*

"An extraordinary job. . . . *States of Grace* is a rare and valuable contribution to the fields of religious studies, spirituality, and social criticism. . . . This rich and complex book will make its mark over time and emerge as a powerful beacon beyond 'the deconstructive-postmodern wake.'"

—*Teilhard Perspective*

"Poise amid the pathos of our times: that is how I would describe Charlene Spretnak's critique of contemporary thought and her vast, healing compassion and guidance for our turbulent and immensely destructive world. Her work reflects one of the finest and most perceptive minds of our times. *States of Grace* is a truly wonderful book for understanding ourselves, the times in which we live, and the deeper mysteries of existence. A spiritual classic."

—Thomas Berry, author of *The Dream of the Earth*

"*States of Grace* is an important and timely effort to bring spiritual and ecological awareness to mainstream intellectual thinking. . . . Spretnak has succeeded in making postmodernism understandable. But more importantly, she challenges the common postmodern assumptions that spirituality has nothing to do with pragmatic concerns and has no place in 'advanced' thinking. . . . *States of Grace* contains a wealth of fresh insights aimed towards healing the pathos of the modern industrial era. It is a bold and incisive work that deserves attention."

—*Turning Wheel,* national journal of the Buddhist Peace Fellowship

"A tour de force! Spretnak's genius lies in the depth of her insights connecting the spiritual traditions to political realities. I do not know of anything like *States of Grace* in its presentation of the wisdom traditions from the inside and its rescuing of wisdom for practical, political, economic, and psychological concerns. This book opened up the world of grace for me."

—Brian Swimme, coauthor of *The Universe Story*

"A sensitive—and political—exploration of the Abrahamic religions (Judaism, Christianity, Islam), Buddhism, Native American spirituality, and Goddess spirituality, and an analysis of their influences on community and social justice."

—*Ms.* Magazine

"In reading *States of Grace,* I feel gratitude for the intellectual sophistication steeped in feminist, spiritual, and political practices; for a sure-footed vision that liberates one at once from the monocentricities of modernism and the aimless decentering of mere deconstruction; and for the narrative generosity and careful clarity of this many-graced teacher."

—Catherine Keller, author of *From A Broken Web*

"*States of Grace* opens the great tree of the world's religions to the self-reflective act of cosmology. Like the manuals of meditation found in the various religious traditions, *States of Grace* orients the contemporary reader to an interior path that is simultaneously the other, namely, the cosmological revelation of the natural world."

—John A. Grim, author of *The Shaman*

States of Grace

Other books by Charlene Spretnak

Lost Goddesses of Early Greece: A Collection of Pre-Hellenic Myths

The Politics of Women's Spirituality: Essays on the Rise of Spiritual Power within the Feminist Movement (Editor)

Green Politics: The Global Promise
(with Fritjof Capra)

The Spiritual Dimension of Green Politics

States of Grace

The Recovery of Meaning in the Postmodern Age

Charlene Spretnak

HarperSanFrancisco
A Division of HarperCollins*Publishers*

 For information address HarperCollins Publishers, 10 East 53rd Street, New York, NY 10022.

FIRST HARPERCOLLINS PAPERBACK EDITION PUBLISHED IN 1993

ISBN 0-06-250697-8

An Earlier Edition of This Book Was Cataloged as Follows:

Spretnak, Charlene.
STATES OF GRACE : *the recovery of meaning in the postmodern age* / Charlene Spretnak.—1st ed.
p. cm.
Includes bibliographical references and index.
ISBN 0-06-250824-5 (alk. paper)
1. Spirituality. 2. Postmodernism—Religious aspects. I. Title.
BL624.S696 1991
291.4—dc20 90-55076
CIP

93 94 95 96 CWI 10 9 8 7 6 5 4 3

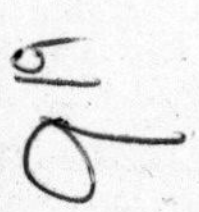

for my mother, Donna Rose,

and

for my husband, Daniel,

great blessings in my life

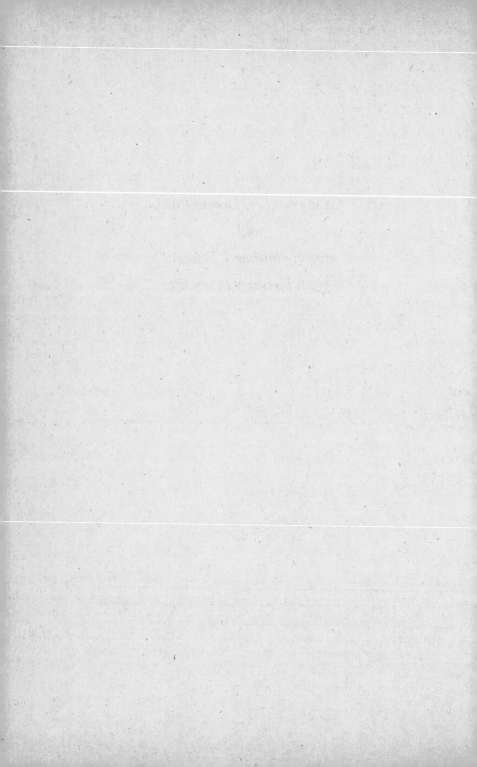

Contents

Introduction 1

Chapter 1 • Saving Grace 10

On the relevance of the wisdom traditions to our times

Our haunted challenge • The promises of modernity • Responses from deconstructive postmodernism • The cosmological context • Ecological postmodernism • The centrality of process/practice in the wisdom traditions • The experience of grace • Beyond the deconstructive-postmodern wake

Chapter 2 • The Center Holds 33

On the nature of mind:
The wisdom of the Buddha's teachings about Dhamma

What is the nature of mind? Whence come fear, delusion, greed, and hatred? • The wisdom of Dhamma • Dhamma in daily life • Grace embodied: Asoka and others • Gandhi and the imperative of nonviolence • Our violent culture • What is required of us?

Chapter 3 • Participation in the Mystery 79

On an intimate relationship with nature:
The wisdom of Native American spirituality

The unfolding dynamics of the universe • What is our responsibility? • Our spiritual relationship to the cosmos • Seeking "green and juicy" spiritual practice • Grace embodied: Native American spiritual teachings • Ecocommunion and the forces of modernity • The ecological imperative • Knowing Gaia, knowing grace

Introduction

I occasionally make a library run up to the university town where I lived for fourteen years. There the stop signs frequently were amended to reflect various political concerns: STOP THE MX. STOP REAGAN. STOP THE CONTRAS. STOP BUSH. STOP ARENA. A couple of years ago I noticed that some of the stop signs read STOP GREED. Greed? The graffiti-oriented wing of the local politicos was now concerned with one of the "seven deadly sins"? They were focusing on a particular state of mind as the villain? That represented quite a shift, for that group of activists generally insisted that socioeconomic, "material" conditions determine consciousness, not the other way around. They previously seemed to think that exploitative economic systems, for instance, had arisen on this planet strictly because of material scarcity or the impact of new technologies, rather than having evolved to serve socially acceptable levels of greed, ill will, and indifference.

In coming to recognize the central role played by qualities of mind in creating, maintaining, *and* altering or abolishing human systems, the stop-sign painters had joined in a grassroots questioning of our assumptions, motivations, and ways of thinking that characterizes the close of the twentieth century. The notions that industrialized societies somehow live on top of nature, rather than embedded within its finely balanced complexities, and that humans have no inherent connectedness with one another are being rejected as ignorant fabrications, which have led to heinous deeds. Turning away from such constricted consciousness has led many people to areas of exploration that are called spiritual.

The contemporary spiritual awakening assumes many shapes: the return of Central and Eastern Europeans, including numerous Soviet citizens, to Christian churches; the return of "assimilated" native peoples to their ancient religions; the spiritual revitalization in Latin America located in the base communities; the sincere piety in fundamentalism and the fanatical political uses of it; the reclaiming of long-lost earth-based spirituality such as that of Mother Earth and other manifestations of the Goddess; the spread of Dhamma from Buddhist countries to the West; the renewal movement within Judaism; the growing interest in Native American spirituality; and, perhaps most widespread, the unnamed personal searching for spiritual grounding in modern cultures, which have quite deliberately denied the importance, if not the very existence, of such concerns. Even some of the most aggressive "Enlightenment fundamentalists," to use Robert Bellah's phrase, have acknowledged in recent years that there might indeed be a spiritual dimension to life. Feeling that mainstream religions devote insufficient attention to an individual's spiritual growth, many people have turned to "New Age spirituality" workshops offering simplified adaptations of ancient traditions or recently invented practices of a therapeutic bent. Often participation in such workshops is a first step toward maintaining a spiritual practice in a more authentic tradition.

Because modern Western culture has enthroned science (or, rather, an arrogant notion of that mode of inquiry) and the "scientific" skepticism toward anything that cannot be quantified, religion has been pushed to the cultural periphery in Eurocentric societies, except for occasional exploitation by politicians. The sense of the sacred—our human perception of the larger reality, ultimate mystery, or creativity in the universe—has become so diminished that we lack the richly nuanced spiritual vocabulary of language and visual arts that is the birthright of everyone born into a traditional native culture, for instance. To make matters worse, the widely acknowledged "dumbing down" trend in American textbooks and education during the past twenty years seems to have spread to religious literacy as well. During a recent visit with a professor of British literature at my alma mater, a Jesuit university, he lamented the fact that many students today have difficulty grasping the thematic structure of Victorian novels because they are nearly ignorant of basic concepts of Christianity. He has to explain metaphors of the fall, grace, redemption, and so forth before he can teach the classic literature! Asked what being a Christian means, his students reply only that it means "to be kind" and "to love people."

Even among people who have a rudimentary knowledge of the major religious traditions in our country, or at least the one in which they were born, spiritual concerns are experienced as increasingly incongruous with the dynamics of a relentlessly orchestrated consumer society in which "you are what you buy." Perhaps "you are what you experience," in which case our ontological range of possibilities may continue to shrink as marketing manipulation increases and our authentic sense of relatedness to other beings decreases. Clearly, modern society is out of touch with the insights of the great wisdom traditions, those rich cultural repositories of thousands of years of human development of relationship with the sacred. Some call them "the great religions," but the Buddha's teachings, for instance, do not fit the standard definitions of a religion, as numerous scholars have noted, and the deeply rooted wisdom of native peoples' spirituality is generally denied a place among "the great religions."

The spirit of modernity shed the wisdom traditions in whatever society it took root because of faith that the truth of "value-free" science and the power of technology would break new ground in social well-being and carry along in its momentum, ethics, morality, and culture—all remade according to the impetus of progress. As we realize now, material conditions improved in many respects, but the trade-offs with the cult of modernity and its uses of science were enormous. The assumptions of that worldview have led to widespread ecocide, nuclear arms, the globalization of unqualified-growth economies, and the plunder of Third and Fourth World (indigenous) peoples' cultures and homelands. The psychological costs have been heavy, as well: loss of meaning beyond consumerism, loss of community and connectedness with other people, and loss of a secure sense of embeddedness in the rest of the natural world. One meaning of "the postmodern age," then, is the transition currently under way in various quarters to create a passage beyond the failed assumptions of modernity and a radical reorientation that preserves the positive advances of the liberal tradition and technological capabilities but is rooted in ecological sanity and meaningful human participation in the unfolding story of the Earth community and the universe. That process entails the creation of what I call "ecological postmodernism." It is that sense of a "postmodern age," meaning the broad-based transition, that I refer to in the subtitle of this book.

Another, more limited meaning of "postmodernism," although the one with far wider currency these days, is a mode of cultural analysis that seeks to reveal the cultural construction of concepts people generally assume to be natural or universal. Proponents of this postmodernism seek to "deconstruct" such influential concepts as humanism, Marxism, God, nature, gender, ethnicity, and so forth in order to break the grip of their control on our thoughts and actions. Deconstructive postmodernists, who are generally clustered in academia but whose influence has spread from there during the past decade, also cite various forms of disorientation and meaninglessness resulting from the ubiquitous simulation of mass media images. They assert that the unreal has replaced the real—except there is no "real" because all meaning is "socially produced," one's relationship to anything, abstract or concrete, being purely contingent.

I agree with the deconstructive-postmodern project to stimulate awareness of processes by which conceptualizations are culturally constructed (a task that African-American and feminist activists were advancing long before deconstruction of contemporary Goddess spirituality are a treasure. In the area of social justice and a sense of community, the core teachings of the Semitic traditions (Judaism, Christianity, Islam) offer a profound sense of the great communion that far exceeds notions of "social contract"—in spite of the fact that those teachings have often been violated by institutions within the Semitic traditions.

At base *States of Grace* is about engagement, an effort to cross lines of compartmentalization that have become habitual in the modern age. It is generally assumed that issues of spirituality have nothing to do with the pragmatic concerns of modernity, or even with a corrective postmodernity—and certainly no relevance to the "advanced" thinking of deconstructive postmodernism. I believe, however, that all three domains can be enriched through interaction with the wisdom traditions. In the final chapter, I suggest some common ground among these areas: the core yearnings of modernity, ecological postmodernity, deconstructive postmodernism, and the sacred.

The book's central chapters (Two through Five) consider four dimensions of human existence in relation to the teachings of the wisdom traditions. The first of these chapters focuses on mind, the second on nature, the third on the personal body and the Earthbody, and the fourth on community and social justice. The structure of that consideration is a weave of engagement. Running horizontally through all four of the central chapters are fibers of modernity, spun of the problematic assumptions and realities of the industrialized, globalized modern age. The other, yet smaller, horizontal fibers running through each chapter carry the subtheme of deconstructive postmodernism, spun of the problematic aspects of its extreme relativism. Within each of the four central chapters are three kinds of vertical fibers. The first is spun of the grounding of each chapter's topic (either mind, nature, body, or community) in the unfolding dynamics of the cosmos. Our knowledge of the universe is incomplete and always in process. In speaking of its "unfolding," my emphasis is on its developmental nature as well as its continuities of interrelatedness, rather than the exact nature of its birth. The second kind of became popular), but I do not agree with their leap to conclude that there is *nothing but* cultural construction in human experience. I admire the courage of their efforts, but they seem spiritually adrift. In addition, they seem not to perceive that certain aspects of the culturally informed "production" of their theories of deconstructive postmodernism constitute not a radical break but a continuation of some of the most destructive and deeply rooted strains in Western philosophy and culture. I consider the deconstructive-postmodern orientation from four perspectives: ecological/cosmological, spiritual, and activist-political (in Chapter Six and elsewhere), and feminist (in Chapter Four, Appendix A, and Appendix B). The combined insights of these perspectives amount to an ecofeminist orientation. (I call the various participants in their diverse movement "deconstructive postmodernists" as a concise way to distinguish them from "ecological postmodernists," who are engaged in developing a constructive transition beyond those assumptions of modernity that have failed.)

When the deconstructive postmodernists stalwartly strip away layers of cultural concepts, they arrive at issues of being that are the central concerns of the great wisdom traditions. Similarly, yet on a much larger scale, when increasing numbers of the promises of modernity and technocratic progress begin to ring hollow for millions of people, many begin to reconsider modernity's flight from the insights of the wisdom traditions. Each of the wisdom traditions addresses the totality of human experience, but each has also invested its greatest concentration of energy and attention in a particular area. If a knowledgeable person considers various contributions to grasping the nature of mind, surely the insights, precision, and experiential transformation contained in the Buddha's teachings stand out. Concerning our relationship with the rest of the natural world, the subtlety, intimacy, and emotional warmth of native peoples' spirituality is unparalleled. (In this book I focus specifically on Native American spirituality.) If one seeks an ecologically grounded response to the Earthbody and the personal body, the deeply erotic sensibilities vertical fiber is spun of awareness of the very real crises and suffering in the Earth community at this time, from which spirituality has too often been discussed in isolation. The third is spun of attention to the effects of the teachings and practices of the particular wisdom tradition in everyday life.

My presentation of what constitutes the core of each wisdom tradition is necessarily a personal perception but one that is informed by experiential knowledge of three of the four traditions that I feel have great relevance to the crises of our times, as well as by research in all four traditions via the printed page. Only a Native American can have full experiential knowledge of Native American spirituality, but I have studied that tradition for years, attended a few ceremonies to which observers were invited, and benefited greatly from the generous attitudes of several Indian friends and colleagues. Although Native Americans understandably find an intrusive raiding of their spiritual culture (especially by members of the dominant society that has treated them so abominably for centuries) to be offensive, many of them also feel that sharing part of their spiritual heritage of ecological wisdom could benefit Western civilization. Regarding the Buddha's teachings on the nature of mind, I have maintained a practice of *vipassana* (insight) meditation for twenty years. Regarding Goddess spirituality, I have been deeply involved with the contemporary expression of that tradition for fifteen years. Regarding the Judeo-Christian traditions, I was born and raised a Roman Catholic. Although I drifted away from Catholicism long ago, I still feel a heart connection with the admirable aspects of that tradition, and I experience the fully unjustified proprietary sense that comes so easily to "retired Catholics": I feel proud of the church, for example, when it aligns its influence with the oppressed and deeply disappointed when it cares so little for the health of the planet as to further human overpopulation. In recent years I have become interested in the renewal movement known as "creation-centered spirituality" (not to be confused with fundamentalist biblical "creationism"), which includes attention to the extremely interesting works of the creation-centered medieval mystics and acknowledges the intricacies of the natural world as the most magnificent source of revelation.

I realize that many people will find my interfaith, cross-cultural approach to reclaiming the spiritual treasures that have been marginalized by modern culture to be uncomfortable because people generally like to believe that their own tradition of being, whether a religion, secular humanism, or any other ideology, has the best answers to every question that might ever arise in human experience. I feel we can no longer afford such parochialism because the "acids of modernity" have eaten away at the fullness of spiritual life to such an extent that modern societies are floundering badly—even at this historical "moment" of reorientation that is occurring within and among so many countries. Because of the resilience of the wisdom traditions, which have survived the rise and fall of countless empires and ideologies, we have the opportunity to reclaim and renew the kinds of sensibilities with which we might cultivate awareness of the sacred processes of the unfolding of the person, the organic community, the Great Family of All Beings, and the cosmic whole. In the absence of such an orientation, many lives may well become focused by default on becoming the Number One consumers in the global shopping mall, while many other lives will continue to be shaped by hunger and privation.

If we wish to explore the richness and depth of human spirituality, we need to embrace its diversity, the treasures at the core of each tradition. The purpose of examining various spiritual paths, however, should not be to pluck out bits here and there to mix in a planetary stew, for each tradition possesses its own integrity. At the very least, even reading about the diverse insights and effects of the practices might suggest to modern and postmodern readers new ways of thinking about the dimension of being that is especially illuminated by a particular wisdom tradition. An interfaith approach also increases understanding, and presumably respect, and often serves to generate interest in neglected aspects of one's own tradition. Most important, a consideration of the wisdom traditions might stimulate spiritual *practice*, for they are entirely process-oriented, the teachings being mere supports for the experience of the practice. Beyond that, I offer this engagement with four of the great wisdom traditions in the hope that the synergy created will spark new possibilities at this moment of spiritual awakening and grave urgency for the Earth community.

I have not attempted an encyclopedic presentation of the wisdom traditions, but only enough of a representation from each to suggest its texture, depth, and resonance. (Readers who desire more information on the wisdom traditions are referred to "Related Reading" at the end of the book.) Neither have I sought a "unified field theory" of spiritual experience. My purpose is to suggest the thesis, woven throughout the book and discussed in the final chapter, that the core teachings and practices of the wisdom traditions—regardless of what sorts of institutional forms may have grown up around them—are thoroughly subversive to the monstrous reduction of the fullness of *being* that the Earth community currently faces through the dynamics of an increasingly manipulative, globalized, consumption-oriented political economy based on rapacious growth and the supposedly pragmatic destruction of being-in-relation. Within the value structure of the intensification of competition in production and consumption that will characterize the focus of life in the global market and mass culture that are presently being constructed, the felt connections between the person and the family, the community, the bioregion, the country, other peoples, other species, the Earthbody, and the cosmos merely get in the way. The materialist worldview of modernity is incapable of offering sufficient support to those felt connections, which have already been under attack for decades by capitalist corporatism and state socialism.

The human family is not without resources in this existential struggle. The core teachings of the great wisdom traditions live in an enduring present. They are relevant, powerful, and accessible. The insights that arise from their core practices yield a paradigm of resistance, creativity, and profound renewal for our time.

1

Saving Grace

On the relevance of the wisdom traditions to our times

As the assumptions of modernity unravel around us and we race the clock against the momentum of destructiveness, we are challenged to create new possibilities and haunted by failures of immense proportion. How is it that we paid so little attention to the steady degradation of our habitat for so long? How is it that the global nuclear arsenal reached fifty thousand cataclysmic warheads before the grassroots outcry became widespread? How is it that many of our landfills reached 90 percent of their capacity before recycling became commonplace? How is it that we have allowed the groundwater to be so recklessly depleted? How is it that hundreds of nuclear power plants have been constructed around the world without safe means of transporting or storing the radioactive waste? How is it that the enthusiasm for the modern nation-state overlooked the fate of some five thousand indigenous or long-standing cultural nations who have resisted the rule of capitalist or socialist states, resulting in hundreds of wars and millions of refugees?

Clearly, we have proven ourselves capable of sacrificing our perception, thought, and behavior to the power of an idea, the Great March of Progress. By now, however, even the most stalwart boosters of modern "progress," in both the East and the West, have had to acknowledge that it is leading us through toxic waste,

fast-eroding topsoil, and bad air. Its powerful momentum, from which we now can barely distinguish our species itself, has brought us from clan members to villagers to citizens of the nuclearized nation-state, from hunter-gatherers to farmers and craftsmen to consumers in the globalized marketplace, from awe at Earth's sacred majesty to scientistic rationalism and the technocrative imperative. The Promethean impulse, so central to the modern era, kicks aside cultural and ecological constraints, assuring us that if we *can* do something, we *should* do it.

While appreciating the comforts, conveniences, and medical benefits of our time, we surely must also wonder at the increasingly ill fit between our nominal values in the industrialized world and the course of our actions. What meaning does the natural world hold for us that we so eagerly sacrifice it to an unqualified growth economy? What is the meaning of national sovereignty when transnational corporations operate at an overarching level? What meaning do we perceive in the fragile unfolding of a child when we consent to raise our young on television violence and models of conspicuous consumption? We say that community means a lot to us, but how tenuous that felt connection has become. We say that the meaning of being human resides in the ability to love and to care—yet when child abuse, violence against women, AIDS, homelessness, and farm foreclosures become epidemic, most of us turn away and hope those problems will be taken care of somehow by someone else. The meaning of life at the close of the twentieth century? According to a joke currently in the air, "You're born. You buy. You die."

The Promises of Modernity

The cult of modernity promised a world of peace, freedom, and fulfillment if we would just trust in an instrumental rationality and never look back at our past, so embarrassingly superstitious, communal, and constraining to the freewheeling, autonomous individual, *homo oeconomicus*. The "natural" belief in the modern era that economics is the driving force behind all other human activities might lead one to suppose that materialism is the creed of modernity. Yet modern states, both capitalist and socialist, have raced each other to impose destructive industrialism on the material base of life—air, soil, water. That material reality was worth nothing weighed against short-term economic growth, from which, according to both classical liberal and Marxist salvation ideologies, would come abundance and fulfillment for all, from which we would have reassuring proof of our power over nature and over any peoples too "backward" to comprehend the historical imperative of the modern state. Modernity stripped down the meaning of life to a struggle between the human mind and the rest of the natural world. Economic expansion promised autonomy and deliverance from the vulnerability of that separateness. (The roots of this orientation predate the modern era, as I explain in Appendix B.)

Because it is now apparent that modernity has failed to fulfill its promises of "a better life" in many of the deepest senses, we are compelled to search for new, or perhaps recovered, modes of understanding our nature and the relation between our species and the rest of the natural world. We face both the external crises of modernity (such as destruction of the natural world, the nuclearized nation-state, the sacrifice of the Third World and indigenous peoples for the needs of the industrialized "megamachine") and the internal crises, including a search for meaning in our lives and relief from a sense of isolation. In this task of sorting and reconsidering, we encounter the confusion of a multitude of analyses, insights, and remedies, as one would expect in times of planetary uncertainty and transition.

One cluster of responses to the internal crises has become quite fashionable in the West: deconstructive postmodernism draws attention to the ways in which overarching concepts are actually culturally constructed and are not the universal truisms that most people assume. In its extreme forms, deconstructive postmodernism declares that meaning itself is impossible, except as relative and essentially arbitrary choices we decide upon and act out in ironic performance. Diverse expressions of this orientation range from sensible defenses of particularity to intense cynicism, denial, indifference, and disengagement.

Responses from Deconstructive Postmodernism

Several streams fed the development of deconstructive postmodernism in architecture, art, and literature, while perhaps the most widely influential stream, actually a torrent, flowed from the (mostly French) academic fields of philosophy, linguistics, literary criticism, psychology, and cultural history, spreading to the rest of the social sciences, to theories of law, to social-change movements, and, in a newly explicit way, to the art world. (In the arts, the influence of deconstructive postmodernism was perhaps strongest during the 1980s; in philosophy and related fields, it is still a considerable presence, particularly as poststructuralism.) The public at large became familiar with the nihilism, randomness, and flatness of the deconstructive-postmodern aesthetic through its influence on commercial art and graphic design. Since the late 1970s, billboards, book jackets, and magazine covers have featured modified versions of *pastiche*—disjointed, unharmonious, emphatically inorganic design, often including starkly contrasting styles of lettering and garish colors. On television the technique of quick-cut editing has produced thousands of commercials and rock videos that present a barrage of clashing, incongruous moving images that "deny meaning."

A sense of detachment, displacement, and shallow engagement dominates deconstructive-postmodern aesthetics because groundlessness is the only constant recognized by this sensibility. The world is considered to be a repressive labyrinth of "social production," a construction of pseudoselves who are pushed and pulled by cultural dynamics and subtly diffused "regimes of power." Values and ethics are deemed arbitrary, as is "history," which is viewed by deconstructive postmodernists as one group or another's self-serving selection of facts. Rejecting all "metanarratives," or supposedly universal representations of reality, deconstructive postmodernists insist that the meaning of every aspect of human existence is culturally created and determined in particular, localized circumstances about which no generalizations can be made. That is, all knowledge is situated within a culture. Even particularized meaning, however, is regarded as relative and temporary, a permutation within our invented language systems, which many deconstructionists regard as merely indeterminant chains of words (signifiers) referring endlessly to other signifiers. Deconstructive postmodernists further maintain that since language systems determine our only possible mode of thought, no ground of meaning—such as God, History, Humankind, Reason—exists outside of our language inventions. (For a fuller consideration of varieties of deconstructive postmodernism, see Appendix A.)

Deconstructive postmodernists speak of "the death of the subject," the harsh truth that the Autonomous Man of Reason, the idol of the Enlightenment, is actually not in control of his possibilities or choices. This analysis emphasizes the partial truth that a human is born into a set of cultural constructions and constraints and lives out her or his life in the embrace, or stranglehold, of various "discourses," socially invented systems of perception, meaning, and knowledge. The deconstruction of the freewheeling "I" as independent agent, or subject, is not a new perception (to anyone familiar with Eastern religion or the Hindu-influenced observations of Schopenhauer, among others). The reason this perspective—particularly in the nihilistic interpretation provided by some postmodern packaging—has engaged the fancy of so many people at this moment in history is surely embedded in the larger dynamics of disintegration and loss of meaning in our time. Although most deconstructive postmodernists consider "nature," "the cosmos," and "the health of the biosphere" to be merely "socially produced" concepts, a collective awareness has gradually taken shape in many sectors of our society such that we can no longer deny the pervasive force of a suicidal disorientation.

Our species, through our dominant cultural and economic institutions, has degraded the health of the biosphere, our home, our very source of sustenance, our greater being. "Death of the subject" sensibilities feel appropriate at this historical moment as we knowingly and willfully continue every day to advance the death of the Primary Subject: Gaia, the wondrous and dynamic ecosphere that is our body. The responses of the industrialized nations to date have been far too little to save the planet. It is increasingly difficult to convince oneself that the majority of human society actively cares about posterity, indigenous cultures, other species, the 4-billion-year-old unfolding of Earth's being, or even our own future a few decades from now. How timely to kick over false assumptions about lordly "pure reason" in politics or philosophy when our carefully constructed sense of humanity is revealed to be radically disjointed from our actions. In the Western, patriarchal societies where deconstructive postmodernism flourishes, deeply ingrained cultural norms of separateness, reactive autonomy, and self-absorption have devoured the sense of grounded, responsible being at the very moment we have finally realized that the destruction of our habitat may have passed the point of no return. In our current situation, where is reason? Where is coherence? Where is truth, beauty, a love of life? Where is even the most basic impulse for self-preservation? What have we become?

In the deconstructive-postmodern play of disintegration and impossibility of meaning, one can merely strike self-conscious postures *as if* one's responses had meaning. Anything more would reveal a dated naiveté. "Enormously suggestive," rather than "accurate" or "truthful," is the highest accolade for an analysis or conclusion. Imagine my surprise, then, to come across a deconstructive-postmodern passage in which the author seems to embrace a famous paleontologist's well-defined organicism: "Maybe in the end Teilhard de Chardin was right to speak of the earth as being an organism." But then the deconstructionist turned in the predictable direction à la mode: "It's not that the earth *is* an organism, or will, necessarily, ever be one, but that this model of the world captures the promise and peril of the coming decades" (his italics).[1] How do we know "it's not that the earth *is* an organism"? Because any data to that effect is, for a deconstructive postmodernist, merely "socially produced" discourse composed of self-referential words and concepts. One may call upon self-interest or utilitarianism for determining in which direction to lean with one's postures or with which models to act as if one were engaged, but the only real commitment is to the ideology of atomized detachment.

I sometimes encounter this attitude—so emblematic, even if extreme, of this age of loss and confusion—when I travel around the country speaking on the "Ten Key Values" of the Green politics movement.[2] In one city where I was invited to address the campus community, the local Greens kindly arranged a potluck supper the following evening; most of the people there seemed to have some connection with the political science department at the university. Some ten of us were seated in a circle, finishing dessert, when a student said to me, "I think Green politics is really the way to go because it's very postmodern. It's a matter of groups with different concerns of the moment coming together, then disengaging, and maybe reforming in different ways according to whatever suits them best at the time." I glanced quickly around the circle and met the eyes of the two professors with whom I had spent the afternoon. Those split-second glances confirmed what each of us knew: here was a bright, earnest young man who had taken a course in the deconstructive-postmodern worldview and had bought the whole package deal.

"No," I replied gently. "That's not at all what we're about. We're trying to reorient human society, including ourselves, to appreciate and live out basic values—ecological wisdom, grassroots democracy, nonviolence, and so forth. To effect that kind of comprehensive transformation will surely require flexibility and creativity but in a much more grounded sense than you seem to have in mind."

He grinned, pleased that I had taken the bait. "There's nothing to be grounded in except what we invent. It's all just discourse—socially produced language games people take for some kind of objective correlation with a fixed outer reality because that makes them feel secure."

"There's no physical reality outside of the language games in our minds?" I asked, playing along.

"There may or may not be, but we can't know anything except what our received forms of discourse allow us to consider," he replied.

"So you would say that our perceptions are not only culturally informed but culturally invented?"

"Absolutely."

"From that, you would dismiss science, I suppose, as a mere accumulation of culturally constrained perceptions?"

"Science is just a narrative. It's a discourse that keeps changing all the time. It's not about the physical world; it's about itself. There's no such thing as "nature"; it's just a tabula rasa onto which people project the concepts of their era in their particular society."

"And we, all of us, have, according to your perception, no real connectedness?"

"That's what discourse is for."

"Is it sufficient?"

"Must be. Here we are."

"Here we are on a planet, a unique habitat, it seems. Let's think about . . . say, *water* on this planet. Every individual manifestation of every life-form, animal or plant, needs water to exist. We have that in common. We are all in relationship through our mutual need for water. There may be other aspects of our existence as well by which we are in relationship—but would you agree at least that we all share in this one undeniable, irrefutable desire, no matter what discourse about it might be invented?"

The young man nodded warily.

I smiled. "Good. Let's start there."

The Cosmological Context

All human experience and knowledge is situated in the unfolding manifestations of the universe, an interactive and genetically related community of beings. Our entire clan, which includes everything in our solar system, is descended from the fireball. The elements in our bodies are the same as those in trees, rocks, raccoons, and rivulets. Those bodies, those myriad forms, are not static, stable objects, but actually consist of trillions of micro-events occurring within the dynamics of self-organization. All the atoms exhibit awareness of each other as they articulate patterns within a vast web of relationship. As the universe acts, resulting in certain manifestations among a tremendous range of possibilities, it continues to create the cosmological story. This is where we live. This is who the human species is—more than 5 billion unique expressions of the dynamism and profound communion that fills the universe.

"That's merely one perspective," a deconstructive postmodernist might scoff. "You could just as easily claim that we're all rigidly discrete, unrelated, unconnected beings. One discourse is as good as the next."

Yet the widespread, cross-cultural occurrence of the perception of interconnectedness makes this perspective far more than a mere "narrative" of projected idealism: It has been *experienced* by an enormous number of people in extremely varied circumstances for scores of thousands of years. The sense that the natural world is alive and that we are inherently connected with that life force is a core perception of most native peoples' worldview, from the cultures of the Upper Paleolithic era to those of the contemporary Fourth World. In Asia it evolved into Taoist, Buddhist, Hindu, and Confucian philosophies of organicism. That perception, that awareness of vibrant interconnectedness, lingered stubbornly despite the challenge of new ideas that spread from Europe throughout the world—first, the assertion that an omnipotent sky-god had actually created everything separate from everything else, then the assertion that the universe is a clockworks of dead matter, which humans can observe and manipulate with detached objectivity. In Europe the more ancient perception of interrelatedness was artfully expressed in statues from the Neolithic era, in the poetry of the medieval mystics, and in much of the folk art of peasant cultures. Even in the midst of

our thoroughly modern culture, the worldview of interconnectedness again appeared in several areas, such as the process cosmology and organic philosophy of Alfred North Whitehead, the epistemology of Gregory Bateson and other systems theorists, and the "twelve principles of the unfolding cosmological story," perceived by Thomas Berry, a cultural historian, and further developed by Brian Swimme, a physicist and cosmologist, to incorporate the latest news from Western science. Contemporary science itself—in the areas of biology, chemistry, physics, and chaos theory—has also concluded that subtle interconnectedness and molecular relatedness are indeed the nature of being.

Ecological Postmodernism

That perception is the core of a second, and quite different, type of postmodernism, one that sees the passage beyond the breakdown of the mechanistic assumptions of modernity as potentially leading to an ecological understanding of the world rather than a nihilistic disintegration of all values. Ecological postmodernism, as this outlook could be labeled, though it is sometimes called constructive, or reconstructive, postmodernism as well,[3] encourages us to expand the gestalt, our perception of the whole, in every situation so that we no longer collaborate in the modern project of fragmentation, with its championing of certain fragments above all else. Just as modern scientists discounted and ignored perturbations observed outside of the accepted model, so modern economists ignored the effects of unqualified economic growth on the "fragment" of the whole that is nature. Modern statesmanship proceeded by ignoring the sovereignty of native peoples, a "fragment" that was clearly outside the accepted model, and modern rationalists denied any spiritual perceptions as anomalous quirks not to be mentioned. With the liberating sensibilities of ecological postmodernism, however, scientists engaged in chaos research now try to absorb into their conclusions *everything* they observe through their measurements; ecological economists consider the *total* costs of production, including the depletion of our primary "capital," the biosphere; advocates of a postmodern world order defend the precious diversity of cultures that comprise the planetary whole; and people no longer boxed in by the tight constraints of highly selective modern rationalism now allow themselves subtle perceptions of the grand unity, the ground of the sacred.

Ecological postmodernism recognizes not only that all beings are structurally related through our cosmological lineage, but also that all beings are internally constituted by relations with others, even at the molecular level. We are not the fixed, thoroughly self-contained entities of the modern model. At subtle levels of perception, we are ever changing and ever aware of our connectedness with other humans, the rest of nature on Earth, and the whole of the universe. Our cultural interpretations of reality, as well as any theories about them, are sorely impoverished if they operate in isolation from the larger context.

Since we have long regarded science as our reality principle in the West, it is curious that society, including the scientific establishment, has kept its distance from the radical implications of postmodern science. The voice of modern science, having displaced the medieval worldview three and a half centuries ago, has been extremely influential, especially through scientistic models of "value-free" authority.[4] In the name of science, earnest crusaders accepted "purely objective" empiricism, "logical positivism," or "scientific Marxism." Claiming to be scientific and hence value-free, time-motion studies shaped the nature of work on assembly lines in the East and West, and doctors strongly urged women to bottle-feed their babies, for instance. The pattern of popular extrapolation from modern science has not recurred with discoveries of postmodern science because the conclusions are so extraordinary to anyone raised in a modern culture that they can barely be absorbed. In the 1920s several of the physicists doing pioneering work in quantum theory experienced great personal distress as they came to understand that nothing, at the subtle level of subatomic particles and wavelets, is as it had seemed in the mechanistic Newtonian worldview. Since then hundreds of discoveries in contemporary science have further indicated a world based on inherent interconnectedness and behavioral relatedness. Science writers have skillfully conveyed these findings with the awe and excitement they deserve, declaring in various ways, "This changes everything about the way we think of life!" It never does, though.

The latest news from science is merely of passing interest to most people it reaches. Perhaps they, like its outspoken enthusiasts, have difficulty imagining what changes the active embrace of such a radically different worldview might effect. Ironically, many of the champions of the "new" worldview, which amplifies the primal perceptions, can relate to it only in a mechanistic, rationalist fashion. Insistent on avoiding any metaphorical mumbo jumbo, so abhorrent to the modern mind, and dedicated to the notion of progress achieved through the rational application of selected facts, they seem to place their faith in declaring a directive to society that is almost charming in its naiveté:

> EVERYTHING IS COMPOSED OF A SUBATOMIC FLUX OF WAVELETS AND PARTICLES, CHAOS AND PATTERN. BOUNDARIES ARE FLUID. POSSIBILITIES ARE ENDLESS. UNRELATED SEPARATENESS IS AN ILLUSION. INTERCONNECTEDNESS IS REALITY. PROCESS IS ALL.
>
> REVISE YOUR PERCEPTIONS, CONCEPTS, AND LIFE ACCORDINGLY.
>
> ANY QUESTIONS?

Just a few. Since modern socialization has taught us to deny subtle perceptions that do not fit within a rationalist, mechanistic model of existence, how are we supposed to instantly develop our atrophied sensitivity in order to grow in awareness of the intricate, moment-to-moment dance of creation, disintegration, and re-creation? Since the identity of modern humankind rests in the belief that the human mind can gain full knowledge and control over the sensate world, how can we afford to accept the sense of mystery inherent in the novel manifestation of subatomic constellations that are the forms and events we perceive? Since intimacy with the material world is fearful to modern, industrialized society, how can we hope to enter into conscious relationship with the unitive ground of the astonishing range of spontaneous subjectivity that is in and around us? How can we expect to achieve such a fundamental deepening of our modes of comprehension without *cultural practices* that encourage us to grow in awareness? How can we come to realize that we live in a participatory universe—that each of us, each minute part of us, is a node within a vast network of creative dynamics—unless we engage in practices that awaken our minds to the realities of such participation? How can we absorb the existential paradox of the universality of processes throughout the natural world that yield the unique patterning of subatomic events giving rise to each of us unless we become experienced in the kind of expression that can handle paradox: skillful metaphor, multivalent poetry, and wise narrative of mythic depth that spark the imagination and reveal the rich unfolding of cosmological possibilities? How can we know the unitive dimension of existence as a felt reality, rather than an abstract concept, unless we experience subtle mindfulness of flux, the palpable connectedness within ritual space, or the music, dance, or drama that activates in us deep awareness, wonder, and awe? Once we have grasped experientially, even for a moment, the astounding unity, what kinds of interactions—with people, trees, animals, rivers—are worthy of it? What kinds of practices will remind us of what we know, even when we encounter little but denial from modern culture?

The Centrality of Process/Practice in the Wisdom Traditions

Surely transformative *process*, the essence of reality in the "new" worldview, should itself be a central focus of our efforts to understand and to connect. Experiential knowledge of the interconnected nature of reality is far more than a decorative complement to intellectual comprehension of scientific observations and philosophical insights. Experience, aided by the development of increasingly subtle awareness, tests conceptual knowledge and

can embody and supersede its linear dimension. Perhaps that is why the controlling institutions and political systems have typically enthroned their favorite concepts while banishing, or firmly proscribing, the importance of individual experience.

The human family is not without impressive resources for the task of achieving a comprehensive transition to an ecological worldview. Not surprisingly, the very traditions that modernity has rejected with contempt are those that contain revelations of ecological communion and dynamic oneness. The core teachings of the great wisdom traditions have much to contribute to the challenge of *how* we might move beyond modernity's sterile, stripped-down model of the nature of the human and our place in the universe.

To partake of the wisdom traditions we need to explore possibilities across parochial boundaries and to appreciate core spiritual insights independently of the institutional religions that may have grown up around them. If we can cross dividing lines and seek honestly and openly, the wisdom traditions illuminate central issues of our time.

In the area of mind, perception, mental suffering, and the cessation of mental suffering, who has gone further than the teachings of the Buddha?

In the area of perceiving an intimate connection with the rest of the natural world, who has gone further than the spiritual practices of native peoples?

In the area of consciousness of the body as intricately embedded in a relational web, who has gone further in ritual honoring of the Earthbody and our personal bodies than the contemporary renewal of Goddess spirituality?

In the area of social ethics as an expression of our comprehension of the divine oneness, who has gone further in the West than the core teachings of the Semitic religions: Judaism, Christianity, and Islam? (In the East, Confucianism developed this area quite thoroughly, giving central importance to the cosmological dimension.)

Each of the wisdom traditions addresses the totality of human existence, but each concentrates its greatest energies on a particular facet. Thanks to the marvels of modern travel and mass publication, teachers and teachings of the wisdom traditions are diffused throughout the world as never before. Due to the modern worldview, however, we have had little use for them. We have long since lost the vocabulary of spiritual practice, the feel for multivalent expression, and a subtle awareness of the grand unity. In modern parlance "myth" is casually used to mean delusion, fallacy, or lie. Meditation or contemplative exercises are regarded suspiciously as nonproductive quietism that "doesn't get you anywhere." Ritual is dismissed as irrational foolishness.

The nature of spiritual practice, the purpose of the wisdom traditions, is to illuminate the truth of being—the flux, dynamism, subjectivity, creativity, and inherent relatedness. Spirituality involves subtle perceptions of our *interbeing*, to use the term coined by Thich Nhat Hanh, a Vietnamese monk. We interare with every entity in the dynamic cosmos. From awareness of that ground, which is nature, arise social constructions that have depth and meaning. In ignorance of that ground arise constructions of human folly, the channeling of human ingenuity into trivial impulses and ignoble goals that are the cause of great suffering.

The Experience of Grace

When we experience consciousness of the unity in which we are embedded, the sacred whole that is in and around us, we exist in a state of grace. At such moments our consciousness perceives not only our individual self, but also our larger self, the self of the cosmos. The gestalt of unitive existence becomes palpable.

The term *grace* comes from the Christian tradition, but the unitive experiences it names are common to spiritual practice in all the wisdom traditions. Catholic and Protestant theologies disagree over whether the Christian notion of grace, the infusion of "God's saving love," is gained through sincere participation in the sacraments (baptism, eucharist, confirmation, penance, matrimony, ordination, and last rites) or directly through active faith. St. Augustine comprehended grace almost entirely in terms of sin and redemption, a private matter in which no external elements are relevant. Unfortunately, his view has shaped much of Western thinking on grace. In contrast, the formative theologians of Eastern Orthodox Christianity perceived divine grace diffused throughout nature.[5] More recently, the Protestant theologian Paul Tillich defined grace as "the impact of the Spiritual Presence," an unexacted gift that is present within this life.[6] The Jesuit theologian Karl Rahner rejected the Roman Catholic church's teaching, following the Council of Trent, that grace is a supernatural structure above humanity's conscious, spiritual, and moral life, a view he called extrinsicalness at its worst. Instead, he perceived nature as enveloped in grace and grace bearing upon our inmost reality.[7]

Grace is considered by nearly all theologians to be a gift that is given to humans by the divine, in whose image we are made. If our image is a clue to the nature of the divine, however, why should we settle on an interpretation that stops at surface perceptions: why should our "image" denote only physical human form and behavior rather than our composition of vibratory flux, subatomic dynamism and creativity, and inherent relatedness? What if the divine is comprehended not as a godhead outside the universe, but as the diffused "mind," or process of subjectivity, that informs the alternatives chosen trillions of times per second at the subatomic level, that makes possible the self-organizing behavior throughout the cosmos, and that informed the evolution of our own form such that we are able to perceive and reflect on all those workings of divine creativity, cosmic subjectivity, or God? Then we see clearly that we are indeed created in the "image" of the participatory universe. We are of it—not by projecting our type of mental processes onto the universe, but by realizing that the human mind participates in the processes of the larger "mind." We are not apart from the dynamic cosmos.

Experiencing grace involves the expansion of consciousness of self to all of one's surroundings as an unbroken whole, a consciousness of awe from which negative mindstates are absent, from which healing and groundedness result. For these reasons grace has long been deemed "amazing." Sometimes the consciousness of grace comes on quite suddenly and so intensely that the moment is never forgotten. More frequently, we experience slight versions of it, as in the act of group singing when the alignment of vibrations evokes in us awareness of the vibratory ocean of flux and form in and around us. Touching the ultimate truth in that way, and many others, brings us joy, release, connection, and peace.

Since ritual has the potential to bring forth the experience of grace in the consciousness of participants, it is easy to understand why Catholicism urged, even to the point of requiring, participation in sacramental rituals. On the other hand, Luther's insistence that grace can be experienced without benefit of institutional rituals is also correct, especially if we understand grace in a cosmological sense, extending beyond denominational faith.[8] Many people vividly recall from childhood unexpected moments of perceiving the grand unity. Some experience the grace of interbeing on extended trips into the deep silence of wilderness. Some know a version of it in the postorgasmic state. Some have reported that such "altered" consciousness occurs suddenly in mundane circumstances. It seems to persist even through our deeply ingrained habits of seeing only separateness and fragmentation.

Persons adept at spiritual practice—meditation, contemplative prayer, or ritual, for instance—experience graced consciousness for extended periods. Perhaps traditional native peoples who regard every act throughout the day as ceremonial practice, or right living, know a certain sense of graced consciousness at all times. That such a possibility is within human reach, even if fitfully, has been the message of the mystics and many poets and artists. It was for Henri Matisse apparently an informing desire. Late in his life, when he agreed to design the stained glass windows for a chapel, he was angrily confronted by Picasso. He reminded Matisse that they had spent their entire professional lives championing the new, the modern, the progressive, the liberated. How, he demanded, could Matisse now further such a backward cause as the church? Matisse replied calmly that they had both been trying their whole lives to regain through art the inner "atmosphere" of their First Communion, a state of grace.[9]

Experiencing grace is only one aspect of spiritual practice, but it is particularly important for a culture that has validated only perceptions of separateness and fragmentation.

Beyond the Deconstructive-Postmodern Wake

We are living through a period of spiritual searching and renewal on many parts of the planet. As the cultural grip of modernity weakens, the insights of spiritual teachings can be shared once again. In the industrialized world, spiritual teachings have been pushed so far beyond the pale of relevance that a large portion of society does not know how or where they might approach them, even for exploratory purposes. For that reason, the desire for spiritual groundedness and growth is often expressed as a vague yearning. A famous biologist declares at an international conference that our global crises call for a "quasi-religious transformation of contemporary cultures."[10] A distinguished nature writer warns that we are about to lose "our sense of what we call God."[11] An authority on international law calls for a "dispersion of spiritual energy."[12] Such sentiments are increasingly common, but there the discussion usually stops. A simple move into institutional religion would be problematic for many people not only because it seems to be a world remote from the demands of modern life, but also because the men in control of its influence have often legitimated oppression, militarism, and the exploitation of the Earth.

We have seen enough of the misuse of the wisdom traditions to be sensitive to any perversions of spiritual impulses in service to nationalism or the oppression of any group. We have also seen slick operators within the human potential movement take from Buddhism certain psychological insights, sever them from their foundation in the precepts of morality, and sell them in training seminars for corporations and individuals who want a mental edge in grabbing all they can in this life. Less revolting but also disturbing are the watered-down versions of the wisdom traditions that are now peddled in our country and allow only for comfortable, shallow participation. The marketable phenomenon of "lite" spirituality, or New Age religion, ultimately deprives people of the benefits of authentic spiritual practice, which requires effort and courage.

Because the wisdom traditions—and not only the four I consider in this book—grew from such varied grounds of human perception, they provide a treasury of modes of thinking about the human condition. They are, of course, far more than tools for thinking about our current situation. They are pathways to spiritual maturity. We of the modern era have often acted as adolescents careless of the consequences of our actions because we were deprived of a sense of communion. We can explore the wisdom traditions not to pluck favorite pieces from each for a syncretic blend but, in respecting the integrity of each, to gain greater understanding of pathways to grace.

How might we approach the wisdom traditions at this postmodern moment of transition? They are indeed "enormously suggestive," but they are much more than that. Understood in a cosmological context, the universe reveals itself to us as we, who are ourselves manifestations of the universe, evolve to the point of perceiving more and more of the nature of ourselves and our surroundings. At the point at which we could perceive gravity, vibration that is music, electricity, atoms, DNA, fission, light years, and so forth, those dynamics were thereby revealed to us and through us by the unfurling universe.

Extrapolating from Thomas Berry's sense of the unfolding story of the universe as a source of revelation,[13] we can consider anew the meaning of spiritual traditions that have roots in the oldest cultural eras of humankind and that have outlasted thousands of passing political systems and ships of state. Each wisdom tradition is complete in itself in that it addresses all aspects of the human condition, yet when we delve into them, we find unequaled depths of revelation in the one area in each that is so fully and richly developed above the others.

I believe the spiritual practices of the wisdom traditions illuminate for us basic processes, or patterns, of the universe, three of which Berry identifies as differentiation, subjectivity, and communion. By *differentiation* he means the diverse manifestations of forms and modes of existence. The universe is amazingly varied in its articulation of energy constellations, from the elementary particles and atomic beings, to the life-forms of the animate world, to the complexities of planetary systems and galaxies. The more intimately we come to know an animate or inanimate expression of the life of the universe, the more we become aware of its differences from other manifestations. Through attention to differentiation, we come to apprehend the enormously fecund creativity of the cosmos.

Berry's sense of *subjectivity* extends beyond the philosophical notion of "agency" (the capacity to be an active agent, that is, an initiating and directing subject of action) to include a being's unique interiority, depth, spontaneity, and creativity. What happens in the universe is "universe activity," which occurs only in and as particular subjects—self-organized, interactive sources of universe activity. The subjectivity of a galaxy, for example, is that which organizes and sustains the galaxy. Subjectivity includes spontaneity, in a wriggling amoeba as well as in a human being, and sentience, in the self-regulating dynamics of a coral reef as well as in a mammal. Through subjectivity, manifestations of the universe present the creative unfolding and ultimate mystery of the cosmos.

By *communion* Berry means the dynamics of inherent relationship, rather than the mere interaction of unrelated entities. The cosmic phenomenon of interrelatedness has been observed from numerous perspectives. The naturalist John Muir noted,

"When we try to pick out anything by itself, we find it hitched to everything else in the universe." The physicist Ernst Mach proposed the principle that every object, or inertial mass, is in [gravitational] interaction with the entire universe. Berry's colleague Brian Swimme cites another example of communion: "The Sun and the Earth awake in a profound embrace of a bonded relationship we call gravitational interaction. With each passing instant this bond deepens so that in time Earth shapes itself into a form that can sing of the Sun's energy. The chlorophyll molecules have the essence of the Sun in their very architecture; the vertebrate eye was shaped using the photonic patterns emanating from the Sun's fusion energetics. . . ."[14] Within the grand communion of the universe, then, countless forms of relationship and community manifest. At one point we humans fell from communion with the rest of the primates, but then entered into a new communion as the human species. The ever-renewing power of communion we experience in our lives is an expression of the creativity of the universe.

(Whenever I work with these processes—differentiation, subjectivity, or communion—in this book, the above definitions are the ones I have in mind. My use of the term "cosmological" refers to the dynamics of the cosmos in its entirety: subatomic particles, cells, DNA, plants, humans and other animals, the Earth, the solar system, the Milky Way galaxy, the whole universe. Any and all of these phenomena are brought about by cosmological processes.)

The cosmological context itself suggests a way out of the deconstructionist impasse of relativism. Berry suggests that these cosmic processes can serve as ethical guides for human behavior: all human actions that enhance the unfolding of the universe through essential patterns of differentiation, subjectivity, and communion are wholesome; all those actions that needlessly damage these essential processes are unwholesome. For example, a totalitarian community, or state, violates differentiation and the unfolding subjectivity of the individual, while a cult of self-absorption thwarts the unfolding of communion. I believe our understanding of these constitutive processes as ethical guides is enriched by spiritual practice. The more deeply we can enter into their dynamics, the greater our participation in wisdom.

Even as the central assumptions of modernity—that mighty *homo oeconomicus* exists to shape nature and society to serve the goal of ever-increasing production, for example—continue to lose credibility, we will hear its defenders repeat firmly from pinnacles of authority that all we need to do is fine-tune the system.[15] Yet it is painfully clear that modern consciousness has taken a detour off the primordial pathways to grace. Day by day people die as victims of this route. The road is getting rougher. At the end lies a cliff. Around us our leaders, good lemmings all, exhort us to stay the course.

The impetus to find other ways of being has spawned ecological postmodernism. The impetus to reveal the card tricks behind the "obvious truth" of rationalist modernity has spawned deconstructive postmodernism. The cultural explosion of the latter in so many fields at this time can be regarded as a wake for the shocking passing of the seemingly stable, objectivist, mechanistic, rationalist worldview.[16] Apparently it is an Irish-style wake with lots of whiskey, food, and verbal virtuosity. Some folks are quite intoxicated and natter on too loudly and too long (do we really need yet another university press announcing a postmodern series that will "expose" everything in human experience as mere self-referential discursive constructions?). Other deconstructive-postmodern mourners are full of rudeness and exaggeration. Still others churn out boring, sterile art, enshrining the futility of it all. In the corner some rowdies chant mockingly, *"Things fall apart; the centre cannot hold."* They smash their glasses and shout that there never was a center. Arrogant and peevish behavior does not hide their fear of living without the smug certainties of objectivist, scientistic delineations of reality. As deconstructive postmodernists continue to "bust up" the furniture at this wake, I suggest we remember that in the grieving period after a shocking death, just as in the minutes or hours before a birth, all rules are suspended. No one expects coherence.

Odd responses are overlooked, and angry outbursts are absorbed. An event of deep transition creates its own rules.

Those who can move beyond cynicism and postures of despair can see that our loss of a determinate, rigidly objective sense of reality is our liberation. Instead of alien manipulators, we now come to understand ourselves as participants in the unfolding universe. Instead of being locked into the tedious debate about whether the universe acts in a thoroughly random manner or strictly according to a master plan of linear development, we can apprehend that the universe offers itself an unimaginable range of possibilities and an intricate play of tendencies from which it fashions its ongoing story. It is a sacred story not of determinism but of creativity, allurement, relation, and engagement—all arising and passing away in lifetimes of a microsecond or longer arcs of billions of years.

We, self-reflexive manifestations of the universe, have the capabilities to enhance the conditions for differentiation, subjectivity, and communion in the Earth community. For these existential possibilities the universe has provided the guidance and inspiration we need: the core teachings of the wisdom traditions. Through their practices, their emphasis on process, we can become sensitive to profound dimensions of mind, nature, the body, and community. The fallacies underlying destructive institutions and practices—including the fatalist view that hostile indifference in so many realms is "just human nature"—then become obvious.

The acute suffering of the Earth community instills urgency in this work. The conceptual liberation of the postmodern moment engenders possibilities. The cosmological context grounds us in the sacred whole. We are ready as never before to appreciate the great wisdom traditions.

2

The Center Holds

On the nature of mind: the wisdom of the Buddha's teachings about Dhamma

As the universe expands, space unfurls. Any point in the universe can be regarded as the fixed point, the center. *You are the center of the universe.*

What transpires at the center? Within a human life, what is the proportion of happiness, contentment, and love to anxiety, craving, aversion, anguish, envy, resentment, greed, and even hatred? If at the end of life one could recall the nature of all the thoughts and emotions that had occupied the mind from moment to moment and sort them into three piles—the loving, harmonious mindstates; the neutral mindstates; and the fearful, negative mindstates—the last pile most often would tower over the others. Our minds simply get caught in inner storms of insecurity, jealousy, craving, or ill will. This inner turmoil is labeled human nature, the human condition, our lot in life.

The fruits of a lifetime of mental agitation and negative mindstates yield a bitter harvest: peace and harmony are elusive while resentment and cruelty abound, their pain fixed grimly in the faces we see around us every day. The expression in the eyes, the way the mouth is set reveal many people halfway to rage and countless others who have swallowed too much sadness. Their pain was caused by others, also with agitated minds—an unloving parent, a spiteful teacher, a callous group of peers. Literally millions were victims of sexual abuse in childhood. Even more met the subtle institutional violence that crushes a child's spirit and the patriarchal constraints that effectively prune the fullness of what a child could become. They came to know the structural violence in an economic system that keeps have-nots in their place and rewards cutthroat competitiveness—or else enslaves everyone to the whims of the state. As adults, their fears and resentment yield authoritarian structures, backstabbing, and more destructive actions than are ever, ever admitted. A daily surge of grim and somewhat deadened faces fills the schools, the workplaces, and the crowded streets of virtually every city in this world.

How cruel, then, the political fraud that promises people *a happy life* in a workers' paradise of either centralized or decentralized socialism, or in a sea of the alleged trickle-down affluence of deregulated capitalism, or any political model at all without attention to the qualities of mind.

At the level of subsistence, some people clearly have greater cause for despair than others. Alcoholism claims thousands of victims on economically depressed Indian reservations of the United States, but it is also a problem in our middle-class high schools. In the homes of both the most privileged and the poorest citizens of Washington, Moscow, Tokyo, Managua, and Buenos Aires, alcoholism, wife beating, and child abuse are not strangers. A particular family structure, whether extended or nuclear, can no more guarantee happiness than can a particular economic or political system. Anywhere an adult family member is consumed by mindstates of anxiety, resentment, and ill will, the entire family is affected.

When families are uprooted and homelands are shattered by war, we naturally expect mindstates of despair and hatred. And yet . . . the happiest people I ever encountered were refugees who had lost everything to Mao's invading army and possessed only what they had been able to carry out of Tibet over the Himalayan

passes in 1959. Some ten years later, the survivors were settled in hill towns throughout the Indian Himalayas when I spent a summer among those in Dalhousie. They lived in poverty, weaving carpets or selling ornate buttons, and frequently received reports that the Chinese occupation forces in Tibet were demolishing the ancient monasteries, imprisoning the monks and others in labor camps, using the sacred *thangkas* (scroll paintings) as toilet paper, and melting the sacred gold statues into bullion for foreign exchange to serve the ambitions of distant Beijing. Surely these were circumstances of crushing despair—but the Tibetans were not crushed. Meeting them on the mountain roads, visiting their simple but colorful rooms, watching them at the tea stalls, I was continually impressed by their cheerful expressions and their almost wry sense of humor that shaped the world for their gentle amusement. The Tibetan women, especially, were remarkable, more free in their carriage and easy laughter, more unselfconsciously outgoing than any women I had ever seen. (All that is lost, I am certain, as the Tibetan refugee girls have since been sent through Indian schools, learning feminine insecurity and perpetual restraint.) I thought often of Abraham Lincoln's homey observation that most people are just about as happy as they make up their minds to be. But how?

An agitated mind creates its own torment. An excessively agitated mind often inflicts physical or psychological damage on family, community, other nations, or other species. With the good of the individual and society resting so squarely on the nature of mindstates—from which historical patterns of political, economic, and aesthetic culture evolve—it is surprising that the modern, rationalist notion of the human is so lacking in subtle perception of the nature of mindstates and an understanding of their inception and dissolution. For that we must look elsewhere: the great wisdom traditions.

Which of the wisdom traditions or schools of psychology and philosophy have gone as far as the Buddha's teachings on

Dhamma,* in perceiving the nature of mind, the nature of mental anguish, and the way beyond these? Who has ever orchestrated so vast an experiment in grace embodied as Emperor Asoka's Dhamma society? Who has ever demonstrated as effectively as Gandhi (though his practice of purifying the mind was Hindu rather than Buddhist) the connection between spiritual states of "pure mind/pure heart" and the power of nonviolent activism? If we examine these graced lives and the practices developed within them, with attention to our contemporary crises and a desire to seek and enhance basic cosmological processes of differentiation, subjectivity, and communion, we encounter new possibilities.

The Wisdom of Dhamma

The Buddha was an empiricist and a spiritual revolutionary. Turning away from the religious dogma and superstitions of his day, he set out to understand—through direct observation—the human condition.

He was born Siddhattha Gotama in a grove of sala trees, probably in the year 563 B.C., a contemporary of Thales, Anaximander, and Pythagoras. His father was the ruler of a province in the kingdom of Kosala, homeland of the Sakya people, on the plains of northeastern India-Nepal. Although he was indulged and elaborately sheltered from the cares of the world beyond his

---

**Dhamma* is a Pali word meaning the way things really are, the truth of flux and being, the law of nature; it also means teachings about the true nature of phenomena, as opposed to illusions of perception at the surface level. The Buddha's discourses are preserved in Pali, a vernacular derivative of Sanskrit used throughout south Asia for Buddhist teachings (for example, *kamma, sutta, nibbana, Siddhattha Gotama*). In the countries where Buddhism later traveled, to the north, and in Hinduism, Sanskrit counterparts are used (for example, *dharma, karma, sutra, nirvana, Siddhartha Gautama*). Northern, or Mahayana, Buddhism—especially Zen—and its Sanskrit terms are much better known in the U.S. To balance things a bit, this presentation of Buddhism focuses on the original, core teachings, which, after all, are the foundation upon which all the rich cultural variations that followed are based. The Zen *roshi* Shunryu Suzuki, for instance, maintained, "We are just Buddhists. We are not even Zen Buddhists. If we understand this point, we are truly Buddhists."

father's walls, Gotama ventured forth as a young man on a series of brief excursions that revealed to him the range of human suffering: anxiety, grief, jealousy, lust, greed, hatred, fear, disease, old age, and death. At the age of twenty-eight he left his life of luxury to devote himself to the ascetic spiritual disciplines then taught in India, in the hope of attaining the liberation from suffering they promised.

Gotama studied with two teachers in succession, excelling in their concentration practices (the eight stages of absorption, or *jhana*), but he eventually saw that their practices did not yield release from misery. Although he left them, he retained respect for the basic truths widely taught by spiritual teachers of that era. First, the need for morality was stressed as the foundation for progress in spiritual purification and liberation of the mind. (Gotama later expressed the moral necessities simply as five precepts: no killing, no taking what is not freely given, no lying, no sexual misconduct, and no use of intoxicants.) Second, the wisdom teachings of his day already contained a good deal of insight into the human condition. They identified four basic mental processes: perception, recognition, feeling, reaction. These teachings also maintained that, contrary to the illusion of solidity, the body and its mental processes are in constant flux at the level of the *kalapa*—or the subatomic level, as we would call it today. Because of that impermanence, the notion of "I" was seen to be illusory, and the notion of real happiness residing in a supposedly fixed body/mind was seen to be negated inevitably by disappointment and anguish. The cause of such unhappiness was identified as the mental bondage of craving or aversion.

Seeing that mere acceptance of those assertions at the intellectual level did not result in the cessation of suffering, Gotama set off with a few peers to move beyond the level of belief to the *experiencing* of truth about the processes of mind and body. For six years he diligently practiced advanced levels of concentration, difficult breathing exercises, self-mortification, and near starvation. Eventually he realized that mortification of the body does not lead to wisdom, a decision that caused his companions to abandon him. He also realized that he had purified his mind at the surface level but was not fully liberated because negativities, impurities, and complexes remained at the deep, deep level of the mind.

Remembering the peace he had felt as a boy in contemplation under a majestic tree as his father plowed the field before him,[1] Gotama, then thirty-five years of age, seated himself under a towering poplar-fig tree and resolved not to move until he had observed the true nature of mind and attained liberation from human misery. He began that long night, he later revealed in his teaching of meditation, by observing his respiration, moving from gross to subtle awareness, and by observing the contents of the mind and the sensations on and in the body. When his concentration brought his conscious mind in contact with the deeper levels of mind, he was able to go deep inside the mental processes until the illusion of solidity was dissected and dissolved by his unwavering attention. He saw that, indeed, mental contents as well as the physical structure of the body were in constant flux and were composed of trillions of microevents, extraordinarily minute particles or movements of energy arising and passing away, arising and passing away with great rapidity.

According to the teachings preserved through the centuries in the southern Buddhist countries,[2] the Buddha then realized that his teachers and peers were working with only apparent truth in claiming that we react directly to stimuli (anything seen, heard, smelled, felt by touch or by heat or cold, or thought) with craving or aversion. He saw clearly that the mental process of reaction arises not because of recognition and judgment of a stimulus ("Oh, very nice! I want more!"), but, rather, because the deep levels of mind are reacting to pleasant or unpleasant *subtle bodily sensations.* Gotama saw that the "unconscious" portion of the mind is vastly larger than the conscious portion and is not unconscious at all: it functions in constant reaction to minute bodily sensations, causing, for example, the body to slap a mosquito, scratch an itch, or roll over in response to the buildup of pressure—all while the conscious mind sleeps. He saw that the "unconscious" mind is not interested in what goes on in the conscious mind, only in the bodily sensations.

Gotama grasped that the ordinary sequence is (1) the conscious mind perceives a stimulus, via the five senses or via a thought arising; (2) the conscious mind identifies and judges it, assigning some negative or positive value (seemingly "neutral" judgments are usually indifference rather than positive judgments); (3) negative or positive sensations arise in or on the body, with subtle or gross intensity in response to the intensity of the valuation; and (4) the deep levels of the mind react to the (usually minute) bodily sensations by generating pleasant or unpleasant emotions and reactions.[3] What is pleasure? It is the feeling of pleasant sensations (or the effect of "neurotransmitters," as recent studies in the biochemistry of the brain would have it) in or on the body, to which the deep levels of mind react with emotions of happiness and contentment. Unpleasant bodily sensations yield emotions of distress.[4]

Gotama saw the futility of trying to repress reactive emotions since the deep levels of mind react blindly to subtle bodily sensations and take no instructions from the conscious level. He also understood then the damage that repression causes, as that aggressive effort generates even stronger patterns of reaction.

Once he understood the "missing link" in the actual chain of mental processes—the response of the unconscious mind to subtle bodily sensations—Gotama was able to work with that knowledge and attain his enlightenment. He saw that human consciousness is by nature completely pure, but becomes marred by defilements of hatred, greed, and delusion that manifest through reactive mental processes. When he was able to bring his conscious mind in contact with the deeper levels, through subtle, direct observation in meditation, he saw that it is possible for the conscious mind to cultivate awareness that the minute, moment-to-moment sensations are transitory; hence there is no point in clinging to them; hence they need not be reacted to. Bare awareness of the subtle sensations, *without judging them bad or good* and thereby calling forth more reactive emotions, breaks the chain reaction and gradually eradicates habitual patterns of response, which are the cause of deep complexes.

As Gotama continued to intervene in his own reactive mental processes simply with unbroken awareness, he saw that the mind becomes purified as the patterns of reaction are weakened and as the judgmental, evaluating process becomes correspondingly less intense. As he progressed and the deep, habitual patterns of reaction were eradicated, his entire mental structure became filled with the qualities of a liberated mind: pure love, infinite compassion, joy in the joy of others, and equanimity.

He experienced the memory of past existences and understood that rebirth is a consequence of deeds. He saw that this life was the final rebirth he would undergo.

He continued to progress to subtler and subtler levels of awareness until he arrived at experiential knowledge of the ultimate truth: that matter and energy—constituting mental contents, the physical structure of the body, and the forms manifested in the surrounding universe—are nothing but vibration and oscillation. He saw that this truth of the entire universe can be experienced within the framework of the body.

Still he went further and experienced the fading away and cessation of craving, the end of suffering, the perception beyond conditions of arising and passing away—the unconditioned state of Nibbana.[5]

At dawn a Buddha arose. Gotama was henceforth called by that title—the Enlightened One, the Awakened One—by all who heard him. Filled with love and compassion for the suffering of all beings, Gotama Buddha spent the remaining forty-five years of his life teaching the practical method by which people can observe the nature of mind, the cause of suffering, and the cessation of suffering. He taught not sectarian "Buddhism" but universal Dhamma, the pure truth, the actual nature of being. (The term "Buddhist" was not applied to followers of his teachings until some five hundred years after his death; rather, they were called followers of Dhamma—*Dhammatho, Dhammiko, Dhammachari.*) Moreover, he claimed no inspiration from any

god or external power, attributing his realization and achievements to human endeavor and human intelligence.[6] He taught that empirical observation of cause and effect regarding the human psyche and behavior, rather than notions of divine intervention, offers a sure path beyond anguish.

The Buddha began his teachings by delivering the discourse called "The Turning of the Wheel of Dhamma" in the deer park near Sarnath. Both of his teachers had died, but he sought out the five ascetic friends who had been with him earlier in order to open for them the "gate to liberation." With clarity and love, he expressed the wisdom of the Four Noble Truths: suffering is with us throughout this life; the cause of suffering is desire (craving or aversion); the way out of suffering is the way beyond desire; that way is the Eightfold Noble Path. The eightfold path consists of morality (right speech, right action, right livelihood), meditation (right concentration, right mindfulness, right effort), and wisdom (right understanding, right thought), each of which strengthens the growth of the others. Together they comprise the path known as the Middle Way, avoiding extremes of asceticism or indulgence.

His former associates then became his first monk-disciples. When the Buddha established his order of monks, and later an order of nuns, he developed a democratic and decentralized model unheard of in that era, which welcomed all strata of society and enlarged roles for women beyond the Brahmanic restrictions. He maintained that the purpose of the monks' and nuns' work was to help as many people as possible to become established in Dhamma, not dependent on an institution or a particular teacher. He asked them to preach the way of Dhamma, as did he, in the vernacular language of Magadhi, which closely resembles the Pali language, rather than in the more elitist, literary language of Sanskrit. He groomed no successor.

The Buddha traveled throughout northern India teaching the truths he had realized during the night of his enlightenment under the Bodhi tree. His means of cultivation (*bhavana*, meditation) of "clear observation" (*vipassana*) he taught in the Great

Discourse on Establishing Mindfulness (*Mahasatipatthana Sutta*). That discourse covers the foundations of mindfulness (subtle awareness of the body, of sensations, of mental states, of mental contents), the means of cultivating awareness, the seven factors of enlightenment, and an explication of the Four Noble Truths. The Buddha taught that consciousness is by nature extremely pure and that *nature* eliminates the defilements that arise if we are able in meditation to observe the mental processes without reaction. He also emphasized the importance of *metta* meditation, the cultivation of lovingkindness and goodwill toward all beings. He spoke often of the causal Law of Dependent Arising (or Dependent Origination or Conditioned Genesis) by which our responses to life—our moment-to-moment existence—are colored by our previous mental reactions. To eliminate the cause of anguish is to eliminate the effect.

Above all, the Buddha admonished listeners not to believe anything he said until they had tried the practice for themselves. Spiritual teachings, he advised, should never be accepted merely because of the weight of tradition or respect for a teacher, but only if they are wholesome and effective. He discouraged speculation of all sorts, as it distracted people from experiential realization. He taught that the purification and liberation of the mind lies within the realm of individual effort; hence the common practice of paying Brahmanic priests to perform rituals on one's behalf was fruitless. This position resulted in enmity toward him throughout the powerful priestly caste. They were also angered at the Buddha's rejection of the caste system and at his teachings that there is no evidence of personified godheads, a permanent soul, or even a fixed entity that is the "self." Instead, all phenomena are impermanent—composed of trillions of microevents yielding continuity but not stasis—and lack any set essence or fixed self-identity.

In spite of Brahmanic opposition, the Buddha's teachings on the wisdom of Dhamma continued to spread. Monks, nuns, and countless lay followers of both sexes experienced through their practice a great lessening of mindstates of haunting agitation. At the same time, mindstates of love, compassion, joy in the joy of others, and equanimity increasingly arose within them. True happiness and gratitude colored their days. Many of the Buddha's followers attained full enlightenment; their names, male and female, are preserved in the Pali Canon, the compilation of discourses (*sutta*), events, and records.

In addition to his teachings on ethical, spiritual, and philosophical problems, the Buddha also delivered discourses on social, economic, and political matters.[7] Many of these addressed the proper conduct of kings, for there were many corrupt ones in his day; we would substitute the word "government." In the *Cakkavattisihanada Sutta* he states that poverty is the cause of immorality and crimes such as theft, falsehood, violence, and so forth. Trying to suppress such crime through punishment is futile, he states in the *Kutadanta Sutta*. Instead, the economic condition of the people should be improved. Among his teachings on "Ten Duties of the King" are nonobstruction of the will of the people, as well as nonviolence.[8]

Leaving a legacy of deliverance and love, of wisdom and compassion, the Buddha died in 463 B.C. Nearing his death, he advised his disciples to "dwell making yourselves your support and refuge, making the Dhamma your support and refuge."[9] He asked them not to grieve, for surely they had learned that all things are subject to change, instability, and loss. Reclining under a canopy of sala trees, he gave last words of encouragement: "Transient are conditioned phenomena. Work with diligence to accomplish your goal [realization, liberation from illusion]." According to tradition, Gotama Buddha then entered a meditative state and progressed into *parinibbana*, the final state of blissful liberation from which further rebirth is unnecessary.

Dhamma in Daily Life

According to Buddhist tradition, Gotama was the twenty-sixth Buddha in a succession that reaches back through distant eons. He is said to have rediscovered the technique that had been practiced in India long before his time, long before the cattle-herding Aryan invaders arrived and installed their omnipotent sky-god on Mount Meru. In his efforts to find that practice Gotama was guided and inspired by his affinity with nature, so it was under a tree—with his hand on the earth, to ground himself throughout temptations to doubt and surrender—that he attained liberation. It was in a deer park that he gave his first sermon. It was under a tree that he entered *parinibbana*. Gotama entrusted himself to nature, and finally he was graced by nature, presented with the revelation of mystery via passage through the illusion of stasis and solidity to the most subtle dance of vibrations. He saw that our consciousness is pure by nature. If we can keep our balance of one-pointedness in meditation and break the reactive chain of mental defilements, nature dissolves the impurities, cleanses and restores us, bathing us in grace.

What does that feel like? Coming out of a ten-day silent meditation retreat, not necessarily with full liberation, one is taken by surprise. Waves of gratitude arise in the mind at unexpected moments for all that is wholesome and beautiful in one's life: the richness of parental love, the blessing of a child, the pleasure of good friends, the bounty of the erotic. One is amazed at how precisely one can see—the vibrancy of flowers and the hundred shades of green, the wing bars on a goldfinch, the exquisite grain in a piece of wood, the shading in the clouds. (It becomes clear then that our usual habits of vision are lazy conveniences that gloss over the particular and the unexpected, the amazing differentiation of the cosmos.) One exists in communion with all life, with every expression of the universe. Happiness is the most frequent mindstate, but, above all, one experiences lightness of the body/mind and a radiant sense of subjectivity. The mind has been freed, even a little, from intensely reactive patterns and so becomes more active in a positive way, anchored in awareness of mindstates and subtle bodily sensations. The weight of predetermination—of reactive resignation, depression, rage, fear—has been lifted. One is no longer a victim of emotionally charged mindstates that seem to take over. That is why the Vietnamese monk Thich Nhat Hanh, when asked how much free will we have, replies without hesitation: "The amount of free will we have depends on how well we practice mindfulness."[10]

For twenty-five hundred years Buddhist meditators, their families, and friends have noticed transformation of character, a gradual movement into ease, strength, and peace. How is it possible that such deep and lasting change could occur, belying theories that our nature is determined for life by heredity and early childhood experiences? Much current research in the neurophysiology of the brain suggests that the Buddha was not speaking metaphorically when he said it is possible to eliminate, not repress, even deeply established patterns of reaction. The brain and the entire nervous system are now understood to function in a state of continuous structural change insofar as the formation of the nerve pathways is plastic and dynamic. Learning and memory, for instance, are dynamic processes that sculpt and resculpt the connections between neurons. To a certain extent, we literally create the structural design of our brains by our mental processes, our habits of response.[11]

The unfolding design of the universe, then, has given us an amazing capacity for evolutionary creativity, or subjectivity, at our very core. That ability does not entertain excuses. We are responsible. No one is trapped ("Gee, sorry I was so rude and nasty, but I've just always been an angry kinda guy"), short of mental illness, as there is a way out of the unskillful mindstates. Because the meditation taught by the Buddha provides the means by which we can create the conditions for our psychological response to events, destructive actions can no longer be accepted as coming uncontrollably from some "dark side," "shadow," or "demonic force" in the mind that is a permanent condition to be "managed." The romanticized "demonic" or "shadow" is simply an unskillful mindstate, a habitual use of particular neural pathways that form the road to a living hell. Using those patterns of reaction only strengthens them. That is why the aggressive act-out or scream-it-out therapies of the 1970s were found to be ineffective over time: mindstates of rage and ill will (if fed with more emotion rather than observed with equanimity) create the patterns for future mindstates of rage and ill will.

Science can tell us why the process of establishing a new habitual reaction becomes easier over time, as the new neural pathways are established, but it cannot explain why a meditation technique that greatly lessens the strength and frequency of negative mindstates, *no matter what the subject matter*, results in the abundance of happy and peaceful mindstates. Why not merely neutral mindstates? Our nature, freed from the torturous reactive modes that we ourselves create, reveals itself to be joyous, loving, and filled with gratitude, the roots of celebration.

When we begin to cleanse the mind of hatred, greed, and delusion and begin to comprehend interbeing at more and more subtle levels of perception, we grasp the Buddha's teaching that *evil is ignorance*. Just ignorance? Isn't that too innocent, too passive a circumstance to account for the massively destructive forces of evil? The failure to know the nature of mind condemns us to the misery of agitated mindstates, a misery we rarely keep to ourselves but inflict on everyone whose life we affect. Militarism, political oppression, exploitative economic arrangements, and a range of other aggressive acts have been traced to defensive psychological reactions stemming from deep-seated fear and self-loathing. The perpetrators are dominated by a stream of negative mindstates. They are pathetically ignorant of compassion, lovingkindness, joy in the joy of others, and equanimity—except in the limited ways allowed by their fear and pain. The ecstatic truth of interbeing escapes them. This is true also of people who exhibit disrespectful, dominating behavior on a smaller scale as well. Ignorance constricts and diminishes them.

A person established in Buddhist meditation perceives—even when on the receiving end of a verbal attack—the mental torment that drives the almost hysterical outbursts of a destructive, dominating person. It is not from theory but from the experience of having watched her or his own mind at thousands of moments when anger or fear or any other emotion has arisen that the meditator knows the nature of mind when flooded by emotion. That in-the-moment clarity during an attack leads to a surprising development: hatred of the agitated attacker has become impossible. Compassion arises. A meditator may, of course, "take a tumble" and allow reactive mindstates of anger or other negativity to take over his or her behavior (which is more likely to happen if he or she has become lazy about the daily practice of meditation), but the negative mindstates do not linger nearly as long as they did before one began to purify the mind.

Even more important, one cannot lie to oneself by rationalizing one's own negative behavior. One's psychological reaction to any event is the meditator's choice; it is not controlled or excused by the event. This does not mean that we control all events that affect us or that we have no control over such events, simply that our response depends on the quality of mind. Without the precise awareness developed in meditation, the subject matter one is thinking about usually overshadows any attention to the condition of one's moment-to-moment mindstate.

When anger, for instance, arises in the mind/body, the meditator is aware of the sensations. "My mind is very agitated. My earlobes feel hot. My gut muscles have tightened. My breathing has become shallow." While paying attention to the content of the event or conversation, she or he is also aware of her or his own body/mindstate, and that very awareness stops—or at least slows—the chain reaction into escalating states of negative emotion. The reason for the anger, perhaps a cruelty or an injustice, can then be addressed, even quite firmly, without the limitations of blind reaction. Even if a strong response is required, a meditator will first try to become certain that no trace of ill will, only compassion, resides in his or her mind.

The formative change over time is simply that many fewer mindstates of hatred, greed, and delusion than before arise in the meditator's mind at all. Surely it is this movement toward grace—the lessening of our private alienation—that explains all the softly shining transformations I have observed over the years among those who live by Dhamma as best they can.

Insofar as we do not succeed in purifying the mind, our experiential horizons are delineated by the First Noble Truth: suffering is with us throughout this life. By *dukkha* (usually translated from Pali too narrowly as "suffering"), the Buddha meant not only the obvious examples of psychological pain and hardship but also the unease caused by the evanescent, imperfect, insubstantial nature of human situations. We experience existence as being unsatisfactory and frustrating, he taught, because of unrealistic expectations resulting from incorrect perceptions of the actual nature of our situation. We crave and imagine stasis, security, and permanence when actually there is only the flux of impermanence.

One response to the human condition is diversion: excessive and often addictive use of alcohol, drugs, television, movies, video games, shopping, spectator sports, amusement parks, and so forth. While focusing attention on such activities does not free the mind from agitation in any lasting way (in fact, it generates agitation through cravings), it does provide temporary relief from painful mental contents, that is, both thoughts and emotional states. Hence there is a huge market for such diversions.

A large portion of our economy caters to the craving for relief from psychological pain, which is often caused by the direct or indirect effects of the even larger portion of the economy that is the growth-manic military-industrial complex: ill health and birth defects from pollution, strains on family life from an every-man-for-himself economy, disintegrative pressures on communities, admitting our destruction of Third- and Fourth-World cultures, mourning for the dying ecosystems, and terror of the fifty thousand nuclear warheads and the stockpiles of chemical and biological weapons. Yet these are crises that can best be addressed with active, rather than reactive, minds that are not trapped in the limiting patterns of denial, depression, or rage. Moreover, such problems are certainly not the only cause of painful mindstates. We begin our reactive patterns when we are very, very young, and we suffer with them for a lifetime if we do not know how to dissolve them and live otherwise. No economic or political system alone can deliver us from suffering.

In a consumer economy in which growth of production levels is the only measure of success, people's suffering through craving and desire must be manipulated and inflamed. Advertising has become a pervasive presence—even in high school classrooms now—that reminds us how much we lack, how much more and better we could own, how much the quality of our existence could be sweetened—if only we will buy. The assault of advertising, in which greed is made to seem attractive, is one of the most shocking aspects of American life one must adjust to when reentering the culture from a wilderness trip, a meditation retreat, a journey to an "undeveloped" country, or some similar absence. The blurring of greed into need is continually projected at us. The last thing the manipulators want is sharp awareness among consumers of the mental phenomenon of greed and craving arising in the mind at the very moment such reactions are triggered by advertising or other means.

Quite a different response to perceiving no exit from the First Noble Truth is to refuse all diversions and stare straight into the face of mental anguish, declaring its horror as the grim reality that the culture at large denies. This is the path of the existentialists, for example. They saw the truth of human nature revealed in moments of experiencing a generalized dread. Anxiety and the shadow of death are the mindstates they dwelled upon. I, with the impatience of a twenty-year-old, found their works in my college philosophy classes to be stupidly pessimistic. Only later, when I had spent many hours of meditation minutely observing the arising of suffering in my own mind, did I appreciate the courage of their truth-telling, even though I had come to see that the roots of anguish are more elemental than "objects" (other people) frustrating one's "projects," as Sartre put it. Moreover, it seemed a tragedy that they had pitched their tents so forcefully in the First Noble Truth but did not perceive a way to get beyond it.

In *vipassana* (insight, clear observation) meditation one experiences what the Buddha called *anicca* (impermanence, flux, insubstantiality) as continuously as possible. By focusing unbroken attention on the subtle sensations arising and passing away in the body and on the thoughts and emotions arising and passing away in the mind, one gradually comes to grasp the universal reality so denied by our bedrock constructs of self, family, nation. All is in ceaseless transformation. Even seemingly static pain in the body is seen to be dynamic and in flux. Our nouns—labeling the apparently solid, permanent, and immutable—are more correctly verbs of becoming. As the Buddha observed, the entire visible universe is fluid.

One's utterly admirable self—so rarely understood, alas, by others—deconstructed, dissolved, dissected at finer and finer stages of perception until only the fact of vibratory flux remains? Unthinkable! That indeed is the problem. *Thinking* about the marvelously constructed attributes of one's mind allows one to throw up walls of denial against the truth of insubstantiality and moment-to-moment impermanence. Discursive thinking is done through concepts, which inevitably make fixed what is actually always in process. Descartes maintained that the essential proof of being was *Cogito ergo sum* (I think, therefore I am), but he could have peeled back one more layer of construct and arrived at the bare truth: thinking is occurring. Where is the "I"?[12] Sartre claimed that we are burdened by the responsibility of having absolute freedom in all our existential choices—but what is the nature of that stalwart being who is claiming absolute freedom? Our being is an aggregate of fluid processes (perceptions, responses, thoughts, emotions, orgasms) occurring within fluid structures. You can spend a lifetime extolling the immutable grandeur of the rational mind if you wish, but it is all just part of the vibratory flow of matter/energy in you, through you, around you.

That contemporary biology, chemistry, and physics have revealed the reality of fluid process at the molecular and subatomic levels of our universe hardly helps because even the weight of Almighty Science is no match for the defenses of ego. After all, are the scientists working in those areas liberated from attachment to the idea of their immutable, personal self with all its "absolutely justified" cravings, jealousy, negativity, and anxiety? Like everyone else, they experience *dukkha*, the pain of denying their own insubstantiality and impermanence. They no more want to consider that their self will cease to exist at some unexpected moment in the future than they want to accept the fact that their created "self" does not exist even now at the level of physical reality.

Who could bear to examine closely with the subtle functions of mind the illusory nature of our image of self as a secure, idealized entity? Why risk the horror? Because we are not abandoned! Inherent in our species' evolutionary design is the potential for deliverance beyond the loss of self—a sense of self first obsessively constructed throughout a lifetime and then seen to dissolve—to a state of grace both buoyant and deeply joyful. The true nature of being, if we stop running from it, is unimaginably sublime. To grasp the truth, though, requires courage, correct effort (not straining), and perseverance.

In *vipassana* meditation, one first must develop the concentration necessary for unbroken attention; then, with increasingly subtle perceptions, one observes the moment-to-moment arising and passing away of mental contents (lots of surprises there!) and subtle bodily sensations. Eventually one glimpses the universal reality of total impermanence and insubstantiality. Too jarring to face for very long at first, perhaps, but as one comes to acknowledge the actual nature of human existence, Dhamma, what is there in one's construct of self to cling to, to prop up, to defend so desperately? When we embrace the truth of being, the illusory constructions of stasis and self fall away, and we are released into the great cosmic ocean of vibration with its exquisite manifestations and dissolutions trillions of times per second.

But what is a second? What is a moment? Our constructs of discrete, immutable beings—including ourselves—existing in discrete units of temporality (the measurement of and by discrete units moving through space) dissolve into the cosmic dance of flux. We are it. It is us. No illusions of separation, so no alienation.

It is precisely this double deconstruction of "commonsense" dualities, argues David Loy, a Buddhist, that escapes deconstructive-postmodern enthusiasts of Derrida's single deconstruction (see Appendix A). Loy sees Derrida's radical critique as incomplete because it does not deconstruct itself and attain the "closure" of metaphysical thinking that could also be the opening to a transformed mode of experiencing the world.[13] Using the Buddhist philosophy of Nagarjuna, who came six centuries after the Buddha and explained the Buddha's teaching in a mode that seems to have been influenced by Greek dialectic discourse,[14] Loy maintains that Nagarjuna would see Derrida's "liberation" only as an illusion in which one remains trapped in a textual "bad infinity." Rather than settling for a mere "change of style," which the deconstructionists advocate and which leads only to more self-conscious "reinscription" of the dualities, Buddhist teachings lead to a mode of existence that is not governed by dualism, to "the utter dissipation of ontologizing thought."[15]

As someone involved in the practice, I have naturally wondered for many years exactly how the process of sitting in Buddhist meditation (*vipassana* in my experience; *zen* in Mr. Loy's) achieves the perceptual dissolution of the "apparent truth" of labels, signs, differences, boundaries, form. I believe that transformation into a new understanding of the world through the Buddha's "clear observation" meditation is so effective because it involves body knowledge. In a long-term *vipassana* meditation retreat, for example, one can arrive at surprising moments of expansive stillness when the apparent boundaries of the body dissolve, and then the subtle vibratory nature of one's form and the surrounding world are experienced as one minutely pulsating ocean of flux. One *feels* this oneness not emotionally but empirically through bodily sensation. Afterward, walking to and from the meditation hall in silence, one sometimes experiences the subtle vibration of the leaves, the grass, the food in the dining hall, as well as in one's own body. Later, after one has reentered society ("Boundaries R Us"), one functions more—much, much more—at the level of apparent solidity and separation, but the body memory of the more subtle perceptions remains. The more one practices the meditation, the stronger that awareness becomes in our organism, gradually liberating perception and behavior—and very often improving one's health along the way.[16]

That is why even the very first steps on the path of Dhamma are achieved only through the experiential, direct-observation knowledge that is manifested during meditation. All the teachings, all the *suttas*, all the discursive embellishments exist only to support the *practice* of meditation. Neither the therapeutic nor the cosmological realizations of Dhamma can be experienced merely through the mode of intellectual description. That is why the Buddha discouraged people from accepting his words until they had tried the process.

Grace Embodied: Asoka and Others

The practice of meditation—simple to explain but challenging to practice—spread less easily throughout Asia than the *idea* of Dhamma. Most of the populace in both southern and northern countries practice "popular Buddhism" by trying to keep the precepts of morality and partaking in rituals and folk customs, such as laying flowers and other offerings before a statue of the Buddha. During this century, there has been a great increase in the number of laypersons practicing and even teaching meditation in Asia, although their numbers are proportionately small. A Cambodian monk, for example, told me that typically only about one-third of the monks and one-fourth of the laypeople, prior to the Pol Pot regime's mass executions of monks and nuns, had a practice of meditation.

There have been, of course, countless people who not only practiced the meditation taught by the Buddha but also acted to spread the benefits of that practice. Their words and deeds reflect grace embodied. Perhaps the best known is Emperor Asoka.

For twenty-three centuries the name Asoka (pronounced Ashoka) has remained alive throughout south Asia. Born roughly 160 years after the Buddha's death, he governed the vast Mauryan empire (much of present-day India and areas to the west) as a *Dhammaraja*, a king devoted to spreading the benefits of Dhamma throughout the land. Historians credit him with elevating the status of the Buddha's teachings on Dhamma, through his own conversion, from that of a regional practice in the Magadha area (on the present-day India-Nepal border) to a religion practiced all across north India to present-day Afghanistan in the west, the Himalayas in the north, and Mysore in the south—as well as Sri Lanka and the Burma-Siam region via his missionaries.

The "establishment" of Dhamma practice in a particular geographic area and Asoka's royal patronage, protection, and partial governance of the institutional *sangha* (order of monks and nuns) were not part of the Buddha's teachings, but have been emulated for centuries, even to this day, by rulers throughout the southern Buddhist countries. Unfortunately, the far greater portion of his program was never duplicated, as meditation came to be almost exclusively the domain of the monks and nuns. In terms of what the Buddha taught, Emperor Asoka's greatness lay in his energetic commitment to making the teachings of Dhamma available to all people and in his emphasizing that meditative practice coupled with morality yielded far greater benefits and happiness than mere rituals. The political models of empire and monarchy are not of much interest to us today, but Asoka's innovations remain noteworthy as creative expressions of the understanding that justice, peace, and harmony in society require liberation from defilements of consciousness: hatred, greed, and delusion.

Heroic legends lace the story of Asoka, especially in the quasi-mythical Asokan chronicles of Sri Lanka. Yet the historical record of India also speaks, and rather directly, as Asoka had his edicts carved onto rocks and forty-foot pillars of hard sandstone throughout his realm. He did not allow statues of himself, but some of the pillars were crowned with carvings of a lotus and the four animals associated with strength and leadership: the bull, the lion, the elephant, and the horse.

Asoka began as a typically ambitious prince, in the empire established by his grandfather, and may have violently usurped a provincial governorship from his half-brother. He ascended to the throne, in Pataliputra (present-day Patna), when he was about thirty, but his coronation took place four years later, in 270 B.C. It was his military conquest of the Kalinga people in 262 B.C. that became the turning point of his life and his reign. Two and a half years earlier, he had converted to the practice of Dhamma, but, as he put it, "had not exerted myself well" (Rock Edict I). After the carnage of the Kalinga war, his first and last, Asoka expressed remorse at witnessing the death and suffering of the combatants, their families, and their communities (Rock Edict XIII). He then "visited the *sangha* [monks] for more than a year and exerted myself greatly" (Rock Edict I). Judging from his later acts, he must have strengthened his practice of meditation and his commitment to moral behavior during that period; he said he "became keen in the pursuit of Dhamma, love of Dhamma, and inculcation of Dhamma" (Rock Edict I).

Subsequently Asoka outlawed war, renounced force, embraced *ahimsa* (nonharming), and advocated only moral conquest over unwholesome acts. He replaced royal hunting tours with "Dhamma tours" to revered sites and sages. He declared an end to ritual sacrifice of animals and to the killing of a long list of protected species. (He did not, however, abolish capital punishment, for reasons never specified in his edicts.) He ordered the entire royal household to become vegetarians, although peacock meat was allowed for several years. He forbade arranged fights between animals for sport. He established hospitals for humans and animals and numerous botanical gardens for cultivating medicinal herbs. To benefit travelers he had rest houses built, wells dug, and shade trees planted.

Asoka left all the adjacent kingdoms unconquered. To them, as well as to Sri Lanka, the Burma-Siam region, and western areas ruled by Macedonia, Syria, Egypt, Cyrene, and Epirus, Asoka sent teachers of Dhamma as missionaries. He also required his ministers and provincial officials to seek spiritual instruction every five years along with their regular duties. Moreover, he established a new corps of ministers called *Dhammamahamatras* whose chief work was to spread the teachings and practice of Dhamma among all sects and all socioeconomic classes. They were also responsible for a vast range of social services, including acting as ombudsmen for accused and convicted persons.

Asoka took a liberal stance toward the religious pluralism of his day—the Brahmans, Shramans (Jains and followers of the Buddha), Ajivikas, and the animistic, tribal mountain people—which was facilitated somewhat by their points of similarity. He "desires that in all places should reside people of diverse sects" (Rock Edict VII), regarding Dhamma, as did the Buddha, as a nonsectarian teaching of the law of nature. In fact, he speaks so generally in his edicts that he does not cite the Four Noble Truths, the Eightfold Noble Path, or the unconditioned state of Nibanna. He advocated a general code of morality based on Dhamma and emphasized the benefits of meditation, referring sometimes to *suttas* about *vipassana*. Even though Asoka's promotion of Dhamma was not exclusive, his prohibition of animal sacrifice was an interference with Brahmanic ritual—and the fees attached to it.

In Pillar Edict VII, written in the twenty-sixth year of his reign, Asoka spoke of the vast welfare programs undertaken by his officials and the royal family "as noble deeds of Dhamma whereby compassion, generosity, truthfulness, purity, gentleness, and goodness of the people will thus increase." Yet he concluded by noting that none of his programs and regulations could do as much to promote progress in Dhamma as the practice of meditation.

How did all this play in Pataliputra and beyond the pale? Apparently, historians tell us, there were grumblings. Foremost, the priestly Brahman caste resented the curtailing and downgrading of their brisk trade in sacrificial rituals. In addition, Asoka's version of divine kingship—that the well-being of a realm depended on the consciousness and deeds of the people, whose progress in Dhamma should be encouraged by their righteous leader—was a radical shift from the Vedic concept of the king's duty being primarily to protect the functioning of the divinely ordained castes in their duties and codes of conduct, a scheme that birthed some rather Machiavellian texts on governing for the *kshatryia* caste. It must be noted as well that Asoka was a bit puritanical in his convert's zeal, for he outlawed festivals with singing and dancing. In any case, there can be no doubt that large numbers of his subjects benefited from his social programs and encouragement to grow in Dhamma in their own lives.

Within several decades after Asoka's death, the huge empire was splintered (not a bad development if one favors local governance), and the Brahmanic reconquest of India was under way, led by Pushametra Sung, who founded a dynasty and established Vedic rule. That counterreformation eventually produced classic texts of post-Buddha Hinduism, which incorporate a great deal of Gotama's teachings incongruously with pre-Buddha Vedic elements that had been introduced by the Aryan (Indo-European) invaders. In them one reads, for example, that there is only the law of Dhamma ("Dharma" in the Hindu texts) and that each person is his or her own master, but also that there is an omnipotent sky-god named Brahma to whom everyone must surrender, especially through obeisance to the priestly caste. Many of the classic Hindu texts also present profound expressions of Dhamma (or "Dharma") framed in the Aryan invaders' scheme of adoration of the warrior, patriarchal-chieftan social systems, and distant gods ruling from the heavens or mountaintops. Brahmanic Hindu texts also emphasize belief in an immutable core, or soul, which is identical among humans, even though the rest of human experience is in flux.

The Brahmanic ministers ruling the lands of the old Mauryan empire made them decidedly inhospitable to Buddhists and

Jains.[17] Eventually, the practice that had been taught by Gotama Buddha was destroyed in India. Dhamma flourished, however, in countries to the north, the east, and the southeast. There Asoka's dream found partial expression through the centuries.

The ideal of the *Dhammaraja* has been emulated, and sometimes hypocritically exploited, by numerous kings and prime ministers in both socialist and capitalist Buddhist countries in the modern era. Not surprisingly, though, it is not from the pinnacle of the nation-state but from the grassroots that most genuine expressions of Dhamma have sprung in our time, with such energy that the force of their integrity proved revolutionary. A call to return to Buddhism and turn away from the imposed religion of the European colonial rulers was often one of the starting points of liberation movements in Buddhist countries during the late colonial period, but the manipulation of Dhamma for nationalist goals took precedence over an actual renewal of the practice of meditation and morality. During the past several decades a number of grassroots Dhamma-based projects and movements have been created that are further examples of embodied grace, even with all their imperfections.

The Sarvodaya movement has brought community renewal to over six thousand villages in Sri Lanka by successfully basing a program of economic and social revitalization on the teachings of Dhamma. For example, *dana* is a term known to everyone in the southern Buddhist countries; it means to give (usually alms or food to monks). The founder of the Sarvodaya movement, A. T. Ariyaratna, gave that common term a twist when he combined it with *shrama* (labor or human energy): *shramadana* is a community work project that includes a sense of spiritual practice. The name *Sarvodaya* itself is from the Sanskrit roots *sarva* (of all) and *udaya* (awakening or arising; Gandhi used it to mean uplift or welfare).

A central belief in the Sarvodaya movement is that all people can change, that is, come out of greed, hatred, and delusion, and serve the common good. With meditation and other spiritual practices, they encourage the transformation of mind as well as collective conditions. The organizers use a chart showing "The Four Noble Truths of Village Awakening," and they interpret the Four Abodes (lovingkindness, compassion, joy in the joy of others, equanimity) as well as the four principles of social behavior (generosity, pleasant speech, social equality, constructive work) in ways that are immediately relevant to communal efforts. They frequently remind the villagers that the Sarvodaya movement's call for self-reliance parallels the Buddha's urging his followers to rely on their own experience and their own efforts. They point also to the historic model of the Sangha (the order of monks and nuns, particularly in the early centuries) as an example of self-reliant, decentralized decision making.

In an insightful study of the dynamics behind Sarvodaya's success, *Dharma and Development: Religion as Resource in the Sarvodaya Self-Help Movement*, Joanna Macy concluded, "Sarvodaya's engagement of people's religious traditions and aspirations is not instrumental to its work of community development, nor is it a means to attract them to the Movement, but rather the reverse. Community development is seen as a means for helping people realize goals that are essentially religious."[18]

In the widely influential book *Small Is Beautiful: Economics as if People Mattered* by E. F. Schumacher, the chapter titled "Buddhist Economics" presents values that the author absorbed during his several years in Burma: "The keynote of Buddhist economics is simplicity and nonviolence. From an economist's point of view, the marvel of the Buddhist way of life is the utter rationality of its pattern—amazingly small means leading to extraordinarily satisfactory results."[19] Schumacher noted that Buddhist economics is necessarily very different from the economics of modern materialism since the Buddhist sees the essence of civilization not in a multiplication of wants but in the purification of human character. The structure of work should encourage one's development.[20]

The three groupings of the Eightfold Noble Path (morality, meditation, wisdom) are viewed by Sulak Sivaraksa, a Thai who is chairman of the Asian Cultural Forum on Development, as vehicles of self-knowledge that can lead to what Paulo Friere calls "conscientization" in Latin America, an awakening and awareness of the dynamics of one's socioeconomic situation. Sivaraksa sees the "awakening into awareness" in a spiritual sense as well as a materialist one, emphasizing that only wisdom can avoid the hatred, greed, and delusion served by partial knowledge.

These are but a few examples of "engaged Buddhism," the practice of wisdom and compassion: the identification of the cause of suffering and the eradication of the cause in such a way that everyone's potential growth in Dhamma is foremost. The quality of mind always matters.[21]

Gandhi and the Imperative of Nonviolence

When the suffering addressed is of a horrifying magnitude, such as the potential effect of the nuclear arms race, it almost seems that no guidelines for behavior could be relevant, that all categories are suspended in the face of mass extinction. How should we respond to the actual and potential amassed violence of the nuclearized security state with its vast cult of militarism in service to an unqualified-growth economy? What response is appropriate to the stockpiling of nuclear, chemical, and genetically engineered biological weapons of devastating capacity? What's a species to do when faced with the rapid destruction of our habitat by acid rain, air pollution, toxic dumping, a hole in the ozone layer, and massive loss of topsoil? When the threat of violence is ever present, as in a dictator's police state, how can the citizens manage to resist? When structural violence is so pervasive that huge segments of the human family are denied justice and opportunity, what kind of action does the humiliation and frustration demand?

The solution to the escalation of direct and structural violence in our time is not more violence. In each of the areas of concern cited above, grassroots movements have successfully altered the situation through nonviolent mobilization. Against seemingly impossible odds, how is that possible? Hannah Arendt suggested that power, by which she meant the power that "springs up whenever people get together and act in concert," and violence are opposites. Violence appears only when power and its legitimation are in jeopardy. "To speak of nonviolent power," she maintained, "is actually redundant."[22]

When the support of the governed—the threatened, the poisoned, the exploited, the ignored—is withdrawn, power goes with it. What then? Mindstates of rage and hatred plant the seeds for further mindstates of rage and hatred. The pioneers of nonviolent resistance saw so clearly the downward spiral of violence that they devoted themselves to finding an alternative. From the quiet dignity and bedrock determination of the women of the Montgomery bus boycott in the early stages of the civil rights movement, to the mothers of "the Disappeared" bearing witness during the Argentine junta's reign of terror, to the throngs of Filipinos marching behind statues of the Virgin Mary up to Marcos's tanks, we have seen the transformative power of nonviolent activism. For their courage and creativity surely the rest of the human family should feel deep gratitude. They created possibilities that allow us to hope.[23]

The very pragmatic necessity of nonviolent social change was expressed eloquently by Martin Luther King, Jr.:

> The old law of an eye for an eye leaves everybody blind. It is immoral because it seeks to humiliate the opponent rather than win his understanding; it seeks to annihilate rather than to convert. Violence is immoral because it thrives on hatred rather than love. It destroys community and makes brotherhood impossible. It leaves society in monologue rather than dialogue. Violence ends by defeating itself. It creates bitterness in the survivors and brutality in the destroyers.[24]

King, like millions of other nonviolent activists worldwide, was inspired by the teachings and actions of "the Great Soul," the *mahatma*, of whom he declared, "If humanity is to progress, Gandhi is inescapable."[25]

It is impossible to understand fully what Gandhi meant by his key concept *satyagraha* without knowing Dharma, particularly the Hindu sense of that concept, but that has not fazed countless nonreligious and antireligion political analysts. They typically downplay Gandhi's spiritual dimension, which is the bedrock upon which everything stands in Gandhian thought, as an embarrassing and shadowy obstruction to the "real" content: political strategy and tactics. One such commentator noted with apparent surprise that Gandhi's religious bent did not seem to interfere with rational thought and his ability to accept empirical evidence! At most, the political analysts usually grant that Gandhi's considerable political success was laced with concern about "ethics" or "morality." Surely Gandhi would chuckle at this "cafeteria Gandhism," for he himself was quite forthright in expressing the overall meaning of his work:

> Religion is to morality what water is to the seed that is sown in the soil.[26]

> To see the universal and all-pervading spirit of Truth face to face one must be able to love the meanest of creation as oneself. And a man who aspires after that cannot afford to keep out of any field of life. That is why my devotion to Truth has drawn me into the field of politics; and I can say without the slightest hesitation and yet in all humility that those who say that religion has nothing to do with politics do not know what religion means.[27]

> Quite selfishly, as I wish to live in peace in the midst of a bellowing storm howling around me, I have been experimenting with myself and my friends by introducing religion into politics. Let me explain what I mean by religion. It is not the Hindu religion, which I certainly prize above all other religions, but the religion which transcends Hinduism, which changes one's very nature, which binds one indissolubly to the truth within and which ever purifies.[28]

He is speaking, of course, of Dharma.

While there is great value in studying Gandhi's political strategies, and some useful guides have been written to aid one in that task,[29] the focus of this study is, rather, to examine Gandhi's "experiments with truth," as he called his life's work, in order to illuminate the extent to which his leadership of a downtrodden nation in its struggle for liberation from an imperial giant was offered in a state of grace. Like Asoka, he envisioned a society in which hatred, greed, and delusion were minimized by spiritual practices of purifying the mind. Gandhi, however, favored *karma yoga* as his practice, selfless service to others.

Gandhi was born into a family of the Vaishnava sect of Hinduism, which is theistic and places great importance on compassion. Tulsida's vernacular translation of the *Ramayana* epic was read in their home by a friend of the family, exposing young Gandhi to the virtuous Rama, who declares that he will accept banishment for fourteen years to honor a rash vow made by his father because truth is the foundation of all merit and virtue. Gandhi was also influenced by the Jain concepts of *anekantavada* (the many-sidedness of reality) and *syadvada* (every judgment of a subject yields only a partial truth).[30]

It was in London, where Gandhi studied law from 1888 to 1891, that he developed a deep appreciation of the wisdom of his own land. He associated with overlapping circles of "Simple Lifers," vegetarians, Fabians, and Theosophists, who were much influenced by Hinduism and whose motto was "There is no religion higher than Truth." He met Sir Edwin Arnold and read *The Light of Asia*, his book-length poem on the Buddha, and *The Celestial Song*, his translation of the *Bhagavad Gita*. From that first encounter with "Gita the Mother," as Gandhi came to call that sacred text, it remained a mainstay of his life. He later wrote many commentaries on it, expounding his sense of its central teaching: the spirit of service without attachment to rewards is the path to self-realization. In South Africa he read the other two books that he said influenced him the most, Tolstoy's *The Kingdom of God Is within You* and Ruskin's *Unto These Last*.

It was also during the South African campaigns, on behalf of the oppressed Indian community there, that Gandhi developed the concept of *satyagraha*. He explained, "Truth (*satya*) implies love, and firmness (*agraha*) engenders and, therefore, serves as a synonym for force. I thus began to call the Indian movement *Satyagraha*; that is to say, the Force which is born of Truth and Love or non-violence. . . ."[31]

To the Indian community, *satya*, from the root *sat*, "being," had a resonance not understood by many Western commentators, who sometimes conclude that Gandhi's nattering on about "Truth" is too vague to be useful. For a Hindu the truth of being is contained in Dharma: that "the world is changing every moment. . . ; it has no permanent existence," as Gandhi wrote;[32] that existence is nondualistic in essence; that there is an ordered moral governance of the universe ("Dharma is the foundation of the whole universe. . . . Upon Dharma everything is founded."—*Taittiriya Aranyaka*, an ancient Hindu text); that one should understand one's place in the cosmos and in relation to others; and that one should cultivate virtuous behavior. The *Upanishads* do not speak of reality in terms of God but in terms of *satya* and Dharma.[33]

The Hindu sense of Dharma also includes "duty" as a primary expression of the core meaning. Duty, which is prescribed minutely in the ancient Hindu "Codes of Manu," relates to their notion of caste and the maintaining of "balance," but also can mean the righting of injustices. Gandhi, who did not find the legalistic work of Manu inspiring, felt that Jesus had given "a perfect definition of Dharma" in the Sermon on the Mount.[34] He wrote that *satya* and *ahimsa* (nonharming action) comprise "the royal road to Dharma that leads both to earthly and spiritual bliss."[35] That would not have seemed an odd message to a Hindu—for the *Mahabharata* teaches, "Whatever is attended with *ahimsa* that is Dharma"—but it certainly must have seemed unusual coming from the leader of a political campaign.

In Gandhi's experience, spiritual growth, which included a large measure of self-purification, led one to a greater understanding of Truth, from which emerged love, tenderness, and humility, a widening of sympathies and their natural expression in the desire to be of service to others.[36] He wrote in the introduction of a biography of Raichand, a Jain sage who influenced him a great deal, that religion serves us as the instrument through which we know our true being and our relation with living things.[37] Gandhi spoke of that true relationship as the "essential unity" of all that lives, a truth of being that he came to comprehend through active love: "I cannot practice *ahimsa* without practicing the religion of service, and I cannot find the truth without practicing the religion of *ahimsa*."[38] "Ignorance," he believed, "is at the root of failures."[39]

Gandhi was convinced that the power of love is the same as the power of Truth, a force without which the universe would disappear. He taught,

> The law of love will work, just as the law of gravitation will work, whether we accept it or not. . . . The more I work at this law the more I feel the delight in life, the delight in the scheme of this universe. It gives me a peace and a meaning of the mysteries of nature that I have no power to describe.[40]

Gandhi never claimed a privileged knowledge of Perfect Dharma or Absolute Truth. He derided the idea of leaving behind a sect called "Gandhism" and insisted that he had originated no new idea or principle: "I have simply tried in my own way to apply the eternal truth to our daily life and problems."[41] He felt that all persons can approach Truth by purifying the mind so that they have a more profound understanding of relative truths. All religions he felt to be true but imperfect, relative approximations of Truth, or *satya*, or Dharma, of which individuals partake. He boldly concluded that there are as many religions as minds,[42] but he did not perceive the pluralism as meaningless relativism: "In Nature, there is a fundamental unity running through all the diversity we see about us. Religions are no exception to the natural law."[43]

Gandhi always referred to God as "He," but he also wrote, "The Soul is one, but the bodies which She animates are many."[44] His conceptualization of the divine was that of a force that pervades all things. In 1925 he wrote that God is a personal God to those who need His personal presence,[45] and four years later he moved so far from the notion of a personal God as to declare not only that "God is Truth" but "Truth is God." He said he came to this new ordering of the equation after meeting with some atheist students in Switzerland and finding their questions to reflect a sincere search for truth, which he recognized as a spiritual quest.

The translation of *ahimsa* has been almost as problematic for many Western commentators as that of *satya*. Translating *ahimsa* as "nonviolence" is not incorrect, but is only partially accurate as the prefix "a" in Sanskrit connotes a more positive state than the mere absence of the root word. *Himsa*, from the root *hins*, means to injure, or destroy, or kill. Gandhi took *himsa* to mean not only the harming of living things but also "hurt by every evil thought, by undue haste, by lying, by hatred, by wishing ill to anybody."[46] Likewise, his understanding of *ahimsa* was expansive: "In its positive form, *ahimsa* means the largest love, the greatest charity. If I am a follower of *ahimsa*, I must love my enemy or a stranger to me as I would my wrong-doing father and son."[47]

Gandhi came to this comprehension, as with most of his spiritual practice, through experiential learning. He once told a friend,

> I learned the lesson of non-violence from my wife. . . . Her determined resistance to my will on the one hand, and her quiet submission to the suffering my stupidity involved on the other hand, ultimately made me ashamed of myself and cured me of my stupidity in thinking I was born to rule over her; and in the end she became my teacher in non-violence.[48]

Gandhi often spoke admiringly of women's competence, firmness, and forgiving spirit in the home, and he also made huge strides in encouraging them to enter the political arena. He considered women the "incarnation of *ahimsa*."[49]

Clearly Gandhi viewed the subjugation of India by the British Empire, as well as the oppression of the Indian poor by the Indian

rich, as violence. He also distrusted the vast centralized power of the modern state. His alternative was "enlightened anarchism": India as a free nation whose structure would be a confederation of "village republics," each largely self-sufficient in economics, government, culture, spiritual vitality, and primary and vocational education (children might have to go elsewhere in the district for secondary school and perhaps even farther for a university). He advocated a redistribution of wealth through a system of trusteeship. He did not wait for independence to begin developing cottage industries, but made all such related work—which he called the Constructive Program—an inherent part of the *satyagraha* efforts.

Gandhi did not favor a scripture-based theocracy, as he felt that religious scriptures, practices, and institutions must be tested by humanity's God-given powers of scrutiny and criticism for correspondence with *satya* and *ahiṃsa*.[50] He vigorously opposed the notion of "untouchability," for example, calling it a perversion of true Hindu teachings and renaming the Untouchables *Harijans*, "children of God." The health of Gandhi's proposed society would be judged by the capacity of its least privileged members to resist any abuses of authority. The purpose of Gandhi's social philosophy was to produce civic structures that would spare citizens the crushing cruelties he viewed as dehumanizing features of the twentieth century and, thereby, to allow cultivation of spiritual growth: "There are two aspects, the outward and the inward. It is purely a matter of emphasis with me. The outward has no meaning to me at all except insofar as it helps the inward."[51]

Gandhi believed that social justice must be attained nonviolently so that a movement does not add to the suffering of this world. He felt that soul-force, or Truth-force, could improve the quality of politics and government because all participants would be operating according to the law of love and so connecting with a deeper level of reality. Yet he judged passive submission to injustice as severely as violent revolt: both expressed moral failure. In fact, he felt that "vengeance is any day superior to passive and helpless submission" if one is incapable of nonviolent action or if an extreme situation arises regarding protecting another.[52] Cowards who hid behind the creed of nonviolence, he maintained, were able to practice only "nonviolence of the weak," a thin imitation of soul-force.

Gandhi developed the concept of *satyagraha* as a pragmatic technique for attaining social change, a disciplined approach of civil disobedience to oppressive laws, a fundamental commitment to community development, and an insightful method of conflict resolution. Those followers who shared Gandhi's concern with "the inward" could see that all of these political aspects of *satyagraha* were expressions of its core meaning: a Dharma activist's way of being. Shrewdly, he did not begin with that understanding as a requirement for participation in *satyagraha* actions, but he hoped that all *Satyagrahis* would grow in Dharma. Like the Buddha, Gandhi invited everyone to test the efficacy of his teachings; he suggested a return to violence if one did not experience *ahimsa* as "a force infinitely superior."[53] He was convinced that the very practice of *ahimsa*—and the willingness to suffer for its truth, such as the essential unity and dignity of all beings—makes one grow stronger.

First among the vows *Satyagrahis* repeated each morning at Gandhi's *ashram*, or center, was the commitment to fear no one. Disciplined nonviolent civil disobedience could never work, of course, if everyone were running about in panicked disarray, but Gandhi's emphasis on fearlessness had a deeper meaning. The starting point of a *satyagraha* action is the radical wrongness of a situation; to achieve correct insight into any situation, one must observe nonviolence of the mind. When the mind is flooded with a negative emotion—most often fear—perception is skewed and the resulting judgment is impaired. The goal of Gandhian conflict resolution is not to defeat one's opponent but to convert him or her to seeing the rightness of your cause. Since a *Satyagrahi* is presumably operating on the basis of truth as well as *ahimsa* ("the greatest love, the greatest charity"), an opponent's coming to see the rightness of such an effort is a victory for her or him as well. Ideally, the truth in each party's position is identified during one or more mediation sessions and a higher truth is acknowledged.

Over the years Gandhi concluded that the consistent, or pure, forms of *satyagraha* are more effective than the less consistent, or less pure, and that an increase in purity is especially favorable when a struggle is already well advanced.[54] "Non-violence," he insisted, "implies as complete self-purification as is humanly possible."[55] A veneer of inauthentic *ahimsa* over hatred, envy, or greed limits one's thought, word, and deed to false "non-violence of the weak."

In the end India failed to meet Gandhi's challenge. At the time of independence from Britain, scores of thousands of people were slaughtered in the riots between Hindus and Muslims. Gandhi was deeply saddened and, for a while, quite depressed. He had long since perceived that the politicians had used him without ever intending to include his concepts and principles into the design of the new nation. After all, most of those men were modern, secular enthusiasts of the nation-state, who had been educated in London. How could such sophisticates take seriously Gandhi's emphasis on cottage industries and self-sufficient villages, let alone his relentless insistence on self-purification, self-discipline, and nonnegotiable *ahimsa*! It was all too quaint, too backward.

He was far more disappointed in himself, though. He wondered if he had failed to be a strong enough example, if some weakness—perhaps his temper, perhaps his pride—had defeated the massive effort. He admitted with resignation:

> I thought our struggle was based on non-violence, whereas in reality it was no more than passive resistance, which essentially is a weapon of the weak. It leads naturally to armed resistance whenever possible.[56]
>
> It is quite possible that my technique is faulty. . . .[57]
>
> That [the unrest and riots in 1942–46] can never mean that the creed of non-violence has failed. At best it may be said that I have

> not yet found the technique required for the conversion of the mass mind.[58]

Gandhi's longtime associate and successor in the Constructive Program work, Vinoba Bhave, concurred with his harsh assessment:

> Gandhi tried to inculcate in us the non-violence of the brave, but the non-violence we showed was the non-violence of the weak. The resistance that was offered was not the resistance Gandhi wanted us to offer. The people had faith in him and followed him. Nevertheless, the battle we fought under Gandhi's leadership was only a haphazard manifestation of non-violence. We had ill-will in our hearts and outwardly affected a non-violent posture. *Swaraj* [self-rule] was gained as a consequence, but there was not the conviction that it had come through non-violence. So the joy of *ahimsa* was denied us. We had a glimpse of the power of non-violence, but it did not blossom in our hearts.[59]

Gandhi's use of the term *swaraj* meant not only self-rule in the sense of independence for the nation, but also in the sense of independence for the mind from dominating patterns of fear, craving, and ill will, allowing love and compassion to arise. It was with this deeply spiritual understanding of how healthy *swaraj* should proceed outward from the individual to the family to the community to the nation to the entire human race that he declared, "I do believe that the most spiritual act is the most practical in the true sense of the term."[60] That is why he insisted, "Means and ends are convertible terms in my philosophy of life."[61] The quality of mind during an action yields the quality of mind when the goal is reached.

With the liberation of mind being so central to all levels of Gandhi's political goals, it seems somewhat odd that he chose *karma yoga* as his primary spiritual practice, combined with some *bhakti yoga* (devotional prayers and songs). *Karma yoga* is the Hindu path of work, of a lifetime of wholesome actions without attachment to reward. The *karma yogi* believes that the practice of eschewing craving, while being of service to others, will gradually yield realization of the truths of Dharma, resulting over the course of several lifetimes of such effort in full liberation.

If he had aimed for less—for instilling in *Satyagrahis* a habit of constructive work, for instance, with a lessening of greed and an increase of love—*karma yoga* might have been sufficient. Gandhi, however, aimed for complete purification of the mind and self-realization. He knew that *ahimsa* could flourish only when the mind had been cleansed of negative mindstates. He could have studied any of the numerous Hindu techniques of *raja yoga*, the path of direct mindwork, and combined those meditation techniques with his *karma* and *bhakti yoga*. (He did not have the option of learning *vipassana* as that practice was not widely reintroduced in India until more than twenty years after his death; besides, he was dedicated to the revitalization of Hinduism.) With the proper method and diligent practice of *raja yoga*, one experiences weakening and eventual fading of the previously obsessive, negative patterns of mind. Instead, Gandhi chose to attempt to whip the mind into shape and tough it out without benefit of a deep-level meditative technique to eliminate the roots of negative mindstates. Gandhi framed the entire process of self-purification as a matter of control and spoke of applying his "indomitable will" in a rather macho sense: ". . . it is always a case of intense mental struggle. It is not that I am incapable of anger, for instance, but I succeed on almost all occasions to keep my feelings under control. Whatever may be the result, there is always in me a conscious struggle for following the law of non-violence deliberately and ceaselessly."[62] Anyone with a practice of mindwork, such as the Buddha's *vipassana* meditation, can see immediately that something is very wrong with the technique when a person of Gandhi's energy and self-discipline is still waging intense battles of "control" in his mind after decades and decades of practice. It would appear that the Mahatma was using the wrong tool for the job. He, however, had other considerations in mind.

Gandhi's decision to ignore the techniques of *raja yoga* served both his political goals and his personal preferences, the latter being informed by the Vaishnava tradition in Gujarat and Maharashtra in which active compassion is valued more highly than mere scholarship or contemplation.[63] It was generally accepted in the India of his day that *karma yoga* was the path for *yogis* who wished to work in the world and that *raja yoga* was for those who wished to retreat to remote meditation centers or hermitages. Work, as inspired activity, was obviously needed if the degenerate, oppressed village culture were to renew itself. Gandhi could have bridged the "either/or" perception of the two paths, as so many of his contemporaries were doing in Buddhist countries, but he, a man of action and deeds, wanted to elevate the status of *karma yoga* and challenge the popular notion that *raja yoga* was the more worthy practice.

Moreover, Gandhi was proud that he had never accepted any man as his *guru*, or teacher of a technique of spiritual practice. He had drawn from inspirational writings—Hindu, Jain, and Christian, among others—but he had a strong sense of having carved out his own way at the level of practice. Sadly, Gandhi, his loyal followers, and all those who "returned to violence" discovered that simply ordering the mind to banish fear, hatred, and craving does not really work over time. For Gandhi in particular, a fixation with the need for celibacy, which he believed gave him greater energy and spiritual power, became a primary struggle of control within his own mind for the last thirty years of his life.

Gandhi admitted near the end of his life that he had never achieved a completely nonviolent action, one without the slightest trace of ill will. He never claimed to be a saint or a *mahatma* (great soul). For those around him, the fruit of his spiritual development was apparent, though, most often in his joyfulness. He experienced prayer, which he regarded as a "heart search" and a call to self-purification, as a powerful tool. He lived as close to Dharma as he possibly could, and that connection carried him in grace: he said that he was led to his acts of *ahimsa* and sustained in them by "the higher promptings of an unseen power."[64] When he died, it was not with a curse on his lips for his assassin, but with the *Ramanama* prayer.

Gandhi did not realize his dream of a renewed India converted to the principles of *satyagraha*. And yet—the very absence of a technique of direct mindwork that would have stimulated the deep rooting of *ahimsa* makes Gandhi's accomplishments all the more extraordinary. Using only compelling exhortations of what *should* be and honest example, Gandhi moved a nation. He showed his own people and all posterity that nonviolent political action does work. He gave us, in the words of Tagore, "a vision of the *shakti* [power, energy] of truth."[65]

Our Violent Culture

When a violent showdown in the Philippines was thought by political analysts to be inevitable as the struggle against the Marcos dictatorship passed the point of no return, Filipino Bishop Francisco Claver wrote, "We choose nonviolence not merely as a strategy for attaining the ends of justice, casting it aside if it does not work. We choose it as an end in itself, or, more correctly, as part of the larger end of which justice itself is subordinate and prerequisite."[66] True nonviolence, or active love, shapes the meaning of nonviolent grass-roots movements and, therefore, the ways in which participants view the world. Once one has experienced communal effort in a caring, respectful, nonviolent mode, one becomes acutely aware of the stark contrast on reentering the larger world.

The perception that life in the United States is becoming increasingly violent is no mere paranoid delusion. The number of violent criminal acts per hundred thousand citizens annually has nearly quadrupled from 1960 to 1988.[67] Rates of rape and assault have climbed sharply in recent years.[68] Every fourteen seconds a woman is battered somewhere in our country.[69] Child abuse, including sexual assault, is coming to light in vast numbers in all socioeconomic classes. Drug-related murders terrorize many urban neighborhoods. Buying a gun, however, in order to protect one's family from crime has proven statistically to be dangerous: a six-year study in King County, Washington, found an 18:1 chance that a gun kept in the home will eventually be used in the death of a family member.[70]

An array of therapies and self-help programs exist to free people from addictions and habitual patterns of violence. When such corrective programs are combined with meditation, the results have proven quite impressive.[71] Yet how many people receive help among the millions who need it? The fruits of violence multiply again and again in society. Who fills our prisons? Most people convicted of violent crime were victims of abuse as children. Who walks our streets selling their bodies for cash? Surveys repeatedly find that most prostitutes were sexually abused as children.[72] Socioeconomic factors play a role in violent and degrading crime, to be sure, but mindstates of self-loathing are a central dynamic.

Surveys indicate that by the time most Americans are eighteen years old, they have watched on television some thirty-two thousand murders and forty thousand attempted murders.[73] American television now averages twelve acts of violence per hour, with several shows featuring twice that many.[74] While the long-term effects of such viewing are undetermined, studies have shown that children are more violent in play after watching such programs.[75] Other studies have found men more willing to inflict sex-related violence on women after viewing violent pornographic films.[76] Violence has reached such proportions that in 1986 Congress and the surgeon general created a special section at the federal Centers for Disease Control in Atlanta to track injuries resulting from violent behavior.[77] Does the fact that we as a society have adjusted to a national murder rate thirty times that of England and fifty times that of New Zealand as if it were merely "the human condition"[78] have any relation to the success our presidential candidates enjoy when they talk like gun-toting toughs in violent movies? *Read my lips: My finger's on the trigger of global thermonuclear war, and I'm* ONE TOUGH HOMBRE.

Our culture of violence is not only reported by our media but reflected in its choice of coverage. In reporting a story, from neighborhood to international levels, most reporters will seek

out conflict, amplify it through a focus disproportionate to the larger context, and feature it prominently. Thus they please their editors, who know as well as the publishers that most unresolved conflict and heated words are low-level violence—and violence is entertainment in this country. "Hard-hitting, tough-minded" journalists in publications left, right, and center often present as "truth" only those facts that suit their model of conflict-as-news. The manager of President Bush's advertising campaign during the 1988 election afterward explained the cynical use of conflict journalism:

> You've got to understand that the media has no interest in substance. Print has a little more interest because they have to fill a lot of lines. . . . There are three ways to get on the air: pictures, attacks, and mistakes. So what you do is spend your time avoiding mistakes, staying on the attack and giving them pictures. You do that and you're guaranteed the lead story on the evening news. If you don't, the other guy gets the lead story. If I were to talk about world peace, pollution, ethics, no matter how good my programs were, I'd be a guaranteed loser.[79]

Even in print journalism, if reporters can get someone to make an embarrassing, damaging, or antagonistic statement during an interview, they usually open the article with it or highlight it in a boldface sidebar.[80] People who want analysis of current events without the macho games and want political commentary and book reviews in which the journalist is not obsessed with scoring off everyone he or she writes about, however, generally find satisfaction in journals in which most of the contributors, and certainly the editors, have a spiritual practice, such as *Sojourners* and *Christianity and Crisis*.

Rudeness, attacks, and insults proved to be popular commodities on television by the late 1980s. Crude, hostile comedy, negative advertising, and abrasive talk-show hosts gained large audiences. Advertising executives have found negative commercials to be clearly effective, especially among young people.[81] After appearing on a typically mean-spirited segment of "The

Morton Downey Jr. Show," a self-identified "Massachusetts liberal" wrote in a nationally reprinted article that he had enjoyed himself a great deal and proposed that the problem in engaging people with political issues today is that "there are so few forums that catch or hold the attention of the average viewer, particularly the nation's youth."[82] Near the end of the article he wrote, "So maybe I'm insane."[83] I cannot but agree. It is madness when a society panders to the fragmentation, callousness, and cruelty that are the inevitable results of failing to comprehend—in an experiential as well as intellectual way—the truth of our existence: the profound communion of all life.

No one is so cynical and hardened, especially not our youth, as to be beyond the reach of that transformative truth, and there are myriad paths to its realization. A convict in the Quakers' Alternatives to Violence Program in a New York State prison wrote of his experience, "I began to grow from a person filled with hate, anger and despair into a person who believes that he, too, is responsible for the protection, preservation and enrichment of humanity."[84]

Without nonviolence—mindstates of lovingkindness and compassion—at the core of our societal constructs, however, even the desire to protect and preserve can be manipulated in service to barbarism masquerading as idealism. Totalitarian regimes exist by convincing their enthusiasts that a lofty social goal is at stake: the preservation of their society, or perhaps the creation of a brave new order. To achieve that goal, it is necessary to root out, contain, torture, and exterminate "bad" people, identified as enemies of the regime's "greater good." The most zealous of the true believers in Stalinist Russia, Nazi Germany, Mao's Cultural Revolution, and the Pol Pot reign of terror were often the youth, violent enforcers sometimes as young as ten steadfastly targeting and punishing the "bad" people so that "good" could triumph. The masterminds of the regime and their more mature comrades seldom had such blind faith in the Great Goal, but a social system built on state-approved cruelty, harassment, and endless violence offered attractive opportunities to act on their deeply ingrained mental patterns of hatred, resentment, and fear. Studies of the childhoods of Nazi leaders have found that they were often made to feel inherently unlovable and undeserving and were granted only a harsh, extremely conditional acceptance; beatings were common.[85]

In contrast, a study of rescuers of Jews in Nazi Europe found that, unlike the control group in the study, the rescuers had almost no memories of being punished gratuitously and had rarely been punished physically. There was generally one parent or parental figure who, in the child's eyes, embodied very high standards of ethical behavior.[86] The child witnessed and experienced a life lived with the truth of interconnectedness. Years later when she or he saw the false separateness of "the Other" called lofty idealism by all the "good citizens," the rescuer knew it was a lie. The courageous acts of refuge that followed were *satyagraha*, holding fast to the truth.

Sadistic regimes are not a thing of the past. Amnesty International reported in 1988 that people, including children, are tortured in one-third of the countries around the world.[87] Are we rescuers?

What Is Required of Us?

We hope that neither we nor our children will ever have to face the horror of a totalitarian regime—although some political observers predict just that as the nuclearized security state moves closer to militaristic control during ecological and other crises. Surely it is not difficult to foresee increasing levels of stress and dysfunctional behavior as ecological uncertainties mount, more nations (and terrorists) join the "nuclear club," and the contradictions of industrialism and the corporate world order become intolerable. Even in the best of circumstances, the breakdown of civility and caring would be worrisome, but it is particularly unpromising when combined with the ecological, economic, social, and political crises we face.

What is required of us in a world where hatred, greed, and delusion fuel ignorance and cruelty on so vast a scale? Neither treaties nor laws nor societal norms have proven sufficient to curb the rise of misery for growing millions. Something more than all the "shoulds" of moral exhortation is needed. They are no match for the agitated mind. Mental defilements are not eliminated through arms limitations, social contract, political ideology, moral norms, or idealized models of family or community, whether religious or secular.

Anguish and mental turmoil are not uniquely Russian, or Kenyan, or Chinese, or Salvadoran, or American. The conditions vary, but everywhere there is the pain of human suffering and discontent. Dhamma offers a path of release open to all.[88] Will everyone then someday practice the meditation technique taught by the Buddha? Not likely. You may prefer a different way. But, please, *find a way*. Find a way beyond the continuous chain reaction of craving, jealousy, ill will, indifference, fear, and anxiety that fills the mind. Find a way that dissolves the deeply ingrained patterns of negative, distrustful behavior caused by past cruelty and disappointment. Find a way that demonstrates to you that ill will and greed are damaging to your psyche. Find a way that grounds your deeds in wisdom, equanimity, compassion, and lovingkindness. Find a way that reveals to you the joy of our profound unity, the subtle interrelatedness of you and every being, every manifestation of the unfolding universe. Find a way that will continually deepen your understanding of that knowledge. Then we could build community without hypocrisy. Then we would have a chance.

3

Participation in the Mystery

On an intimate relationship with nature: The wisdom of Native American spirituality

Fifteen billion years ago, our universe was born in a vast and mysterious eruption of being. Out of the fireball came all the elementary particles of the cosmos, including those that later formed our home galaxy, the Milky Way, and our planetary home, the Earth. All the land, the waters, the animals, the plants, our bodies, the moon and stars—everything in our life experience is kin to us, the results of a cosmic birth during which the gravitational power of the event held the newborn particles in a miraculously deft embrace. Had the rate of expansion of the infant universe differed by even one part in 10^{60}, it would have either collapsed into a black hole or dispersed entirely, the possibility of our being and that of the hundred billion galaxies around us never to have found form. Moreover, nothing but light would have existed but for the saving asymmetry that one in each billion pairs of protons and antiprotons had no partner.

The gravitational embrace, some 4.6 billion years ago, gathered a richness of elements eight light minutes from a blazing star, our sun, and layered them by weight into a sphere, with iron at the core. The elements sought their own positions in the layers that formed, creating among themselves all the minerals in Earth's body. On the smaller celestial bodies nearby (such as Mercury, Mars, our moon), the electromagnetic interaction overpowered gravity's pull; on the larger ones (such as Jupiter,

Neptune, and Uranus), the opposite relationship developed. Only on Earth were the two in balance.

On Earth's crust, molecules continually broke up and recombined into new and larger molecules. Lightning created the possibility of amino and nucleic acids by providing intense heat framed by severe cold. Molecules that assembled themselves from amino acids became protein, while others formed of nucleic acids and sugars became ribonucleic acid (RNA) and deoxyribonucleic acid (DNA). The long chains of RNA, DNA, and protein molecules found themselves drawn into various partnerships, creating a dynamic bioplasm of bacteria in warm mud and shallow seawater. From Earth's store of potential, the great mediator chlorophyll later developed, enhancing our planet's relationship with the sun through the wonder of photosynthesis. A rambunctious bursting forth of Gaian life stretched over millions of years and continues today with new speciation and the unpredictable moves of Earth's body. With the emergence of humans, the universe had created a life-form that could reflect on the cosmic mysteries. (It does not seem to me that this occurrence justifies the claim made by some that the universe was preparing with every previous development specifically for the advent of humans.)

Slowly the part of the cosmos that is human has become aware of the vast web of life that organizes itself toward increasing complexity in an ongoing weave of novelty and continuity. We have become aware of its processes of self-regulation, such as the regulating of Earth's unique atmosphere via the response of Earth's organisms, or biomass.[1] Moreover, we have finally seen that we, too, are participants in the metabolic dynamics and the unfolding adventure that is the life of the universe. The rigid charade of the supposedly detached Newtonian observer has been rendered obsolete by postmodern physics (though the psychological reasons for desiring that kind of "objective" distancing in certain cultures have not). The assumptions of modernity positioned us on top of nature, imperiously heedless of its integrity. We now have accumulated sufficient data to indicate to even the most smug champion of the mechanistic worldview that we are, as every primal culture has always understood, inherent participants in the processes of the universe at very subtle levels. What responsibility does such participation carry? What meaning does it bring?

As for those deconstructive postmodernists who dismiss all attempts to align our consciousness more clearly with the rest of the natural world as merely groundless, culturally constructed "discourses," scientific or otherwise, they might consider that, cultural choices aside, they themselves exist embedded in the "metadiscourse" of the universe. They can ignore the larger reality or actively engage with it, but they do not exist apart from it. That is, every worldview does indeed create its own internal logic, as the deconstructionists maintain, but all human systems of logic exist within the grand cosmologic. Granted, our perceptions are often shaped and shaded by culture—although moments of graced consciousness so intense that they bring revelation are usually experienced as being joltingly *outside* of cultural frameworks, making it nearly impossible for one to discuss the occurrence afterward except in oblique approximations. Granted, our knowledge of cosmic complexities is woefully limited. To shrink from the human challenge of attempting to come into awareness of the larger reality as fully as possible, however, is a sterile retreat.

What Is Our Responsibility?

To traditional native cultures, the intricately balanced relatedness of the Earth community obviously calls forth awareness and sensitivity on the part of humans. Native people find the extent to which modern citizens are oblivious to the rest of the natural world incredible. Since the birth of modernity, Eurocentric cultures have seized on technological prowess to insulate ourselves not only from any limits imposed by nature, but also from the fearsome treachery we projected onto the rest of nature. If we let down our guard, it was felt, surely we would be engulfed by chaos and destruction. Having had no regard for the ways of our planetary home, though, destruction is precisely the fate that awaits us—unless we effect fundamental changes in our behavior.

Since environmentalists began bringing various facets of the ecological crisis to the public's attention more than twenty years ago, we have witnessed a range of responses. Theologians suggest that we take better care of God's creation (though most cannot solve the conceptual problem that results when divinity is located outside the creation and humans are believed to enjoy a special relationship with the godhead, so that we humans are thought to partake of divine transcendence *over* the rest of the natural world).[2] Ecofeminists note that destructive actions toward both nature and the female are related and are the results of attitudes instilled by patriarchal culture.[3] Deep ecologists, drawing on relevant streams in Western philosophy, propose that we humans recognize our "ecological self" and that we have no right to damage the habitats of other species except to fulfill our vital needs.[4] Bioregionalists urge us to "reinhabit," to learn to live attentively "in place," rather than seemingly above the ecocommunity.[5]

These and other disparate calls for collective soul-searching have brought angry reactions from defenders of modernity, primarily from the strange bedfellows who identify with humanism, including many conservatives, socialists, liberals, New Age champions of "human potential," as well as numerous Christians and Jews. They view human autonomy and control over nature as unquestionable, dismissing pleas for the integrity of the Earth community as unsophisticated and absurdly sentimental at best or even pathologically misanthropic. Countless expressions of this view have appeared in print, nearly always interpreting complaints about humanity's treatment of nature as self-loathing on the part of the ecological activists. Among the most remarkable was a book review in 1989 by the editor of a prestigious national magazine that answered an author's sadness over human-caused destruction with a triumphant recitation of human accomplishments, citations of praise for the human from Sophocles and

Shakespeare, and a passage from Pericles on the character of the Athenian citizen: "self-reliant, loyal, public-spirited, resourceful, versatile, marked by refinement without extravagance and knowledge without effeminacy." Left unaddressed by the passionate crescendo was the matter of whether the reviewer accepted or denied the book's detailed presentation of evidence that there is a large hole in the ozone layer, that we are beginning to undergo potentially catastrophic global warming, and that various forms of animal life seem destined to be replaced by genetically engineered versions.[6]

Religious humanists regard our species as the "crown of creation," God's most impressive piece of work. Secular humanists, although derisive toward the idea of any transcendent power, do indeed believe in a transcendent power: the unbounded potential of the human, set above all others as the controlling force in this world. Both varieties embrace a managerial ethos for our species, which, they fear, would be dangerously compromised by humility and respect toward other species and our planet. Hence they support environmental adjustments "within reason." They are deeply affronted by the suggestion that human population, for instance, should be limited, in the industrialized countries as well as worldwide. That too many *humans* could constitute a causal component of ecological breakdown is unthinkable! Why, it must be solely capitalism, or industrialized socialism, or undemocratic government, or faulty economic projections, or too much centralization, or inadequate technology. *Anything* but excessive human presence as part of the problem. We are to know no bounds.

Whether one feels that modern society's interactions with nature have demonstrated arrogance and callous disregard or a forward-looking thrust of progress with a few problems that require some fine-tuning, surely it is embarrassing that our collective sense of alarm arose not over shame that we have driven more than a hundred thousand species into extinction in recent decades, or that we have clear-cut most of the old-growth forests in the entire temperate zone, or that we have filled in much of the wetlands on which 75 percent of American bird species depend for roosting, or that we have blown apart entire mountainsides for a relatively small amount of ore, but only when it became apparent that our own survival and quality of life were in jeopardy.

Currently we live among, and support in various ways, ecologically destructive dynamics of vast proportions. Most environmental scientists agree that there is still time to reduce and halt the damage—but not a great deal of time, perhaps a decade or two. If we were to become seriously committed to allowing an ecologically healthy existence for the Great Family of All Beings and our progeny, we would focus our collective energy and attention not only on urgently needed ecological restoration projects, but on achieving fundamental changes in the world's economics. A program that is to be effective over time would have to address the following issues, among others. First, a global market composed of unqualified-growth economies, whether capitalist or socialist, is madness on this rather finite planet. As the pioneering ecological economist Herman E. Daly notes, "It is widely believed by persons of diverse religious traditions that there is something fundamentally wrong in treating the earth as if it were a business in liquidation."[7] Rather than supporting the accumulation of money and material gain by converting the biosphere into trash as rapidly as possible, Daly, Hazel Henderson, James Robertson, and other astute analysts suggest ways to distinguish qualitative "development" from merely quantitative "growth."[8] Second, it is increasingly apparent that we need to decentralize economic power—shifting control from corporate headquarters, which continually demonstrate disregard for the health of both the U.S. and Third-World communities and ecosystems in which they operate, to worker-owned businesses in community-based and regionally oriented economies. Third, energy efficiency should be recognized as the cheap way to halt global warming and ease other damage as well.[9] Fourth, we need to conserve the earthstuff we use, hence to require less and produce less. Life-style changes, such as recycling and eating less meat,[10] are a subset of the necessary structural changes.

Such basic concerns lie beyond the intentions of nearly all governments today, which see their role as safeguarding and engendering economic growth. It is not at all clear that they even consider survival to be affordable as they press on with business-as-usual in their growth economies. Advocates of various alternative systems of government who fervently believe that *everything* would be all right if only we had political and economic decentralization, or democratic socialism, or laissez-faire capitalism might consider that no particular political and economic structure alone will result in a polity informed by ecological wisdom. After all, the renowned Mondragon cooperative enterprises in Spain, which are in many ways admirable, polluted their river without concern. Closer to home, the paper mill workers at Champion International in Canton, North Carolina, adamantly defend their right to pollute the Pigeon River, which flows through their town and then carries dioxin downstream into Tennessee. One cannot say with any certainty that the Champion International employees would automatically think ecologically were they to gain collective ownership of the factory.

While it is heartening that recent polls find a high percentage of American citizens favoring much stricter environmental standards, it is difficult to feel optimistic that survival-only responses (that is, responding to the ecological crises in such ways as to assure merely our own species' physical survival) will necessarily partake of wisdom and avoid still more error. Moreover, what of all the ecologically problematic situations that may await us in the future? What we require is a sense of grounding in our context, our larger reality.

Our Spiritual Relationship to the Cosmos

To consider our relationship to the cosmos is to engage with primary issues of being. Why are they understood to be spiritual?

The universe is laced with mystery, undulating in rhythms of novelty and unity. Its self-organizing, self-regulating magnificence is informed by diffuse powers of subjectivity we call by various names: Cosmic Consciousness, Ultimate Mystery, the divine, God, or Goddess. When one experiences consciousness of the exquisite interrelatedness and subtle vibratory flux of the life of the material world—a perception that extends our understanding of "sentient" beyond the animal kingdom—one is filled with awe. One has experienced immersion in ultimate value, the sacred totality. Hence one has known grace. Reverence for the grand communion and gratitude follow, the roots of worth-ship, or worship.

This primal experience, in all its variations, precedes culture—not the other way around. That is why vastly disparate primal cultures on all the inhabited continents developed around core concepts that the natural world is alive and that reverence toward the sacred whole is the obvious response. Many such indigenous, tribal cultures still exist, referred to collectively as the Fourth-World peoples. Culture, as we know from our mechanistic, nature-fearing modernity, can do much to devalue and block such primal experiences of revelation. It can also encourage spiritual practice that creates conditions in which they are likely to occur. Culture cannot, however, create or duplicate genuine revelatory experience.

When we experience our cosmic self, we see that the gestalt notions of foreground and context are one: it makes sense to speak of nature as our "context" only if we remember that our seeming separation from the rest of the natural world is a matter of perception, a view that does not hold up at subtle levels of awareness. Atoms exhibit responsiveness to other atoms. Chaos moves into pattern. Subtle mind is aware that nature is aware.

Knowing the unitive dimension of existence, the human still ponders over the puzzle of what our function might be in the sacred whole. One possibility that is eliminated after a revelatory experience of the inherent relatedness of the cosmos is that of the detached controller. That is not our being, not at all. What then? I resisted for some time "geologian" Thomas Berry's assertion that we humans have not only a reflexive but a celebratory function in the universe. How do we know that our species is to do anything more than sit around and refrain from being boors in the eco-neighborhood, I wondered. However, the very next time I emerged from intensive spiritual practice, a meditation retreat, there they were again: the mindstates that arise when mind is in a relatively pure condition—cleansed of fear, anger, craving, ill will, and such—in which the natural world is perceived as surprisingly vivid and wondrous. Gratitude and celebration indeed fill the mind, frequently and when least expected. One feels brimming over with thankfulness and joy for life on Earth. We have a celebratory function in the universe not because we aspire to that role but, rather, because we allow it to manifest itself, shining forth from within our being. The more we purify the mind, the greater the clarity with which we perceive our meaning, the finer the perception with which we comprehend interbeing, the deeper our entry into mysteries of vast range and power.

Seeking "Green and Juicy" Spiritual Practice

Spiritual practice that has developed from a sense of the sacred whole, rather than sacralizing the human story apart from the larger reality, can help us cultivate increasingly subtle awareness of our true nature. Such a focus has not been central to Eurocentric religions, yet growing interest in recent years in the contemplative prayers of creation-centered medieval mystics such as Francis of Assisi, Hildegard of Bingen, Mechtild of Magdeburg, Meister Eckhart, Julian of Norwich, and Nicholas of Cusa, as well as some of St. Thomas Aquinas's work, has evoked an understanding of interbeing for many Christians.[11] St. Hildegard, the gifted poet, composer, artist, and biologist of twelfth-century Rhineland, coined the term *viriditas,* the greening power of the divine, to describe her perception that the optimal spiritual condition is to be green and juicy, warm and moist, rather than cold and dried up.

It is all too obvious, even if one does not know church history well, that the cosmological focus of the creation-centered mystics did not carry the day. Most of them lived under the threat, or actuality, of ecclesiastic condemnation. Their ecstatic, "green and juicy" prayers were not taught to us in Sunday school or catechism class. Their sense of sin as the rending of the cosmic fabric was not preached from the pulpit. Now, when ecological destruction has reached critical levels, church leaders of many denominations finally issue creation-centered pastoral letters and encyclicals.[12] We could have been there all along. The flowering of creation-centered concern, from "stewardship" to "co-creation," has grown mainly from grassroots initiative, such as the efforts by the Jewish group *Shomrei Adamah* (Guardians of the Earth) to focus attention on the creation-centered wisdom teachings in the Hebrew Bible and the Talmud.[13]

In October 1986, representatives of "the great religions"—Buddhism, Hinduism, Judaism, Christianity, and Islam—were invited by the World Wildlife Fund to convene in the Umbrian hills of Italy and issue the Assisi Declarations, highlighting the ecological wisdom in their traditions.[14] Each of those faiths contains cosmological riches, expressions of the sacred whole and the love it calls forth from us. Such teachings, however, do not seem to have been made central in the *practice* of "the great religions" thus far. Hence members of the religious grassroots seeking "green and juicy" spiritual practice in their own faith might be particularly interested in the rich possibilities suggested by considering those traditions that do hold the cosmos to be primary.

Taoism undeniably focuses its teachings and practice on the inherent intelligence, "the way," of the unfolding potential of the universe, although the conceptualization in philosophical Taoism is sometimes rather impersonal. (Translations of philosophical Taoism are the form best known in the West; popular Taoism, which includes worship of numerous deities, thrives in Taiwan and elsewhere.) Yet who has gone further than the spiritual traditions of native peoples in terms of a familial and even intimate sense of our subtle interrelatedness with the rest of the natural world?

On our continent the Native American nations have maintained unbroken practices of earth-based spirituality for more than twenty thousand years. Since contact with the European invaders, beginning five hundred years ago, native peoples' spiritual practices have often been targeted for eradication so that their cultural fabric might unravel and the Indians might then become properly atomized team players in the modern world. Not only have hundreds of the native nations maintained their spiritual practices against great odds over the centuries, but they are even willing to share some of their teachings with the dominant culture, believing it is not too late, even now, for all peoples to cultivate a loving awareness of the rest of the natural world and change our ways accordingly. Striving to repair modernity's severed connection from the rest of nature, longing to heal our deadening alienation, we can take inspiration from ways of being that are artfully infused with sensitivity, humility, and love for the great web of life.

Grace Embodied: Native American Spiritual Teachings

Documentation of early contact between Europeans and the native nations of North and South America reflected a similar temperament even amid a great deal of cultural diversity. Christopher Columbus, Sir Francis Drake, and numerous Spanish chroniclers in Mexico and Peru noted that Indians enjoyed offering extensive hospitality, shared a passion for rich color, valued giving over getting and cooperation over competition, and lived by a spirituality that found a diffuse sense of "God" everywhere.[15] In North America that spiritual power was called *wakan* (Siouan), *orenda* (Iroquoian), *manitou* (Algonquian), or other names. Its translation as "the Great Spirit" seems to have been influenced by Christian contact. Many Indians maintain that an adjectival form more accurately conveys Indian usage: the Great Holy, or the Great Mysterious.

The cosmic union of humans and the rest of the Earth community, including the stars and moon, is central to the Native American worldview. The Hopi term *navoty* expresses the concept of being in perfect harmony and balance with the laws of the universe. Harmony requires careful attention to life's processes and events. It requires a sense that human communities are a cooperative part of the order and rhythms constituting this world. The Lakota spiritual teacher Black Elk explained that peace lives in human minds "when they realize their relationship, their oneness, with the universe and all its powers, and when they realize that at the center of the universe dwells *Wakan-Tanka,* and that this center is really everywhere; it is within each of us."[16] Indians believe that such understanding is realized only if one can feel perfect humility before the sacred whole.

Native peoples, in general, perceive "the environment" as a sensate, conscious entity suffused with spiritual powers. Hence their interactions are a respectful and spiritual exchange. "Everything we do is a prayer. Our religion is a way of life," an Absaroke (Crow) woman, Vera Jane He Did It Half, once explained to me in Montana.[17] In fact, there is no word in Indian languages for "religion," the closest concept usually being "the way you live."

For the Tukano Indians of the northwest Amazon basin, "the way you live" follows from their perception that the entire cosmos participates in an exchange of procreative energy that flows continuously between humans and animals, between society and nature. Hence they exhibit little interest in information about modes of exploitation that would lead to obtaining more food or raw materials than are actually needed, but they are always extremely interested in accumulating more factual knowledge about biological reality and, above all, about knowing what the rest of the physical world requires from humans. They feel that human society must fit its demands to nature's availabilities if it is to exist as part of nature's unity.[18] This attitude is common among native peoples. Spiritual teachers among the Dineh (Navajo), for example, maintain that "the greatest sacred thing is knowing the order and structure of things."[19]

The awareness that our very presence affects the interplay of natural forces around us is also common to Indian sensibilities. In explaining why so many of the Dineh people refuse to cooperate with the federal government's forced relocation order at Big Mountain in northern Arizona, Ruth Benally Yinishye has stated, "Here nature knows us. The earth knows us. We make our offerings to certain trees, certain rocks, to natural water springs, on top of hills. . . . We have songs and prayers. Our history cannot be told without naming the cliffs and mountains that have witnessed our people."[20] *The earth knows us.* Its atoms are aware of our atoms (as reflected in Bell's theorem in quantum physics).[21] The manifestation of its wavelets and particles is affected by our presence (as reflected in Heisenberg's Uncertainty Principle in quantum physics).[22] A people rooted in the land over time have exchanged their tears, their breath, their bones, all of their elements—oxygen, carbon, nitrogen, hydrogen, phosphorus, sulfur, all the rest—with their habitat many times over. *Here nature knows us.*

Qualities of the divine are often seen reflected in the lives of animals. Some native cultures believe that animals were once humans; others believe that humans were once animals. Either way, a strong, respectful connection is maintained, in viewing certain animals as spiritual guides, for instance, or as knowing and powerful beings. (The most economically useful animals are not necessarily those perceived to have the most spiritual power, contrary to materialist theory.)[23]

Native people's cosmological spirituality is frequently dismissed by both secular and religious critics as "nature idolatry." Addressing a recent conference on the Native American ministries of the Episcopal church, a Choctaw Indian and Episcopal priest, Steven Charleston, explained that the kind of "harmony" and "balance" within the circle of life that Indians speak of is like the warm relationship between members of a family. "Non-Native people often look at this part of our theology as nature worship," he continued. "They do this because they have never experienced a personal relationship with the natural world."[24]

The Koyukon Athapaskan people of Alaska view the environment as a second society and express a fondness or affection toward the Earth community through the poetry of the riddles they compose:

Wait, I see something: We are sitting all puffed up across from each other, in coats of mountain sheep skin.
Answer: duhnooyh, *snow clumps on the tree branches.*

Wait, I see something: My end sweeps this way and that way and this way around me.
Answer: Grass tassles moving back and forth in the wind, making little curved trails on the snow.

Wait, I see something: We whistle along the hillside.
Answer: Loose, half-peeled bits of birchbark, hissing in the wind.

Wait, I see something: It has taken the color of cloudberries.
Answer: The bill of the white-fronted goose.

Wait, I see something: Tiny bits of charcoal scattered in the snow.
Answer: The bills of ptarmigan.

Wait, I see something: They are like bushes bending in the wind.
Answer: The "ears" of the great horned owl.

Wait, I see something: We are wide open in the bushes.
Answer: The snowshoe hare's eyes.

Wait, I see something: It looks like a bit of charred wood waving around in the air.
Answer: The short-tailed weasel's tail in winter.

Wait, I see something: Far away yonder a fireflash comes down.
Answer: A red fox, glimpsed as it dashes brightly through the brush.[25]

Since the invasion of military and clerical missions determined to conquer and assimilate Native American peoples, many have had to make accommodation to the imposed culture, often taking their cosmological sensibility with them into the church and giving birth to syncretic creations. The Mayan Indians of Guatemala, for example, have found places in their ancient eighteen-month calendar of religious ceremonies for the Catholic holy days honoring various saints and the Virgin Mary, whom they associate with their "Grandmother Moon." Such accommodations result not only from foreign pressures but also from the Mayans' deep respect for all spiritual practice; nothing spiritual is denied. Whether native peoples have maintained their traditional ways, or become Christian, or blended the two, they generally have exhibited a religious tolerance and wry live-and-let-live attitude that they surely must find lacking in the dominant culture. How familiar the following recorded exchange must be to native peoples everywhere: An Eskimo asked the local missionary priest, "If I did not know about God and sin, would I go to hell?" "No," said the priest, "not if you did not know." "Then why," asked the Eskimo earnestly, "did you tell me?"[26]

Not surprisingly, native peoples' languages reflect the cosmological focus central to their cultures. Hence they provide a (now) rare opportunity to consider possibilities of human conceptualization that are rooted in awareness of our cosmic reality. The linguist Benjamin Lee Whorf contended that the emphasis on process, becoming, and happenings in Hopi language encourages speakers to understand the world more in terms of events than things. It follows, he felt, that the Hopi language is better suited than English to express the discoveries of contemporary physics. He described the Hopi term for "subjective," *tunatya,* as referring to "the state of the subjective, unmanifest, vital and causal aspect of the Cosmos, and the fermenting activity toward fruition and manifestation with which it seethes—an action of *hoping,* i.e., mental-causal activity, which is forever pressing upon and into the manifested realm."[27] The Hopi see this "burgeoning activity," Whorf noted, in the maturing of plants, the forming of clouds and their condensation in rain, the careful planning of communal agricultural and architectural activities, and in all human thought, including hoping, striving, and especially prayer.[28]

The language of the Wintu Indians of northern California reflects a worldview in which, according to studies by the anthropologist Dorothy Lee, reality, or ultimate truth, exists irrespective of humans. Human experience is felt to help actualize this reality, but not to otherwise affect its being.[29] Such an orientation contrasts sharply with that of solipsistic postmodernists, who maintain that reality is contained within the bounds of human perception—which, they add, is nothing but a cultural construct anyway.

As might be expected, the Wintu take a more modest view of their interaction with the larger reality than does someone steeped in worldviews of either objectivist mechanism or rigid deconstructionism. Lee found the Wintu relationship with nature to be characterized by intimacy and courtesy. They speak only by implication of reality not within their experience, avoiding a stark declaration of "This is." Rather, the Wintu say, "I call this bread." Lee observed that, by contrast, the Eurocentric dominant culture is "aggressive toward reality."[30]

Every Wintu is constantly aware of an encompassing reality existing beyond his or her delimiting experience. Just as the cosmos is primary to the Wintu, with human society regarded as a participant in the larger reality, so society as an unpartitioned whole is primary, with the individual regarded as a delimited part of the social whole. Lee found the Wintu tenets of an original oneness and a pervasive continuity to underlie not only linguistic categories but "thought and behavior throughout."[31]

Native Americans are known for their ability to weave stories that encode lessons about life, tribal sensibilities, and spiritual teachings. The stories are generally allegorical in form and can be symbolically unfolded through each listener's reflections, seeking, and spiritual grounding.[32] Through repeated listening over the years, more and more of the coded knowledge is revealed. An Indian child's first memory is often one of receiving a story. An O'odhdam (Papago) woman, Maria Chona, recalls how a child learns among her people: "My father went on talking to me in a low voice. This is how our people always talk to their children, so low and quiet, the child thinks he's dreaming. But he never forgets."[33] Skillful storytelling can create ritual space, a consciousness in which boundaries are arbitrary and connectedness is deeply felt.

The concept of symbolism that infuses Indian stories, art, architecture, and sacred geography is far more subtle than the contemporary semiotics that understands a sign, or symbol, to *represent* a concept or phenomenon, sometimes as an emotionally charged icon. Indians from various cultural orientations speak of symbols as aspects of the symbolized reality itself: "It is important to note that to the Plains Indian the material form of the symbol is not thought of as representing some *other* and higher reality, but *is* that reality in an image."[34] "The symbol is, in a sense, that to which it refers."[35] Symbols participate in knowledge so primal in form that they are themselves "the ineffable, structured into images."[36] "The language of the circle . . . unites vision and reality."[37] "Without symbols, the spiritual could not be expressed or might not be perceived."[38] After hearing many such similar statements from various native peoples, Dorothy Lee concluded that they regard a symbol as part of a whole, a component of a field that also contains the so-called *thing,* as well as the process of symbolizing, and the apprehending individual.[39]

Tasks necessary for survival—sewing clothes, making utensils, building shelter—are also regarded as processes of symbolization. The results are spiritual extensions of the sacred whole. The Pima and O'odhdam peoples, for example, consider their acts of basket making, including the gathering of grasses and vegetable dyes and the weaving itself, to be a ritual recapitulation of the total process of creation. The completed basket is the universe in an image.[40] The Dineh blanket weaver, in creating the dynamic interrelationship between warp and weft, participates in acts that evoke the ongoing creation of the cosmos. A Plains Indian woman, as a member of a women's quillwork sodality, fasts and prays before beginning her work, which she then performs in a contemplative state of mind. The quills, arranged in geometric patterns established by tribal tradition, participate in the creative principle, as does the sun, which is associated with the porcupine. The ritual quillworker captures sacred rays of the sun, understood as a spiritual principle, on the garment.[41]

Living symbolism of the larger reality also informs Native American architecture in the construction of both dwellings and ceremonial structures. All such structures as the tepee, the domed sweat lodge, the Sun Dance lodge of the Plains, the wickiup of the Apache, and the longhouses of woodland peoples such as the Iroquois and the Menomomini are created so as to imitate the process of the creation of the world itself. Hence all are sacred. The Plains tepee, for instance, is a model of the universe. Its circular floor plan represents the world or, microcosmically, the human. The fire at the center of this world is the presence of the Great Mysterious at the heart of the human.[42] The Dineh hogan also represents the cosmos, with a post "planted" at each of the cardinal directions and two framing the doorway, facing east. The roof is domed, the dirt floor "ever in touch with Mother Earth."[43] Moreover, the Four Sacred Mountains are considered posts of the tribal hogan for all Dineh: "We are on our Mother Earth's lap inside the hogan, and she is protecting us," explains Roberta Blackgoat, an activist grandmother resisting the forced relocation at Big Mountain.[44]

Personal entry into the Earth community is the goal of an Indian child's upbringing. A newborn child, in the Omaha tradition, is lifted in presentation to the creative powers of the cosmos with this prayer:

Ho! All ye of the heavens, all ye of the air,
all ye of the earth:
I bid you all hear me!
Into your midst has come a new life.
Consent ye, consent ye all, I implore!
Make its path smooth. . . .[45]

In order that knowledge not get separated from experience, nor wisdom from the mysteries, or great powers, elders in traditional Indian cultures encourage the children to listen and observe, rather than ask *why*. Among the Lakota, the children are taught to sit very still and use their senses, to perceive when all is seemingly quiet and nothing apparently is happening. A Keres man, Larry Bird, recalls, "You watch and listen and wait, and the answer will come to you. It's yours then, not like learning in school."[46] A woman raised at Taos Pueblo, Soge Track, remembers that asking direct questions of her elders would have meant that she was learning nothing: "Having been raised not to ask why but to listen, to become aware, I take for granted that people have some knowledge of themselves and myself—that is religion. Then when we know ourselves, we can put our feelings together and share this knowledge."[47]

At puberty an Indian youth may go on a first, or only, vision quest, a solitary retreat during which an individual fasts, usually on a mountaintop, and seeks the blessing of sacred power that can come through a dream, or preferably a vision, of some aspect of nature, possibly an animal who offers guidance for the future direction of the person's life. Essential to this practice is the Indian belief that within the solitude of nature one may ultimately hear the "voice" of the Great Holy and experience the awakening of spiritual power within.[48] Puberty is also a time of menarche ceremonies in many Indian cultures. In Apache tradition, a girl's elaborate ritual passage into womanhood ends with a tribal prayer of blessing: "The woman will walk happily upon the path of pollen."[49] In the Luiseño tradition, an intricate sandpainting representing the universe is the focal point of ritual acts celebrating menarche.[50] All the various Indian initiatory rites are informed by a sense of personal awareness as the heart of responsible participation in the cosmic community.

An Indian child also may absorb spiritual teachings through witnessing or receiving healing rituals. In the Blessing Way ceremony of the Dineh people, the patient is identified with the outer forms of the Earth and restored to harmony (*hozhooji*) through ritual participation in the sacred "way":

Earth's feet have become my feet;
by means of these I shall live on.

Earth's legs have become my legs;
by means of these I shall live on.
Earth's body has become my body;
by means of this I shall live on.
Earth's mind has become my mind;
by means of this I shall live on.
Earth's voice has become my voice . . .

Before me it will be harmony as I live on.
Behind me it will be harmony as I live on.
Below me it will be harmony as I live on.
Above me it will be harmony as I live on . . .

After identification with the Earth's outer form, the Blessing Way ritual reinvigorates the union of the patient's inner being—what we might call her subjectivity—with that of the Sacred Mountains, the Earth:

It is surprising, surprising . . . yi ye!
It is the very inner form of Earth
that continues to move with me,
that has risen with me,
that is standing with me,
that indeed remains stationary with me. . . .[51]

Throughout adulthood a traditional Native American participates in numerous communal ceremonies. They serve to keep the community in balance with the rest of the cosmos, to renew attitudes of respect and gratitude, to fulfill obligations toward the land. Often such practices are misunderstood by non-Indians as attempts to coax or prod nature in desired directions. Rather, native peoples regard nature's gifts, such as needed rainfall or a bountiful hunt, not as favors bestowed in return for supplication, but as natural occurrences that come to pass when a people has taken care to avoid negative, disruptive mindstates, is cognizant of the spiritual powers in Earth's dynamics, and is full of care for the Earth community. Grace leads to right living, and right living leads to grace. Many Indian cultures believe that even one person's generating hateful or greedy thoughts destroys the communal balance with the cosmos and impairs the web of life.

A wide variety of ceremonies celebrate events within the year's cycle of unfolding creation. The Iroquois, for instance, offer communal gratitude for the manifestation of maple sap, green corn, and strawberries. Other ceremonies, such as the sacred dramas danced throughout the year by the Pueblo peoples, are renewals of nurture, power, and union with the sacred whole. The O'odhdam respond to the Sonoran desert as if it were a sacred calendar, celebrating their place in the cycles of change. In all instances, Indian ceremonies are regarded as spiritual responsibilities, human expressions of the reciprocal interdependence that constitutes the cosmic processes.

In the Cheyenne ceremony of the Medicine Wheel, the spiritual teachers place small stones within the circle to symbolize individuals, families, communities, hawks, buffalo, elk, wolves, religions, governments, philosophies, and entire nations. The Medicine Wheel thus contains the entire universe. The teachers explain that all beings within the Universe Wheel know of their harmony, or balanced relatedness, with everything else and know how to "give away"—except humans. Of all the creatures of the universe, we alone do not begin our lives with knowledge of this great harmony. To become whole, the Cheyenne believe we must find our place in the Medicine Wheel of the universe by learning to seek and perceive through the practice of a vision quest. The "determining spirit" of humans can manifest wisely only if we know how to realize our harmonious relationship with the world around us.[52]

In the Plains peoples' ceremony of the sacred pipe, the pipe itself symbolizes humans, the long, wooden stem being the breath passage leading to the stone bowl, which is the spiritual center, or heart. Macrocosmically the pipe also symbolizes the universe, the stem as an axis joining and defining a path between the Earth community and the larger reality. As the pipe is filled with the sacred tobacco, prayers are offered for all the powers of the universe and for the myriad forms of creation, each represented by a grain of tobacco. The rites of the pipe declare that each of the indefinite number of grains of tobacco placed into the bowl ritually symbolizes, or really *is*, a specific form or possibility of creation. There follows the act of smoking as a rite of communion. When the fire consumes the consecrated tobacco with the aid of human breath, the ritual act affirms the absorption of all creation in the fire, which is the presence of the Great Mysterious. Through the agency of human breath the apparent multiplicity and separateness of phenomena yield ultimate unity. In concluding the ceremony, the participants often recite, "We are all related." This ceremony is commonly called a "peace pipe" because each person who gives breath to the sacred fire is reminded that his or her own center is the same as that of every other person and of the universe itself.[53]

Traditional native peoples pass their lives in uncluttered communion with the simple and the profound. It is humans' *responsibility* to the cosmos, they feel, to know grace, to know as intimately as possible the mysterious interrelatedness and the spiritual powers that infuse being and to live our lives accordingly. In the fulfillment of that responsibility lie meaning and purpose, as reflected in this statement by a contemporary Maidu man, Frank LaPena: "We live our lives by the turning of the seasons and the passage of the Milky Way. We direct our actions by the fullness of the moon and the need to do ceremonies, to put things to rest in winter and awaken them in spring. With our lives and our work we create a metaphor of the universe; all things are one with us."[54]

Ecocommunion and the Forces of Modernity

In creating our own metaphors of the universe, our own personal and communal expressions of our understanding of the sacred whole, we non-Indians need not mimic Indian ceremonies. Indeed, Native Americans would prefer that we do not. John Mohawk, of the Cattaraugus Senecas, told me, "I do not want people to adopt Indian rituals because I want people to own their own rituals. I want them to come to ownership out of experiences that are real to them, that mean something to them. Then I'll come and celebrate it with them."[55] The difficulty lies in ascertaining what really does "mean something" to us when our inner and outer landscapes are so relentlessly colonized by forces of modernity that seek to whip nature triumphantly into shape.

A few years ago, while visiting my family in Ohio, I had an urge to return to the mysterious earth structures created by the Adena and later the Hopewell Moundbuilders some two thousand years ago, which my parents had shown to my sister and me in our childhood. The sensuous Serpent Mound, in the south-central part of the state, is the most famous, but on that trip I convinced my mother to come along for a ride to the Newark Earthworks, closer to home. We found one grouping of the mounds, long embankments that wind through a parklike setting. Studying a map of the entire array of earthworks, my eyes were drawn immediately to an earthwork remarkably similar to the surviving outline of a womblike goddess temple on Malta: a round anteroom, enclosing about twenty acres, is connected by a narrow passageway to an octagonal inner room, enclosing about fifty acres. "Let's go there," I said, pointing on the map to the outline that resembles a womb and birth canal. (I did not elaborate on my suggestion as my mother is a sweet Midwest mama of a generation that becomes slightly disconcerted to hear words referring to the reproductive system.) We drove to the other side of Newark and followed a narrow street away from the center of town, past Victorian houses set on large lawns. At the end of that gravelly street, we came to a parking lot and a puzzling sign: Moundbuilders Country Club. I could not see any state park signs or trails. We climbed up a grassy rise before us since the only path out of the parking lot led to the sprawling clubhouse off to the left. What we saw at the top of the embankment caused my stomach to tighten and spread a dull shock throughout my body: a golf course had been created not adjacent to but directly over the ancient earthworks. That afternoon men were driving hard little missiles within the huge womb, a sterile exercise from which nothing would issue. Wave their clubs as they might, she yielded nothing, shared no secrets, offered no communion. Even more horrifying, I saw that we ourselves were standing on a section of the sacred mound. "Let's get out of here," I said, taking my mother's arm, "before we get hit by a golf ball."

Driving home, my mind was filled with recollections of communion with the unitary presence that infuses the natural world—and the subsequent paving over of such graced consciousness by the forces of modern culture and "regular life." Why had there been no correspondence during my youth between those luminous moments of connectedness I experienced intermittently at summer camp in the Appalachian foothills of southern Ohio and the life I returned to in an orderly suburb that clearly considered itself, and the rest of modern society, to be beyond nature? Why had my spontaneous presentation of my newborn daughter to the trees, the grass, the flowers, the air, the stars, and the moon when we sneaked out of the hospital one night for a cosmic coming-out party in the adjacent garden later seemed so quirky an impulse, so unrelated to the modern concerns about childrearing that I forgot entirely about it until sixteen years later when I heard the Omaha presentation prayer recited? Why do silent moments on wilderness trips when the membrane between inner and outer mind seems to dissolve and one experiences the vast, ecological self later seem so remote from the possibilities of daily life?

There is no cultural support for the experiencing of self beyond the human-centered confines of a culture that is hostile to nature. The stubborn recurrence of such experience is derided or ignored. The very ways in which a modern society views itself serve to marginalize contact with the sacred whole. In the materialist view, production and other economic activity are central to human society, social constructs are a related tier of developments, and the so-called epiphenomenal concerns such as spirituality and cosmology cluster around the edges of "real life." To a traditional native person, of course, that conceptualization is utterly inside out: at the center of human life are experiences of deep communion with the cosmos; from those, a people understand and honor their relationships and seek to retain the revealed wisdom through cosmologically oriented cultural practices that inform their performance of such basic tasks as putting food into the stomach and clothing and sheltering the body.

Modernity holds that our natural role is to function in opposition to nature, to "master" it and thereby hold chaos at bay. Ecological versions of the managerial ethos hold that the unfolding dynamics of the natural world, as understood through evolutionary biology, are indeed extraordinarily complex, resiliant, and worthy of awe—but that the role of the human is to intervene, beyond fulfilling our vital needs, to manage and direct the further evolution of other species. What accounts for that sharp turn at the bifurcation point of awe toward the urge to control rather than toward humility and the urge to protect? The cause seems to be a deep fear that one's being might well be absorbed and annihilated by a larger whole unless that whole is broken down into areas of human control—the land "resources," the waterways, production animals, the space frontier, and so forth. In addition to the fear that nature unchallenged would physically destroy us, the notion of experiencing oneness with the natural world is feared by many as a horrifying engulfment: either one guards his individuality, freedom, and particularity *or* he surrenders his being to an overarching monster, oneness. This highly charged dualism is so central to the sensibility of modernity that cultural commentators who wish to be considered sophisticated and urbanely modern routinely mock expressions of communion with nature as sophomoric, embarrassing, sentimental, or boring. Deconstructive postmodernists add that the "narrative" of experiencing oneness is politically incorrect because it "totalizes" or "colonizes" multiplicity, or "difference." Both of these objections are locked into a framework of dualism: either particularity *or* ultimate unity. They can be held only in ignorance of the *experience* of being at one with the world, in which one perceives in an instant the sacred whole, the vast organism in which we are embodied without separation, the larger self. Knowing the wonder of the larger reality, the experience of grace, all particularity is then understood to be exceedingly precious, the unimaginably diverse articulation of the dynamically creative cosmic body. Moreover, the unique abilities of the human species are understood to participate in responsibility for developments in the great unfolding.

Since there are myriad paths, many unmarked, to the unitive experience, it is in no way exclusive. When a culture hostile to nature disdainfully ignores children's and adults' experiences of cosmic grace, however, deep communion is discouraged and ultimately denied. Is this not a thwarting of evolutionary potential? There is much support for the view that the *telos* of the universe is toward ever-increasing subjectivity and complexity—but why not toward increasing communion as well? The emergence of self-reflexive consciousness in humans introduced the possibility of rich, subtle, and endlessly creative communion with the larger whole. Since "progressing" beyond primal worldviews of the spiritual relatedness of all phenomena, though, we have walled off that evolutionary path.[56] The substitutions—communing with an anthropomorphic deity said to orchestrate the sacred whole, or guarding against communion with nature as a dangerous (and unscientific!) act of vulnerability—have left us atrophied, lacking a deeply personal connection with the natural world around us. Hence the modern denial of our larger self not only confines and diminishes us, but is cosmologically irresponsible.

"But it was either us or nature!" defenders of the mechanistic, invasive, technocratic worldview insist. They maintain that we never could have achieved all the modern conditions and conveniences we enjoy without separating ourselves from the natural, cosmological processes as much as possible in order to advance our levels of manipulation. "Blurring the lines between human and nature would sink us back into the Stone Age," they often warn. (Ironically, the Stone Age, with its verdant wealth of flora and fauna flourishing in unpolluted ecosystems, will look most appealing from the devastated wasteland toward which industrialized growth economies are leading us, unless fundamental change is accomplished. Assuming the role of arrogant taskmaster with nature has turned into a suicidally bad joke.) There is no inherent reason that scientific inquiry and technological innovation could not have been informed all along by a spirit of communion with the sacred whole (rather than church politics or expansionist economics). Basic research into cosmological dynamics could be conducted not as part of a massive campaign to conquer nature but as part of a spiritual practice to enter into the mysteries of the universe's web of life as deeply and reverently as possible. Applied research as spiritual practice could develop ecological design in order that our species might interact lightly with the Gaian ways of being and so express our awe, humility, and love. Regarding the cosmos as primary would not stop wise progress, only senseless destruction.

Communion with the cosmos, from the deconstructive postmodernists' perspective, is nothing more than a "discourse," an example of an arbitrary "logic" we construct for a particular situation in order to interpret events and shape responses. Bioregionalists, who take inspiration from native peoples' sensitivities toward the land and the ecocommunity, would counter that there is a "logic of place" in which the endless variety of cultural constructions should be rooted. That is, the cosmos is indeed primary, and the bioregion, the home neighborhood, is not at all unintelligible. Its land forms and water establish boundaries; its soils have a particular character; its microclimates are hospitable to some crops, but not others; its winds move in certain patterns; its flowers keep their seasons; its air is laced with the sounds of certain songbirds, frogs, and crickets. Our perceptions of all these cosmic manifestations weave together a complex ground for our sense of being and our imaginative range. The more we pay attention to the bioregion's ways of being, the stronger that grounding becomes for us. From familiarity grows relationship, from which spring creative possibilities for our approach to education, religion, economics, politics, and social structures in communion with the bioregional presence. If we are sufficiently attentive, we arrive "home" with the primal sense of awe and thanksgiving.

To hone our awareness of the ecocommunity, most of us need to begin with basics, such as learning to recognize a dozen native plants, a dozen birds, and other local animals. Professional naturalists in city and regional parks can be of assistance, but it is also worth the effort to seek out the amateur naturalists in one's community. In both my former and present homes, I have enjoyed many half-day bird walks with white-haired ladies who were extremely knowledgeable and encouraging to novices. (All the naturalists I have known were good-natured and wore their knowledge lightly, perhaps because long periods of immersion in the larger reality have imbued them with an existential security that requires no grandstanding. In any case, getting out into nature seems to be good for the disposition, and even beginners find it nearly impossible to return home from birding in a negative mood.) Having a sense of one's bioregion may someday be considered as essential as knowing the local streets and highways. Newcomers might ask their neighbors, "On what day of the week is the local farmers' market held around here? What time of year is the all-species parade?[57] Oh, and who are the local naturalists—we don't want to remain know-nothings for long!"

As we begin to develop a sense of the ecocommunity in which we live, we grow to cherish it. Without much forethought we find ourselves creating personal rituals of communion—making visitations to a particular spot, suspending thought for a long moment at the beginning of the day to let the backyard bird song fill our mind/body, or feeling drawn to observe the daily progress of a budding tree. As our sensitivity increases, certain narrowly focused rituals within the human community seem to cry out for greater fullness. While saying grace before a meal, why not express gratitude not only for our food but for the presence of the animals, plants, landforms, and water? Participating in worship services, why not suggest various ways that the presence of the

bioregion can be included? Celebrations of baptism, confirmation, Bar Mitzvah, Bat Mitzvah, and weddings could all include the ritual planting of a tree. Certainly the annual slaughter of millions of firs to celebrate the birth of Christ could be replaced with purchasing live firs, or, better still, native trees, which could later be planted or donated to a regional park.

Beyond that, each of our religious rituals, those that mark the stages in an individual's spiritual life as well as those that are communal celebrations in the liturgical cycle, could be enriched by greater recognition of the cosmic web of life.[58] In this era of ecological awakening, the living presence of the ceremonies of native peoples—inspiring acts of regeneration of their sense of interrelatedness with the sacred whole—is a great gift. Perhaps the growing appreciation of their embodied wisdom will lead to an interfaith deepening of the spirituality of Earthlings.

While some people work to "cosmologize" organized religion, others have taken to grow-your-own ceremonies of cosmological celebration, especially at the solstices and equinoxes. The two days with the longest and shortest gift of light from our sun, plus the two days with light and darkness of equal length, plus the midpoint days between those four were celebrated in pre-Christian Europe as natural markers in the majestic cycles of Earth's body. Two of the midpoint holy days are preserved in modern times as May Day and All Saints Day (or All Hallows Day, preceded immediately by Hallows Eve, or "Halloween").[59] Today the solstices and equinoxes have become occasions for groups of friends and family to gather in celebration of the Earth community and to focus awareness on the particular turning of the seasons. With friends, I have given thanks at autumn equinox for the bountiful harvests of the soil and in our lives, turned inward on the long night of winter solstice to look directly at the dark, known regeneration at spring equinox as Earth's exuberance burst forth, and felt the fullness of fruition at summer solstice when Earth's day is long and sensuous.

Of all those images, the most beautiful that remains with me is the spring equinox ritual we evolved over time.[60] A group of some forty people in spring colors walk from our cars in procession to a gentle rise in a spacious park, carrying armfuls of flowers and greens, food and drink, and burning incense. Musicians among us play instruments as the children toss a trail of petals. We form a circle and place the flowers and greens at our feet, forming a huge garland for the Earth, one foot wide and half as high. In the center on colorful cloths we set baskets of food and objects of regeneration—feathers shed by eagles and other birds, a bowl of water, a small statue of a pregnant female, and several sprays of pink and white blossoms. We breathe together and plant our feet squarely on the warming earth, drawing up its procreative powers into our being. Working mindfully, we take some flowers and ivy from the Earth garland and make individual garlands with trailing ribbons for ourselves, then weave together the stems and greens in the grand garland. Standing, we call upon the presence of the East and the cleansing winds that clear our minds. We call upon the presence of the South and the fires of warmth and energy that enliven us. We call upon the presence of the West and the water that soothes and renews us. We call upon the presence of the North and the earth that grounds and feeds us. We sing, perhaps the Indian song "The Earth Is Our Mother." We seat ourselves around the garland and offer into the circle one-word poems about spring in our bioregion. Someone reads a favorite poem. A storyteller, accompanied by soft drumming and bird-song flute, tells an ancient tale of the meaning of spring. We sing a lilting song with her. A second storyteller tells another story of spring. We sing a rhythmic chant with him. The two bards put on masks they have made and dance and leap around the circle, sprung with vernal energies. In counterpoint, the men sing his song, the women hers. We rise and sway like saplings as we sing. We move as the spirit moves us, dancing, turning. When we come to rest, we sit, emptied of song, on the ground and let the flute song fill our bodies. We pass around a bowl of berries, each person taking one and offering into the circle thoughts of thanksgiving for particular gifts of spring. Brimming with love for the embodied wisdom of Gaia, we bid farewell to the presence of the four directions and break the circle. Then come feasting and visiting. Thus do we welcome spring.

The Ecological Imperative

The philosopher George Santayana wondered, "Why should we not look on the universe with piety? Is it not our substance? Are we made of other clay? All our possibilities lie from eternity hidden in its bosom."[61] Yet the shrunken, narcissistic focus of the modern human locates all our possibilities in *our* bosoms, freewheeling creatures without a past or relations. In the absence of any comprehension of the sacred whole, meaninglessness and destruction are as acceptable as anything else to many people. An operator of a timber-harvesting company in the Pacific Northwest stated a few years ago, "It is natural for man to manipulate his environment and ruin it. And it may be natural that we are going to go through the process of ruining the land and we are going to die and there is going to be nothing left. That will be the end of it."[62] Others feel that there can indeed be something left once we have run through the health of the ecosystems: an artificially created replacement world with soil, rocks, trees, crops, and animals created by nanotechnology (molecular engineering) and genetic engineering. Enthusiasts would explain, "Once humans have remade the physical world to suit our preferences more closely, scarcity of resources and other insulting ecological limits to human population will be behind us!" Also gone will be the unfolding differentiation, subjectivity, and communion of billions of unique manifestations of the cosmos. "Extinction is natural," they counter. "This is a participatory universe, and everyone knows you have to break a few eggs to make an omelet. What's the problem?"

The problem is hubris, the rending of the cosmic web of life through arrogance, fear, and an emptiness so deep it is wrenchingly painful to observe. Our species is but one expression of the cosmos. We have always played an interactive role with the rest of the Earth community. There is no possibility that we could refrain from intervention; even walking down a street, we probably crush countless tiny creatures. Our bodies require food, warmth, clothing, and shelter—all of which we take from earth-stuff. The *problem* is the denial of humility and care that marks the modern and ultra-modern revolutions against the integrity of Gaia, a dynamic unfolding that was well established long before our emergence. Our species' ethics should include the fulfilling of our vital needs with minimal damage to our cosmic relations. If that were our guideline, we would surely have to admit that our knowledge of the intricacies of Gaian life is so far from complete that we should make far-reaching changes in the ecosystems only with great caution.

Since the dominant culture continues to rush in the opposite direction—cleaning up a few production processes, for example, while still maintaining ravenous growth economies that devour habitats with dazzling efficiency—Gaian spirituality calls for "action prayers," activist engagement with those human systems that are furthering the gratuitous destruction of the Earth community. Much "green" activism in the industrialized nations as well as the Third and Fourth Worlds has been sustained by spiritual commitment.

Commitment, to be effective, must also be informed. Understanding basic principles of ecology—interdependence, diversity, resilience, adaptability, and limits—is necessary in opposing unwise human intervention.[63] People with untempered faith in the supposedly value-free, objective life of technology often insist that environmental dynamics are so complicated that the public should back off and let commissions of scientific experts make all decisions, which would then be enacted by government. If memory serves, that course of action gave us scores of dangerous nuclear power plants; numerous disastrous assaults on the ecological integrity of watersheds by the U.S. Army Corps of Engineers; approval of hundreds of toxic compounds for agricultural, industrial, and medical uses; and a flood of federal research funding for the development of genetically engineered animals, pesticides, and crops without adequate testing of *dynamic* interaction, such as will occur in a real ecosystem once a new microorganism leaves the lab. The burden of proof (of safety) should be on the people pushing for novel, substantial change in the ecosystems, not on the citizens calling for caution.

Not only is it difficult for concerned citizens working through existing channels in modern technocracies to defend sustainability against destructive projects that will boost the GNP (a tally that includes costs of attempted environmental cleanup as if it were merely part of value-free production and services), but the voices of millions of other residents are not heard at all. In a parliament of all species, humans' expansionist schemes for industrial mastery of the biosphere would no doubt be hooted off the floor as too unbearably callous, greedy, and murderous to merit a formal vote. Because the existing governmental channels in societies with growth economies are not designed to welcome sustainable earth ethics in more than superficial ways, grassroots movements have had to mount direct, usually nonviolent, challenges to ecocide. Such campaigns demand much time and energy and often yield frustration. Yet, for increasing numbers of people worldwide, that work is experienced not merely as attempts to save enough of the biosphere for human survival, but as moral acts that embody our felt connection with the sacred whole. John Seed, a defender of the rain forests in Australia, has described the Gaian spiritual transformation he underwent in the course of his activism: "'I am protecting the rainforest' develops to 'I am part of the rainforest protecting myself. I am that part of the rainforest recently emerged into thinking.'" Through continuing engagement, he has found, one's Gaian memory improves.[64]

Knowing Gaia, Knowing Grace

We are haunted by the question of how much recovery is possible for human consciousness formed in modern societies hostile to nature. Will we ever experience anything like the nuanced, richly detailed sense of the sacred whole known to traditional native peoples? Will we ever know that pervasive sense of intimacy with the rest of the natural world, we who have lived in exile so long? Chief Seattle warned in mid-nineteenth century that humans would die of a terrible loneliness if all the animals on this continent disappeared, yet how many of us even notice the gradual disappearance of songbirds, for instance, as fewer return each spring from their ravaged winter homes in the Central and South American rain forest? The diminishing bird counts are items we read about in the newspaper and then turn the page. Or are we dying, slowly, of a terrible alienation?

We are not abandoned. Nature will receive us into communion once again and make our sterile consciousness fertile if only we will bring bare attention to its wonders. Recovered awareness, patient and precise, is the taproot of Gaian spirituality. In a garden, at a park, or on a wilderness retreat, we can open our senses and learn. Just as in the meditation practice of observing with precision whatever arises in the mind or the body, bare attention to the rest of the natural world requires setting aside preconceived notions, such as the view of nature as a dumb mechanism. In unexpected moments I have witnessed the prolonged eroticism of garden snails and the exuberant play of two sanderlings bodysurfing repeatedly down the rivulets of a freshwater stream that cut across a beach while the rest of their flock splashed around more sedately downstream. We have underestimated our animal relations because we felt we had no use for them. In truth, we need them deeply to heal us, to initiate us, to spark our possibilities.

Once we no longer feel like tourists in the natural world, more and more of the intense vitality and intricate interrelatedness of the sacred whole is revealed to us. Its wonders, if we have sloughed off at least some of our implanted fear, evoke celebration, hence the flowering in recent years of personal and communal rituals of gratitude and joy. Gaian spirituality is nonsectarian, sprouting up in Hebrew tree-planting ceremonies, bioregional liturgies, the United Nations' interfaith Environmental Sabbath, the imaginative burst of homegrown solstice and equinox celebrations, and much more. Alas, disapproving glances still shoot between some members of these groups, as if there could be only one correct way to attempt to express the ineffable. Were we and the rest of the world set here by Raven the creator? By the Great Holy, the creativity of the cosmos? Were we modeled by God the Father? Did we grow from the body of Mother Earth? *We are here*—inextricably linked at the molecular level to every other manifestation of the great unfolding. We are descendants of the fireball. We are pilgrims on this Earth, glimpsing the oneness of the sacred whole, knowing Gaia, knowing grace.

4

Embracing the Body

On honoring the personal body and the Earthbody: the wisdom of Goddess spirituality

The universe unfolds through diverse processes that weave novelty and preservation. Some one and a half billion years ago, the creative possibilities on our planet were enhanced dramatically by the emergence of sexual reproduction, the uniting of DNA from more than one parent. For two billion years, bacteria, single-celled beings that propagate by dividing, had graciously produced such gases as oxygen and methane. These gases, interacting with the rest of the atmosphere, the oceans, and the rocky crust of Earth's surface, created a habitat for the more complex cells that followed and, eventually, for a multiplicity of fungi, plants, and animals. Species became delineated as mating populations, and most organic life-forms were divided into female or male.

If we had gone the way of paramecia—single-cell organisms that can still reproduce the old way by cloning or by developing as many as eight sexes[1]—imagine what cultural responses might have emerged. Instead of seeing situations as "black or white," perhaps we would habitually perceive eight gradations. As it is, human societies have responded to the bodily differences between the two sexes in dualistic ways that shape the life experience of every individual. Born into a particular culture, most people regard that orientation as "the natural way," or at least, if they become aware of other cultural choices, "the proper way."

What is seen as the "natural" conceptual foundation for constructing culture seems to reflect a society's perception of its relationship with nature. The anthropologist Peggy Reeves Sanday studied the cultural context of sex-role configurations in anthropological data on 156 tribal societies and found that they operated according to an "inner orientation" or an "outer orientation."[2] In societies where the forces of nature are sacralized, a reciprocal flow is perceived between the power of nature and the power inherent in women, a power dynamic in which men can participate through ritual. Mediating both of those forces with ritual is felt to be a function of women's being representatives of nature's power. Sanday labels such relationships an "inner orientation," generally found in situations where most of a people's food comes from the earth or water. Nature is regarded as a partner, rather than an opponent. There is a good deal of mingling between the sexes, fathers play a nurturant role in childrearing, and rape is a rare occurrence.[3] In such cultures, which exhibit a ritual focus on female reproductive powers, the creation myth usually features a sacred female creator or a divine couple.

Where a society's interaction with nature revolves around the necessity of migration and the pursuit of large animals, Sanday found an "outer orientation" to be prominent. Men hunt animals, engage in interpersonal violence as a norm, make weapons for those activities, and pursue power that is "out there." In such cultures, male dominance in myth and everyday life is associated with "fear, conflict, and strife." Sanday observes,

> In these societies, males believe that there is an uncontrollable force that may strike at any time and against which men must be prepared to defend their integrity. The nature of the force and its source are not well defined, but often they are associated with female sexuality and reproductive functions. Men believe it is their duty to harness this force, with its power over life and death, to prevent chaos and to maintain equilibrium. They go to extraordinary lengths to acquire some of the power for themselves so that they will not be impotent when it is time to fight. Men attempt to

> neutralize the power they think is inherent in women by stealing it, nullifying it, or banishing it to invisibility.[4]

In such cultural configurations, fathers are more distant from childrearing, rape is not unusual, and men often forbid women to use certain ritual objects, musical instruments, or meeting places. Sanday found that the sexes tend to separate from each other in situations where nature is defined in hostile terms and that the sexes must be physically as well as conceptually separated in order for men to attain dominance.

Once in place, cultural patterns tend to have great tenacity. Although many modern citizens of our country would bristle at any comparison with tribal customs, it is obvious that the historical processes resulting in Western civilization preserved a good deal of the orientation exhibited by those cultures in Sanday's "outer" category. Nature is not considered sacred or a partner; ultimate power resides "out there" with a sky-god; and men traditionally proclaim numerous cultural "spaces" (the priesthood, higher education, law, medicine, business, government, the art world) to be off-limits to women. In a cultural orientation where the elemental power of the female body—by which I mean the capability to grow people of either sex from her flesh, to bleed in rhythm with the moon, to transform food into milk for infants—is considered somewhat frightening by males, a tremendous amount of effort goes into preventing women from acquiring cultural power in addition to the disquieting elemental power. The female is contained by belittling and controlling her. Our culture can be classified as "patriarchal" (meaning literally "ruled by the father") not because power is reserved for biological fathers, but because men and women are socialized to understand that males should legitimately act as controlling cultural fathers, while females should appropriately act as dependent, obedient minors.

Patriarchal Dynamics

"Oh, how dreary. Patriarchy is such a seventies topic," one hears in certain circles today. "Let's just drop that whole tedious gender-conflict business and get on with ecology [or global networking, or making a lot of money]." One also hears, from some deconstructive postmodernists, that analyzing the power dynamics of oppression by gender (or race or class) is passé since the mechanisms of domination are now understood to be too subtly diffuse for any analysis. I do not feel that attention to patriarchal dynamics can be dismissed as long as one of every three women in the United States will be raped during her lifetime,[5] or a woman is physically beaten every fourteen seconds in our country,[6] or our youth get the message early on that (patriarchal) men's sexual "needs" take precedence over the "wants" of women and children. The average age of young male sex offenders and their victims is decreasing, and growing numbers of college students today feel that forced sex on a date is not rape. A random survey of women in Los Angeles in 1986 found that 62 percent had been sexually abused at least once before age eighteen.[7] A survey of teenage mothers in Illinois in 1987 found that 61 percent had been sexually abused as children.[8] Studies consistently find that most prostitutes, and many people convicted of violent crimes, were sexually abused as children. Even the crisis in homelessness, generally thought to be solely an economic problem, disproportionately afflicts women who, according to a recent study, are to some extent dysfunctional because they have experienced physical, sexual, and emotional abuse since early childhood *and* who are caught in the economic crunch.[9] A study of Third-World women, which was not intended to focus on "battering" by men, repeatedly found it to be a common thread among women's experiences in a variety of patriarchal cultures.[10] Moreover, the female body is not only abused but exploited: women worldwide contribute two-thirds of the work hours, earn one-tenth of the income, and own one one-hundredth of the property.[11] Patriarchy is real.

In a patriarchal society, cultural forms evolve to ease the fears of nature and the female felt by the dominant group. The compensatory dynamics identified in Sanday's survey of patriarchal cultures are abundant in our own. Traditionally, dominance-or-submission has been the model for interactions. Chaos is avoided by a chain of command, not only in military and corporate subcultures, but in the very perception of being: a hierarchical configuration with God at the top, followed by angels and white men, on down to animals. The "sacred blood of the female," as it is regarded in "inner-oriented" cultures, becomes a source of embarrassment to women in patriarchal cultures, a shameful function that must be hidden and denied. Yet the blood mysteries of the female have extremely ancient associations with honor, sanctity, and power. For example, at prepatriarchal, Neolithic excavation sites, red ocher has been found smeared on the entrances to caves in which ritual objects, often Goddess statues, were found and on the statues themselves. Sometimes this association is maintained even in patriarchal societies, such as the tradition of brides in China and India marrying in red, not white. Honorable access to flowing blood is available to men in patriarchal societies through participation in imitative rituals such as religious circumcision (in which blood is drawn from the male genital),[12] drinking the transubstantiated blood of Christ, or earning the "red badge of courage" on a battlefield.[13]

Like menses, pregnancy under patriarchy is treated as a disability, one requiring the power of the male medical establishment, who pushed midwives out of practice in most areas until recently. Lactation, too, has been disparaged by modern physicians as a rather pointless, animallike function of women; between the 1930s and the mid-1970s, doctors almost succeeded in phasing out breast-feeding, which passes antibodies of immunity as well as nutrition to the infant, in favor of more modern, "civilized" bottle-feeding. The hundreds of thousands of unnecessary hysterectomies performed in the United States, especially during the 1960s and 1970s, constitute a devastating assault on the womb. Patriarchal men often experience discomfort at having to be around pregnant women—in boardrooms, classrooms, or factories. Ernest Hemingway, for instance, reportedly could not stand the sight of pregnant women.[14] Did his macho sensibilities perhaps perceive "the great round" as a competitively superior erection?

Social structures and attitudes in our society draw legitimacy from the central assumptions of Western religion and philosophy. Creativity in the universe, ultimate mystery, the divine—all are symbolized by the distant father-god, ruling in transcendence far above Earth's realm of blood, mud, birth, and death. The goal of most Western spirituality has been to transcend nature and the flesh (which meant primarily man's escaping the "lure" of woman's flesh). Western philosophy, following the Pythagoreans, identified man with mind, subjectivity, determinate form (substance), and potential transcendence. It has identified woman with body, passivity, indeterminate and disorderly form (process), and "dumb" matter. Throughout the history of Western philosophy, three vital concerns of men raised in patriarchal culture continually appear: separateness, reactive (defensive) autonomy, and control. What is accorded value is that which is situated within the bounds of "reason," a mode of cognition that disallows gestalt sensibilities, feelings, or subtle perceptions called intuition.

Patriarchal socialization shapes the consciousness of both sexes, not with uniform results among individuals, of course, but with an informing orientation. In general, women raised under patriarchy received the message from myriad sources that we have the wrong body to be taken seriously in matters of culture, commerce, medicine, government, and so forth. "Feminine nature" is found wanting by the dominant culture; hence insecurity abounds. Even within the delineations of patriarchally approved presentations of the female body, cultural messages tell woman she is inadequate—in need of bound feet or high heels, corsets, padded bras, dyed hair, and even plastic surgery. Depression, fear, self-loathing are common psychological themes for women raised under patriarchy. For men raised in such societies, the informing obsession is to be "not-woman"—not emotionally invested in relationships, not "vulnerable" through empathy, not weak in physicality (especially upper body strength), not docile. Autonomy is the goal, and there is great pressure to distinguish oneself from the pack. Life is often experienced as competitive, atomized, and alienating. Cultural messages tell man that his body is somehow treacherous, issuing from a woman's vagina only to eventually cause his death by breaking down and failing. Rage, fear, and loneliness are common psychological themes for men raised under patriarchy; detachment from feelings is the acceptable coping strategy.

Society generally evolves controlling structures and behavior patterns that diminish culturally implanted fears. When patriarchal man's deep-seated fears of the elemental power of the female, his own body, and his emotions are indulged, however, by a supposedly strong leader calling for even more intensely patriarchal social structures, fascism can result. Contrary to German Marxists' insistence that National Socialism was simply the natural progression of capitalism, aided by the intrusion of "the irrational," a recent study by Klaus Theweleit, *Male Fantasies*,[15] found in the Nazi dreams of mythic grandeur an attempt to escape the personal and the intimate. Studying recruiting posters, popular novels of the post–Great War era, and journals written by officers of the proto-Nazi *Freikorps* units, many of whom went on to become officers in Hitler's SA and functionaries in the Third Reich, Theweleit discovers the fantasy urge to stay dry, erect, and rigid versus an imagined female liquefaction and flowing, a feared and yet desired "flood." Desire becomes mutated into the desire for violence against desire. The cultural artifacts Theweleit studied reveal fantasy as a means of killing and protecting: the more lifeless, regimented, and monumental reality appears to be, the more secure the men feel. He concludes that the core of all fascist propaganda is a battle against everything that constitutes enjoyment and pleasure, so that the only remaining "erotic" fantasy is one in which soldiers destroy a mob of supposedly evil and lascivious enemies and are rewarded by distant and stiff dream-figures: kings, generals, and idealized women. He found the diaries of the *Freikorps* officers to be rife with dreamy scenes of brutality and passionate dedication to a quest, a beloved commander, and hallucinated vision-queens without female genitals. Fascism, according to Theweleit's study, is a set of violent fantasies and acts meant to protect (patriarchal) man from his body, his desires, his emotions, and his immediate and local relations with other people. While fascism is an extreme form of the patriarchal shaping of life, its themes are recognizable as intensifications of the leitmotiv that recur throughout such cultures.

A Patriarchal Dream: The Disembodied Worldview of Deconstructive Postmodernism

Within the context of patriarchal culture, deconstructive-postmodern philosophy has emerged during the past twenty-some years, not only focusing attention on the cultural construction of our most dearly held "natural" concepts, but also making the leap to declaring that there is *nothing but* cultural construction in human experience. A problematic aspect of this mode of analysis is its seeming lack of attention to the ways in which its own cultural context, Eurocentric patriarchy, has shaped its perspective. In many regards, it continues certain thematic concerns of Western patriarchal philosophy and culture, such as autonomy from relationship, separateness, and control through abstraction (see Appendix B). In patriarchal societies the fundamental orientation toward the two primal power-mysteries—nature and the elemental power of the female—is fear because those powers are conceived of as power-over and threatening, rather than as cosmic presence, a dynamic and transformative power in which males participate. This fundamental response infuses all social constructions. For patriarchal men in particular, who have traditionally shaped Western culture, all relationships, and even the very nature of relationship, are potentially dangerous. Safety lies in guarding one's autonomy and dominating others whenever possible.

Throughout Western patriarchal history each era has shown a particular genius for meeting these challenges, with variations on the themes in each society. Modernity's thrust of will over nature promised a seemingly invincible protective shield of technology, but the felt danger of the elemental power of the female, the fear of being engulfed by her sexuality, was still omnipresent. The macho strikes of much modernist literature and painting had not succeeded in smashing the female threat and containing "the new woman."[16] Structuralism later conceptually squeezed the female into a mere complement of the male, but the popularity of that analysis has faded.[17] Into this struggle was introduced the dazzling tactic, far less engaged and hence less risky, called postmodernism, or poststructuralism: simply declare the elemental power of the female null and void on the grounds that *anything* associated with the female (or anything else) is merely a cultural invention! Any mention of the elemental capabilities of woman can be dismissed as merely a "valorizing narrative"! Since such concepts as "woman," "man," "nature," and "body" are regarded as nothing more than the cultural projections of a particular time and place, their "presence," or substantive validity, is "erased" by seeing through and deconstructing their cobbled nature.

Because "the body" is so strongly associated with woman in patriarchal cultures (man/mind/spirit as opposed to woman/body/matter), the deconstructive-postmodern "erasure of the body" is foremost the erasure of the female body. Derrida asserts that everything in human experience, including nature and human physicality, is "always already," that is, always an already "supplemented" entity that has been shaped into cultural perceptions. Hence any search for origins is deemed absurd, as there was no foundational experience. That is, deconstructive postmodernists seem intent on denying there was a point at which the bodies of female proto-humans transformed from cycles of both estrus and menses to cycles of menses alone, when human consciousness developed. Among other phenomena, the new human consciousness encountered day, night, water, edible plants, weather, animals, and wombs from which issued both males and females, breasts from which issued life-sustaining liquid, and vaginas that bled, even though no cut had been made, in rhythm with the moon. (They also encountered two kinds of liquid issuing from penises, but apparently semen was not connected with birth for a long while. That connection was probably apparent in many societies at least by the Neolithic era, when animal husbandry was common, but even well into the modern era aboriginal peoples in Australia, for example, believed that women are impregnated by the wind.)

Although we, with our own culturally informed concepts, cannot know the cognitive processes of the earliest humans, they obviously had some sort of psychological response to physical phenomena, and those responses set in motion the dynamic orientations of culture. Myriad responses would be possible, of course, but anthropological examples of the alternatives can be considered in two groups. According to Sanday's study, peoples who found it rather easy to fulfill bodily needs perceived their surroundings (nature) to be benevolent and the elemental capabilities of the female to be the locus of benevolent mediation of great power, while peoples in more difficult and nomadic circumstances perceived nature to be unreliable and harsh and the female powers to be sources of danger. From such responses to physicality grew cultural orientations, which have proven remarkably stubborn even through changes in a people's physical situation. *Within* the framework of a people's cultural response—principally fear or love—to the power-mysteries, the insights of the deconstructive postmodernists are quite valid: all our concepts are indeed socially constructed. "Woman," "man," "nature," "body" are all infused with meaning that varies from era to era and place to place. The conceptualizations, however, remain within the fundamental cultural orientation. (Cultures in transition from one orientation to the other, of course, exhibit elements of both.) "Woman" in patriarchal societies may be considered a madonna or a whore, weak or dangerous (or all of those), but she must be contained by cultural constructions and made as inconsequential as possible.

Foucault painstakingly brought attention to the historicity of the acculturation processes by which human beings are shaped into particular kinds of acting subjects. He also illuminated the diffuse and multicentered nature of societal control. Such dynamics, though, are not the enforcement of arbitrary abstractions. They are always situated within a fundamental cultural orientation. Foucault was well aware of expressions of cultural continuity through epochs—the recurrence of determined practices and "discourses," which he called "generalities"—but did not emphasize these as streams of a cultural orientation. He focused instead on the "transformable singularities," the particular manifestations of power relations within a time and place, because his mission was to awaken people to the socially constructed nature of the received concepts we consider to be natural. Foucault did not deny the possibility that singular forms of experience "may perfectly well harbor universal structures" (a position many of his more aggressive followers seem to overlook), but he insisted that the "putting into play" of any universal forms is always done via thought, which has a historicity.[18] Unfortunately, his conclusions, like those of other deconstructive postmodernists, often fulfill core desires of patriarchy, such as the negation of the female body: Foucault proposed that rape be reclassified as simple assault since, after all, our notions of sexuality are merely an arbitrary social construction.[19] This is an example of the "desexualization" he recommended to the feminist movement as a comprehensive goal.

The patriarchal desire to disempower the body is served by the deconstructive-postmodern assertion that abstraction, or conceptualization, is all. Foucault proclaimed that we are "*nothing but* determined historical figures"[20] (my italics), our bodies being mere docile recipients of various power-laden "discourses" and diffuse practices of cultural discipline and self-discipline. The deconstructionist insistence that socialization "goes all the way down," as the philosopher Richard Rorty puts it, champions human endeavor above the larger dynamics of the universe. Yet extensive studies of identical twins raised separately, which have been conducted at the Universities of Minnesota, Ottawa, and elsewhere in recent years, reveal idiosyncratic and extremely resilient expressions of the genetic coding carried in every cell of the human body. In short, our evolving inheritance from the fireball constitutes a drama unfolding in the midst of cultural construction. Since we possess limited understanding about the vast web of cosmic dynamics—that is, our inherent participation in the larger reality, which subtly affects one's experiencing of life—humility is in order. Instead, deconstructive postmodernism calms the patriarchal anxiety about containing "hostile" nature by shrinking the awesome creativity of the unfolding universe into the realm of (hu)man's invention. Nothing matters, or even is real, except the projects of human society. "There is nothing outside the text," Derrida announces.

Within that realm men raised under patriarchy are taught, directly or indirectly, that relationship is always a threat to one's prized autonomy. Images of "oneness" or "unity" trip an alarm in patriarchal consciousness that dangerous forces (religion? woman?) are trying to swallow up male autonomy in an annihilating "sameness." Patriarchal man believes he must always guard against being colonized via relationship, so Derrida is embraced for "proving" that language itself, a primary tool of relationship, is inherently unreliable. The (patriarchal) horror that even the very personal interior monologue in a man's mind is composed of language invented by *other people* is deflated by Derrida's assurance that language has no power because it refers to nothing except endless chains of "signifiers" and "signifieds." "The play of difference" is the only reality for the insular subject. Relationship is held at arm's length. In the deconstructionist worldview, one's sense of fixed "identity" also must be denied as a hopelessly ignorant and reactionary concept, but deconstructionist men are nominally willing to sacrifice identity because they experience their own, in patriarchal culture, as reactive and insecure, continually projected in opposition to nature and the female. Since it is all a house of cards anyway, why not knock it down? Foucault felt that once the nature of social relationship, to self as well as others, was revealed and demolished as being other people's power plays and "discourses," we could face the task of constituting ourselves as "autonomous subjects."

To be truly free for autonomous self-creation, one must be free of any received or inherited determinations, tendencies, or associations. Deconstructive postmodernism, growing out of Western philosophy, addresses this issue by employing Aristotle's sense of "essence," that which is most irreducible and unchanging (as opposed to "accident"). Deconstructionists apply the derogatory label "essentialist" (or "cultural imperialist") to anyone who speaks of commonality by using words such as "woman," "women living under patriarchy," "we," "the African-American experience," or "the service-sector working class." Deconstructionists are genuinely concerned that the particularity (or "difference") of individuals and groups is disregarded in the construction of generalities. They feel that by speaking of even qualified commonality, "essentialists" are guilty of "grammatical violence" that squelches individual differences. Moreover, deconstructionists maintain that speaking of commonality assumes that the group is composed of a fixed essence that supposedly supersedes the historically and locally determined production of conceptualizations. Such an interpretation of perceiving the relationships of commonality is clearly an exaggeration; to speak of common socialization and cultural attitudes does not deny individual particularity. A further problem is that the deconstructionists have once again opted for the assumptions of patriarchal Western philosophy: the focus on substance (Aristotle's fixed characteristics) rather than process. Hence they arrive at a dualistic conceptualization: *either* fixed essence *or* social construction.

This dualistic perception has led to a one-way "debate" within feminism between deconstructionism and alleged essentialism. The question posed, however, is skewed to support the deconstructive-postmodern retreat from engagement with the wildness, the amazing novelty, the vast and relational flux and evanescence of the cosmological *processes* of being, which cannot be captured and pigeonholed by conceptualizations. They can only be alluded to with metaphors of art, including language and ritual. The female, like other cosmological life-forms, consists of a flux of microevents rather than stasis, or a fixed essence, yet to deny the particularities of the female body is to serve the interests of patriarchy. Deconstructive postmodernism promises freedom for all, but elements of its internal logic continue the patriarchal project by authoritatively declaring *NO!* to the female body, the Earthbody, and the larger reality that is the cosmological scope of existence.

What is particularly worrisome about many current expressions of deconstructive postmodernism, especially in analyses of contemporary culture and politics, is the utter glee at citing evidence of violation and cultural dismemberment of all sorts. Many postmodernists' observations about the effects of commodification and mass media are telling (although quite a few of the more extreme conclusions would be justified only if each of us passed our days with a small television set strapped in front of our faces so that mass media constituted our *sole* reality). I find it eerie that one rarely encounters an (apolitical) deconstructive-postmodern analyst who is the least bit wistful over what has been lost. Instead, the attitude is one of triumph at naming the perceived disempowerment of everyone and everything (except the corporations running the mass media, as political postmodernists note) and a "sophisticated" passivity that mocks any attempt to change the situation. A deconstructive-postmodern "advanced" attitude in a recent anthology is typical of the syndrome: "Why then be sad as the body is unplugged from the planet? What is this if not the more ancient philosophical movement of immanence to transcendence as the body is on its way to being exteriorized again?"[21] Indeed, it is the ancient patriarchal dream: transcendence beyond the body.

Cultural Feminism and the History of Goddess Spirituality

Since the midseventies a movement of spiritual renewal that honors nature, the female, and the body has flourished in our society: the reclaiming of Goddess spirituality. The genesis of this recovery was part of the movement by many women from radical to cultural feminism, although there is still much overlap. In the initial burst of the current wave of feminism, the source of women's oppression was located in "male chauvinism" and "white males." Some feminists still cite the latter term as the cause of social ills. Many of us, however, came to focus attention on the dynamics of *acculturation* that maintained attitudes devaluing women. We located the problem in socialization rather than in oppressive types of supposedly inherent masculine behavior. Hence there is a good deal of common ground between cultural feminism and certain aspects of deconstructive-postmodern feminism.[22]

In my own life, I can recall the exact moment of the shift to a cultural analysis. I was traveling to a meditation retreat in 1974 in New Mexico from southern Illinois in a Volkswagen "Beetle" with two friends from our local women's center. Someone had recommended *The First Sex* by Elizabeth Gould Davis, which I had purchased and was reading in the backseat. Over the engine noise I would call out, "Amazing! Listen to this!" and read passage after passage. Davis revealed countless examples of how woman's cultural and legal status declined as Christianity gradually transformed the Celtic societies in France, England, Ireland, the Rhineland, and elsewhere. She also noted that Christian conversion succeeded in Celtic Europe only when the people agreed to accept "Mary" as a new name for the Goddess. As I read on with sustained astonishment, the fixed entity that had been taught to me as "history" disassembled along Interstate 40, and I saw for the first time that *patriarchy is a cultural construct*—although I did not conclude, as deconstructionists do, that there is *nothing but* cultural construction in human experience. (Even though I could see that Davis made a number of unwarranted leaps in her conclusions, I hope her memory will be honored as a catalyst for the more careful studies that followed.)

Cultural feminism has focused on prepatriarchal culture (such as Neolithic Old Europe), nonpatriarchal culture (such as the Hopi), dynamics of oppression in patriarchal culture, and creative possibilities for postpatriarchal culture. From this branch of feminism the terms "patriarchal culture," "patriarchal religion," and so forth have spread to the others. That the informing expressions of the prepatriarchal Neolithic era stood out in our readings, fixing the attention of women who had been raised in patriarchal religion, is not surprising. Feminist critiques of the Jewish and Christian traditions were already in the air,[23] but they did not offer the spark of possibility that we found in poring over statues, symbols, and mythic narratives from the age of the Goddess. We discovered powerful female bodies of all sizes honored and revered; statues that were half bird and half female, linking humanity with the rest of nature; ritual figurines of female bodies incised with representations of life-giving water; symbols of the sacred pelvic triangle of the female; and sacred myths of the transformative powers of the Earth and the female celebrated in ecstatic dance and holy rite. Imagine our surprise.

During that period of awakening I became engrossed with reconstructing the pre-Olympian myths of early Greece, the sacred stories and symbolism of the pre-Hellenic goddesses, whose artifacts, shrines, and other historic documentation long predate the arrival of the Indo-European thunderbolt god, Zeus, and his patriarchal soap opera on Mount Olympus.[24] The shift from the pre–Indo-European religion (centered on goddesses, who were enmeshed with people's daily experiencing of the energy forces in life and who were powerful sources of compassion and protection, as well as inspiration for divine wisdom and just law) to the Indo-Europeanized Greek religion (centered on a chieftain sky-god who was "up there" and remote, judgmental, warlike, and often involved in local strife) was well established. Yet I and other "spirituality feminists" were curious to know more about the societal transformation in which the disempowerment of the Goddess was embedded.

Over the years numerous studies have appeared documenting widespread occurrences of Goddess spirituality in Old Europe, the Middle East, Asia, Africa, and the Americas. It would be most interesting if an international task force of cultural historians were constituted to assemble and synthesize all the evidence regarding the myriad incidents of societal shift from Goddess to God, from matrifocal to patriarchal culture. (Most feminist cultural historians interested in the long era of the Goddess in various societies avoid the term "matriarchal," since the archaeological findings usually indicate a roughly gender-egalitarian society or are inconclusive regarding sex-role dominance—although many excavated sites clearly do reflect the centrality of women's social roles. Because "matriarchy" connotes the inverse of a power-over, male-dominant society, cultural feminists and several archaeologists prefer to use *matrifocal, matristic, matricentric, gynecentric,* and so forth, since the cultural artifacts demonstrate a focus on the transformative powers of the female regardless of whatever the exact form of government may have been.) Eventually, many matrifocal, matrilineal cultures were pressured to shift to patriarchal arrangements when they were confronted with dominant forces of Christianity, Islam, or Eurocentric colonialism.[25] Male-dominant cultures certainly existed before those powerful forces of social, economic, and religious conversion spread out over the world, but they did account for a sizable boost in the incidence of patriarchal societies.

For cultural feminists with European familial roots, the archaeological record indicating the patriarchal shift in Old Europe is particularly engrossing. Evidence indicates that waves of nomadic horsemen, examples of the cultural model Sanday classifies as having an "outer" orientation, migrated from the Eurasian steppes into east-central Europe, arriving first in the Danubian basin, and imposed their rather crude culture onto the existing agricultural settlements, which exhibited an "inner" orientation and produced an impressive array of artwork. The horse had not become extinct on the steppes, as it had in Europe. (Recent findings in archaeozoology indicate that horses were ridden with a bit and bridle on the steppes at least as early as 4000 B.C., although many archaeologists expect the date to be pushed back even further as more research is conducted.)[26] According to the archaeologist Marija Gimbutas, who has excavated several

pre–Indo-European sites in southeastern Europe, the horse-riding "Kurgan" pastoralists from the Eurasian steppes migrated west in three major waves: c. 4400–4300 B.C., c. 3400–3200 B.C., and c. 3000–2900 B.C.[27] Their initial arrival in Neolithic Bulgaria, Yugoslavia, and Romania caused waves of refugees to move west and northwest into hilly terrain where no human community had settled since Paleolithic times. The Kurgans also moved outward from the steppes in southern and southeastern directions. In India they became known as "Aryans," warlike Indo-European cow-drivers who imposed worship of the sky-god Brahma and instituted the caste system. Most probably they moved beyond their original pastoral range because of climatic or other environmental change.

The cultures of Old Europe (Gimbutas's term for pre–Indo-European Europe) were matrifocal, sedentary, peaceful, earth- and sea-oriented, and appreciative of numerous art forms. They revered various manifestations of the Goddess. The Indo-European (Kurgan, or Aryan) invaders abided by a patriarchal chieftain system and were mobile, warlike, and indifferent to art. They revered warrior gods: the light-of-the-sky god, or sun god; the thunderbolt god; and the god of death and the underworld. The upheaval of Old European civilization is registered in the archaeological record by the abrupt cessation of painted pottery and figurines and by the disappearance of shrines; matrifocal, matrilineal culture; Goddess religion; and symbols of cosmogony, generation, birth, and regeneration. The Kurgans used a primitive stabbing technique to impress their main symbols, the sun or a fir tree. They exulted in the making of weapons, rather than art, and believed that a glorious death was visited upon heroes who died in battle, touched by the spear of the god of death. After the Indo-European incursions, burial patterns shifted from roughly egalitarian graves (with females having somewhat more burial objects, though age seems to have been the major determinant) to chieftain-centered barrows (burial mounds), in which one man apparently owned, or dominated, the other buried men, women, horses, and objects. Almost all Old European settlements before the middle of the fifth millennium were unfortified, and no evidence of warfare (extensive fortification of hilltop settlements, caches of weapons, large numbers of skeletons killed by wounds at the same time) has been found from that era.

Transitional cultures, such as the Mycenaean in Greece and the many Celtic cultures across Europe, exhibited the dominant Indo-European elements (a patriarchal chieftain system, hill forts, reverence for warriors, worship of a sky-god), but also maintained traces of Old European culture, such as matriliny, Goddess symbols, and rituals at sacred springs and groves. In time, the Indo-European societal characteristics triumphed and still figure largely in all Eurocentric cultures. Yet the old ways, the Earth-based sensibilities, proved extremely resilient among the folk cultures in rural areas, even into the present time. In a few areas of Europe where the people speak a non-Indo-European language, such as the Basques, those linguistic patterns are thought to be survivors from the pre–Indo-European era.

Cultural feminists' attention to the radical shifts indicated by the archaeological record in Europe brought intense, if unexpected, reactions from various ideological quarters, each of which insisted that patriarchy must have arisen internally in all societies. Had it come into Europe or elsewhere via migrations, their informing theory would be shaken. Jungian cultural historians, such as Erich Neumann, maintained that all societies naturally "progress" from "immature matriarchal consciousness" to "mature patriarchal consciousness." Marxist feminists asserted that patriarchy universally arose with the development of private property. A group of antireligion anarchists even held that shamans (animistic healers), rather than warrior-chieftains, were the cause of all domination! Another curious development was that materialist feminists (Marxists, neo-Marxists, socialists, and anarchists) dismissed cultural feminism as "ahistorical," even though it has been the source of scores of books and articles tracing patriarchal dynamics, and resistance to them, through history. Following Marx, materialist feminists considered real history to be economic history. Cultural history, they felt, was merely a dabbling in the "superstructure" extruded from economics, utter pablum unless it was the type of analysis that treated contemporary culture solely as an outgrowth of capitalism, specifically "the forces and relations of production." In contrast, cultural feminists tend to view a society's fundamental orientation to nature, women, and issues of autonomy, interrelatedness, control, and complementarity as the forces driving its particular development of religion, community, economics, education, health care, and so forth. Efforts to radically transform all institutions in a society must necessarily fall short if the deepest informing assumptions go unexamined. Only if the powerful dynamics and historical tenacity of the core values are understood can the depth of the transformative task be embraced.

Earthbody and Personal Body as Sacred

The contemporary renaissance of Goddess spirituality draws on a growing body of knowledge about historical Goddess religion but is shaped and energized by the living practice, which is both personal and communal, ancient and spontaneous. The initial response to learning of the historical presence of Goddess religion, at least for myself, was wonder, followed by gratitude that the entire phenomenon, which had nearly been paved over by patriarchal culture, might now be known. That wonder was followed by puzzlement at what Goddess religion might mean to the spiritual lives of women in contemporary circumstances. Poring over the hundreds of photographs of Goddess figurines, bas-reliefs, and frescoes, one could not fail to grasp the centrality of the elemental power of the female body, jarring as that was to any reader raised under patriarchy.[28] Absorbing even a little of that orientation made it easy to see why our Neolithic, and probably even our Paleolithic, ancestors perceived the bountiful manifestations of the Earth as emanating from a fertile body—an immense female whose tides moved in rhythm with the moon, whose rivers sustained life, whose soil/flesh yielded food, whose caves offered ritual womb-rooms for ceremonies of sacred community within her body, whose vast subterranean womb received all humans in burial. It is not difficult to understand why they held Her sacred.

To even attempt to surmise the Neolithic thought processes that informed the artistic expressions of female forms and the ritual practices that must have surrounded them, however, was more difficult, even though Gimbutas's work has helped to sort the multiplicity of forms and focus on the recurring symbols of water, birth, regeneration, and so forth.[29] Stare as one might at, say, a small sculpted circle of ritual female dancers, one could not know, more than five thousand years later, what the actual and entire practice had been. Hence the contemporary expressions of Goddess spirituality, including its flowering in the arts,[30] are not simply attempts to replicate the extremely ancient religion that long preceded "the lost weekend" of patriarchal culture. Rather, they are creative spiritual practice, which is embedded in a profound historical tradition and, more fundamentally, in the female dimension of being.

Some forms of contemporary Goddess spirituality are entirely "free-form," creating practices by drawing directly on inspiration from the artifacts, myths, and other remnants of Goddess religion in early Greece, the biblical lands, Africa, Asia, and the pre-Columbian Americas. Other forms involve participation in mediating traditions, that is, systems of worship such as Goddess-centered "native European" witchcraft or the African-based folk religions of the Caribbean and Brazil. Some ancient traditions of Goddess spirituality, such as that of the Goddess Akonedi in Ghana, have spread to Europe and the Americas in recent decades through immigration. While there is great diversity within contemporary Goddess spirituality, the common threads among the forms that grew out of feminist renewal are the desire to honor the Earthbody and one's personal body via an ongoing birthing process of cosmological unfolding—the intention to articulate as deeply and fully as possible one's ontological potential as an embodied Earthbeing, a weaver of the cosmic web.

The honoring of the female embodiment that takes place in Goddess-oriented women's spirituality rituals has much in common with many of the concerns of postmodern French feminism's *écriture feminine* (also known as "writing the body"), which seeks to create nonpatriarchal "discourse," or modes of knowledge, regarding the nature of the female body. Although a few of the French feminist theorists have devoted a good deal of energy to refuting Lacan's absurd Freudian claim that women naturally function with a biological sense of phallic lack,[31] the more interesting aspects of *écriture feminine* address deep structures in patriarchal culture of suppression of women's subjectivity, body, and desire and the need to recover women's authentic voicing of pleasure, or *jouissance*. They reject the binary dualism of male and female (so essential to the theory of structuralism) as a concept framed in patriarchal culture, which they call the phallocratic symbolic order. Patriarchal culture teaches men to perceive an opposition between self and other and then neutralize the other as being the same or complementary. As Luce Irigaray declares, however, "Women have sex organs just about everywhere."[32] Because even the most radically body-oriented of the French feminist theorists were responding within the forum of intellectual exchange to poststructuralist patriarchal philosophy, their focus has remained in the areas of critique and suggested possibilities. In the United States, however, the *experiential* flowering of radical women's body-oriented spirituality from the midseventies on, generally uninfluenced by the rumblings in Paris, arrived at many of the same postpatriarchal conceptualizations of the female body—and embraced them as vital elements of a "new" religion and culture to be lived daily.

The contemporary practice of Goddess spirituality includes creative participation in myth, symbol, and ritual. Because this spiritual orientation particularly honors the elemental power of the female and its embeddedness in nature, it was perceived as regressive, embarrassing, or even horrifying to liberal and material/socialist feminists, who apparently accepted the patriarchal dualism of nature-versus-culture and had internalized the patriarchal rationalization that the reason women had traditionally been blocked from participation in culture was their bodily "plight" of being mired in the reproductive processes of nature. Investing their consciousness within such an orientation, it is quite understandable that "modern" feminists recoil (I use the present tense here because it still occurs today) when "spiritual feminists" celebrate our bodies and our elemental connectedness with nature. If one subscribes to the patriarchal view of culture as human endeavor pursued in opposition to nature, drawing attention to such connections automatically places women outside the realm of culture as "biological agents" *instead of* "cultural agents." The renewal of Goddess spirituality, however, rejected the patriarchal dualism from the outset. Like countless prepatriarchal and nonpatriarchal societies, we women who had drifted out of patriarchal religion[33] view culture not as a struggle in opposition to nature but as a potentially harmonious extension of nature, a human construction inclusive of creative tensions and reflective of our embeddedness in the Earthbody and the teachings of nature: diversity, subjectivity, adaptability, interrelatedness. Within such an orientation—let's call it ecological sanity—the bodily affinity of females and males with nature is respected and culturally honored, rather than denied and scorned.

The central understanding in contemporary Goddess spirituality is that the divine—creativity in the universe, or ultimate mystery—is laced throughout the cosmic manifestations in and around us. The divine is immanent, not concentrated in some distant seat of power, a transcendent sky-god. Instead of accepting the notion in patriarchal religion that one must spiritually transcend the body and nature, it is possible to apprehend divine transcendence as the sacred whole, or the infinite complexity of the universe. The Goddess, as a metaphor for divine immanence and the transcendent sacred whole, expresses ongoing regeneration with the cycles of her Earthbody and contains the mystery of diversity within unity: the extraordinary range of differentiation in forms of life on Earth issued from her dynamic form and are kin. A second aspect of contemporary Goddess spirituality is the empowerment experienced by people as they come to grasp their heritage and presence in terms of the cosmological self, the dimension of human existence that participates in the larger reality. Such empowerment is far different from a dominating "power-over," the binding force of social constructions in a patriarchal culture. Rather, it is a strengthening of one's capabilities of subjectivity and cosmic unfolding within a web of caring and solidarity that extends backward and forward in time, drawing one from the fragmentation and lonely atomization of modernity to the deepest levels of connectedness. A third aspect of Goddess spirituality is the perceptual shift from the death-based sense of existence that underlies patriarchal culture to a regeneration-based awareness, an embrace of life as a cycle of creative rebirths, a dynamic participation in the processes of infinity. It is a commonplace in patriarchal society that men often spend their lives striving to create cultural achievements, including male heirs who will bear their name, in order to beat death by achieving a measure of immortality.[34] As Heidegger put it in *Being and Time*, one's constant awareness of his own death is the ground for an authentic existence; "being-toward" death is the nature of consciousness of the future. As is often the case, that "profound" philosophical insight is a projection of men's experience under patriarchal socialization, not a universal perception of human existence. (The contrast in images between a dead man on a cross and a bountiful, living goddess-body reflect two distinct perceptions of the core of being.) Goddess spirituality celebrates the power of the erotic as the sparking of cosmic potential, rather than wrestling with the erotic as a process that potentially yields a new generation and hence the signal of one's approaching end. The erotic and the sensuous, expressed through the aesthetic, draw forth not only physical generation but unpredictably creative waves of spiritual, intellectual, and emotional renewal.

Grace Embodied: Body Parables, Symbol, Myth, and Ritual in Goddess Spirituality

Consciousness of the larger reality, through the practice of body-oriented *vipassana* meditation and body-oriented Goddess spirituality, led me eventually to perceive the erotic processes of female being as "body parables," expressions of the subtle dimensions of existence that underlie supposedly fixed delineations of separateness. A woman often experiences a sense of soft boundaries of her body on the first day of menstruation. In the postorgasmic state, many women experience a peaceful, expansive mindstate of free-floating boundarylessness. (Many men, particularly young men, describe their postorgasmic state as a sensation of weakness and vulnerability; some call it *le petit mort*, the little death.) In pregnancy and childbirth, the delineation between me and not-me is blurred and somewhat elusive. In nursing, while cradling the extension of her flesh to her breast, a woman again may experience a dreamy sense of soft boundaries. All of these immersions into the "oceanic feeling," which I have experienced as grace, teach one that, although boundaries can be important in this life, they are altogether relative and temporary in the larger field of the grand communion.

For feminists delving into the history of Western culture and religion, one of the most surprising discoveries was the closeted erotic meanings of common symbols or cultural objects. The rose, like the lotus and chrysanthemum in the East, originally represented the female genitals, the red rose being rich in the sacred blood. (Imagine my perverse delight to open the morning paper a few years ago and read that Congress had voted to make the rose, an emblem of the elemental power of the female, our nation's official flower.) The custom of a woman painting her lips with red stain alluded to the red riches of her nether lips. (How incredibly constricted a culture is ours that such an obvious

connection escaped me for twenty years of applying lipstick until I read about it.) The Holy Grail, and all chalices, are symbols of the womb. The throne evolved as a symbol of the seated body of the sacred queen, as succession passed matrilineally to rulers in many ancient cultures. As for that most famous negative symbol of the female, "vagina dentata," it apparently is not universal but found only in patriarchal cultures.

The Virgin Mary, chaste and docile, is actually a direct descendent of the Goddess, producing her child parthenogenetically (that is, by herself), a son born with the coming-of-light at winter solstice and renewed, even after death, at the vernal equinox. As was commonly the case, her procreative power was inverted by patriarchal culture: Saint Augustine added to church doctrine the "fact" that Mary's hymen was not ruptured in the birthing of Jesus, so she was not responsible for any "pollution" entering the world from her womb! She was made into a physically passive and nearly neuter symbol of a patriarchal dream-queen, often presented by clergy as a model of subservience against which women should measure themselves. Nonetheless, Mary retained her considerable power, as the Great Mother, in the spiritual lives of Catholic women, an extremely resilient phenomenon some church authorities try to curb as "Mariolatry." In Latin America, where Mary is sometimes still called by the old pre-Columbian Goddess names, her image is the central one in many Catholic churches, while the statue of Jesus is found on a side altar.

As with symbols, feminist research into the myths of patriarchal culture also revealed long-hidden meanings. The goddesses of Greek Olympian mythology turned out to be degraded images of their far more ancient selves: Hera, the disagreeable and jealous wife of Zeus, was a powerful deity of women and all fecundity long before his arrival; Athena, the cold, boyish daughter of Zeus, was formerly a protector of home and the arts; Artemis, who had been made the sister of the new god Apollo, was formerly the wild forest presence in Arcadia and the protector of women in childbirth in her manifestation at Ephesus; and Pandora, who was made into the troublesome, treacherous source of human woes, was actually the maiden form of the Earth Goddess who poured bountiful gifts from her earthen jar. Similarly, every element in the biblical story of Adam and Eve has been inverted from its earlier meaning: the serpent had been a positive symbol of renewal and regeneration in the old, Earth-based religion; the sacred trees were not forbidden but sites of worship and celebration; and the female was not the cause of a fall from grace but was a respected manifestation of the sacred cycles of life. The serpentlike dragon slain in the legend of St. George was actually the Old Religion being destroyed by "the one true Church." So powerfully rooted was the ancient religion, however, that the dragon's head often grew back in folk tellings of the tale. The metaphorical boast that St. Patrick had rid Ireland of "snakes" was also a story of the imposition of the new religion over the old, as the Goddess Bridget was transformed into a Christian saint.

Such symbolic legends of political conquest are twisted descendents of the far more ancient and primordial processes of myth that apparently informed the era of the Goddess and most certainly inspire its contemporary renaissance. Since the divine is understood to be immanent (dynamic creativity in the cosmic unfolding) as well as transcendent (as the sacred whole, or ultimate mystery), one approaches spiritual practice in this orientation as an awakening of possibilities. Engagement with myth and symbol, as participatory fields of relation rather than fixed artifacts, suggests a shaping of our continuity and groundedness while evoking a sense of our larger self, the fullness of our being. It is the aesthetic path to grace.

Many who follow this path assemble a home altar bearing symbols of the Goddess. It may be no more than a shelf in a bookcase covered with a cloth on which stand Goddess figurines, shells, stones, or other gifts of the Earthbody, but its affective power is remarkable. Even a passing glance at the symbolic forms of the Goddess reminds a woman that she is heir to a lineage of deeply grounded wisdom and inner strength and a weaver of the sacred whole. Sarasvati stands sensually poised on a lotus blossom, playing a sitar as She guides knowledge and the arts. Our Lady of Guadalupe stands on a crescent moon, clothed in a blue robe of the starry heavens and radiating a full-body aura of golden light. Yemaya, mother of the sea, the great womb of creation, stands draped in blue and white, a beautiful, dark woman of deep mystery. Quan Yin, smooth and serene, dispenses from her open hands the vast power of compassion. On many women's altars "the little snake Goddesses of Crete," their names long lost, stand as we moderns never could have imagined: planted firmly on the earth, baring breasts proudly, their outstretched arms hold writhing serpents, symbols of shedding and growth in endless regeneration. We sustain the mythic presence of the Goddess in our lives as She evokes our creativity and depth.

The telling of myth is a ritual creation of sacred space. It actualizes the narrator and the listener as engaged witnesses, weavers of a web of being that grows outward from the principals, avowing existential bonds of community in an eternal present. Far more than arbitrary "social constructions," the articulation and cherishing of unions and separations, creations and destructions in mythic drama are acts of relation that place all participants in deep accord with the life processes of the unfolding universe. Myth is sacred narrative evoked by a totemic presence, a manifestation or empowered bearer of cosmic energies. The more a narrative evolves in elaborations distant from the totemic presence, the more it loses vitality and may fade in time to formulaic allegory. There are those myths, though, that do not fade. In the sacred stories of the Goddess—replete with totemic serpents, deer, owls, spiders, bear, and more—the body of the Goddess is itself a totemic presence.

By way of example, let the mythic presence of Artemis dance in your mind:

When the moon appeared as a slender crescent, delicate and fine but firm in the promise of growth, Artemis roamed the untouched forests of Arcadia. On each night of the waxing moon Her animals and mortals came to dance with the Goddess. They encircled a large tree that stood apart from the others, its smooth bark and leaves seeming silver in the fresh moonlight. Artemis moved toward the tree and silence followed, but for Her doves cooing softly in the boughs overhead. The Goddess crouched as the Great She-Bear She once had been and touched the earth. From the roots, up the trunk, along the branches to the leaves She drew Her hands. Again. And again. With each pass She brought forth new life: pale blossoms unfolding and falling away, tiny globes of fruit shining among the branches, and finally ripe, glowing fruit hanging from the sacred boughs. Artemis gathered the fruit and fed Her animals, Her mortals, Her nymphs, and Herself. The dance began.

The animals were drawn to the tree. They rolled over its roots and encircled the trunk. In a larger ring the dancers raised their arms, turning slowly, and felt currents of energy rising through their trunks, turning faster, through their arms, turning, out their fingers, turning, turning, to their heads, whirling, racing, flying. Sparks of energy flew from their fingertips, lacing the air with traces of clear blue light. They joined hands, joined arms, merged bodies into a circle of current that carried them effortlessly.

Artemis appeared large before them standing straight against the tree, Her spine its trunk, Her arms its boughs. Her body pulsed with life, its rhythms echoed by the silvered tree, the animals at Her feet, the dancers, the grass, the plants, the grove. Every particle of the forest quivered with Her energy. Artemis the nurturer, protector, Goddess of the swelling moon. Artemis! She began to merge with the sacred tree, while the circle of dancers spun around Her. They threw back their heads and saw the shimmering boughs rush by. When Artemis was one with the moon tree, the circle broke. Dancers went whirling through the grove, falling exhausted on the mossy forest floor.[35]

When a woman raised in patriarchal culture—which tells her she has the wrong type of body/mind, unlike males, to share a sexual sameness with the divine Father God—discovers the sacred stories of the Goddess, identification with Her female dimension of being is an immediate perception. When a woman—who has been told by patriarchal culture that female power is somewhat shameful, dirty, and downright dangerous if unrestrained—immerses herself in sacred space where various manifestations of the Goddess bring forth the Earthbody from the spinning void, bestow fertility on field and womb, ease ripe bodies in childbirth, nurture the arts, protect the home, guard one's child against forces of harm, issue guidance for a community, join in ecstatic dance and celebration in sacred groves, and set love's mysteries in play, then the woman's possibilities are evoked with astoundingly joyous intensity. *She* will create the ongoing completion of each mythic fragment. *She* is in and of the Goddess. *She* will body the myth with her own totemic being. *She* is the cosmic form of waxing, fullness, waning: virgin, mature creator, wise crone. She cannot be negated ever again. Her roots are too deep—and they are everywhere.

In the present coming of the Goddess, we have recovered ritual. The presence of ritual circles at gatherings of the radical women's spirituality movement during the seventies spread to political actions such as the women's peace encampments at Greenham Common in England and at Seneca, New York, in the United States; the Woman's Pentagon Action, held simultaneously in Washington, D.C., San Francisco, and other cities in 1980 and 1981; and numerous actions at sites where design and production of nuclear weapons take place and at nuclear power plants. By the second half of the eighties, it was common practice to open and close meetings of a wide range of organizations in alternative politics with ritual circles of singing, or brief meditation, or a moment's silent "centering" and bonding.[36] More elaborate rituals of mourning and empowerment, for instance, came to be included in political conferences on social justice and ecopeace.

Ritual practices have also spread to the fastest-growing branch of the men's movement, the "mythopoetic" wing.[37] In workshops and longer gatherings, they use myth, ritual poetry, and drumming to spark a recovery of an "earthy masculinity" that is not constructed of insecure, fearful reactions to the female and to nature. They seek to identify men with the Earthbody once again and with the processes of healing—particularly healing themselves of the pain of being only minimally fathered in patriarchal culture and denied close friendships with other men, who are culturally positioned as constant competitors. Perhaps the bodily dimension of ritual is particularly effective in dissolving the emotional numbness that many men have identified in recent years as oppressive patriarchal socialization.

Ritual has also spread in a third direction: honoring Gaia, the living Earth, on the solstices and equinoxes. As mentioned in the previous chapter, these rituals are communal celebrations by men, women, and children around the country who give thanks for the cyclic renewal of our Earthbody and who seek to align their awareness with seasons of initiation, growth, fruition, and repose—a perception that balances the cultural pressure to regard one's life solely as a linear trajectory. These ceremonies focus on the seasonal "moment" of the bioregion by bringing into the ritual circle found objects—feathers, leaves, rocks, flower petals—that activate the participants' sense of relationship with the Earth.

Although the concept of Mother Earth as a sacred whole is extremely ancient in many parts of the world, objections have been raised in recent years to the projection of female identity onto the planet. The most obvious problem is the ill fit between carrying forth concepts that were regarded as a locus of honor and admiration, such as symbolism of the elemental power of the female, into patriarchal contexts, where those concepts are feared, resented, and degraded.[38] A second objection is that patriarchal culture feels that "Mom" (Mother Nature) will always clean up any ecological mess we make and, besides, she would never really kill off her children no matter how badly we treat her.[39] The argument that it is unfair for either sex to claim primary identification with our Earthself may be the most compelling objection. (Curiously, that call for fair play did not occur to men during more than two thousand years of patriarchal religion.) Then, too, there are poor reasons to reject the female metaphor for Earth: A man insisted to me that such identification is "very dangerous," alluding to the patriarchal fear that women are always just a hairsbreadth away from turning into monstrously powerful biofascists. Personally, I find the notion of Mother Earth to be an image far more subtle and grand than a literal extension of woman's processes and particularities, but I am not bothered by people's declining to use a female metaphor as long as they understand this planet to be a body—a celestial body, an interrelated body, a unitive body of intricately balanced and dynamic systems of circulation and generation. It is the Earthbody that we celebrate and cherish at seasonal rituals of the Earth community.

Consciously or not, we exist as participants in the greatest ritual: the cosmic ceremony of seasonal and diurnal rhythms framing epochal dramas of becoming that are composed of a constant dance of subatomic manifestations of matter-energy. When people gather in a group to create ritual, they form a unitive body, a microcosmos of differentiation, subjectivity, and deep communion. To enter ritual space is to feel a palpable sphere of attunement among the energy fields of the participants. Such ritual presence, if successfully created at the outset, by singing, invocation, meditation, or other body-prayer, is at once calming and energizing. It is so pleasing to our body/mind that participants often experience reluctance to move away from the ritual space even when the circle has been formally broken at the conclusion.

Just as myth and symbol are aural and visual religious communication, ritual is whole-body communing that evokes personal emergence within the palpable whole. Ritual process often expands the awareness of one's bodily presence, along with all the other bodily presences within the circle; participants may experience their presence and form becoming merged with the circle or the ritual space it encloses. One's sense of group-being becomes as large as the whole, yet one is not lost in diffusion. On the contrary, the expansion of self to the larger group-body intensifies one's unique sense of capability and energized subjectivity. This simultaneous expansion and intensification is the ecstatic gift of ritual, a mystery of the erotic. It remains as a body memory that shapes new possibilities in a life increasingly understood to be thoroughly relational and endlessly creative.

In the contemporary renaissance of Goddess spirituality, women have formed ritual groups in order to mark passages in their lives, to affirm their emotional and other mind/body experiences, to heal and to celebrate, to explore new possibilities of being, to empower their efforts and desires, to renew commitment to ongoing social-change work, to enrich their spiritual lives, and to strengthen bonds of communion in this fragmented, atomized society.[40] At times these rituals are wrenching, raucous, or sweetly rapturous. In my own life I have participated in many rituals over the years with a rather fluid configuration of sisterly ritualists: an intimate group of four, a larger group of a dozen or so, and a full tribal gathering of both sexes who assemble irregularly for solstice, equinox, wedding, and funeral rituals that include a multiplicity of friends and relations.

Although it is impossible to convey the experience of ritual on the printed page, I offer brief accounts of two ceremonies that may serve as examples of affirming the female dimension of being even in the midst of diffuse cultural mechanisms that degrade it. The first is a menarche ritual, the second a bride's prenuptial ritual. (This selection is not intended to slight other rites of passage; I look forward to attending lots of truly great menopause rituals in the future!)

Some months after the daughters of two of us had their first menstrual periods, seven women plus the two adolescents spend a weekend at a hexagon-shaped house in the country with an open deck in the center. On Saturday afternoon the mothers prepare an altar in the womblike round enclosure, a cloth on which they set red candles and a pot of big red Gerber daisies, along with Goddess figurines, pine cones, an abalone shell filled with dried cypress needles, and other favorite objects that people had brought. The group silently drifts toward the circle from various doors and is seated on cushions. We listen as the order of the ceremony is explained. We begin by lighting the dried needles and passing the shell around the circle, breathing in the purifying smoke and fanning it gently to surround each body. We invoke the presence of the four directions and sing a melodic chant: *We all come from the Goddess and to Her we shall return like a drop of rain flowing to the ocean.* We tell the girls about some of the many, many cultural responses to menses as a visitation of transformative power, a sacred time set apart from the mundane. We tell them of the cultural degradation of women's procreative power to potential danger and then shameful uncleanliness. We tell them of the invention of counting, the Paleolithic bone-calendars etched with twenty-eight marks, the cycle of women's blood and the moon. We read them a poetic myth of Hera, goddess of women and the powers of fecundity, who draws forth the lunar blood. We sing again: *She changes everything She touches, and everything She touches changes.* Then, one by one, the women tell the story of their menarche, that first visitation of Hera—the excitement, the embarrassment, the confusion, the family's response. After each story, the speaker receives a crescent moon painted with berry juice on her forehead. Some women also speak of their first sexual experiences, of how they hope the girls might think about their bodies and their womanhood. The girls tell their stories last, tales of red blood on white slacks during the middle of movies! The circle is filled with laughter and tears, blessings and hope. We sing a final song, *Listen, listen, listen to my heart's song. . . .* Then the women stand and form a birth canal, an archway with our upraised arms. The two mothers stand at the far end of the passageway, near the opening of the deck into the outer world. One at a time the girls pass through our arch of arms as we chant their names and kiss their cheeks. As they emerge as women, the mothers paint a crimson moon on their foreheads and hug them. Then come gifts and feasting. That was my daughter's menarche ritual.

When two women in our group married in recent years, we created a prenuptial ritual that draws on the ancient association of women and water. In pre-Olympian mythology, the goddess Hera returned each year for her ritual bath of renewal at the spring called Kanathos, just as the goddess Aphrodite returned to the sea at Paphos. They renewed their sense of virginity, which originally meant one-in-herself, independent, and self-directed. In our ritual the women form a circle, seated around a low table that has been transformed into a visual feast with flowers, candles, Goddess figurines, shells, and other favorite objects. We begin by invoking the presence of the four directions and passing a large shell containing smoldering sage sprigs for purification. We ask the blessing of the waters that love might flow, the blessing of fire that passion might burn, the blessing of the air to cleanse a new beginning, and the blessing of earth that the lovers might stay grounded and sure. We sing a chant of the Goddess's names: *Isis, Astarte, Diana, Hecate, Demeter, Kali, Inanna.* We invoke the spirit of Hera and Aphrodite. Each woman offers a blessing for the bride, the union, and her new state of being. We close our eyes as one of us leads us on an inner journey of transformation in which one's old identity, as old clothes, is sloughed off on the bank of a stream one crosses to enter a bower of eros. Someone reads from the myth of Aphrodite about her return to Paphos for her sacred bath of renewal: *"There She was attended by Her Graces: Flowering, Growth, Beauty, Joy, and Radiance. They crowned Her with myrtle and lay a path of rose petals at Her feet. . . ."*[41] Then we crown the bride with laurels and lay a path of rose petals before her as, humming a chant, we lead her to the grotto, that is, the transformed bathroom, filled with a profusion of flowers, numerous candles, and fragrant incense. Her warm bath of water and scented oils is sprinkled with petals, and she is left alone to immerse as gently lilting music plays. When she rejoins us, the bride reclines and we encircle her, massaging oil into her warm, soft body while we take turns reading favorite poems of eros softly near her ear, poems of opening one's heart and mind and body to the beloved. Then we dress the bride in our gift, an extravagantly beautiful sleeping gown. With still more blessings and radiance, we break the circle. We eat voluptuous fruits and cake.

I was given that ritual before my remarriage. The following day, still enveloped with the glow of grace and transformation, I thought back to the bridal showers I had attended during my college years and just after: ladies in cheery frocks playing parlor games, partaking of tea and cake, chatting of just about anything on the eve of a marriage except the elemental bounteousness of the female, skimming on the surface of our lives.

Recovering an Embodied Epistemology

The contemporary renaissance of Goddess spirituality is not merely a protest demonstration against patriarchal hegemony in Western religion or even against the broader cultural negation of the female body. It is the practice of an embodied way of knowing and being in the world. We have immersed ourselves in the erotic realm of myth, symbol, poetry, song, dance, and ritual for more than fifteen years in order to *come to our senses*. Having been educated within the patriarchal framework of tightly bound "reason" and supposedly detached "objectivity," we hungered to feed our capabilities of perceiving subtle, encompassing, scrumptious connectedness emanating from every direction of our being. We longed for authenticity, the truth of our being. Boxed in by cultural denial, we dissolved the boxes by forming a circle, an ever-widening circle of the empowering realization that being is being-in-relation, that we come to know the larger reality of humanity, Earthbody, and cosmos through the body, not by escaping the personal to an abstract system, and that apprehending our dynamic embeddedness in the unitive unfolding brings wisdom and grace to our subjectivity—including our conceptualizing and theorizing.

These metaphysical observations, considered so elementary in nonpatriarchal, nonmodern cultures, challenge the entire defense system that has been erected by patriarchal, disembodied epistemology, the seemingly inviolable split between the knowing subject and the passive object about which data is gathered. The

Western notion of "reason" placed gestalt sensibilities and *feelings* of interrelatedness beyond the pale of relevance. That orientation evolved not because of constitutional imperatives of the male, but because of the profound cultural shift away from a worldview in which males as well as females felt a secure sense of connectedness with the dynamics of the sacred Earthbody to a worldview in which males were set apart from the "dangers" of nature and the female and became focused on reactive autonomy, separateness, and control. Because of the perceived threat posed by emotion, desire, and sexuality to rational control, a fundamental opposition was established between eros and cognition and, hence, between women and rational thought.[42] In the analyses of Hobbes, Rousseau, and Freud, for example, reason emerges under the authority and pressure of a patriarchal father.[43] In Plato and Descartes, reason emerges only when nature, which was strongly associated with the female, is posited as oppositional with an "inevitable" moment of domination.[44]

The patriarchal norms for reason and objectivity have been constructed as the (male) triumphant dismissal and containment of the (female) senses. The sense of sight, which allows measurement and instrumentation, has been the most highly valued mode of obtaining information since, as Plato noted, it is thought to be less entangled with the "prison house" of the body than are the other senses. Deconstructive postmodernism continues the patriarchal project of distrusting and devaluing the body by regarding it as a dumb receptacle of power-laden invasions, an unreliable and even treacherous collaborator. Within that framework of perception, any bodily sensation is suspect: It is most likely the result of devious invasions of culture and community. Hence, the body must be resisted in order to protect autonomy.

The advent of Cartesian rationalism, which has been called a "super-masculinization of rational thought,"[45] initiated the development of modern philosophy. Susan Bordo has proposed that the "great Cartesian anxiety," his epistemological insecurity that is resolved via rigorous processes of doubt, was actually a dimension of anxiety over separation from the organic female universe of the Middle Ages and the Renaissance.[46] She posits Cartesian objectivism as a defensive response to that separation anxiety, an aggressive intellectual flight from the feminine rather than simply the confident articulation of a positive new epistemological ideal. Descartes published his *Meditations on First Philosophy* in 1641, at the close of a century that had seen an extreme food crisis, wars, plague, and devastating poverty. It was also an era of intense gynephobia, which was expressed in the prevailing ideas on the need to bring the untamed natural power of female generativity under male control. The patriarchal hysteria that resulted in the witch burnings and related persecution was fueled by nightmare fantasies about female power. Kramer and Sprenger's *Malleus Maleficarum*, the authoritative text widely used by the prosecutors, accuses witches of a plethora of natural and supernatural crimes involving sexuality, conception, and birth. Just as Bacon identified nature as needing forceful male control, so the gradual male takeover of birthing by obstetrics was said to resolve the "disorder" of birth.

The medieval sense of oneness, continuity, and organic justice was replaced by the sense of the universe as an indifferent home. Nature came to be perceived as an unruly and even malevolent virago. Instead of organic unity, one perceived only "I" and an unpredictable "she." The passions behind the Cartesian revolution burned not merely to replace the enervated, legalistic system of scholasticism, but to tame the female universe. The practitioners of empirical science used metaphors that express heady delight in assaulting nature in order to reveal her "secrets,"[47] while rationalism philosophically neutered her vitality. With the cosmos reduced to dead matter functioning as mechanically as a clockwork, the modern era grew confident of conquering nature through "objective" knowledge.

Modern faith in the patriarchal sense of reason and objectivity, based on detaching oneself from the treacherous emotions and relational thinking, has shaped the development of science, medicine, scientism in the social sciences, law, commerce, and government. The grand edifice of rationalism and objectivism stood, of course, on the extremely subjective procedure of selecting certain bits of information from the gestalt field that encompasses every situation and then shining the light of "reason" on those "objectively" considered "facts," which were "quite obviously" the only noteworthy aspects of the situation. People ignorant of, or resistant to, the cultural rules of what is and is not engaged within patriarchal rationalism might argue that much more of the gestalt awareness, including feelings, must be considered to attain even a rudimentary systematic knowledge, but, on the whole, citizens in modern Western societies have abided by the orthodox patriarchal cultural messages concerning the proper shaping of rational consideration.

Because distancing oneself from the relational gestalt assuages the culturally imposed existential fears of men under patriarchy, the restricted awareness required by patriarchal rationalism feels quite natural and generally becomes habitual with them. In a well-known set of experiments to determine whether there were differences correlating with gender in the way people perceive a figure embedded in a surrounding field, H. A. Witkin and his colleagues in 1962 designed a procedure whereby the subjects could either separate out the figure from the surrounding field or see the whole, that is, see the figure as part of the surrounding field, or the gestalt. In many of the experiments the researchers found women more likely to see the embedded figure and surrounding field as a whole, while men were more likely to separate out the figure from its context. Reflecting the values of patriarchal culture, Witkin labeled this phenomenon with a positive term for the detaching behavior of most of the men ("field independent") and a pejorative term for the relational behavior of most of the women ("field dependent").[48] Relational perception, so threatening to the patriarchal touchstones of autonomy, separateness, and control, is simply devalued as dependent and hence inferior.

The gender-based differences in patriarchal culture concerning relational cognition—either avoid it like the plague or embrace it—account for gender-based differences in the use of language. According to feminist linguistic studies, women tend to view conversation as the relational glue that holds everything together, while men tend to view it as yet another form of competing for control, protecting independence, or negotiating for status.[49] Perhaps that explains linguists' findings that, although women are societally perceived as nattering on endlessly, monitored mixed-sex conversations show that men, in fact, talk more, interrupt much more, and usually set the topic of discussion, often ignoring subjects raised by women.

It is not surprising that men often experience more difficulty than women in breaking the grip of patriarchal conceptualization when they try to shift to a worldview of holism and interrelatedness. I have heard a cognitive biologist explain that cognition, and life itself, far from being a rigid matter of stimulus-and-automatic-response, is actually a mutual, creative interaction between organism and environment—from which he concludes that the organism is "autonomous"! Would not "creative interaction" be a more accurate term for the process than "autonomy"? I have heard a cultural historian extol the new perceptions of our interconnected universe and the dynamic play of unimaginable multiplicity only to conclude that "opposites are basic and opposition essential." Surely the holistic discoveries in many areas of science recently, like the insights of the wisdom traditions, indicate that the cherished patriarchal notion of dialectic struggle as the universal norm for creativity and survival must yield to awareness of far more complex "multilectic" interactions. I have heard various male lecturers tout interactive, contextual epistemology—extrapolated from constructivist philosophy and general systems theory—and arrive, not at a sense of the extended self and a network of interactive bonding and caring, but at the comfortably patriarchal conclusion that since no one any longer can claim to perceive or know anything as objective reality, they have no grounds to impose their perceptions, judgments, and values on others: everyone will be free of everybody else!

The first time women hear—from members of the sex having an excess of privilege and power in our society—that "new thinking" declaration of independence, many of us experience a bodily reaction, a tightening in the solar plexus and the groin, a tension throughout the body. *What becomes of ethics and morals?* That rape or battering is a violent assault might be the perception of the victim but not the attacker. That a rape took place at all might be regarded as the "cognitive construction" of the victim and even a witness, but that would be merely their respective idiosyncratic interaction with other organisms and phenomenon.

I once watched a seminar of graduate students listen to a lecturer who first discussed the interactive nature of being and then drew relativist, pro-autonomy conclusions. Expressions of concern were manifested on most of the women's faces, and some began to question the speaker; the men saw no problem with the presentation until the discussion, and then most of them agreed that the women had raised sound concerns. When asked how a community with such a worldview could even pass laws against assault and other crime, the lecturer responded that such laws could be enforced, but they would no longer be associated with "right" or "wrong," merely the preferences of that particular community. Since we now know that all human behavior is part of a larger dynamic, he explained, "wrongdoing" or "evil" or "culpability" can no longer be located in any one being or group. Our being is interactive, but everyone creatively constructs his own reality, so our behavior is essentially autonomous, he asserted. If ever there were a case of *a little knowledge is a dangerous thing,* such patriarchal conclusions drawn from systemic analysis must surely qualify. If one cultivates a depth practice in a spiritual tradition, one experiences not only the epistemological phenomenon of interactive subjectivity but also deep empathy and constitutional connectedness with all being. The patriarchal obsession with ultimate freedom *from* everyone else then seems a comical notion. Hearing someone's joy or pain, one *cares*, one's whole-body sensitivity receives it, rather than shrugging it off as just another perceptual construction, holding relationship at arm's length once again.

Nurturing an empathetic and affectionate "feeling for the organism," the geneticist and Nobel Laureate Barbara McClintock spent decades insistently cutting through the patriarchal dualisms of *either* rationality *or* emotional warmth, *either* objectivity *or* bonding, *either* truth *or* involvement, *either* science *or* love. She discovered genetic transposition, the ability of "regulator" and "operator" genes to change positions on a chromosome, by cultivating pure mindstates of absorption with openness to "hearing" what the cells of corn plants had to tell her, "letting" it come to her.[50] She observed the markings and patterns of coloration on the leaves and kernels, as well as the configurations of the chromosomes as they appeared under a microscope. She became aware that each plant was unique and yet was in relationship with her and with the larger reality. Long ignored and ridiculed by her scientific colleagues, she proudly calls herself a mystic. She performs ritual arts of the Earthbody through a microscope.

A feeling of empathetic connection with a corn plant, a member of an endangered species, a homeless person, or a family member is not an attractive option to men whose psyche is shaped by patriarchal fears that any emotional "entanglement" can render one vulnerable. One cannot experience embodied ways of knowing in a universe of dynamic intersubjectivity and unitive being if one is locked in a lifelong psychic struggle with the body—one's own physicality, one's mother's womb-body, all womb-bodies, the Earthbody, the generative cosmos. The ritual arts of Goddess spirituality have attracted men as well as women because they are healing and radically reconstructive. They evoke possibilities for realizing one's uniquely felt relationship with divine creativity and ultimate mystery in the universe.

Some feminists have called this embodied and deeply connected way of knowing "lateral transcendence"[51] or "dynamic objectivity."[52] In Goddess spirituality we call it a blessing, an aura of grace. When we part we say, "Blessed be."

5

Who Is the Other?

On social justice and community: The wisdom of the Abrahamic traditions

All being on our planetary home is descended from the supernova that gave birth to our solar system. The birth date of our particular species, the evolutionary "moment" at which we differentiated our being from that of other primates, is unclear. Paleoanthropologists believe we became human about 5 million years ago, spreading out from Africa more than a million years ago. A group of biochemists, however, have deduced from studies of mitochondrial DNA, which is passed only from mothers to offspring, that all humans now living are descended from one womb, from a woman who lived in Africa about two hundred thousand years ago. Their findings are known as "the Eve hypothesis."[1] Whether or not the entire human family is literally one clan, the fact of our amazing diversity (no two faces exactly alike, except for identical twins, out of 5.3 billion manifestations!) can mask our internal relatedness. The indications from contemporary science that our reality is an interactive and genetically related phenomenon amplify the unitive experience at the core of the great wisdom traditions.

In the absence of experiential knowledge of the unitive ground of being and our interrelatedness, a narcissistic fallacy shapes both consciousness and culture. The inflated "I" becomes the informing reality, while that which lies beyond the self is perceived to be less than fully real. For the narcissistic "I," the only valued collective is the tightly proscribed "we." People outside the "we" group are seen as deserving of less concern, or no concern at all, being merely "the Other." (In discussing social justice later in this chapter, this is the meaning of "the Other" that I use.)

The philosophical notion of the Other, as meaning any and every individual other than the "I," came into popular parlance through the existentialist works of Sartre. He built on Hegel's peculiar perception that one grows into selfhood only *in opposition to*, in antithesis of, another self-consciousness (an understandable conclusion for a man raised under patriarchy, but hardly a universal truism for humanity). For Sartre every relation is essentially conflictive because to be regarded by an Other, by a regarding "subject," reduces oneself to an object—unless one can either "absorb" the Other's freedom or reduce him or her to an object. Although a grotesquely constricted perception of human relations, Sartre's theses were considered a profound analysis for a couple of decades in various patriarchal cultures and "hip" subcultures.

In deconstructive-postmodern political philosophy the Other is any group or individual that has been marginalized by the dominant group(s) at the "center" of society, the locus of greatest control. More so than the French postmodern concept of "the Other," the American version emphasizes the vitality, subjectivity, and inherent power of such marginalized groups as African Americans, Asian Americans, Hispanics, women, and gays. The rush to celebrate difference, however, has resulted in an extreme hostility among deconstructive postmodernists to any expressions of commonality whatsoever, which they consider a mode of colonization. Everyone is thoroughly Other to everyone else, they feel, and should make this "fact" the basis of all interactions in order to safeguard one's psychological freedom, political independence, and subjectivity. Theirs is a reaction to hurtful and oppressive insensitivity, but, like most reactive sweeps, it flattens complexity.

Existential otherness, or unique subjectivity, is not an absolute dimension of our being, but a singular aspect of our larger reality. Each of us exists in a matrix of being that is the universe. We are constitutionally connected with the manifestations of being that surround us. None of us exists in isolation from the vast web of relationships that are gravitational, genetic, vibratory, and much more. Everything that appears in the cosmos emerges into this web. A manifestation of being is a concentration of energy, allurement, elemental communion. The subjectivity of each being, its depth and interiority, is a face of the ultimate mystery of the universe. Each of us is unique but not apart. Our differentiation yields otherness, while our unitive ground of being is dynamic oneness.

The subtle interconnectedness underlying our apparent separateness becomes apparent as an experiential realization in the great wisdom traditions. In Buddhism the process of purifying the mind and cultivating lovingkindness leads one to a desire to alleviate the suffering of others. In Native American spirituality the desire for balance within the community and with the rest of the cosmos leads to communal concern for well-being. In Goddess spirituality, as well, active care for the personal, familial, communal, and cosmic embodiments grows from spiritual practice that encourages awareness of the web of life. In the Semitic, or Abrahamic, cluster of religions, however, the quality of one's faith is thought to deepen through a sincere practice of righteous acts; that is, waging justice is not an outgrowth of the spiritual practice but an inherent component of the core teachings. A sense of connection with those who suffer poverty and oppression is particularly emphasized. The origins of the Semitic traditions were not among the privileged, as in the case of Prince Siddattha Gotama, but among shepherds and carpenters: Abraham, Moses, Jesus of Nazareth, Muhammad. Their scriptures teach that active opposition to exploitation, evil, and corruption is a matter of fulfilling a spiritual mission: justice and righteousness are the ongoing conditions of a people's communion with the divine creativity of the universe—called Yahweh, or God the Father, or Allah in the Semitic traditions.

The Imperative of Active Social Concern in the Semitic Religious Traditions: Judaism, Christianity, Islam

A central focus in the development of Judaism was the understanding that the divine is manifested not only in nature, but also in the dynamics of human history. The miraculous exodus of the enslaved Israelite tribes out of Egypt into Canaan demonstrated the presence of divine creativity and guidance. Two related elements in Judaism—prophetic anger and social legislation—have deeply influenced the responses in Western civilization to suffering, cruelty, and oppression. The prophets of Hebrew scriptures vigorously denounce acts of inhumanity, including causing suffering without deliberation. Their vigilance is an example of naming and condemning oppressive practices. In addition, a large portion of the law in the Torah (the first five books of the Bible) prohibits injustice and inhumanity as violations of the community's relationship with God.

The manifestation of the divine in Hebrew scriptures responds especially to the poor and disadvantaged—the sojourner (outsider), the fatherless, the widowed. (Such concern is especially strong in the Book of Deuteronomy.) Hence in the evolution of Judaism, as well as those religions that grew from its foundation, Christianity and Islam, active social concern is an imperative linked with the quality of one's spiritual practice. The Hebrew term for the commandment of "charity," *zedakah*, means righteousness and is derived from *zedek*, justice. The relationship between spiritual health and social concern was expressed by Rabbi Israel Salanter as, "A person should be more concerned with spiritual than with material matters, but another person's material welfare is his own spiritual concern."[2]

The "Jesus movement" within Judaism continued and amplified the Hebraic tradition of active compassion for the poor and awareness of the blessings of *hesed*, God's lovingkindness, or grace. The core concept of Christianity is the incarnation of the divine in the person of Jesus the Christ (meaning the Anointed One, the Messiah), whose gospel of love and resurrection offer humankind redemption from the state of sin and new life in communion with the divine. His being was a lesson, a reminder, of divine immanence in the creation, of the ultimate mystery that pervades the cosmos. His inviting people to follow him beckoned them toward a way of life rooted in what has become known as the "social gospel": active communion with all people, with particular respect, compassion, and protection for the poor and oppressed.

The New Testament contains many accounts of such acts and admonitions by Jesus,[3] but the summation of much of his teaching appears in Chapter 25 of the Gospel According to Matthew. In that text he predicts the fate of his followers: either eternal punishment (alienation from the divine, "hellfire") or eternal life (union with the divine). The deciding factors are no lists of sins or legalistic proscriptions but, rather, the questions of whether they had failed to give food to the hungry, drink to the thirsty, shelter to the homeless stranger, clothing to the naked, or to visit the sick and the imprisoned. "Truly I say to you, as you did it to one of the least of my brethren, you did it to me." The immanence of the divine is inescapable. To deny this, to violate the communion, yields misery, the alienation of one who has cut him- or herself off from the family of being. To recognize and honor divine immanence by loving and caring for the manifestations of cosmic creativity is to grow in the experience of grace.

Some six hundred years after the life of Jesus Christ, the third of the Abrahamic religions was founded. Islam, meaning submission (to the guidance of Allah), traces its descent from Abraham's son by Hagar, Ishmael, rather than the Hebraic lineage from his son by Sarah, Isaac. Muslims recognize six chief prophets—Adam, Noah, Abraham, Moses, Jesus, and Muhammad—the last of whom they believe was the greatest, as he received divine teachings that supersede the "preambles" that are Judaism and

Christianity. These teachings are gathered in the Qur'an. As with its predecessors, Islam makes caring for the poor and disadvantaged a central expression of one's faith: *zakat*, a communal almsgiving, is a sort of annual religious tax on certain types of property and wealth above a minimal level. Since Allah the Merciful graced the creation with abundance and wealth, one's enhancing the community through sharing prosperity is considered an act of gratitude and worship. Interrelatedness is emphasized by this teaching from the Islamic *Hadith*, for example: "No one of you is a believer until he desires for his brother that which he desires for himself."

The core concept of Islam is *tawhid*, the divine unity of the cosmos. A oneness, both immanent and transcendent, is understood to infuse the dynamics of the universe. The Qur'an repeatedly addresses humankind's ingratitude for the cosmic blessings they have received in this life. Muslims feel there is something wrong with a person who fails to acknowledge with wonder and gratitude all the gifts of the creation. Such a person ignores, or, as the Qur'an says, "covers" or "hides" the divine blessings and thus fails to enjoy the close relationship with the Creator (or creativity in the universe, or Ultimate Mystery) that is his or her birthright.[4] Islam emphasizes negligence more than sin as the fundamental human failing; each of us has free will and can turn away from our *fitra*, natural connection with the divine. If cultivated, however, one's *fitra* can also guide one to experiencing the grand communion.

These basic tenets of the Abrahamic traditions place active social concern within the central focus of spiritual practice. They have inspired countless beings through the centuries to individual acts of lovingkindness and participation in correcting oppression, the rending of communion. Moreover, the understanding of social justice as a dimension of spiritual awareness in Western religion has also influenced many people outside those traditions.

In appreciating the wisdom of these teachings, however, one cannot overlook the unfortunate fact that the Semitic traditions, from their inception, have demonstrated a rather harshly limited sense of divine community. The Other, as an individual or group less worthy than the inflated "I" or "we," was frequently subjected to armed aggression. For both the Jews in Canaan and later the Muslims in Arabia, the neighboring "idolators" they attempted to exterminate were the faithful of the "old religion" of the sacred earth, people who still worshipped in sacred groves and at sacred springs. The oldest of their deities were manifestations of the Goddess,[5] although in the later periods, in Arabia, these were joined by so many "idols" that by Muhammad's time there was one for each of the 360 days in the Arabic calendar. The Christian conquerors in the New World treated the Indian nations and their nature-based spirituality in a similar way.

It is clear from the first commandment in both the Judeo-Christian and Islamic traditions that expanding allegiance to "the one god" by forced conversion of "idolators" was considered an imperative in claiming religious and political turf during the formative periods. Yet the situation today is far different. What is under threat of extinction now is not those institutionalized religions but, rather, the precious diversity of the creation, including the cultural diversity through which the human family expresses its subjectivity and spiritual awareness. Both Christianity and Islam have, in the past, coerced the conversion of large numbers of the Other through economic, political, and military pressures. Insistent conversion campaigns continue even today, such as that of the Mormons aimed at the Dineh (Navajo) and Hopi peoples. Perhaps the best way for the major religious institutions to safeguard what is left of cultural diversity within the integrity of the creation would be to cease any further proselytizing and follow the example of Judaism, which accepts sincere converts but does not recruit them.

Another common thread running through all three Semitic traditions is their effort to cast women in decidedly inferior roles to those of men. This bias, which was present from the beginning,[6] has proven to be an obsessive campaign over the centuries, resulting even in witch-burnings. For the past two decades, however, increased attention within Christianity and Judaism to

false constructions of Otherness have initiated a difficult process of renewal that holds great promise.[7] Women, African Americans, Native Americans, and gays have identified many streams of ideology (that is, the elevation of one group's interests to the theoretical norm or supposedly universal perspective while masking structures of domination) in the institutional development of the Semitic traditions. Various practices, teachings, and symbolization have been challenged as unjust, exclusive, and in violation of the core spirituality. While the failings of the traditions have been clearly identified, a strong commitment also has been made to carry forth the prophetic identification of faith with social justice. The Jewish feminist theologian Judith Plaskow has noted that the prophetic writings of Hebrew scripture are full of contradictions, but the fact that the prophets failed to wholly live out their commitment to justice does not invalidate that commitment, any more than the commitment justifies its violation. "Feminists can affirm our debt to and continuity with prophetic insistence on connecting faith and justice," she suggests, "even while we extend the prophets' social and religious critique beyond anything they themselves envisioned."[8]

The cross-fertilization of concerns that has occurred among the liberation theologies in Christianity is vital and inspiring. Focusing on the history of Jesus and the early church from any of the marginalized vantage points illuminates the Christian challenge on behalf of *all* people who have been shunted aside, exploited, and relegated to peripheral importance whether in the church or society. The call for a deeper faithfulness to the spirit of the gospel of love in institutional extensions of that "good news" could potentially revitalize the entire Christian tradition—unless reactionary and fundamentalist groups succeed in defending hierarchical orderings that devalue the Other.

Naming Structural Violence

The spiritual imperative in the Semitic traditions to work for the relief of the poor and oppressed has often been reduced to comfortably manageable proportions by sins of omission, by giving donations to charity while withholding a willingness to engage with the causes of perennial hardship for the oppressed. Expressing the commitment reflective of engaged spiritual practice in recent years, the German theologian Dorothee Soelle has declared that everyone has "a duty to know." Turning away and trying not to think about the evidence of acts of inhumanity, as so many "good Germans" did during the Holocaust, does not render one innocent. We have a duty to know about the death by undernutrition and infection of forty thousand children per day worldwide, the North-to-South (Hemisphere) exploitation, the dynamics of the nuclearized security state, the sacrificing of the urban underclass, the federal and corporate squeeze on the family farm, the destruction of native people's cultures, and much more. Rabbi Abraham Heschel taught that to remain silent in the face of great social evil is to be an accessory to injustice. Naming the evil, the rupture of divine community, is an act of spiritual practice.

To gain a sense of the shape of suffering on our planetary home today, one must consider the effects of regional wars, the modern model of development for the Third World, and the emerging global market. Our own country is involved in all three areas, as well as in creating a number of domestic circumstances that inflict hardship. A duty to know requires attention to such "structural violence" (or *violencia blanca*, as it is called in Latin America), as well as the more obvious violations of human rights by torture and waging war against impoverished civilian populations.

Fifteen million people worldwide have been driven from their homes by war in recent decades. Most are living in overcrowded refugee camps with little hope of being resettled. Seventy-two percent of the wars currently being waged are freedom fights by long-standing or indigenous cultural nations against the socialist or capitalist states that have been created around them.[9] In other cases, imperialist reach—such as the Soviet invasion of Afghanistan, the Chinese occupation of Tibet, and the many acts of American intervention in Latin America and elsewhere—is the cause of endless grief. Most civil wars since World War II have involved the economic interests of one of the megastates.

The Third World—which, if counted with the Fourth World (native peoples), accounts for more than 75 percent of the global population and so should more accurately be called the Three-Quarters World—has been pressured by the former colonial powers to accept the modern model of "development," a notion embraced for the most part by the privileged members of Third-World societies, primarily in the cities. It is they who have benefited by "progressive" development, while most of the rest of the populace lives in poverty. The development model rests on agricultural exports, for which local self-reliance is destroyed as more and more arable land is claimed for export-crop plantations. Falling commodity prices on the world market (which the futurist Hazel Henderson calls the global gambling casino) have made it impossible for the "developing" nations to pay even the interest on the enormous loans from banks in the industrialized countries that are part of the development package. Commercial enterprises in the development model are usually capital-intensive, energy-intensive, and centralized—exactly the opposite of the small-scale, decentralist projects and enterprises that would further village-level and regional self-reliance and ecological sustainability. (Vandana Shiva, a policy analyst in India, has concluded that modern "maldevelopment" is antidiversity and hence reflects the values of patriarchal, technocratic culture, which is destroying the forests, soil, water, and air that have supported diverse cultures and rural women's economic patterns in particular.)[10] As "developing" countries fail to service their debts, the International Monetary Fund orders them to cut spending in social services. Because of displacement and gross inequities in the development model, plus the related squeeze on public services, the poorest people in the Third World suffer the most from such "modernizing" of their economies. A report cosponsored by the U.N. Environmental Program and UNICEF in 1990 stated, "Fourteen million child deaths around the world each year make a mockery of our rhetoric of sustained development. . . . A large part of the developing world is moving backwards."[11]

The development model is linked to an overarching phenomenon, the emerging global market, in which every country is to specialize in producing one or more commodities or types of labor services and hence becomes largely dependent on international trade. This model is enthusiastically embraced by most business and government leaders in our country and elsewhere in the industrialized world. Yet a "free trade" global market obviously throws everyone into a global wage competition in which manufacturing moves to the countries with low wages, low standards of environmental protection, child workers, and government-controlled labor. We have witnessed this phenomenon in our own country as factories have been moved "offshore" in recent years, leaving displaced workers to scramble for low-paying jobs in the "service sector." Amid the ubiquitous boosterism for worldwide prosperity through endless, unqualified economic growth, one finds not the slightest admission that a model of ever-increasing use of "resources" on a rather finite, crowded, and ecologically strained planet is a devastatingly bad idea.

Also not mentioned is the implicit understanding that the Third World is to be slowly sacrificed to the interests of the economic superpowers. The response of a French executive of a corporation producing petrochemical fertilizers to a meeting of French ecologists, government officials, and other executives in 1989 was alarming but not atypical: After listening to a factual, convincing presentation on unsustainable agriculture that documented the eventual ruin of French soil by petrochemical fertilizers and noted their high costs, he finally exclaimed, "All right! All right! But at least let us have the Third World!"[12] *Give me your tired, your poor, your huddled masses yearning to breathe free.*

The emerging oligarchs of the new world order are the transnational corporations who recognize no accountability to any workforce, community, elected body, or nation. The occasional candor of executives of the transnationals is sometimes related in the press, thereby startling those citizens who assume some loyalty in the corporate world to one's homeland. For example, the chief financial officer at Colgate-Palmolive told the *New York Times*, "The United States does not have an automatic call on our resources. There is no mindset that puts this country first."[13] Similarly, a Japanese director of the Tokyo office of a transnational consulting firm explained to the Institute for International Economics in Washington, D.C., in 1989 that the single motivation of the transnational corporations is profit, adding that concerns about national security belong to an outdated generation.[14] The new global order is increasingly centralized within a tightening circle of partial mergers.[15] In short, to the transnational corporations virtually everyone outside their enterprise is the Other. Curiously, U.S. taxpayers are still told that our huge defense budget is necessary to protect the access of American-based corporations to foreign resources and markets[16]—a bloodstained apologia for interventionism that is no longer certain even to benefit the American worker.

It seems likely that our government will continue foreign intervention, especially in the funding of "low-intensity" warfare against those residents of the Third and Fourth Worlds who decline to be team players in the global market. That was the recommendation in *Discriminate Deterrence*, a report composed in 1988 by the Federal Commission on Long-term Strategy, which included Henry Kissinger and Zbigniew Brzezinski. To aid "fledgling democracies" (not the sort dedicated to land reform and regional self-reliance, certainly, but those committed to the modern model of development and American corporate interests), the commission recommended covert actions, training of police forces, and maximizing use of advanced technologies to fight opposition. The application of such strategic ideals would create scenarios in which, for example, the indigenous freedom fighter on his ancestral lands would be traced by heat-seeking "smart" bullets and other explosives supplied by state-of-the-art defense industries in the United States. Nor is this scenario entirely a futurist projection, as American weapons have already killed thousands of Indians and peasants in Guatemala, El Salvador, and elsewhere.

We have a duty to know.

In our own country, attention to structural injustice can hardly overlook the fact that the richest 1 percent of American families own more than 40 percent of the net worth owned by all American families.[17] The top 20 percent of American households hold nearly 90 percent of net financial assets.[18] The poorest 50 percent of all American families combined, many of whom are single mothers and their children, own roughly three cents of every dollar's worth of all the wealth in the country.[19] Whites' median net worth is 11.7 times that of African Americans.[20] The median income of families with young children fell by 26 percent between 1973 and 1986, a loss virtually identical to the 27 percent drop in per capita personal income that occurred during the Great Depression.[21] In addition, Federal Reserve economists have determined that a permanent unemployment rate of 5.75 percent is necessary to prevent excessive inflation, which is caused, they claim, by employers having to bid for scarce labor.[22]

Hardly anyone concerned about social justice in the United States still dismisses ecological concerns as a middle-class hobby since three-fifths of the toxic waste sites identified so far are located in poor people's neighborhoods and waste-management corporations are increasingly choosing poor, mostly African-American counties in the South for dumping grounds. Poor air quality, from nearby polluting industries, and leaded soil are much more common in low-income neighborhoods than middle-class suburbs. While various types of pollution and other ecological degradation are "great levelers"—the rich and the poor together at last—several are concentrated in communities with the least political and economic clout.[23]

Many communities have been devastated by the "restructuring" of our economy that resulted from all the "buy, slash, and liquidate" hostile takeovers and leveraged buy-outs in the 1980s. As jobs were liquidated by new owners, or moved "offshore," or lost for other reasons, hardship increased—along with a boom in "hate crimes" against minorities. At the very time when so many people were displaced and desperate, our lawmakers approved ever-widening holes in the "safety net" of health and social services for the disadvantaged (yet tripled the federal debt by doubling the defense budget and reducing taxes for the well-to-do).

Grace Embodied: Spiritual Practice in Recent Social-Change Movements

The more we learn about structural violence, the more we come to understand the far-reaching meaning of the verb in Christ's central admonition: "Truly I say to you, as you did it to one of the least of my brethren, you did it to me." We participate in cruelty and oppression by supporting the systems that perpetuate them. We *do* it to others by our acquiescence.

In recent decades, spiritually motivated activists have played a large role in challenging systemic injustice. Numerous church groups have contributed to finding alternatives to the modern development model by assisting with community-based projects in the Third World such as village-level water and energy systems, cooperatives, and other enterprises. Such movements toward community self-reliance and away from the grip of the export-crop plantations and transnational corporations have been labeled "the barefoot revolution."

In the United States, religious groups and individuals created the sanctuary movement (protecting Central American refugees who are refused asylum here because they are fleeing from countries in which our government supports and supplies "low-intensity conflict") and the Witness for Peace campaign (pledged to oppose a U.S. invasion of Nicaragua). Religious activists also have demonstrated solidarity with the Free South Africa movement. In the peace movement, they have been a prominent force in war tax resistance, Nuremberg Actions, anti-nuclear-bomb testing, and the entire moral and political progression beyond the deterrence strategy of M.A.D. (mutually assured destruction). By the mideighties even so decidedly secular a journal as *The Nation* published an estimate that three-fifths of the people engaged in substantial social-change work in our country were religiously motivated.[24]

Nearly all of them, as well as countless other activists worldwide, draw lasting inspiration from the spirit and conduct of the civil rights movement. Beginning with the quiet dignity and bedrock determination of the women who launched the Montgomery bus boycott in December 1955,[25] the American people witnessed a movement in which the prophetic righteousness of biblical faith found form and the philosophy of nonviolence gradually increased public support and disarmed opponents. Every encounter was an opportunity for conversion, spiritual as well as political. "We have come," said the Reverend Martin Luther King, Jr., "to redeem the soul of America." Early in the movement, he asked the Fellowship of Reconciliation, an interfaith activist coalition, to develop guidelines for nonviolent campaigns, which were widely circulated. The dual emphasis on clearly stated objectives as well as the realization that destroying people acting within an oppressive system is not the way to dismantle the system infused the movement with the power Gandhi called "truth-force" (*satyagraha*). Building on that dual tradition, Cornel West, an African-American philosopher and Christian activist, has suggested recently that we must speak truth *with love* to power.[26]

In recent years most Americans have learned a good deal more about the civil rights movement through books and documentary films than we knew at the time. We have a fuller grasp of the roles of the Southern Christian Leadership Conference, the Congress on Racial Equality, the Student Nonviolent Coordinating Committee, and other groups—especially the community churches, where activists met every week, and sometimes every evening during a boycott or other campaign, to sing and hear inspiring oratory and sing and hold strategy meetings and sing.[27] Pastor Will Herzfeld of the Evangelical Lutheran Church, who was the

S.C.L.C. coordinator of Alabama for five years, has explained, "The *Magnificat* [Mary's song of praise at the very beginning of the 'Jesus movement,' after the angel Gabriel told her she will give birth to the divine incarnation] told us not to begin a movement without a song."[28] "We Shall Overcome" became the anthem of the struggle.

As I was a high school student during the early 1960s, my sense of the civil rights movement was mostly limited to the aspects selected by the national media, that is to say, Dr. King with a backup cast of thousands. I suppose I was hardly alone among the television viewers that day in August 1963 in the feelings I experienced during the crescendo of Dr. King's "I Have a Dream" speech at the March on Washington:

> From every mountainside, let freedom ring. And when this happens, when we allow freedom to ring, when we allow it to ring from every village and every hamlet, from every state and every city, we will be able to speed up that day when all of God's children—black men and white men, Jews and Gentiles, Protestants and Catholics—will be able to join hands and sing in the words of that old Negro spiritual, "Free at last! Free at last! Thank God almighty, we are free at last!"

Suddenly I understood that he was not referring only to the freedom to secure voting rights or lunch-counter service or university admissions for black Americans: he wanted *all of us* to be *free* of the sin of participation in oppression. It was the most electrifying theology lesson I had ever received.

A Consideration of Liberation Theology and Catholic Social Teaching

Today Jewish, Christian, and Muslim activists in our country work within their communities and in broad-based movements to challenge injustice. One movement, however, has inspired such widespread possibilities of grassroots renewal in Latin America, the United States, Africa, and Asia that it deserves considerable attention in any discussion of contemporary forms of enspirited social-change work: liberation theology. Shaped by the conditions of extreme maldistribution of wealth and well-being in Latin America, both the "base communities" within the Catholic church and this new theology framed by priests, nuns, and lay theologians focus attention on the impact of the living gospel on the poor and oppressed.

The notion of creating theologies from the vantage point of "the least of my brethren" has inspired creativity and renewed vitality among Christian women and minorities throughout the church.[29] Moreover, the example of grassroots Christians acting to live their faith in a social context, rather than remaining passive until or unless instructions came down from a distant church hierarchy, has had far-reaching effects. The new sensibility was explained well by a woman at an international conference in October 1989 on "Strategizing the Gandhian Way": "When we practice depth politics, we unite organization with spirituality, drawing strength from covenant community and basic community organizing. We build on the models of the base communities of Latin America and the ashrams of India rather than on those of the gatekeepers of the status quo, some of whom are in organized religion, corporations, academia and partisan politics."[30]

The base communities of the Catholic church in Latin America, particularly in Brazil, the country in which they are the most numerous, have simultaneously revitalized and challenged the institution through a process of mutual empowerment among the poor that is spiritual as well as political. A base community is composed of a group of people, usually about twenty or fewer, who come together every week or so to read a Bible passage, pray, sing, and reflect on the meaning of Scripture in relation to events in their daily lives. A leader, or "delegate of the Word," guides the discussion of Scripture in ways that dispel the fatalism and passivity traditionally encouraged by the church in Latin America. The participants learn that God does not want them to be poor, to live in conditions of relentless hardship, to watch their children die of malnutrition. On the contrary, holy Scripture in both the Old and New Testaments, it is emphasized, condemns oppression, celebrates the exodus from slavery, and champions the cause of those who are marginalized, abused, and kept in poverty. Although God loves all creation, the oppressed repeatedly receive preferential attention in the Bible.

Perhaps the primary outcome of participation in a base community is the discovery of self-worth. This process is illustrated by an account of a session that took place with poor women in Sao Mateus, Brazil. The theme of the meeting was "that Jesus was born poor and humble and shares our life," and the question for discussion was "Why?" A one-minute reading of Luke's account of the nativity—trials of a poor family on the move whose baby had been born in a stable—stimulated a one-hour discussion of the hardship and daily humiliation in the lives of the participants. The catechist then asked, "Why did Jesus choose to be born poor and humble?" A woman ventured that it was "to show those rich people that we are important, too." A ripple of excitement passed through the room. Was God really making such a clear statement about *their* humanity? A charged discussion followed. After half an hour, a young woman said, "I think we still haven't got the right answer to the first question: I think God chose his son to be born like the rest of us so that *we* can realize we're important."[31]

In a similar discussion of Scripture led by Ernesto Cardenal at the Solentiname community in Nicaragua, participants considered the story of Jesus' staying on in the temple at age twelve to teach. One of the peasant discussants observed that Jesus was "developing in love," growing up and maturing in love for people. Another added, "And he didn't just grow once. He grows and develops in a community every time that love and unity among everyone in the community develop and grow. And so now here among us Jesus is growing."[32]

The dual roots of the base communities were the shortage of priests, resulting in huge parishes where scores of thousands of people received almost no religious instruction, and the desire on the part of a number of clergy to address the conditions of extreme suffering. An influential precursor was the Catholic Action movement, which imported from Belgium the model developed by Canon (later Cardinal) Joseph Cardijn: three largely autonomous branches (farmers, workers, students) recruited young people and taught the program "See, Judge, Act." In small groups they were to observe and describe the situation in which they worked or lived, judge the situation according to Christian principles of justice and charity, and then act realistically to correct or enhance the status quo. This model was informed by Saint Thomas Aquinas's teaching on wise judgment in practical matters. Numerous grassroots organizations grew from Catholic Action, but eventually its impact dissipated in failed experiments of Christian Democratic parties that called for modest reforms and supported the modern model of development, which by the late 1960s had widened the chasm between the rich and the poor.

The base communities that began in the early 1960s drew on the experimental work of José Marins and other priests and on the vision of Bishop Helder Camara, who believed the church should move beyond working *for* the poor to working *with* the poor to empower themselves. Influenced by Scripture, Catholic social teaching, and Gandhi, Dom Helder emphasized the dignity of the human person and the role of humanity as cocreators with the divine of the evolving world. The methodology he chose for his Movement for Grassroots Education, a cooperative venture with the government, was "conscientization," a program developed by Paulo Freire for teaching literacy with a strong component of consciousness-raising that encourages poor people to shift from "fatalist thinking" to "transformative thinking." In many respects the clergy, both nuns and priests, became the students as they learned about the vitality of the folk culture and the sensibilities and spiritual depth of "the people," the "base" of a hierarchical society.

Today there are between eighty thousand and one hundred thousand base communities in the Brazilian Catholic church (comprising only a small percentage of the population, however) and several thousand others throughout Latin America, as well as the Philippines, Kenya, and Zaire. Many meet solely for spiritual sustenance, but most also initiate self-help projects within the community. Some go further and enter the political arena to support various campaigns for land reform and other structural change, but often they have felt used or absorbed and then disregarded when they have worked with political parties, many of which are run by secular-left strategists who perhaps harbor the traditional Marxist scorn for religiously motivated activists as "useful idiots." At any rate, experience has shown many in the base communities the need to remain an independent force, while still exercising political influence.

A parallel development to the grassroots flowering in the base communities is the intellectual work created since the late 1960s by Latin American theologians. Although several of the well-known theologians have direct contact with base communities or the many types of related self-help organizations, inspiration has generally flowed from the "base" to the theorists and not vice versa. In fact, an attitude called *basismo* among many base-community participants locates value solely with "the people's process," activism that is grounded in the culture of the marginalized people.[33]

For their part, the theologians have always considered the base communities to be the central focus of liberation theology and their theological reflection to be a "second act" that elaborates solidarity with "the least of my brethren." At the historic meeting of the General Assembly of Latin American Bishops in Medellin, Colombia, in 1968, three "options," or choices, were affirmed: for the poor; for integral "development," or liberation (spiritual and social); and for the base communities in particular. These themes were given fuller articulation in the document that emerged from the assembly's conference in Puebla, Mexico, in 1979, although support for liberation theology is far from unanimous among the bishops of Latin America.

The basic tenet of this theology is that liberation must be integral. One seeks freedom from sin and alienation while moving toward deeper communion with God's love, the experience of unconditioned grace. At the same time, such spiritually grounded love is concerned with efficacy, the actual liberation of the oppressed from socially constructed suffering. Each aspect of the dual focus—spiritual depth and active concern—is weak without the other: a purely interiorized spiritual practice thwarts the naturally extending circle of love, while a spiritually barren activism leads to sins of arrogance and alienation. A central image in liberation theology is the biblical exodus from oppression to liberation. To further such a process in Latin America, the church cannot merely adopt a stand of neutrality because it has always aligned itself with empire, first with the church-state axis of the colonial era and, since then, with the wealthy and powerful families, who benefit from the exploitative export economies. Neutrality would aid the unjust status quo, which the church historically helped to sustain. Rather, the liberation theologians insist, the church must use its power to be the voice of the voiceless, to amplify the presence and liberatory efforts of the disregarded Other.

During the first twenty years of the liberation theology movement, until the second half of the 1980s, most of the theologians engaged in a romance with Marxism that had predictably negative effects. In wondering how their biblical faith might find concrete form in a situation where the needs of "the national security state" were framed to support highly concentrated forms of ownership and exploitation, they turned to the social sciences. There they found encamped, as in the universities of Europe and North America during the late sixties and seventies, Marxist ideology presenting itself as an objective science of history. Perhaps these theologians, themselves immersed for years in systematic theologies, were attracted by Marxism's promise of a systematic, comprehensive analysis, one that had much in common with biblical concepts such as "idolatry" ("fetishization") and the notion of an apocalyptic deliverance (revolution) to a new life. Some liberation theologians concluded that state ownership of the means of production was the only way to secure the type of material liberation called for by the social gospel. Accepting

Marx's interpretation of history, they announced that they were "walking with history," encouraging the poor to "irrupt into history" by rising up to intensify class struggle and seize their fair share of the economic bounty. Many of these theologians declared that the meaning of the base communities was that the locus of the church had moved from the center (of power in society) to the margins and that henceforth the true church was located in the *barrios* and poor rural villages.

Not surprisingly, the Vatican took a dim view of all this, but largely for the wrong reasons. Their objections, cited in 1984 in a critical public letter, "Instruction on Certain Aspects of the Theology of Liberation," by Cardinal Joseph Ratzinger, head of the Vatican's Sacred Congregation for the Doctrine of the Faith, included many critiques that had become commonplace among post-Marxist activists by the 1980s. It was also apparent, however, that a power struggle was involved. As expected, the Instruction rejected the reductionism and "economism" of Marxian theory and practice and the notions that Marxism is a "science of history" and that ethics is shaped by fidelity to a particular interpretation of history. Also expected was the criticism that the liberation theologians' overemphasis on social sin devalued attention to the spiritual condition of the individual. In pointing out that economic structures are more consequences than causes, Ratzinger was echoing the objection of numerous activists to Marxists' claim that consciousness arises from material conditions, never the other way around. Ratzinger asserted that evil is perpetuated by free and responsible persons who can be converted through the experience of grace (which he limited to "the grace of Jesus Christ"). He objected to the liberation theologians' seeming absorption of the Marxist belief that universal love is possible only after the revolution and that even violence is a means to a loving end. Moreover, he objected to dividing the faithful into class blocs. Looming large in the 1984 letter and other declarations from the Vatican, however, was implicit disapproval of the base communities and liberation theologians as troublesome outbreaks of independence running counter to the current pope's and Cardinal Ratzinger's program of "restoration" to an earlier era of hierarchical control and obedience. Even though a 1986 statement from the pope was much friendlier toward the liberation theology movement, especially the base communities, the Vatican's sudden division and gerrymandering of Archbishop Arn's diocese in Sao Paulo, Brazil, in 1989 revealed hostile sentiments. It also has been suggested that Cardinal Ratzinger dislikes liberation theology's emphasis on the continuation of themes from the Old Testament, such as Exodus, since he adheres to the "supersessionist" view that Christianity is a radically different path.

The Vatican's 1984 instruction on liberation theology was met with angry denial and charges of exaggeration. The theologians' initial response was to point out that theirs was a more nuanced use of Marxism and spiritual teachings than Cardinal Ratzinger had presented. Nonetheless, by the last few years of the decade nearly all the leading liberation theologians had publicly distanced themselves from Marxism and its scientistic modernity. I do not believe this shift was due primarily to Cardinal Ratzinger's many heavy-handed actions, as force and disrespect tend to yield only redoubled resistance. It is more likely that the intellectual and activist streams in the 1980s beckoned these theologians beyond the unraveling assumptions of Marxism, just as the corresponding forces in the late 1960s had attracted them to that path. In many cases their disaffection with Marxism began several years before the Vatican's instruction was issued. For example, in 1978 José Comblin published a deconstructionist critique of Marxism, challenging its aura of scientism and rejecting it as an idealist philosophy that replaces free human activity with an underlying movement that supposedly shapes history.[34] In *Faith and Ideologies* (1984), Juan Luis Segundo was much more critical of socialism than in his earlier works. José Porfirio Miranda, author of *Marx and the Bible* (1974) and *Communism in the Bible* (1982), rejected Marxian analyses in an essay published in 1985.[35] In 1988 Otto Maduro summarized several points of departure in an unpublished paper, "The Desacralization of Marxism within Latin American Liberation Theology." Although he and his colleagues value certain Marxist analytical concepts, or "tools," they have come to find many other aspects unacceptable, such as the condescension with which Marxism treats the poor as victims of an illusion in their maintenance of religious faith; the model of elitist, "vanguard" leadership imposed on the poor in the Marxist-Leninist state; and the authoritarian government inherently necessary in Marxism. Maduro notes that a pluralism of approaches is needed to account for all the important cultural factors and values that Marxists neglect or disparage,[36] and he urges "epistemological vigilance" in using the social sciences to avoid building an analysis on "partial truths."[37]

Gustavo Gutierrez, widely acknowledged as the father of liberation theology, expressed several aspects of the post-Marxist shift in his new introduction, "Expanding the View," to the fifteenth anniversary edition of *A Theology of Liberation* (1988): the steadfast attention to the suffering that results from "institutional violence" and the need to analyze its cause; the absence of Marxist assumptions or vocabulary; a broadening of dependency theory (which is not necessarily Marxist) to include internal factors in Latin American countries, as well as international exploitation by the "developed" nations; an appreciation of the resilience and vitality of the poor (the majority of whom are labeled *lumpenproletariat* in Marxist analysis); an acknowledgement of racism and patriarchal oppression; an emphasis on the universality of God's love as well as God's predilection in Scripture for the oppressed; regret for having imposed categories on the poor that were foreign to them and can lead to impersonal interactions; the theological analysis that only liberation from sin gets to the very source of social justice; and the centrality of prayer and reflection as correspondent acts of Christian solidarity with the poor.[38] (The last several elements are not new in liberation theology, but are now given greater weight than in the past.) In an interview in February 1988, Gutierrez stated, "Socialism is not an essential of liberation theology; one can support liberation theology or do liberation theology without espousing socialism."[39] In Peru the "summer school" led by Gutierrez in 1975 included some two hundred pages of reading material on Marxism; in the 1988 sessions of the same summer school, Marxism was not even mentioned.[40]

Gutierrez has said often that liberation theology's selective use of Marxism has been "misunderstood." With all due respect, for I find your work among the most soulful in the movement, Father Gutierrez, how could you have thought it would be otherwise? A sympathetic analyst has concluded that liberation theologians have shown little interest in early or late Marx, but have (at least until recent years) adopted concepts from the "middle Marx": a theoretical analysis yielding a dramatic view of social and political conflict and a particular interpretation of the conceptual formations, or ideologies, that accompany and support social inequalities and injustice.[41] Certainly such distinctions are possible in a university or seminary classroom—but in the political arena during an era of cold-war frenzy? Were the forces of repression expected to appreciate that liberation theologians espoused only Marxist analysis and had no use for Marx's solution of a communist state? During the late sixties and seventies many liberation theologians stated that they had turned to Marxism because it is the most "effective" analysis. Surely that is a debatable claim, not only in terms of its limiting assumptions but also considering the practical effect the Marxist linkage may have had on the movement during the cold-war era. The reactionary forces—that is, the right-wing governments and the wealthy families who keep them in power—had an easy time recruiting militia and goon squads "to defend Christian civilization against Communist infiltration" by murdering some 850 bishops, priests, and nuns, as well as scores of thousands of peasants and Indians. Because the forces of repression in Latin America have long been quick to label *any* type of community organizing as "Communist," however, it is impossible to say whether liberation theology's embrace of Marxism provided the excuse for even one more murder than would have occurred anyway. As Dom

Helder Camara, the Gandhian archbishop in northeastern Brazil, has noted, he was called a saint when he fed the poor, but was suddenly labeled a "Communist" when he asked why they were poor.

Considering the goal of actually effecting structural change, it seems that a powerful inclusiveness was lost by adopting the Marxist notion of clashing class blocs as the only relevant reality. Some writings by liberation theologians in the 1970s almost implied that the middle class and the rich were barely welcome at the Communion rail during Mass (who needed them anyway since the uprising of "the people" was inevitable?). Nothing was expected of them in terms of living the social gospel because they were, more or less, the bourgeois enemy. Today that attitude has faded, but how many possibilities like the following were lost?

An Irish priest of the Columban order working in the Philippines, Niall O'Brien, was asked to attend an urgent meeting of sugarcane plantation owners on the island of Negros in 1989. The plantation owners were simultaneously being pressured by the Marxist guerrillas, the New People's Army, to pay certain taxes and by their peers to arm the cane-cutters on their land. The Irish priest and three Filipino priests attended the meeting, opening it with a reading from the Sermon on the Mount. One by one, the landowners told their stories, and soon the group was divided in two: those who refused to take up arms and those who felt there was no other way. The priests sat silently "in great anxiety" through the discussion. O'Brien was inspired by the way some of the group came up with answers, and finally he spoke about Jesus' agony in the garden and how the apostles tempted him to take up arms. Next, someone proposed that every landowner present pay the minimum wage and check to see that neighboring plantations were also paying it. Someone else noted that the minimum wage is not a living wage, so the landowners should pay more. They then discussed land reform and decided that land should be given to the workers, a transfer that should be accompanied with necessary support and follow-through. O'Brien remarked later, "The whole evening was very grace-filled for me and I believe for them, too."[42] According to the Marxist worldview, the outcome of that meeting was decidedly extraordinary because people are expected to act as automatons for their class interests, generally resorting to violence and repression rather than accepting a loss of wealth. The notion that a group of privileged people could reflect together on their faith and then take concrete steps toward justice lies beyond the Marxist script—which is precisely why the *challenge* of the social gospel is so powerful and creative. "When you're being ideological," O'Brien has pointed out, "new information is irrelevant."[43]

Only the participants in the liberation theology movement—the hundreds of thousands of struggling activists in the base communities and the self-help organizations, plus the theologians—can predict what forms and actions might come next in their movement. The situation has been further complicated by the strategic deployment of U.S.-funded right-wing evangelical Protestant conversion campaigns, especially in Central America, where they are protected by the reactionary governments in exchange for never mentioning the social gospel. The possibility of attending church services without being labeled a "Communist" and being shot at by the army has understandably found wide appeal among peasants and Christianized Indians, who, after all, have been terrorized for years by "low-intensity conflict" supported by U.S. military aid. In some areas, such as the Guatemalan highlands, right-wing evangelical groups have reportedly worked with the military to destroy the ancient Mayan religion by harassing, and sometimes murdering, the medicine men, whom the tormentors label "witches."

Since the liberation theologians increasingly speak of seeking "new alternatives" or a "third way" (although the latter term is somewhat tainted in Latin America because it was used by the failed Christian Democrat reformists), perhaps the time is ripe for them to take Catholic social teaching more seriously. Pope Pius XI's 1931 encyclical *Quadragesimo anno*[44] established three cardinal principles: subsidiarity (no organization should be bigger than necessary, and nothing should be done by a large and higher social unit than can be done effectively by a lower and smaller unit), pluralism (a healthy society is characterized by a wide variety of intermediary groups freely flourishing between the individual and the state), and personalism (the goal of society is to develop and enrich the human person; the state and society exist for the person, not vice versa). In *No Bigger Than Necessary,* Andrew Greeley argues that Pope John XXIII's major encyclicals in the early 1960s, *Mater et magistra* and *Pacem in terris,* continued the strong, positive defense of the integrity of the person and the social rights and obligations of that person in the modern world, but that Pope Paul VI's 1967 encyclical *Populorum progressio* (often cited by liberation theologians) marked a "decisive shift away from the distinctively Catholic social theory to watered-down Marxism."[45]

Rooting themselves in the communitarian, decentralist tradition of Catholic social teaching would not produce an instant model of a third-way economy and government, but it would provide guidelines with which to analyze various possibilities. Certainly the model of decentralized ownership of land would align more closely with current calls for land reform in Latin America than would huge collective plantations owned by the state. Moreover, a commitment to the democratic, communitarian decentralization of economic power—the realization that justice cannot thrive when the economic fate of millions is controlled by a centralized state, or transnational corporations, or a cabal of the very rich—would place the liberation theology movement in the growing company of Green-oriented, community-based, third-way activists and economists, who are developing a wide range of possibilities that could be considered for adaptation in Latin America. The pioneering works of the New Economics Foundation[46] and its affiliated T.O.E.S. ("The Other Economic Summit") international networks, for instance, continue to demonstrate the richness of third-way approaches. Clearly, there is a great deal of common ground between Catholic social teaching and the emerging Green economics and its affiliated beyond-left-and-right politics.

The concept of personalism cited in the 1931 encyclical was born in Paris in the early 1930s under the influence of the Russian exile Nikolai Berdayev, who was an early critic of the Leninist state; the Thomist Jacques Maritain; and the charismatic Emmanuel Mounier. Personalists were "of the party of the Spirit against the materialists of both East and West."[47] Personalism criticized communism from the humanist perspective suggested in Marx's early, philosophical manuscripts, and it maintained that Marxism was as incomplete and one-sided in its understanding of the human person as were the individualistic cultures in which liberal capitalism flourished.[48] Personalism also drew on certain Nietzschean existential themes and German phenomenology to shape "a defense of the transcendent dignity of the person in the face of twentieth-century ideologies."[49] It reflected a determination to decentralize modern state structures into more meaningful communities.

The personalist movement in France, which was centered around the journal *Esprit,* attracted prominent intellectuals and artists throughout the 1930s, such as Jacques Ellul, Jean Lacroix, Maurice Merleau-Ponty, Jean Guitton, Father Marie-Dominique Chenu, Marc Chagall, and Eugene Ionesco. Personalism was brought to North America by Pierre Trudeau and his friends who founded the journals *Cross Currents* and *Cité Libre* and by Peter Maurin, Dorothy Day's mentor in the Catholic Worker movement. In Poland personalist philosophy became influential during the Resistance and the postwar decades. Father Josef Tischner, chaplain of the Solidarity movement, frequently discusses personalist concepts in his sermons. The former prime minister and Solidarity activist, Tadeusz Mazowiecki, is a personalist, as is Pope John Paul II, formerly bishop of Krakow, the center of the personalist movement in that country. Both the French and Polish personalists sought a model of distributive economic justice and developed the outline of a "third way" whose deepest inspiration was spiritual.[50] On his way to the Vatican the present pope wrote numerous monographs and sermons with personalist themes, the best known being *The Acting Person* (1969). He has incorporated personalist vocabulary and themes into his encyclicals, but he has also magnified the doctrinal orthodoxy that was adopted by the early French personalists (Maritain, for example) so as to head off near-condemnations from the church hierarchy at times. What kind of a liberation movement rigidly sacrifices the liberation of women, for instance, in exchange for its own acceptance and protection from the ecclesiastical power structure? Under the current pope, personalism has shown itself to be patriarchal personalism.

If liberation theologians were to partake of the richness and radical third-way orientation of Catholic social teaching, yet help to advance its breadth and depth, they would do well to pay attention to the women in their movement, whose insights were not sought for the first fifteen years but have more recently been heard. Since 1979, when the Latin American bishops' Puebla statement mentioned the "double oppression" of women who are poor, that observation has appeared rather frequently, if briefly, in books by male theologians. Female liberation theologians note that the model of the dominant father-figure ruling over supposedly childlike women is as operative within the Bible and the church as throughout the rest of society, but they also go far beyond naming the sins of oppression to explore authentic expressions of their spirituality. The collective statement from a conference held in Buenos Aires in 1985 cited certain themes that need to be deepened via women's perspectives such as "the image of God, the incarnation, the experience of God, the Trinity, community, the body, suffering and joy, conflict and silence, the ludic and the political, tenderness and beauty."[51] In "The Concept of God: A Feminine Perspective," Alida Verhoeven suggests that contemporary Latin American women are called to begin an exodus from "a fraudulent era" and fill the vacuum with a consciousness of the "creative spiritual force" that can never be trapped by language, images, or symbols and that manifests itself only in "vital-creative presence" for life.[52]

Often the female theologians' writing contrasts with the men's emphasis on divisions and exclusiveness (especially the men's Marxist-influenced rejection during the seventies of what they called "a fictive and formalistic unity" that masks the one reality: class struggle). While they describe themselves as "militant" about issues of injustice toward the oppressed, most of the female theologians are firmly rooted in a sensibility of organicism. Consuelo del Prado, writing on spirituality as a way of following Jesus, "I Sense God in Another Way," observes that "women tend to live things out in a more unified way, and they value daily life without giving undue emphasis to isolated moments."[53] Ivone Gebara proposes in "Women Doing Theology in Latin America" that the theological work of women reflects an ability to view life as the locus of the simultaneous experience of oppression and liberation, of grace and lack of grace. This orientation, not the sole property of women but extremely common among them, enables women, Gebora concludes, to avoid taking dogmatic and exclusive stances.[54] Alida Verhoeven believes that women, through "the creative fullness that is produced in our very beings," have the ability to "feel the pulse of the cosmos," to extend in ever-growing circles of awareness among all people the "creative-recreative spiritual force, the source of love and life."[55]

A deepening of cosmological sensitivity in liberation theology might also yield new perspectives on the native peoples of Latin America. Just as issues of discrimination against women and blacks have entered the discussion, the abuse and virtual enslavement of the Indians by the Spanish and Portuguese agents of Christendom is often lamented today. Expressions of shame and regret for the Indians' economic exploitation are common in the writings of liberation theologians, yet I have never seen an apology for the destruction of their ancient religion in the name of Christ. Even though native peoples' earth-based spirituality is extremely resilient and has found syncretic form within the Eurocentric religious framework, often to the dismay of missionaries, the theologians' robust *mea culpa* over economic domination of the indigenous peoples without any mention of the spiritual domination is sadly inadequate. Since liberation theology places much emphasis on interpreting the gospel from one's "concrete historical reality," one might expect a greater understanding from the theologians of the reason many Christianized Indians reading the biblical story of Exocus identify not with the followers of Yahweh migrating into Canaan, but with the Canaanites, the land-based native people who are being invaded, whose sacred groves and images are destroyed.[56] Honoring the earth-based spirituality and cosmological wisdom that native peoples bring into the church could yield an enrichment of liberation theology beyond anthropocentric boundaries to a commitment to the entire Earth community.

No matter what directions liberation theology may follow in the future, Gustavo Gutierrez reminds us that all the theologies of hope and liberation are not worth as much as one act of solidarity with the poor. The courageous example of the base communities, and all who support them, is a gift of inspiration, a creative possibility of living the social gospel. "The least of my brethren" have shown the world a movement toward grace.

Reflections on Community and Communion

> Jesus said, "I was hungry, and you gave me nothing to eat. I was thirsty, and you gave me nothing to drink. I was naked, and you didn't clothe me. I was a stranger, and you didn't take me in. I was sick and in prison, and you didn't come to see me."
>
> And the people said, "Lord, Lord. When did we see you hungry and thirsty and naked, a stranger, sick, and imprisoned? We didn't know it was you. Had we known it was you, we would have done something. We would have responded. Had we known it was you, we would have at least formed a Social Action Committee. But we just didn't know it was you!"

That prayer, based on Matthew 25, is frequently offered at the Sojourners Community Center in Washington, D.C., by Mary Glover, an African-American volunteer, just before the doors open to some three hundred needy families who each receive a bag of free groceries on Saturday.[57] There is no end, Mrs. Glover suggests, with gentle exasperation, of what people *might* do for others if they understood the presence of the divine, the face of ultimate mystery in all beings.

Mrs. Glover's prayer, and the teachings of Jesus on which it is based, would be dismissed by deconstructive postmodernists as merely another culturally invented narrative, hence no more or less meaningful than a national anthem or an advertising jingle. At the same time, however, deconstructionists who are beginning to be bothered by their "logic" of passivity in the face of very real suffering have begun to suggest the need for some agreed-upon "glue" that might hold together an atomized world of difference sufficiently to foster a functioning sense of community.

We do not need to invent a ground of connectedness, but only to realize it. Interrelatedness has been experientially grasped in myriad cultural contexts and variously expressed as the core perception of the wisdom traditions. Yet the forces of modernity continually deny and degrade it.

Human society needs grounding in the unitive dimension of our existence. We can surmise that a countervalent effort to decentralize institutional structure, for instance, would do much to correct modernity's shattering of community through its dynamics of large-scale economic, governmental, and academic organizations. Yet appropriate scale alone does not create community bonds of care and concern. The thwarting of structural violence would not eradicate callous acts of freewheeling individualism.

What if we were educated to nurture awareness of our inseparable relatedness? In effect, young children would be allowed to continue their natural perception of the world as a realm of inherent relatedness instead of suffering through the educational process of displacing holism with what Bateson called "the epistemological error" in Western culture, the notion that mind is totally discrete in each of us rather than being immanent in the larger biological network. Young children feel a magical connection with other people, animals, trees, and flowers that could, through the progression of years in a cosmologically grounded educational system, be gradually enlarged to include knowledge of the ways relatedness is explored by mathematics, science, literature, the social sciences, music, fine arts, and so forth.

Since there is widespread recognition at this historical moment that the American system of public education has become shockingly ineffective, a sweeping reorientation seems possible. A curriculum that built on fundamental processes of the universe—differentiation, subjectivity, and communion—would honor and encourage both the particular and the communal.[58] It would ground creativity in awe and respect for the larger reality, the web of life. Instead, alas, we hear nothing but talk about educational reform that will meet the demands of the global market. The only goal seems to be to shape our children's minds in ways that will allow us to "beat the competition" in Japan and Europe. It does not require much imagination to envision the dismal future that will result if ecological depth, critical thinking, and creative unfolding continue to be passed over in a reorientation of our educational system for the narrow demands of the technocratic imperative.

Not only education, but the very nature of work itself would be challenged by a revitalized sense of community that is cosmologically grounded. If we understood being as participation in an internally related unit, an unfolding whole, we would view our labor as a gift given to the community and the cosmos. We would probably come to see types of work as roles of interaction with earthstuff, animals, and people, rather than simply as jobs isolated from any larger meaning. The subjectivity of a worker would be appreciated as a gift to be shared. The unfolding of the person within the context of the ecocommunity would be nurtured. What we have instead is a cult of unqualified growth, promoted with language that disallows concern about accountability, community control, and the quality of life. Functioning within that ethos, business people today, according to a recent study, demonstrate less social responsibility than in previous decades and feel that if they meet the requirements of the law, there are no further ethical restraints on the ways in which they conduct business.[59] "He who dies with the most toys wins," declared a yuppie slogan of the eighties.

Why, in a society where there is so much suffering, where 5 million children under age six, the most vulnerable Other, live in poverty, is it not a matter of shame to have far more money than a person or family could possibly need? Since abusing the environment (nature as the Other, posterity as the Other) has gradually come to be perceived as shameful behavior, is it too wildly unrealistic to expect that harmful hoarding might come to be regarded as a rending of communion? Only in a culture desperately estranged from its own depth of being could maximizing one's income be embraced by so many people as the major goal in life. One of the brokers convicted in the insider-trading scandals on Wall Street in the late eighties, Dennis Levine, recalled the teaching of his favorite business professor: "Greed is a nice religion. If you are greedy, you are going to keep your shoes polished, you won't run around on your wife or get drunk. You will do whatever it takes to maximize your lifetime income, and that doesn't leave time for messing up."[60] In the drive to keep on increasing one's assets far beyond what is needed to fulfill reasonable desires of living comfortably, having enough retirement income and medical coverage for old age, and leaving some money to one's children, the magic number identifying one's financial net worth becomes a label of one's personal worth for all those "major players" who simply cannot bear to stop playing.

While it is true that some wealthy individuals give generously to charities and other worthy causes, the ideal of sharing, of caring deeply for community, has little place in an atomized culture. Since the various studies cited earlier indicate that the richest 1 percent of American families own between 28 and 40 percent of the net worth owned by all American families, is not a sharply graduated income tax necessary to adjust the extreme maldistribution? (In 1977, before the Reaganite scam of "supply-side economics," the richest 1 percent of households had 7.3

percent of the national income after taxes; by 1990 it was about 12.6 percent.)[61] Such tax revenue could be used to restructure the economy by building up community-based economics, providing training and seed grants for ecologically sound worker-owned businesses of appropriate scale that serve a regional market. Even in a community-based economy with no banks (replaced by nonprofit, county-level credit unions), however, the kind of callous attitude expressed in instructions to employees selling junk bonds in Charles Keating's now-defunct Lincoln Savings and Loan—"Remember the weak, meek, and ignorant are always good targets"[62]—would still be with us unless we can cultivate awareness of the communion inherent in community. Structural change alone cannot save us from estrangement.

During the past decade we have seen just how tenuous a sense of community is when it is based only on proscriptions against base behavior as understood in the social contract. The civil agreement that citizens will not harass other citizens unravels when the Other comes to be seen as a handy scapegoat for collective fears. From the outset of the Reagan administration, the message was put forth in many ways that "*those* people"—minorities and women—could fend for themselves while legal protection against discrimination, aid to the poor and disadvantaged, student loans, public housing, and equal-opportunity measures were drastically reduced. Once the tone of sacrificial community went out from the highest levels of government, minorities and women gradually became targets of harassment and attack with increasing frequency. By the closing years of the decade college students, who had come of age during the Reagan years, widely used racial and ethnic slurs and cheered comedians who expressed contemptuous, degrading views of women, people of color, gays, and the disabled. White supremacist groups are now a presence even in many of our high schools. As of this writing, the incidents of harassment are increasing, and history shows us that frenzied hatred of the Other, once cultivated, does not necessarily dissipate when employment levels rise again. It is literally nauseating to witness a resurgence of bigotry and violence, even replete with Nazi symbols, finding such fertile ground in our country once again. In the absence of comprehending the inherent, even if denied, communion in the human community, the inflated "I," or "we," justifies doing unto others before they can do unto you. Cycles of destruction continue to come 'round, often draped in claims of existential nobility: the rightful role of a master race. Big Daddy again.

Perceiving differentiation while failing to perceive communion can be a deadly error for a society. When there is seemingly nothing but difference, everyone outside one's group is alien, odd, and of lesser value. College students today "are separating themselves in unhealthy ways" as old prejudices deepen, according to a report issued in 1990 by the Carnegie Foundation for the Advancement of Teaching, "Campus Life: In Search of Community." I suspect we are witnessing the effects not only of adult-induced bigotry, but of the breakdown of various community institutions that used to mix up various groups of children in pleasant situations. Some of the happiest memories of my youth are from the portions of eleven summers spent at a Camp Fire Girls camp in the Appalachian foothills of southern Ohio that drew girls from every part of Columbus. Many of the girls were from families who could not afford the $25-per-week fee. They were there on "camperships," but no one, not even the counselors, knew who they were, as that was all taken care of by the countywide office. Nature's bounty and a challenging, loving program revealed to us the dynamics of differentiation, subjectivity, and communion among ourselves in ways that we made our own. Today, however, the opportunity for such formative experiences is dwindling. Around the country, much of the middle class, who provided the base of financial support for such programs, has pulled out of Scouting and Camp Fire in favor of tennis camps and the like. My own camp's annual season has been reduced to only a few weeks, and the Fourth of July parade in my hometown suburb, which used to feature four Camp Fire floats plus a couple each from the Girl Scouts and Boy Scouts, now often has not a

single one. (Even worse, military planes buzzing over the parade route have been added. A telling, if disheartening, swap.)

The after-school and weekend youth programs existed because certain adults, usually mothers, had the time and caring inclination to help children develop their unique potentials. In most families today both parents must hold jobs, as must nearly all single parents. In addition, the real purchasing power of many family incomes is less now than it was twenty years ago, so parents are stretched thin. The "extra" time available for community commitments is largely gone. Professional programs to fill the gap have often proven unsatisfactory, but indictments of such efforts sometimes embrace nostalgic yearning without acknowledging the labor that traditionally sustained community. For example, several years ago I listened to a lecture by a "hip" professor of public policy who mocked the idiocy of a hypothetical young woman who had trained in college to be a "bereavement counselor" and had set up shop in a small town to aid the community in psychologically helpful modes of grieving for their dead. His theme was that community functions are being devalued and pushed aside by the new helping professions and that we were better off with the old ways. The first of the invited respondents to his lecture, the feminist author Elizabeth Dodson Gray, walked up to the microphone, looked out over the audience, and asked in stately tones, "How many men . . . in this hall . . . have ever made a casserole . . . and taken it . . . to a grieving family?"

Expecting a rich community life to flourish once again through women's now taking on the equivalent of three jobs—employment outside the home, most of the housework and child-rearing, and nearly all the caring work to nurture community bonds—is neither a realistic nor appealing vision. Perhaps the thirty-five-hour workweek, recently won by some major unions in Germany, will be widely adopted in time. Jobsharing is also making more part-time work available for those who can afford the reduction. The additional free time, along with a perception—on the part of both sexes—of labor as a gift to one's community, could fuel the growth of community-run food co-ops, service-trade networks, child care, youth programs, senior programs, literacy programs, and so forth.

The fragmentation and weakening of community by economics and bureaucracy have proven damaging but not irreversible. Among the most ambitious attempts to restore community today are several "beyond development" efforts in the Third World in which people focus on their community needs, often drawing from precolonial cultural constructions to restructure the social dynamics, with economics reduced to a support service. They insist they are not "doing community-based economics"; they are "doing community." As elsewhere, the failed assumptions of modernity are evoking fundamental reassessment.

Veterans of spiritually motivated social-change work often come to regard the community self-help projects as an opportunity, or "stage setting,"[63] for the unfolding of people's inherent capabilities and the inner journey that may take place. An Italian priest, Prosperino Gallipolli, who has worked with rural co-ops in Mozambique for more than thirty years, explains, "The economic part is only a way to help people gain self-esteem. Underdevelopment is a spiritual problem; it's a lack of active, critical thinking, initiative, self-confidence. People here still have complexes left over from colonial days."[64] The diminishment of the person by structural violence, in every disadvantaged community in the world, is violence against the sacred because the fundamental processes of the unfolding cosmos, the larger reality, our extended being, have been thwarted and suppressed. Differentiation is scorned rather than celebrated; everyone must try to look and act like the oppressor group. Expressing one's interiority, or subjectivity, is dangerous; submission, repression of feelings, and passivity are necessary for survival. Communion between the oppressed and oppressors is profoundly denied. Social justice, then, restores the possibility for fundamental life processes to flourish.

The process itself can yield joy ("subversive joy," as Cornel West has suggested) and graced communion. Yet a sense of spiritual hunger sometimes dogs activists in church-based social-change projects. Jim Wallis, editor of *Sojourners* magazine and an activist minister, suggests that "works righteousness" arises whenever one mistakes actions for grace or whenever "Christian ministry or leftist ideology" use the poor "to make capital out of their suffering," rather than desiring to be their friend.[65] He believes that grace helps us overcome the temptation to believe we are better than those who need convincing and converting: "The marks of grace are gentleness, hope, and faith. The most dependable sign of its presence is joy."[66]

No matter what spiritual path one prefers—including the free-form variety in which one has suddenly, unexpectedly experienced the unitive dimension of all being and preserved awareness of that perception against the modern forces of denial—the core teachings of the Semitic traditions remind us that our spirituality is always tested: If you allow injustice, you fail to grasp the depth of communion. If you fail to offer the gift of your creative subjectivity to struggles against oppression, your spirituality is a self-serving delusion. If you cannot honor and cherish the face of ultimate mystery in every being, your sense of the sacred is a pale imitation. If you deny interrelatedness and mutual humanity with people considered the Other, you have detached yourself from communion. To know—deeply know—the nature of the sacred web of life is to live a life of cosmological integrity.

6

The Recovery of Meaning

On cosmological grounding for humanity's creative possibilities

The paradox of modernity, for all who believe in the forward march of rationalist, science-based progress, is how the modern project could have yielded so many destructive dynamics for the person, the community, the nation, and the biosphere since it was fueled by a Promethean urge to escape from superstition, ignorance, and subservience to the constraints of the omnipotent church-state during the Middle Ages. As the cultural history of Western Europe is commonly understood, Renaissance humanism, followed by the Scientific Revolution and then by the Enlightenment, jointly delivered Western civilization from darkness into light. Modernity supposedly unleashed the freedom and ingenuity of humankind so that we could come into our rightful role as objectively knowledgeable, powerful, gloriously unbounded rulers of ourselves and all life on Earth. What went wrong? Was there perhaps an inherent flaw in this schema of liberation that led us to regard meaning and value in dangerously constricted ways? In the current effort to determine what postmodernity should preserve or discard from the Enlightenment tradition, a fuller understanding of its formative influences is helpful.

One effect of the Scientific Revolution during the seventeenth century was to divide the intelligentsia into two camps, the "ancients" and the "moderns." The "moderns" became convinced that basic principles of natural science were applicable to all areas of human endeavor and could produce new insights and knowledge that would replace ignorant and distorted perceptions. Hence they relegated even Petrarch and Vasari, who had been so instrumental in establishing many foundational concepts of "modern man," to the "dark ages" because their efforts were not based on science. Recent studies in the history of the Renaissance and the Scientific Revolution, however, reveal numerous cracks in the monochromatic interpretation of these eras as a movement from sacred to secular society. Stephen McKnight, for instance, demonstrates in *Sacralizing the Secular* that the function of science, rather than its presence alone, is a key to understanding the new epoch.[1] He traces the considerable influence of a body of esoteric religious texts called the *prisca theologia*, or Ancient Wisdom (or "pseudoscience"), on the evolution of modernity in general and the social sciences in particular. McKnight speaks only of the "sacralizing" effects of the esoteric pseudoscience's popularity, but clearly the dominant orientation of the *prisca theologia* led to a very particular (and peculiar) sense of the sacred: a self-aggrandizing sacral humanism. The core concept of the Ancient Wisdom is that man [*sic*] is a terrestrial god who can shape his own destiny and control nature.

The texts of the Ancient Wisdom were widely considered by Renaissance philosophers and theologians to be the earliest and most complete divine revelations to non-Christian wise men, such as Pythagoras and Zoroaster. The teachings of "Hermes Trismegistus" in particular became the most highly revered of all ancient revelations during the fifteenth century. When a manuscript of the *Corpus Hermeticum* was brought to Florence in 1460, Marsilio Ficino, head of the famed Platonic academy, was ordered by his patron, Cosimo d'Medici, to translate it immediately, before proceeding with his interpretations of Plato. "Hermes Trismegistus" was thought to have been an Egyptian magus who, curiously, was believed to have been the spiritual mentor of both Moses and Plato. Hence his works were prized as the connecting link between Judeo-Christian theology and classical philosophy. Initially, the objective of Renaissance scholars in studying the Ancient Wisdom was to determine the unifying core of the revelations and demonstrate its compatibility with Christian truth. A growing conviction developed, however, that the *prisca theologia* contained "a deeper and purer truth about man, God, society, and the world than was found in Christian theology or classical philosophy."[2] By the sixteenth century, the Ancient Wisdom was a fundamental element in the mounting criticism of traditional theology and metaphysics and in the call for a thorough religious reorientation and political reformation.

Although it was established as early as 1714 that the texts in the *Corpus Hermeticum* date from the second or third century A.D. (containing elements of Platonism and Hellenistic Judaism, possible Persian and Christian elements, and various esoteric teachings), the "Egyptian" myths and symbols of human divinization remained influential. Their presence is evident in the utopian dreams that developed in the sixteenth and seventeenth centuries and in the programs of social reformation in the eighteenth and nineteenth centuries. Even our country's founding fathers, stalwart sons of the Enlightenment, thought enough of the "Egyptian" wisdom to make a (Masonic) pyramid the dominant image in "the Great Seal" of the new political order, dated 1776, which appears on our one-dollar bills.

Those contemporary historians who continue to discover a blurring of the lines between "sacred" and "secular" in the birthing process of modernity have uncovered not a simple movement from the City of God to the City of Man but the intertwining of both of those perspectives on the meaning of the individual and society. In the secular worldview, society is no longer considered a microcosm of the divine macrocosm, and nature is considered to be independent of divine providence. Nature is ruled by Fortune and Necessity, as in the works of Bocaccio and Machiavelli, or it is a self-contained system indifferent to humans, as in the work of Galileo. God is considered to be remote from this world or dismissed as irrelevant. In the sacralizing worldview of modernity, man [*sic*] lost his creaturely limitations, regarded as backward medieval constraints, and became a terrestrial god capable of creating an earthly paradise.

Ficino and the other members of the Platonic academy in Florence were particularly interested in the text in the *Corpus Hermeticum* known as the *Pimander*, or the "Egyptian Genesis." In a dream Hermes learns that God the Father instructed the Demiurge to create the natural world, but that man himself was created directly by God the Father and formed in his image; hence man exists in a divine Father-son relationship superior to the realm of nature. In the second major book of the Hermetic texts, the *Asclepius*, Hermes explains that the most marvelous aspect of man is his ability to discover the nature of the gods and reproduce it via magical power, enabling him to participate in the maintenance of cosmic order and create a microcosmic social order. When man realizes his true role as magus, thereby attaining his full humanity, the world will be restored to its original beauty and will again be worthy of reverence and admiration. Nature provides man with the means of expressing his God-like creativity.

This view was presented by Ficino in the *Theologica Platonica* and *De vita triplici*, which assert that man's discovery of his own ability to know and recreate the world demonstrates that he shares with God the attributes of comprehensive knowledge and creativity and, further, that man can draw upon the *spiritus mundi*, the world spirit, to enhance his own condition and control nature as did the ancient magi. Giovanni Pico della Mirandola's famous *Oration on the Dignity of Man*, generally considered a pivotal break with the theological "dark ages," actually presents a variation on the Hermetic theme that man is the *magnum miraculum* of creation. Eliminating the Demiurge of the "Egyptian Genesis," Pico declares that God first created the world and then created man with unlimited potential to be whatever he decides, having the ability to purify the soul via "natural magic" in order to "become He Himself Who made us." According to Pico, only the accomplished magus who follows "many teachings taken from the ancient theology of Hermes

Trismegistus, many from the doctrines of the Chaldaeans and of Pythagoras, and many from the occult mysteries of the Hebrews," as well as classical philosophy, can fully contemplate the wonders of God and so love and worship him properly.

McKnight's study traces this perspective as the emphasis shifts in the sixteenth and seventeenth centuries from self-divinization to utopian dreams of religious reform: Cornelius Agrippa called for the recovery of a pristine Christianity that was esoteric and cabalistic; Giordano Bruno called for a reinstitution of Hermetic religion as a replacement for Christianity (and was burned at the stake); and Tommaso Campanella attempted to engage rulers in a utopian revolution to establish a Hermetic City of the Sun and, for a while, had considerable influence with Pope Urban VIII and then with King Louis XIV of France. Their writings served as a source for the advent of modern messianic figures who proposed to lead society from an alienated condition to a utopian paradise.

McKnight also proposes that this tradition contributed "sacralizing" elements to the secularizing, modern patterns found in the works of Bacon, Comte, and Marx: the consciousness of an epochal break with the past, a conviction that this break is due to an epistemological advance, and a belief that this new knowledge provides "man" with the means of overcoming his alienation and regaining his true humanity. Francis Bacon, father of the scientific method, incorporated the myths, symbols, and basic yearnings of the modern "sacralizing tradition" into his utopian works. His *New Atlantis* includes many references characteristic of the Rosicrucian movement, which blended the Hermetic and cabalistic traditions of the Renaissance "magi" with alchemy and mystical Christianity. Auguste Comte, regarded as the founder of social science and positivist philosophy, believed that a new age of positivism could be achieved by a radical reformation of education and religion, although he certainly had no interest in Hermeticism. He urged replacing traditional philosophy and theology with a new religion of humanity in which science would lead society to spiritual renewal and social reformation. Karl Marx's critiques of philosophy and religion have close affinities with Agrippa's, Bruno's, and Bacon's criticisms and with Ficino's and Pico's new understanding of human nature. Like the Renaissance "magi," Marx was convinced that he had reached an unprecedented understanding of the human condition and could employ instrumental knowledge to reshape the conditions of existence to create a heaven on earth. For Bacon, Comte, and Marx, science functioned as a new, improved version of the old "pseudoscience."[3]

Labeling the two formative traditions in the emergence of modernity the "secularizing" and the "sacralizing" may provide a handy pair of labels for some historians, but the latter is inadequate since a very particular sense of the sacred was involved: the texts that comprised the Ancient Wisdom, which were compiled during the late Hellenistic period, combined surviving practices and perspectives of nature-based spirituality, astrology, and other esoteric practices, as well as spirituality based on an omnipotent sky-god. As such, two formative influences guided the development of modern "sacralization." First, it is framed by a patriarchal power structure. Hence the obsessive goal of the tradition is to further perspectives that wrest power from the Father-God in the sky and declare the male's true role as God-like controller of nature. Second, the Ancient Wisdom contained not only pseudoscience but also some pseudospirituality, that is, esoteric practices that promise one extraordinary powers and are self-aggrandizing derivatives of ancient disciplines of mindwork and deep communion with the natural world. These were most enticing to "moderns" bent on outdoing God at the power game. Throughout the "modern" interpretations drawn from the Ancient Wisdom, one observes the influence of both the self-aggrandizing pseudospirituality intermeshed with the extremely ancient cosmological, nature-revering spirituality. Examples of the latter abound, for instance, in Ficino's last work, *De vita triplici*, in which he declares that humans may partake of the *spiritus mundi* by preparing and cleansing ourselves through reverent interaction with and absorption of nature. In a similar vein, Newton believed that his discoveries in science and mathematics would allow humans greater knowledge of God through more accurate understanding of the creation. However, in time the power of communion was ignored in favor of the power of dominating nature through acts of God-like control. After the seventeenth century, the remnants of the ancient philosophies honoring nature's subjectivity were displaced in the sciences by the "new mechanical philosophy."

Because of the "sacred" Father-son power struggle that shaped the modern sacralizing tradition and because of the secular perception of nature as an indifferent, closed system, the modern project did not result in a biocracy dedicated to the well-being of all species but in a replication of the power-over model of interaction with nature. We tend to think of that orientation as the "obvious" human response because modernity has always maligned the premodern and nonmodern alternatives and denied their wisdom regarding reciprocity and responsibility toward the sacred whole. The twentieth-century Tukano Indians of the Amazon basin, for instance, are as eager as were the "high priests" of the Scientific Revolution to learn about the workings of nature, not to "bind nature into service" and make it a "slave," as Bacon said, but to comprehend with ever-increasing precision what is required of the human to fit into the greater dynamics.

The modern worldview has long been infused with the arrogance of power-wielders, triumphal self-proclaimed titans rather desperately denying the existence of a larger reality sparked by diffuse creativity of which human intelligence is only a part. According to the modern attitude, nature exists to be "perfected" by humans, and what meaning there is in this world is imparted by humans.

Spiritual Concerns in Secular Modernity

As the development of modern technocracy progressed and spiritual concerns were increasingly displaced by the forward thrust of scientistic pragmatism, bureaucratic standardization, materialism, and industrialization, oppositional forces emerged in the arts. In the reaction against the rationalist mind-set, which began to appear even in the works of some Enlightenment proponents in the second half of the eighteenth century, the Romantics redefined the central ideas of reason, nature, and progress. They celebrated reason that is informed by intuition and depth, nature as wild and varied, and progress as an organic unfolding. The Romantic poets sought to learn how to marry their minds to nature "in love and holy passion," as Wordsworth put it.

Other writers of the nineteenth century, such as Balzac, Hugo, and Baudelaire, as well as a large number of visual artists were influenced by a revival of cosmological spirituality that drew from the *Hermetica*, Paracelsus, Robert Fludd, Jakob Boehme, and Emmanuel Swendenborg. This time the emphasis was not on humans realizing their true nature as terrestrial gods but on attaining subtle awareness of the universe as a unitary, living phenomenon and on grasping the interrelatedness of mind and matter. Various notions of spiritual progress and evolution were circulated at the same time as those proposing "progress" through social Darwinism.

Following the symbolist painters of the late nineteenth century, who felt that art could transform modern society by offering spiritual alternatives, such pioneers of abstract painting as Kandinsky, Kupka, Malevich, and Mondrian moved from figuration to pure abstraction in order to express cosmological imagery, vibration, occult notions of duality and the union of opposites, synesthesia (the overlapping of senses, such as hearing color vibrations and seeing sound shapes), and sacred geometry. Their work, including Kandinsky's book *On the Spiritual in Art* (1912), which presented theosophical theories on the human response to color, influenced scores of other artists.[4] (Figurative painters were also influenced; Matisse said of the pre–World-War-I period of his work, "It was a time of artistic cosmogony.")[5] In 1945, two hundred of Kandinsky's paintings were exhibited in New York, and his book was reissued. Postwar abstract expressionists such as Barnett Newman, Mark Rothko, Jackson Pollack, and Adolph Gottlieb continued the abstract exploration of what they called "the world mystery" and "metaphysical secrets" of the sublime.[6] Their spiritual sources were not Madame Blavatsky's theosophy or Rudolf Steiner's anthroposophy, which had been so influential with earlier cosmological abstract painters, but Native American art (especially from the northwest coast), Zen Buddhism, and Carl Jung's theories of the mandala and other archetypal forms (plus, for Newman, Jewish mysticism). Even many art critics ignored these artists' statements of cosmological intent; certainly to the public at large, "modern art" seemed an odd fixation on form, color, and spatial arrangement for its own sake.

Within the framework of nineteenth- and twentieth-century modernity, spiritual quest manifested more freely among certain artists than in numerous religious institutions. Many Christian denominations attempted to become more "rational" by emphasizing the historic Jesus at the expense of the cosmological dimension and by closeting the "embarrassing" cosmological mystics of their traditions.[7] Both art and religion are accorded only marginal value in a technocracy, but spiritual quest—albeit in atrophied form—can also be found at the very heart of foundational modern thinking. While most of the architects of modernity were in open revolt against organized religion, their own work often exhibited spiritual concerns.

Nietzsche, for example, was contemptuous of both church and state as sources of intimidation and conformity. (He felt that Christianity was a false extension of the teachings of Christ.) He was quite interested in the Buddha's teachings, proclaiming him a "physiologist" par excellence and lauding Buddhism as the only genuinely "positivistic" religion in history, strictly "phenomenalistic" and pragmatic in its outlook.[8] Though he eventually pronounced that path too "weary" for his taste, several aspects of his notion of the superior person (*Übermensch*) share common ground with the transformation associated with Dhamma: someone who is free of resentment of the ignoble acts of others and can respect and love his enemies, someone who has mastered his passions so that he can affirm life creatively. There is also a Dhammic sense of the fullness of the present moment in Nietzsche's notion of the suprahistorical (*überhistorisch*) individual, who realizes that the world is complete in every moment, not in some projection of a distant, salvific goal for the human species.[9] Many other aspects of Nietzsche's work, however, depart radically from the wisdom of Dhamma, revealing an extremely agitated mind and an aggressive mood of frustration.

In Marx, too, one finds spiritual concerns, especially if one looks beyond the formalistic parallels that have often been noted between Marxism and the Judeo-Christian tradition: the prophetic railing against exploitation, the promise of apocalyptic deliverance, the Day of Judgment (of the bourgeoisie by the proletariat after the revolution)—and the rather frequent emergence of religious fanatics, who settle arguments by quoting chapter and verse of salvific texts and who are absolutely positive about the inevitability of the historic course perceived by their tradition. Although millions of people have been crushed for the sake of communist ideology, Marx's early philosophic and economic manuscripts, which are still considered inspiring by many non-communist socialists, addressed existential concerns that are widely recognized as spiritual issues, specifically subjectivity (understood as the unfolding of one's creativity or profound interiority) and communion. Marx felt that the deepest essence of an individual, his or her creativity, is turned into a possession (of the capitalist employer). The worker becomes alienated from his or her true nature and becomes a mere commodity as a wage laborer in the marketplace. Marx believed that private property reduces the richness of our senses to the poverty of the one obsessive "sense of having" and that only in an economic system whereby human beings are reduced to such "absolute poverty" are they willing to yield their "inner wealth" to the outer world. He also felt that capitalist production estranges the worker from active communion with the rest of the human species because such work is deprived of the social and universal quality that enables one to produce for the sustenance and development of society rather than the desires of the owner of a company. (One might argue that if products were not filling a need on the part of society they would fail to sell, but it is clearly apparent by now that mass advertising *creates* the demand for various products, even unhealthy ones, by relentlessly stimulating desire.)

Another giant of modernity, Sigmund Freud, is accurately associated with opposition to Jewish and Christian worship of God the Father. Freud felt that religious ideas are largely a matter of "wish-fulfillment" and that the religious doctrine of an omnipotent father-god was a compensatory response to society's historical memories of having displaced the "primal father." He believed that modern individuals should "proceed" from the "neurosis" of religion into "education to reality," by which he meant, at least in *The Future of an Illusion*[10] (1928), a science-based exploration of human experience. The psychoanalyst Bruno Bettelheim argued in *Freud and Man's Soul* that the English translators of Freud's work fixated on the early state of his thought, when he was inclined toward science and medicine, and disregarded the more mature Freud, whose orientation was "humanistic" and focused on "broadly conceived cultural and human problems and with matters of the soul."[11] Freud's use of *Seelentätigkeit* (activity of the soul) was translated as "mental activity," for example, and his use of "homey" German terms was replaced with scientistic Greek or Latinate words, such as "ego" and "id" for "*ich*" and "*es*." While most scholars maintain that Freud was more mechanistic than soulful, he certainly believed, in common with such spiritual traditions as Buddhism and Hinduism's *raja yoga*, that observing the dynamics of one's mind can free a person from patterns of response that are detrimental to oneself and others and that hinder relationship. Freud's opinions about the causes of self-harming mental patterns, as well as his method of alleviating them, however, were quite different from the teachings of the spiritual traditions.

These enormously influential shapers of modernity—Nietzsche, Marx, and Freud—were engaged with many of the spiritual concerns that lie at the heart of the wisdom traditions, but their explorations of those issues were skewed by two fundamental orientations of modern thought: they were patriarchal in style as well as core assumptions, which closed them off from a great deal of life, and they focused largely on the human drama as set apart from the "backdrop" of nature, often regarding human culture as the triumphal opposition to nature. The best intentions of many pioneers of modernity were compromised by their own patriarchal attempts to smash the inescapable bonds with the Earthbody, the female body, and the "stifling" female realm of the domestic. After attacking and displacing the old ways, they established themselves as the controlling fathers of the new, the daring, the disconnected. Bombastic certitude was their style, indulging a flair for Nietzschean "creative destruction" and "destructive creation."

Perhaps the public and private ailments of "the modern condition" stem from our personally and socially atrophied state: the self-defeating modern, Eurocentric containment of the person and society apart from Gaia and the universe, as the cosmologist Brian Swimme has suggested.[12] It is unlikely, he notes, that any civilization has ever isolated itself so profoundly from communion with the cosmological dynamics of our larger reality. Our felt connections with each other and the rest of the Earth community have been pruned to pathetic proportions. We have converted more earthstuff into the fulfillment of human desires than ever before, yet we are uncomfortable, dissatisfied, and disappointed as we continue to support systems and institutions that will provide more of the same. We simply cannot experience the fullness of being by continuing to banish the existential dimensions that modernity has denied.

The Nature of the Revelatory Experience

Within a cosmological orientation, revelation is acknowledged whenever an individual experiences direct awareness, purposively or unexpectedly, of the larger reality, which includes the perceiving being and is not something apart from him or her. In such moments the universe reveals a dimension of its nature that is inaccessible to mundane, discursive consciousness. One perceives being as a unitary ground of form, motion, time, and space, such that one experiences an enormously spacious sense of the immediate. Perceptual boundaries between the "inner" and the "outer" dissolve, and an intense awareness of the whole, as a benevolent and powerful presence, is common. Revelation may be *extra*ordinary, but it is not *super*natural. It would more accurately be labeled *ultra*natural, a journey into the cosmic nature that lies within the world we tend to perceive as an aggregate of discrete fragments bound by such forces as gravity and electromagnetism.

In William James's classic study *The Varieties of Religious Experience* (1902), he concluded that our encounters with "transmundane energies" are among the most important biological functions of humankind. That area of physiology has hardly been a strong focus of scientific research in the intervening decades, but in the 1970s a British biologist, Sir Alister Hardy, established the Religious Experience Research Unit at Oxford University and collected over four thousand firsthand accounts of people's spiritual experiences. He and his staff explained through solicitations in newspapers, pamphlets, and questionnaires that they were interested in experiences with a nonphysical presence, or power, that were not necessarily connected with "God" or any particular religion.

Hardy opens his book on their findings, *The Spiritual Nature of Man*, with the following typical example:

> One day as I was walking along Marylebone Road I was suddenly seized with an extraordinary sense of great joy and exultation, as though a marvelous beam of spiritual power had shot through me linking me in a rapture with the world, the Universe, Life with a capital L, and all the beings around me. All delight and power, all things living, all time fused in a brief second.[13]

While revelatory experiences are often moments of amazed perception in which emotion seems stunned, rather than conventionally "happy," the largest category of the accounts, when classified according to "cognitive and affective elements" was the one labeled "sense of security, protection, peace."

When Hardy and his staff classified the experiences according to the phenomenon that had "triggered" them, they found the largest three groups of antecedents to be despair, prayer or meditation, and natural beauty. The most characteristic feature of the accounts was the perception that a transcendental element in life is fundamental, that an individual can "have communion" with a spiritual reality that *appears* to be beyond the conscious self. Awareness of the presence often "gave new meaning to life." Many people reported strong feelings of a pleasant nature, including a transformation from despair to unbounded joy. Hardy's successor, Edward Robinson, notes that the great majority of the correspondents he studied are persons in whom the original childhood vision of the "Something More" never faded.

Scholars of religion generally divide spiritual experience into two types. *Numinous* experience involves awareness of a holy presence apart from the self, whether it is an encounter with an awesome *numen* (the holy) or a loving relationship with a personal "other." *Mystical* experience involves a sense of unity in multiplicity ("extroverted" mysticism) or unity devoid of all multiplicity ("introverted" mysticism).[14] My own hunch is that the unitary, or "mystical," experiences are primary. The experience of a "wholly other" power, both fearful and attractive, was named "numinous" by Rudolf Otto in 1917, a definition of the sacred that was adopted by Mircea Eliade and many other scholars. It seems probable that partial perceptions of ultimate mystery can come to be shaped by the religious metaphors that develop within a culture, such as a "wholly other" judgmental father-god. Yet such influence is neither automatic for all cultures (that is, there is no universal "progression" toward religion with a godhead) nor universal within a culture: many spiritual traditions recognize the great unity but not a separate godhead, and many individuals in cultures where a religion with a godhead is the dominant orientation (such as the Semitic traditions) have unitary mystical experiences that do not include a "wholly other" presence. Moreover, the scholarly categories do not seem adequate for describing contemporary Goddess spirituality, in which people experience a "loving relationship" with the presence of the Goddess, but that presence is perceived as unitive, as the immanent and transcendent cosmic creativity *within* the self and the great whole. That sort of relationship, with God, is also experienced by people who share the orientation of creation-centered Christianity (not to be confused with fundamentalists' biblical "creationism").

Scholars of religion also puzzle over the question of whether mystical experiences cultivated within disparate religious traditions are the same, or entirely different from one another, or share common ground as well as exhibiting particularities. Certainly the religious metaphors and framing orientations differ widely. Initial Western scholarship influenced by missionary work often sought to establish that various male deities were "just like" the Judeo-Christian God and that all mystical experiences were the same. Subsequent studies have suggested that mystical experience is the same everywhere but that descriptions of it vary according to culture and spiritual tradition. Another hypothesis is that all mystical experience is contained within a few cross-cultural types and that descriptions of those types are culturally determined. Academic discussions of these possibilities and others proceeded rather quietly for years until the first deconstructionist moved onto the block and declared the new reality to his colleagues. In a breathtaking article a young professor announced in 1978 that all previous scholarship on mysticism was "unsophisticated" and "mistaken" because *"There are* NO *pure (i.e. unmediated) experiences"* (his italics and capitalization).[15] That is, the content of every mystical experience is epistemologically constructed because everything in human experience is "socially produced," as the deconstructive postmodernists put it. This interpretation has become the dominant orientation within many academic circles. The deconstructionists (also called philosophical "constructivists") do a fine job of calling attention to particularity, but when they make *that ol' totalizing decon leap* to concluding that there is *nothing but* cultural construction, their argument takes a tumble. The kind of unitive experience recalled by the person who was strolling down Marylebone Road, for instance, is a cross-cultural occurrence widely reported. Such moments seem to be jarringly other than the comfortable framework of one's spiritual and cultural orientation, more like the energy of the universe bursting into the consciousness of one of its human manifestations in such a manner that the amazing unitary ground of being is revealed.[16] Can the deconstructive postmodernists prove that this type of experience is not a biological function? Can they account for novelty, that is, cosmic creativity? Even in the cases of mystical experiences that are cultivated through particular practices within a spiritual tradition, the goal is often the *de*construction of perceptual "crutches" provided by social context.[17] It has been suggested that such practices amount to a "deautomatizing" of our culturally implanted habits of perception.[18] Moreover, even mystics working within traditions often report surprise at their experiences. The similarity of many of their accounts, though vastly separated by time and place, is worthy of attention. Perhaps an attitude of open-mindedness—indeed, a learning mode—is the most sensible approach to considering revelatory occurrences.

Awareness of the cosmological processes—at least three of which we can recognize as differentiation, subjectivity, and communion—also arises in human consciousness in myriad ways that are less intense than the "grand moments" discussed previously. All of them are experiences of grace, felt connection with the universe as a glorious dance of being. When our minds are grasped by the display of differentiation in a field of wildflowers, or the depth of a child's emerging subjectivity, or the communion of love that swells within us at unexpected moments, our sense of interbeing is activated and the universe draws forth relationship. If we deny grounding in the revelatory experience, we shrink further and further inside ourselves, increasingly uncertain of the wisdom of our thoughts and the depth of our feelings.

That dynamic of shrinking from the world beyond the human, whether through a belligerent distancing or a wall of indifference, has been a central component of the modern project. Value was recognized solely within human history. Now, as the natural world beyond human society has become critically degraded and dysfunctional, the possibility that the meaning of the human is anchored in the meaning of nature is frightening to many people. That is why, I believe, the radical denial of meaning has recently found widespread appeal and intense emotional support. (Since the deconstructive-postmodern orientation amplifies certain nihilistic elements inherent in modernity, it is called "most-modern" by some.)[19] Yet the deconstructionist declaration that truth is merely "socially produced" and hence artificial misses the point. Truth is pluralistic in that it is relational and intersubjective—but humans are not the only subjects in the universe. Indeed, the universe itself is a grand subject. When we cultivate sensitivity toward other forms of being, we begin to recognize the value, requirements, and movement toward satisfaction that are located in plants, animals, communal structures, events, and place. In such a condition of receptive awareness, the truth we grasp has greater depth than that arrived at through a denial of engagement. In wondering about the "loss of nerve" causing the current "surrender to interpretation theory," the philosopher Robert Cummings Neville observes, "Like it or not, the actual world with its real normative possibilities is the standard against which our interpretations measure up well or badly."[20] He suggests that the philosophical task for our civilization is "to cultivate the critical disciplines of piety before the real."[21]

I suggest that the wisdom traditions meet that very need. They lead one to an inner poise that allows vivid awareness and relational insight into all we may observe and experience in and around us. They yield revelation, not on demand but according to the rhythms and creativity of the cosmos.

The Spirit of the Body Politic

What kind of human interactions are worthy of the sacred whole? When humans realize that we participate in the great unfolding and that our contributions of culture and society can either hinder or enhance the dynamics of differentiation, subjectivity, and communion, we understand meaning as meaning-in-relation. Then a sense of caring and responsibility for self and others (inorganic as well as organic) becomes central, and rights are regarded as integral with responsibilities.[22] Modern citizens are taught to conceive of society as an aggregate of individuals bound only by a Lockean sense of "social contract" guaranteeing rights, but the perennial tension between the individual and society is reframed by the experiential knowledge derived from a depth practice in the wisdom traditions. One comes to understand the person as a unique but integral manifestation of the social whole and the cosmological whole. Since interbeing is the nature of existence, measures of reciprocity are the "internal logic" of life. One comes to experience them as extensions of states of grace and to cultivate greater awareness of what is drawn from and contributed to the creative unfolding of the person, community, and society, as well as the bioregion and the entire Earth community. Within such an orientation, community structures, education, and governance exist not only to provide basic services and protect citizens from one another, but to facilitate opportunities for such unfolding in ways that honor both freshness and continuity. In contrast, a society that guarantees civil rights, for instance, but allows the trivializing of coming-of-age as simply the absorption of its youth into the vacuous world of mass media and a consumer culture is cosmologically irresponsible.

Human culture is part of the integral articulation of the sacred whole, but when societies have claimed a privileged relationship to the cosmos or cosmological creativity (called "God" or any other name), their spirituality has been perverted to serve nationalism and transformed into a civil religion that has excused, and even encouraged, the torture and slaughter or enslavement of millions of people throughout history. Each Native American nation traditionally considered its society and its lands to be the cosmological center—which is true, since the universe is expanding away from any given point—yet many of them did not seem to extend that sense of authenticity to all the other Indian nations around them. A number of them lived by a warfare mentality and took pride in torturing and enslaving their conquered neighbors. The Judeo-Christian and Islamic traditions, both born of violent campaigns against neighboring peoples in present-day Israel and Saudi Arabia, later conceived of themselves as expansive empires of territory and frequently conquered by the sword. A religion of nationalism was promoted in Japan during World War II and the preceding decade, as was the case in Nazi Germany. In both countries, political leaders declared that the trees and soil are sacred, which they are, but why did the populace accept the further declaration that all such participation in the sacred stopped at the nation's borders? Such absurd "logic" is adopted only where the cultivation of hatred, greed, and delusion meets with insufficient resistance.[23] Our own government, like those of Western Europe, has frequently claimed God to be "on our side" during imperialist actions and invasions.

Following the dissolution of communist states in Eastern Europe (or Central Europe, as they prefer), we again witnessed the linking of religion with nationalism. Members of long-standing cultural nations who had been forced to conform as modern citizens in a communist state, often one with newly drawn borders, were understandably elated to be able to worship without persecution and to express their cultural identity. Because these two regained freedoms were joined in some instances to support exclusionary and sometimes hateful attitudes, numerous political observers concluded that "unleashing" religion always breeds strife and oppression. Why not focus attention on the ways in which nationalism, like patriarchy and racism, perverts spiritual impulses and causes people, including some clergy, to accept a severed sense of communion with others as if it were a religious truth? In our own country this is the essential question concerning the Christian Right, who insist that the nation should be run by fundamentalist Christians (a notion that surely would have horrified the founding fathers with their eighteenth-century sense of "natural religion" and nonsectarian Deism).

In the "revolutions of 1989" in Central Europe, including the decade-long struggle that Solidarity began in Poland, people in increasing numbers withdrew the power of their cooperation from the communist states and bore witness in massive vigils of resistance. They demanded the end of regimes that had been born and maintained with violence, and they demonstrated, in general, an insistence that the process of liberation be itself the foundation of new possibilities, not a murderous prelude. That same year the bicentennial commemoration of the French Revolution inspired considerable debate over whether the excessive violence in the Vendée region, where civil war wiped out one-third of the population, as well as the ongoing terror in Paris and elsewhere had actually been "cleansing" and "ennobling" or whether the revolutionaries' enthusiasm for exterminating everything and everyone perceived as oppositional to the new order had left a crippling legacy for subsequent generations.

Those of us who were raised with Eurocentric acculturation are not accustomed to focusing careful attention on process. Predisposed by an Aristotelian framing of reality, which was preceded by the desacralizing of the Earthbody's processes, we see primarily substance and structure. The new attention to process in recent decades is an expression of the spiritual awakening of postmodernity. Indeed, the father of general systems theory, the biologist Ludwig von Bertalanffy, was inspired by the creation-centered mystic Nicholas of Cusa, and numerous scientists working in postmodern directions of theory and experimentation grapple with issues of being and becoming that have long been central to the wisdom traditions.

The news from chaos theory and related areas of scientific inquiry that even a slight alteration in a dynamic open system can cause overwhelming changes has been embraced by many political activists as an inspiring perception. Yet the more urgent aspect of process for politics is surely the ways in which it is conducted that repulse such a large segment of society. Patriarchal models of behavior—competitiveness, control, negation, "combative integrity"—dominate not only in Tweedledee-and-Tweedledum politics (that is, the Republican and Democratic parties and their counterparts worldwide), but also in environmental and other public-interest organizations and in alternative political movements. Many feminists experienced a heightened awareness of such dynamics during the 1980s when they moved into mixed-gender activist groups and organizations, after working primarily in women's groups during the 1970s, to address crises in ecology, the arms race, and social justice. Repeatedly I heard from women friends in various movements and different parts of the country that a large portion of the men acted out domineering or endlessly contentious process, or did nothing to stop it—even though a good number of those men did not cling to patriarchal behavior outside the political subculture. "They compete with each other even when agreeing!" observed a friend in New England. At first, many of these women believed that lack of awareness of other people's actual opinions was the main problem, but they discovered that, even after broad areas of consensus were identified, many men had no interest in placing discussions about differences within a context of common ground. They exhibited what seemed to be a rather desperate desire to define themselves in opposition to others and to bolster their own perception of their position with verbal aggression, ludicrous straw-man arguments, and continual strategic maneuvering for one-upmanship.[24] The women painfully discovered—in business, the arts, and academia, as well as alternative politics—that underneath all the rhetoric about building community and working together, all the denigration of individualism and "ego trips," and especially all the shocking elbow-in-the-gut maneuvers by some male colleagues whenever recognition was at stake, reverberated that classic sermon on the patriarchal mode of being by

Vince Lombardi: "Winning isn't the most important thing: it's the only thing."

Like every other social endeavor, politics could be structured to enhance the great unfolding, drawing forth the creativity and deep interiority of the individual as well as the bonds of communion in many directions. To do so, we would need to develop relationships that are evocative and to realize that our developmental nature calls for a learning mode of behavior.[25] Such an orientation would also call for the cultivation of wisdom and compassion. Only if one can free the mind of agitation, or at least be aware with some precision of its effects, can one perceive something of the fullness of another being without the usual veils of self-serving illusion. Spiritual practice generally increases one's ability in these areas, which is perhaps the reason Gandhi declared that the most spiritual act is the most practical one. It is perhaps also the reason the Iroquois Indians state in *Basic Call to Consciousness*, "In our ways, spiritual consciousness is the highest form of politics."[26]

Beyond Nihilism: Postmodern Quests

Observers have often wondered at the messianic zeal of deconstructive postmodernists, at their triumphal denial of nearly everything. Clearly, the postmodernists feel that culture has failed them, and they are not willing to live out lives of quiet desperation in the face of alienation, emptiness, dead ends, and received "natural truths" that are slyly constrictive. They care deeply about awakening everyone to awareness of the manipulations of being. This, too, is a spiritual quest. Moreover, their intensive focus on *difference* within human society can be appreciated as a celebration of the cosmic process of differentiation (although the processes of subjectivity and communion do not fare as well in their worldview).

As the initial passion propelling deconstructive-postmodern theory has cooled in recent years, many adherents have come to acknowledge problematic paradoxes within the content and expression of its critique.[27] In addition, I have suggested a few other elements of that orientation that pose thorny problems. First, I find troubling their internal logic that "proves" that nothing, including the Earth community or the cosmos, can be more influential than human constructs; hence, an individual's worldview is etched by society upon her or him as a tabula rasa. No consideration can be given to the dynamics by which a child's natural and magical felt connection with aspects of the world of nature is *subtracted*, or systematically disdained and repressed, in order that a cultural distancing from nature can be implanted—except in most traditional native cultures.[28] I also feel that insufficient attention is granted by deconstructive postmodernists to the genetic coding inherent in each individual; certainly such coding, *along with* socialization, affects behavior. A researcher involved in the study of hundreds of pairs of identical twins recently observed, perhaps overzealously: "The interesting question today is 'Are there any traits that *aren't* significantly affected by genetics?'"[29] (He believes, by the way, that he has identified one: "niceness." Whether a person is agreeable, trusting, sympathetic, and cooperative or cynical, callous, and antagonistic appears to be more influenced by early environment than by genes.)

A second problem is that deconstructive postmodernism is shaped by traditional concerns of a patriarchal orientation toward life, as I have suggested in Chapter Four and Appendix B. No distinction is made between social constructions that enhance the unfolding of the person and those that repress. Relationship itself is regarded as a treacherous cap on "unconditionality" and, hence, must be circumscribed. Communal process (such as language) is felt to be stifling (a "prison house"), as is communal context (history as "gossip"). Nothing is treasured so deeply as the "nomadic, unregulated freedom of pure difference."[30] This is the Lone Cowboy fantasy, the realm of a maverick "undomesticated" by bonding with family, society, or the Earth community. What has often followed is a subculture of indifference and the (patriarchal) heroic stance that the "repressive code" cannot be resisted but by death, as Jean Baudrillard declares. If the (patriarchal) project of separation is one's frame of reference, every relationship—including the spiritual and cosmological—will be perceived as a power struggle. Every manifestation of the unfolding universe with which one might achieve "metaphysical" communion is warily regarded as an ominous power to be guarded against and rejected. Therein lies truly the most "repressive code," the cultural construction of the deepest loneliness.

A third constraint in deconstructive-postmodern analysis is its heritage from the "metanarrative" of Renaissance humanism and the Scientific Revolution, which sacralized (or "valorized") the human story apart from the larger reality. Hence Baudrillard, for instance, can admire the "noncommodified and continuous symbolic exchange in primitive cultures,"[31] but he cannot acknowledge the *presence* of the sacred, or reverence for the divine whole, as well as the *absence* of commodification as informing influences in those cultures. Moreover, postmodernists are hindered by their inheritance of habits from Marxist economism; although they do not view culture as a mere superstructure that extends from economics, they seem to feel that economic terms are the proper way to describe just about everything. Why should we speak of the "libidinal *economy*" rather than the "*ecology* of the erotic"? Why should all forms of human creativity be jammed into the term "production" (as in "social production")? An analysis that does not discern any difference between producing a tractor and creating a menarche ritual as an act of evoking the powers of cosmic creativity is crudely limited. In a cosmologically based society, such as that of traditional native peoples, culture is not autonomously "produced" but extended from their inevitably partial apprehension of the divine.

Interestingly, some of the most prominent deconstructive-postmodernist thinkers have begun asking the sorts of questions that bring them to the threshold of the wisdom traditions. Whether they could possibly avail themselves of such perspectives depends on their degree of attachment to the "totalizing" deconstructionist dismissal of all religious and spiritual "discourses" as unacceptably dependent on a "transcendent signifier" (God, the Creator, Providence, or any type of "metaphysics of spirit") outside of the "system of difference," or realm of (language-based) human events. Although many religious persons do conceive of the divine as an "outside" reference point, or controller, that perception is not the "universal narrative" of spirituality that deconstructive postmodernism assumes. A great number of participants in the wisdom traditions apprehend "God," "Goddess," "the Great Holy," "ultimate mystery," and so forth not as a force set apart from the world but as the presence of divine creativity *in* the universe (hence within "social production"!) that continually manifests and passes away, that is in and of us all, that is at once the larger reality and the tiniest micro-event. Of course, fundamentalist deconstructionists reject the very perception of an embedding larger reality, however vaguely apprehended, as a "totalizing" and oppressive affront to the human. Derrida despairs that all political beliefs, including struggles against racism and tyranny, are complicit in "the metaphysics of spirit," in that they acknowledge higher, unifying forces. He seems to yearn for a clear-eyed moment in which people could think without recourse to spirit or metaphysics.[32] Yet the newly declared "modesty" of many deconstructive postmodernists would seem to necessitate an open stance toward this matter: perhaps politics is necessarily "muddled" by an illusive metaphysics due to persistent cultural fallacies—or perhaps there actually is a sacred whole toward which human existence is drawn and the necessarily partial apprehensions of the larger reality have often been manipulated as culture and politics in ways that hinder subjectivity. Perhaps the more thoroughly a society denies wisdom traditions that enhance participation in cosmic processes such as differentiation, subjectivity, and communion, the greater the "muddle" of constriction that results.

Many deconstructive postmodernists with a sense of social responsibility seem now to be seeking a way beyond the denial of relationship and meaning to the possibility of *grounding* their insights on freedom, in ways that incorporate their sense of process, fluidity, and reclaimed subjectivity. Such postmodernists have begun struggling with perhaps the most basic contradiction in their worldview: they maintain that only difference, multiplicity, and centerlessness are valid and valuable—while the theoretical justification for that conclusion is their "totalizing narrative" that ironically condemns all "socially produced discourses" for imposing an invented commonality of values. A few deconstructive postmodernists themselves have admitted that free negotiation among multiple centers of interest needs an overarching principle, or, as they would say, a "valorized, universal" perspective. Should it be "justice" or "rights of self-determination" or some other "socially produced" construct? *Consider fundamental processes of the universe—differentiation, subjectivity, and communion—as guides for whether a "negotiation" impedes or enhances the great unfolding.*

Ihab Hassan sees the postmodern quest as an effort "to apprehend reality more immediately" and to struggle while at the same time "struggle to empty all struggle."[33] *Try Dhamma.*

Jean-François Lyotard and other postmodernists have urged a turning away from (doctrinaire, constricting) theory to narrative. *Look into native people's knowledge of the power of story to evoke and awaken possibilities. Examine without prejudice the power of sacred story in Goddess spirituality to strengthen simultaneously communion and subjectivity.*

Fredric Jameson is concerned that postmodernism lacks the means by which one could order him- or herself spatially in the newly globalized culture. *Try the bioregion.* He sees the problem for postmodern cultural theory to be the constructing of a "map" of the world from inside that world. *Try cosmological awareness* of the full effects of the emerging global influence of transnational corporations. Our current condition, he feels, is one of perceiving perpetual presence without depth.[34] *Try openness to the immense and profound processes in and around you.*

Chantal Mouffe argues that, rather than retain "abstract Enlightenment universalism," radical democracy should create and depend on new, "decentered subject-positions" that would create openness, indeterminacy, and ambiguity in the articulation of "intersubjective relationships."[35] *Try the ecological model: soft boundaries, diversity, adaptability, novelty—and interrelatedness.*

Steven Connor ends his admirable study *Postmodernist Culture* with the concern that postmodernism needs "new and more inclusive forms of ethical collectivity."[36] *Try awakening your sense of profound communion via the depth practices of any of the wisdom traditions.*

Spiritual practice, in short, leads to a more subtle and far more radical deconstruction of the received world of appearances than fixation on "social production." That mode of exploration might perhaps become of interest to those postmodernists who perceive the inadequacies of language as a function of our being awed witnesses of the "unpresentable," as Lyotard puts it, rather than viewing language simply as a "prison house" of oppressive games of textual play. In fact, traces of the inheritance from Kant and Nietzsche of the desire for (or "will to") the sublime, or the "aspiration towards the ineffable," can be found in the writings of such deconstructive postmodernists as Derrida, Lacan, Foucault, Kristeva, and Barthes, according to a study by Dick Hebdige.[37] Lyotard feels that, while postmodern art shares in common with modernist art the "gesturing" toward those things that lie beyond the possibility of representation, the latter "still allows pleasure in the capture of the sublime" while postmodern art goes further in imparting a stronger sense of the sublime by searching for new presentations.[38]

In the wisdom traditions there are ways to approach the inexpressible that are not language-bound or dependent on "gesturing" beyond form. Yet there is something far greater to consider regarding such paths: what is it about, say, the meditation practice taught by the Buddha, which strips away all constructions regarding the present moment, just as the courageous dimensions of postmodernism attempt to do, yet ends up in love and compassion? Moreover, is it sufficient to focus, as deconstruction does, on the "subject," or self, as unstable, in process, and "constituted" (I would prefer "affected") by the received language in interior monologue and exterior discourses? Or is it useful to attain some experiential sense of *how* consciousness, the body/mind, the "self," is continually formed by the arising and passing away of microevents? Dhamma, like deconstruction, reveals that we do indeed live in a state of "false linguistic confidence"—not because human reference beyond "social production" is impossible, but because language cannot express the flux that underlies the illusion of stasis.

A number of deconstructive postmodernists have condemned, exaggerated, and seemingly surrendered to the pernicious effects of ubiquitous advertising and mass media. While some see no solution, others now call for resistance. The practices of the wisdom traditions help us to nourish wonder and hence to appreciate difference, the unique subjectivity of every being and community, thereby subverting the flattening process of mass culture. Such awareness keeps hope alive. It protects consciousness from becoming so beaten down that it loses a grasp of what is worth fighting to defend.

I realize that many deconstructive postmodernists will rule that my suggestions of some common ground between their efforts and the perspectives of the wisdom traditions are thoroughly unacceptable. They will maintain that the internal logic of any communal system is always oppressive. One can cling to a belief that holism is merely an empty "narrative" or open him- or herself to the immensities of life and consider the possibility that perhaps the millions of people in thousands of cultures over the years who have perceived life in this way were, after all, grounded in the cosmological processes. Perhaps a theory that denies those larger processes is the empty narrative.

It seems to me that many deconstructive postmodernists might now be willing to consider holistic perspectives that lead not to closed systems and tamed responses but to open-ended, unpredictable evocation of cosmological powers of creativity in and through the person. Perhaps some attention might be focused as well on skillful means, to consider whether the inadequacies of language require "deconstructive violence" and whether the "false constructs that constitute subjectivity" require harsh "neutralization" so that "unconditionality" can flourish. A depth practice within the wisdom traditions reveals other ways.

States of Grace in States of Grace

Ours is an age of fading utopian dreams and looming dystopian nightmares. State socialism yielded deprivation and totalitarian controls. "Free" enterprise has allowed huge concentrations of wealth and the dominance by large corporations, while communities and individuals have been victimized in recent years by abandonment to "offshore operations" and destructive kinds of development. Under both systems the Earth community has been brutalized by the cult of industrialism, which requires enormous sacrificial offerings to sustain unqualified industrial growth and is still supported, with minor quibbles, by our large institutions, not only corporations but also government agencies, academia, and the media. The Earth cannot sustain the current rates of destruction, yet the plan for the immediate future is to increase them, especially in the Third World, through the machinations of the "global market."

The sense that we are living through a time of great loss is pervasive. We hear about astounding rates of species loss and habitat loss; sometimes we see and feel it around us. Community and family ties have been weakened. The entire stream of human culture—the adult world of history, politics, economics, religion, literature, and the arts that I so longed to join as I was growing up—has been reduced for most of our young people to the two-dimensional, extremely limited stream of images that appear and disappear on the television screen, often encouraging a cultural proclivity for indifference and violence. Children today play less in nature and more at video games. Even reading, it seems, is being lost to many. College instructors note that many students do not seem to know how to reason morally, to guide themselves with such considerations as honesty, integrity, and responsibility. Adults are concerned about the shallow engagement with the world that so many of our youth exhibit, but the problem is more widespread, as potentially involved adult citizens have been transformed into passive receivers of several hours of corporate-directed television programming every day.[39]

A few months after the collapse of state socialism in Central Europe, the Polish theorist Adam Michnik wrote in an American newsmagazine, "A striking characteristic of the totalitarian system is its peculiar coupling of human demoralization and mass depoliticizing."[40] That sounded awfully familiar. In our country half of the people do not vote, teachers complain that parents are apathetic about their children's education, and community involvement is unusual. In spite of all the significant differences between life under a Marxist-Leninist government and a democratic one, I wonder if the survivors of state socialism realize that passive detachment among citizens is the desired goal of the modern state whether it is the long arm of a centralized government or the corporate culture reaching into the inner landscape of the individual.

For the past couple of years, national pollsters have found that the portion of the American public who say they favor stronger controls and more action to protect and restore the environment hovers around 79 percent. Yet we do not witness 79 percent of the public entering citizens' environmental organizations that prod the government to take appropriate measures. Such organizations have learned to distinguish the uninformed citizen from the uncaring citizen. The latter are so numerous because the progressive stages of modern "liberation" from supposedly backward clan, community, and Earth ties have atomized society to the extent that many people feel almost no connection to the existing Earth community or to posterity. I have marveled at executives of chemical corporations insisting (successfully!) to the U.S. government that millions more tons of ozone-depleting chlorofluorocarbons should be produced during the coming decade—even though their own grandchildren will be at increased risk for skin cancer along with everyone else. Surely theirs is a pathological response. I believe there is so much steadfast refusal to "be bothered" by the ecological crises not because of a "death wish" inherent in the human psyche but because so many profoundly unconnected modern individuals privately feel that the ecosystems will hold together for at least thirty, forty, or fifty more years—until they get out of this beleaguered place.

The quality of life for hundreds of thousands of communities across the country and the ecosystems in which they are embedded are currently under assault by developers and complicit local governments who cling to the orientation that growth is always good.[41] The inertia of growth at any cost to the public good is still a powerful force in our land. A similar kind of thinking at the international level seems determined to turn the whole world into a "company town" run by the transnational corporations.[42] From many perspectives, it appears that a strong communitarian ethic is the most sensible antidote to the modern state.

The third-way, communitarian option eschews both the sacrifice of community to an atomized society of competing "free" enterprisers (in which the huge concentrations of wealth and power render most people's possibilities far from free) and the sacrifice of the individual to a communist regime of totalitarian controls for "the good of all." Communitarian economics encourages regional economies, employee ownership, mostly local and regional circulation of capital, and a variety of cooperative ventures. Communitarian government includes citizen participation in decision making, open processes of governing, and full accountability of elected officials.

Tracing a partial family tree of third-way, communitarian advocates, Theodore Roszak suggests in *Person/Planet* that the transcendent delight in the creative possibilities of human fellowship and the sense of a politics grounded in self-discovery make the communitarian tradition inherently spiritual, in spite of some blustery railing against religion by certain of its philosophers.[43] One might also note that this tradition has not

always displayed skillful means, including nonviolence; that many expressions of its ideals have been patriarchal; or that its premodern aspects must be combined with subsequent possibilities. In fact, these considerations, and others as well, are part of the contemporary development of the communitarian ethic in such grassroots expressions as Green politics, ecofeminism, bioregionalism, steady-state and community-based economics, and community opposition to nuclear arms, toxic environments, economic displacements, and social injustice. Far more than mere localism, this weave of movements recognizes the need for coordinated protection of the oceans and the biosphere, as well as indigenous and Third-World peoples.

The wealth of creative ideas about particular issues approached from an ecological-communitarian, or Green, perspective is impressive and continues to grow as a clear challenge to the forces of concentrated economic control, ecological destruction, and the nuclearized security state. In addition, the numerous single-issue, grassroots victories in communities nationwide are encouraging. Yet the comprehensive transformation of culture, politics, and economics that such a challenge requires is slow in coming, especially in our country. Perhaps too many people have been "liberated" beyond caring by the insular values of modernity, too many others care but feel that engagement in social-change work is a waste of time, too many others are daunted by the scope of the crises, and too many others are consumed by a daily struggle to make ends meet. Perhaps the problem is simply that the proper "linkage organizing" among groups has yet to be done. Even among the earnestly committed, however, it sometimes seems that people are holding back, as if this were merely a dress rehearsal for crises threatening the person, society, and the entire Earth community.

The most gripping wake-up call I ever heard concerning the role of the individual in these perilous times came not from any theorist but from an activist, one with roots in her community in central Mississippi. A few years ago I was invited to participate in a weekend conference sponsored by the Mississippi 2020 Network, a group dedicated to analyzing the fate of their state and seeking creative alternatives to destructive courses of action. At the close of the conference, an "open mike" session allowed participants to express their thoughts. Following the first few speakers, an African-American woman of substantial form and poise walked on stage and told of her response to a workshop on cosmological awareness that had been led by Sister Miriam Therese MacGillis.[44] She said that she now understood herself to be a unique expression of the magnificent unfolding of the universe and that it would have been incomplete without her. She said she realized that her own special being was part of the life of the Earth and that the story of the Earth's being is also the truth of her being. She told us that when people think about the Earth community, they are the Earth thinking about itself. She made it clear that each of us can spend our life paying attention to the Earth's unfolding story and taking care of its ways or failing to do so. She spoke with great enthusiasm and love.

When she finished, the audience sat silently, still embraced by the moment of grace that had just ended and perched in suspension on the rim of the return to the mundane. Then a long round of applause began, after which the stream of speakers continued their progression to the microphone. I, however, sat nearly catatonic, so moved by her presence. What arose in my mind was "There it is!" I had wondered for years about ways in which the new awakening might be expressed so as to spark political engagement. I was reminded of my mother's experience as a young woman when she had stood on a crowded platform in Cleveland's railway terminal to hear President Franklin D. Roosevelt deliver a campaign speech from the back of a train: "He made you feel you were really part of something very important!" I thought of the frequently reported response to Dr. Martin Luther King, Jr., from African-American veterans of the civil-rights movement: "He made everybody feel like a Somebody." This Mississippi woman had sidestepped the charisma of temporal leaders and drawn her meaning, importance, and political strength from the Earth community itself. She inspired all of us to live our lives as a calling, a meaningful response to our larger self and the grandeur of the ongoing story.

The ecologizing of consciousness is far more radical than ideologues and strategists of the existing political forms, including the received communitarian model, seem to have realized. They often try to tack ecology onto programs born of instrumental rationality, scientistic reductionism, and the modern belief that further advances in the manipulation of nature for human ends will deliver a future filled with peace, freedom, and goodwill. It seems quite unlikely that political versions of democracy that are steeped in those values of modernity that have proven so deficient can serve as the vehicles of transformation to carry humans into a new relationship with the entire Earth community and our own potential. It is already clear that visionary political developments lag behind the ecological and spiritual awakening. Increasingly, moral authority resides less in official position than in wisdom, in an experiential sense of the interrelated nature of our reality. A widely respected head of state, Vaclav Havel, observed in his address to the U.S. Congress in 1990 that "we are still under the sway of the destructive and vain belief that man is the pinnacle of creation and not just a part of it" and that we still do not know how to put a morality that includes "responsibility to something higher than my family, my country, my company, my success" ahead of politics, science, and economics.[45] No political model will win popular support if it aims to shape a brave new world by dragging along all the broken processes rent by the cult of modernity—ecology, spirituality, community, family, and self-in-nature—to fit in as best they can. Rather, a new politics, economics, education, medicine, and culture that are responsive to the healing and empowering ecospiritual awakening will be integral with it.

We are living through a time of great discontinuity in the Earth processes, social processes, and personal processes, yet we have deep pools of resources from which to draw guidance for our courage and creativity. When we embody the core teachings of the wisdom traditions, we are eased from mental anguish to inner balance, from debilitating exile to the embrace of the Earth community, from denial of the body to the ecology of the erotic, and from dread or indifference toward "the Other" to active love. These four effects of practices in the wisdom traditions are not fixed goals of a radical transformation beyond the constrictions of modernity; they are fruits of *processes* that can help us develop new modes of enhancing differentiation, subjectivity, and communion in the Earth community.

What chance have we to heal ourselves and move beyond the constrictive parameters and broken processes of modernity unless we can find practical ways to ease mental agitation, recognize kinship with nature, honor the body, and cherish justice and community? We may find ways entirely different from the practice taught by the Buddha, but we know that the human family need never settle for less than the benefits Dhamma yields in the task of diminishing fear, hatred, greed, and delusion. Hence we need not be defeated by the misconception that inherent egotism is a fixed human trait and will always erode and finally destroy efforts to create a better world. Similarly, as we seek to renew a sense of deep connectedness with the rest of the natural world, the native peoples' intimate relationship with the cosmological processes shows us what is possible. As we seek paths beyond the patriarchal constriction of the body, the depth of ritual experience in Goddess circles shows us that our search can be grounded in the Earthbody itself. As we seek ways to address the oppression of those rendered vulnerable in this world, the core teachings of the Semitic traditions remind us that the great communion is enhanced by conditions of justice and righteousness and is violated by their absence.

The wisdom traditions can be appreciated for their respective benefits, but also for their potential to bring to a multicultural dialogue about significant issues and ideas a depth of understanding that has been denied by the boundaries of modernity. I believe that ecological postmodernism—the cultural passage beyond the failed aspects of modernity—might itself become a wisdom tradition, contributing to that dialogue the fruits of in-depth exploration of process in various areas. Twentieth-century religious philosophers as disparate as Alfred North Whitehead and Mary Daly have concluded that the divine is more accurately considered as process, as the verb "becoming," than as a noun. All the wisdom traditions address processes of relation and interaction of some sort, but their valuable insights have not exhausted the manifestations of ultimate mystery. The Eurocentric focus on substance, form, and surface observations of motion suppressed attention to subtle process as long as possible—until the shocking advent of postmodern physics and quantum mechanics. We are only now beginning to grasp many of the subtle processes of the body, such as the dynamics of "brain" receptors on white blood cells. Our hospitals have only recently learned that infants who are not touched and held later suffer impaired development. We are largely ignorant of the processes that cause markedly increased rates of depression, mental hospitalization, terminal cancer, and other premature death among people who are socially isolated. We cannot explain why studies find that life expectancy often is extended among people who participate regularly in volunteer work. We have only a rudimentary sense of the subtle effects of group process. We have hardly begun to incorporate attention to processes of epistemology in science and the humanities. Perhaps ecological postmodernism will illuminate the play of intersubjectivity, chaos and pattern, systemic dynamics, and multivalent meaning in ways as yet undreamed of. Perhaps its practice will include the new forms of nonviolence that Gandhi predicted. Perhaps it will help to heal our culture of truncated perceptions that block love.

In the work now required of us, both the immediate and the long-term, a seeming flood of pressing needs demands attention—recognizing our kinship with the Earth community and acting to protect it, nurturing and protecting that which cannot be commodified, and replacing politics of denial with a renewal of coherence based on wisdom and compassion. In reflecting on the insight, commitment, and joy that the wisdom traditions can yield in the tasks we face, I experience once again the habit of gratitude that seems to accompany spiritual practice. Gratitude arises for all the people working from various directions to give birth to ecological postmodernity—the holistic scientists, the communitarian grassroots activists, the process philosophers, the visionary artists, and, yes, all those deconstructive postmodernists who warn us of the shortcomings of human systems of knowledge yet search for engagement with the ineffable. Gratitude arises for all the Jews, Christians, and Muslims who now and in the past have challenged institutional failures to enhance the great communion and who have courageously acted to shape their traditions by advancing justice and love. Gratitude arises for all people who now and in the past have kept alive a sense of the Goddess—through the images in village women's crafts, through preservation in the face of historic persecution, through the rebirth of ritual arts of the Earthbody and the personal body. Gratitude arises for the steadfast guardianship of native peoples, preserving their sacred trust with the Earth community even through centuries of forced assimilation, exploitation, and genocide. Gratitude arises for the Buddha and all true teachers of Dhamma, gently spreading release from anguish and ill will.

Gratitude arises for their bounteous gifts of grace and for the possibilities before us.

Appendixes

Appendix A

The Merely Relative: A Brief Survey of Deconstructive Postmodernism

The various manifestations of deconstructive-postmodern thought and their popularity are emblematic of our anxious transition beyond the failed certainties of objectivist modernity. Deconstructionists courageously proclaim that the emperor's new clothes—the grand belief systems, or "metanarratives," of modernity—are illusory and were "socially produced" to exert diffuse means of control. Hence what most people mistake for valid apprehensions of reality, they maintain, are nothing more than received cultural constructions. In making this partial truth the focus of their genuine quest for freedom, many deconstructive postmodernists find themselves in the paradoxical situation of championing "difference, multiplicity, and centerlessness" via a theory that is itself "totalizing" because it dismisses all other perceptions of reality. Linguistic and philosophical deconstructionism; social deconstructionism; postmodern feminism; the postmodern mood in architecture, literature, and the visual arts; the Santiago theory of cognition; radical constructivist psychology; and certain applications of general systems theory and cybernetics have all contributed to a worldview of extreme relativism and a cultural posture of "savvy" disengagement. Far from escaping the atomized, alienated sensibility of modernity, the new relativism intensifies it.

A cursory survey must begin with the philosopher Jacques Derrida's perception known as deconstruction. In building on the structural theory of language proposed by Ferdinand de Saussure—that meaning is produced by the difference between "signifiers" (words, which have an arbitrary but fixed connection with the "signified") in the "language chain"—Derrida maintains that every word is divided into a phonic "signifier" and a mental "signified" and that language is a system of *différance* (from the verb meaning both to differ and to defer) between those two phenomena, not a system of independently meaningful units. His term for what he perceives as the fallacy of the self-presentation of meaning or "presence" is *logocentrism,* which represses the "lag" of *différance* inherent in the act of using phonic "signifiers" (words) to express mental "signifieds" (ideas, concepts, perceptions, or emotions). Moreover, Derrida denies that "signifiers" can have any fixed meaning since the meaning of a word or concept occurs only in a specific context ("textual location") every time it is used. We, of course, can never know the precise mental context in which a writer used a word, but her or his intention is not important anyway, according to Derrida, since all language is merely self-referential, a chain of signifiers referring to other signifiers so that language is always indeterminate. Hence, he concludes, meaning and consciousness do not exist outside language; all meaning is temporary and relative; and there can be no central, original, or transcendental signifier (for example, God, History, Man, Reason) outside the invented language system of differences, which determine our only possible means of thought.[1]

While deconstruction has been critiqued by a growing chorus of linguists, philosophers, and literary critics,[2] it has attracted a large following in Europe and the United States, for reasons I shall suggest later. Its supporters seem to overlook the fact that there is no room in this rigidly language-based theory of human existence for all the kinds of experiences that are not "repressed" into total denial simply because they do not fit well into our interior monologue of language when we attempt to label them or reflect on them—a child's quirky, magical perception of the world; spiritual experience; the orgasmic state; substance-induced altered states of consciousness; the artistic process; and *feelings*. We realize that we approximate such experience with language, in our interior monologue and elsewhere, but we know that those experiences are other than language can relate. The experiences themselves have a presence far stronger than the emphasis given by deconstructionists to the "difference," "gap," "lag," or "interval" between words and the partially described phenomena.

In the social sciences and some arenas of social-change activism, one encounters social deconstructionism (sometimes called "constructionism" or "constructivism," as it focuses attention on the ways in which worldviews are constructed). Social, or cultural, deconstruction seeks to reveal the "social production" of all meaning, constructs, and "objectivity." The central focus of social deconstruction is a "suspicion of metanarratives," as Jean-François Lyotard puts it. This analysis rarely goes so far, however, as to assert that no meaning is ever possible anyway since language is just the self-referential play of indeterminate signifiers, as Derrida's deconstruction would have it. Still, the belief that all assertions of truth, or even relevance, are merely "socially produced" means that no analysis or conclusion can be accepted beyond being "enormously suggestive." All systems of knowledge are perceived as operating with an internal logic that cannot be legitimated outside the particular system or orientation. Moreover, many deconstructionists maintain that one must continually "recontextualize" one's own perceptions—that is, resist interpretation via a particular worldview—in order to escape any "totalizing" concepts. (Yet deconstructive postmodernism's "antiworldview" of denial functions as an informing worldview for adherents. Their cry of "No more worldviews!" is based on an intensely held set of presuppositions about life.)[3]

Seen through the lens of social deconstruction, which draws heavily on the work of Michel Foucault, a cultural historian (or "archaeologist of knowledge," as he preferred),[4] *all* interactions are expressions of power relations. Foucault contributed valuable studies on the relationship between rationalization and political power, but if the diffuse exercise of power is the "new" focus of attention, it is curious that social-deconstructionist authors, who are often tenured professors, ignore earlier expressions of similar analyses by marginalized groups. For example, a recent, typical article on social deconstruction in a social-change journal, written by a law professor, presents the "revolutionary" insight that so-called pure reason is a social construction that has been used to exclude "voices that have been diminished as 'primitive' or 'passionate' or 'emotional' in the march of 'enlightenment' and 'progress.'"[5] Is this supposed to be news to cultural/radical-feminist, African-American, or Native American activists? We have been saying just that for decades, independent of what was being cooked up in Paris; in addition, the counterculture had made the same critique. Still, one has to appreciate the fact that social deconstruction has worked wonders in deflating ideological arrogance born of those theories now rejected as "totalizing" and hence oppressive, thereby transforming countless dogmatic Marxists, for instance, into rather open-minded post-Marxists. Of course, many veteran activists with a preference for actually effecting *change* are cool to the passivity that can logically follow from "the death of the subject," the postmodern view of the self as merely a site of conflicting "discourses" (systems of knowledge), all predetermined by social construction and none participating in any overarching truth. Even the deconstructionists' championing of "diffuse centers of power" is difficult to translate into political strength if all principles, such as economic democracy or ecological wisdom, are disallowed as "totalizing."

Postmodern feminism seeks to protect women from "metanarratives," which, it maintains, are always oppressive to the individual. Toward that end, commonsense warnings that white, middle-class feminists must be careful not to project our experience onto women of color and working-class women have now been transformed into deconstructionist assertions that feminism can be *nothing but* "a politics of difference." (Beyond the realm of theory, of course, commonalities, often quirky and unpredictable, become apparent whenever women of color and white women—whenever *persons*—actually work together over time on shared goals.) To speak of any commonality among women is to commit the deconstructive-postmodern sin of "essentialism," the "failure" to perceive that every single aspect of human existence is supposedly "socially produced" and determined in particular, localized circumstances about which no generalizations can be made. Hence some white postmodernist-feminist academics criticize their African-American peers for speaking of "the African-American experience," which postmodernists judge a false commonality, and they are skeptical of the very concept of gender-based analysis in feminist theory.[6] Even to speak of common dynamics involving women in cultures that are patriarchal is rejected as "totalizing." Some postmodern French feminists are adamant in insisting that naming the political subject of feminism *the female sex* reproduces the biological essentialism and the binary logic that have relegated women to an inferior role.[7] Their acceptance of the patriarchal formula that "necessarily" ranks the biological female as inferior unfortunately reflects the influence of the postmodern psychoanalyst Jacques Lacan and the legacy of Simone de Beauvoir's assimilation of so much of Sartre's expressed revulsion toward the "immanence" of the female body and his preference for "masculine" transcendence via projects of rationalist consciousness.

That deconstructive postmodernism disallows speaking of commonalities renders much analysis and activist theory impossible, a conservative aspect that has been addressed by a number of political deconstructionist feminists who seek a modified version suitable for activists.[8] Even more promising is the movement of some deconstructive-postmodern, post-Marxist feminists toward ecofeminism because they have come to appreciate its view of the world "as active subject, not as resource" and its linking of "meaning and bodies," which was inherited from cultural feminism.[9] Certainly the somewhat amazing insistence by some feminists that race and class each have a "material base" that gender lacks can be seen as participation in the patriarchal and postmodern project of "erasure" and denial of the elemental power of the female body. No matter what kinds of "social production" shape gender within a culture, the physicality of the female body with its elemental capabilities (to grow people of either sex from one's flesh, to bleed in rhythm with the moon, to transform food into milk for infants) is a core reality to which culture *responds,* usually with considerable elaboration, in negative or positive modes.

Deconstructive-postmodern aesthetics features a sense of detachment, displacement, and shallow engagement. Postmodern literature in particular has been characterized by such practitioners as John Barth and Umberto Eco as using traditional forms in ironic or displaced ways to treat perennial themes.[10] Two derivative genres, minimalist fiction and "video novels" (written by "the TV generation"), shift the focus of displacement to a fascination with flatness of perception and characters bound in a passionless, hopeless, nihilistic existence. One critic asserted that the characters in such "antiseptic novels" are "insanely oblivious to what's going on around them."[11] Other critics have celebrated the "cool language and cool surfaces" of television-influenced literature as "the aesthetic of a new age."[12] In a muscular defense of minimalist fiction, Frederick Barthelme maintained that flat valuelessness (for example, perceiving the stench of a refinery as merely "interesting" rather than destructive) is the only justifiable art, since social context, or cultural history, is merely "the shifty thumbnail sketch, docudrama, the primary apparent use of which is self-defense—it's a kind of high-tone P.R.," just someone's lineup of selected facts, hence bearing no weight.[13] (Do deconstructive postmodernists, I have always wondered, dare to "run this rap by" survivors of the Holocaust, pogroms, slavery, the Armenian genocide, the Pol Pot terror, the ruin of native cultures?)

Postmodern architecture claims to have "a complex relation to the past, or pluralism,"[14] but that theory did not translate well into practice. Neoclassical postmodern architecture, which became the most prevalent version of the genre, exhibits the very flattening that disallows complexity. Reaching back into history and plucking out classical forms as if from a consumer catalogue and affixing them to the roof or doorway of an urban skyscraper reflects a self-absorbed dismissal of the context and meaning of the earlier forms in their own culture. But, then, if history can never mean more to deconstructive postmodernists than the self-serving selection of facts by one group or another, limited "complexity" of ironic, superficial engagement is the logical outcome.

Postmodernism in the visual arts was extremely influential in the 1980s. As in architecture, it often features earlier cultural emblems detached from their context and juxtaposed to create an aggregate present. This approach is an act of bravura imposture designed not to heighten but to buffer engagement with experience.[15] In various media the deconstructive-postmodern focus is often authority, how to command attention and dominate others.[16] Frequently, postmodern painting and photography have shown a fascination with slick consumer art: since all meaning is tediously relative and manipulated by mass culture, why not devote one's attention to bold, aggressive art that claims no meaning beyond the demands of mass media and advertising? In that way one can demonstrate awareness of the "totalizing" processes of manipulation, but do so with ironic detachment.[17]

The extreme groundlessness so central to deconstructive-postmodern thought is also found in the "Santiago theory of cognition," recently constructed by Humberto Maturana and Francisco Varela, two Chilean neurobiologists.[18] They hold that "nature, the world, society, science, religion, the physical space, atoms, molecules, trees . . . only exist as a bubble of human actions floating on nothing."[19] They posit that our nervous systems are operationally closed and that meaning is attributed to perturbations in our environs only through "languaging," by which they mean "the consensual coordination between people's individual consensual coordinations of distinctions or actions."[20] Hence, they maintain that objects do not pre-exist language.[21] This theory has been critiqued as "neuro-idealism."[22] A less extreme but related worldview is found in radical constructivism, a school of thought in cognitive psychology that does not deny a physical reality, but asserts that no such reality can ever be known because the world we experience is merely our own ordering and organization of selected stimuli, that is, our own "cognitive creation."[23]

One can also consider general systems theory and cybernetics as contributors to the deconstructive-postmodern mood, not because they doubt the existence of objective "information" (indeed, it is their mainstay), but because of the flattening that can result when human behavior is "mapped" in their schemata.[24] After describing the interactive principles of process expressed in general systems theory, which are quite interesting in many respects, enthusiasts sometimes declare triumphantly that it is "no longer possible to locate evil," since primitive perceptions of one-way causality have been replaced by the more sophisticated systems view of power as feedback, correction, homeostasis, and so forth. Perhaps—but a hypothetical Third-World woman, for instance, can rather easily point to two seats of power that radically limit her "free" choice of "feedback": the nearby exploitative plantation owner, who operates in partnership with a transnational corporation, and her husband, who may beat her or otherwise enforce his dominance over her body and her choices.

The problem of addressing power relations is particularly apparent in the derivation from general systems theory known as "family systems therapy." This mode of analysis often treats wife-battering as merely one component charted on a circular map of interactive loops, a component that is perceived to have equal weight with such abstractions as "lack of individuation," "sex role polarization," and so forth. As a few feminist therapists have noted critically, regarding violence as anything other than provoked "feedback" (rather than, say, a vicious control mechanism that seeks the slightest excuse for display and discipline) or observing that unequal power distribution in a dysfunctional family may be structured by gender "offends the systemic aesthetic."[25]

Among all the varieties of deconstructive postmodernism, groundlessness is a constant. Whether the postmodernist experiences life as the solipsistic creator of "the world" (via "neuro-idealism" or constructivist psychology) or as a diffused pseudoself (via social deconstruction), meaning is considered quite arbitrary and ethics is extremely problematic. There are, of course, well-intentioned deconstructive-postmodern declarations of a new ethics born of total freedom, but a corresponding focus on active caring and concern does not often manifest after such grand claims. One deconstructive postmodernist who tried to avoid what she sees as "the apolitical nihilism that so frequently seems to follow the postmodern undermining of the foundations of modernity" argued for a sense of "the self in community," yet could arrive only at the conclusion that such an orientation "would allow us to be responsible while acknowledging that there is nothing beyond ourselves to be responsible to."[26]

Perhaps the contemporary experiencing of relationship, of all sorts, as tenuous and arbitrary lies at the heart of the popularity of deconstructive-postmodern sensibilities. When a speaker at a recent academic conference on historical treatments of fascism was challenged on his Foucauldian observation that power is now so dispersed (even atoms against atoms!) that it makes no sense to speak of Third-World or gender or class power, his painfully honest justification, after a moment's silence, was that perceptions of breakdown and alienation seem right since our era lives with the breakdown of the family. Others have suggested that the seven hours of television per day in the average American household have accustomed people to news and information without context and to a flat relativeness.[27] A neo-Marxist analyst insists that postmodernism is simply the logic of "late capitalism" with its "decentered" global network of transnational corporations.[28] Some have noted that French intellectuals, in particular, embraced deconstructive postmodernism so enthusiastically because of their traumatic experiences of being psychologically "decentered" by the Nazis, the Vietnamese, and the Algerians. (One might add that the French would perhaps be more inclined than other peoples to view language as a "prison house," as Derrida calls it, since the French language is tightly controlled by the rulings of the French Academy.) The disproportionate number of newly minted college graduates among deconstructive postmodernists is probably due to their recent exposure to deconstructionist professors, their rejection of the "failures" of the sixties, and the desires of youth to be iconoclastic. Especially appealing would be a bold rejection that outdoes the partial rejections of every past young generation: the denial of meaning itself!

All these somewhat plausible yet peripheral explanations are embedded in a much larger event and have roots deep in the cultural history of the West. Foucault's postmodern notion (after Nietzsche) that we can trace the genealogy of a body of knowledge, that is, the construction of concepts, can be applied to deconstructive postmodernism itself. Since it is indeed "situated" in a particular mode of thinking, we would do well to be aware of its long evolution (see Appendix B). It is there we find the reason that postmodernism seizes on denial as its path to authority.

Such denial of meaning, connectedness, and embodiment can elicit exasperation certainly, but also an aching too deep for language to shape. After listening to a panel of deconstructionists hold forth on women and art, an artist friend of mine told me that she walked directly home, growing increasingly furious, went straight to a mound of clay in her studio, and found herself shaping a number of female bodies. The lines were crude, hurried. The affirmation was fierce.

Another friend, a professor of anthropology and women's studies in Ohio, was surrounded for a time by particularly aggressive deconstructionists. One day she picked up her young niece without much advance notice and drove far out of town to a woods, to a stream, to a muddy shore where they dug their toes into the cool ooze, silently going deeper. She felt she literally had to stay grounded to survive.

More often, exasperated responses to postmodern absolutism are articulated with language, yet one still finds an insistence on basics. Reviewing a book on deconstructionist philosophy that claims that socialization "goes all the way down" and that the best we can do is play within the confines of imaginative "liberal irony," a British philosopher, Jenny Teichman, recently wrote:

> The creative, ethnography-reading imagination tells us, surely, that these dogmas represent nothing more or less than the tribal mores of teen-age human males. As such they can be explained in terms of the evolutionary history of the human race, just as the temporary "loner" behavior of the adolescent male lion can be explained in terms of the evolutionary history of lions. Why do philosophers elevate the temporary instinctual behavior patterns of the human male teen-ager into (allegedly) self-evident truths? The creative imagination readily suggests an answer, but it is not a very polite one.[29]

Less politely English but equally unamused is the response from defenders of the political modernism that has roots in Marx and Nietzsche. The "modern nihilism" these people advocate is merely a temporary stage in the dialectical struggle, not a total and permanent denial of meaning, they insist. The mode of transformation that so delights in continually smashing, degrading, and annihilating the old—guided by the "invisible hand" of macho values—in order to proclaim and enforce the new is thwarted by the deconstructionists' cool dismissal that "there is nothing outside the text," as Derrida puts it, to smash.[30]

A more profound complaint than the loss of the sport of smashing is the denial of very real dynamics of suffering that deconstructive-postmodern logic often demands. As various manifestations of Foucault's deconstructionist conclusion that "there is nothing to analyze"[31] have appeared in arenas of social change, many activists have rejected the new posture with frustrated appeals to basics, such as the obvious rightness of acting to save the planet, defend human rights, and challenge exploitation.

These sorts of pleas for a "reality check" are of great concern to many postmodernists but cut no ice with others, who may agree to the need for social-change activism but reduce it to a slightly ridiculous charade. In the end, many deconstructionists maintain, one can merely act *as if* one embraced "universal narratives" such as justice, compassion, and the dignity of the individual. Deconstructive postmodernists who consider such a "charade" too unbearable a compromise act out, instead, the postmodern rallying cry of Jean Baudrillard: "We must conquer the world and seduce it through an indifference that is at least equal to the world's." Anything less, they feel, would mean succumbing to one sort or another of "uncritically accepted metaphysics."

Appendix B

A Feminist Consideration of the Philosophical Roots and Attractions of Deconstructive Postmodernism

Deconstructive postmodernism prides itself on the bold novelty of its insights about the contemporary condition, but many of its thematic concerns and conclusions have always been central to patriarchal philosophy and culture. The objects of its denial fall into familiar patterns. It is possible to trace the politics of separateness, reactive autonomy (from relationship), and control (often via abstraction) through Western cultural history to its current manifestation in deconstructive postmodernism. From that perspective, certain of the "heroic" declarations of deconstructive postmodernism, which I examine in Chapters Four and Six as well as the appendixes, constitute yet another swing of a rather tedious pendulum motion—this time from patriarchal modes of control to patriarchal notions of autonomy.

Since the Neolithic age, the European cultures, which have influenced the entire world from the colonial era onward, have turned away from the organicism of felt connections between humans and the rest of nature, a worldview that honored the bountiful dynamics of the natural world as the female processes of periodicity and procreation writ large. After the establishment of patriarchal chieftian systems in which warrior cults were central, the Earth was desacralized in favor of a sky-god, and female sexuality, like the larger forces of nature, came to be regarded by men as potentially chaotic, engulfing, and devouring.

Once that kind of acculturation cuts off males from the mother/female and nature, they must address the vulnerability of unconnectedness. If everyone is a discrete, unconnected human being, then competitive self-preservation is a logical response since it is likely that other people's desires will eventually impinge on one's own. Hence protective autonomy—especially from women and nature, but also from other men—becomes an existential ideal for males. Unlimited freedom for every male, though, would lead to dangerous, possibly chaotic bullying by some, so controlling as many of the unconnected, discrete, competitive beings as possible becomes a second ideal. Moreover, when the mother/female and nature are viewed with resentment and fear, the male must invent himself as extremely different from the dreaded Other. Because of this reactive mode, male-dominated, patriarchal culture is never authentically "male"; rather, the core obsession of men under such socialization is to be "not-female" and "not-nature." Endless social constructs of "femininity" and "masculinity" are created to serve this need. (Fortunately, a large portion of the men's movement focuses on contacting and cultivating positive male energy, presence, and power that is not contorted by the reactive demands of patriarchal culture.)

The major shifts in Eurocentric history are often characterized by a tediously narrow range of motivation: rather than a dynamic spiraling of increasingly subtle and sophisticated understanding of organic, interconnected realities through various eras, we usually see the alternating embrace of two poles of the worldview of separateness—a new burst of reactive (male) autonomy or a new mode of control. This reactive type of autonomy is a defensive response to culturally induced fear of the mother/female, nature, and other men as competitors. It is a diseased imitation of the type of self-definition, freedom, and creativity that can unfold within an individual whose society encourages him to recognize the web of organic interconnectedness and relatedness.

Both reactive autonomy and reactive control share in common a subtheme of reinvigorating a patriarchal vigilance: society should be run by those whose behavior emphatically proves them "not-nature" and "not-female." While no single set of dynamics can explain the entire complexity of historical development, denying the influence of this particular orientation yields a sense of history that is decidedly lacking.

Even when alternative ways of thinking have been introduced, they usually have been crushed, marginalized, or corrupted into yet another form of control. Some of the most organic and holistic thinkers sadly capitulated to the strong influence of patriarchal socialization such that their prescriptive worldviews take a surprising turn into the comfort of a patriarchal hierarchy controlling that ever-looming chaos. Examples are Heraclitus's preference for monarchy over democracy, Spinoza's ideal of democracy run by men who own property, Hegel's admiration of the Prussian state as the ideal manifestation of the informing World-spirit, and Heidegger's support of the Nazis.

The patriarchal model of the autonomous warriorlike hero is a pervasive figure in Western culture—from Odysseus to Saint George, from Hitler to Ronald Reagan, from the western gunslinger to the corporate takeover heavy. The cult of the warrior-hero was introduced into Europe in the Neolithic age by invading nomadic tribes, the "Kurgans," horse-riding Indo-Europeans, who, probably for climatic reasons, migrated from the Eurasian steppes west into east-central Europe (entering the Danubian basin initially), south into the Near and Middle East, southeast into Pakistan and India, and east toward Mongolia.[1] The Indo-European migrations into Europe were concentrated in three waves: c. 4400–4300 B.C., c. 3400–3200 B.C., and c. 3000–2900 B.C. Archaeological excavations of the agricultural settlements of Old Europe, that is, Europe prior to the Indo-European presence, have revealed no evidence of warfare such as caches of weapons, concentrations of skeletons all killed by battle wounds at the same time, or extensive fortification of hilltop settlements.

After the migrations, hill forts became common and the patterns of burial changed dramatically: whereas pre-Indo-European graves were roughly egalitarian between the sexes (females having somewhat more burial artifacts, but age being the major determinant), the Indo-European gravesites (barrows) reflect a patriarchal chieftain system. A number of the Kurgan barrows indicate the sacrifice of women, men children, and animals to accompany a wealthy male.

The Indo-European pastoralists exulted in the making of daggers, swords, and shields, rather than pottery or sculpture. They had one main symbol, the sun, which was usually impressed with a primitive stamping technique, but sometimes they also used a fir tree. Old European artifacts, in contrast, were richly symbolic of cosmogony, generation, regeneration, the Goddess and minor gods, and sacred animals, as well as sculptures of half-animal and half-human forms. The upheaval of Old European civilization is registered in the archaeological record by the abrupt cessation of painted pottery and figurines, the disappearance of shrines, the termination of their symbols and signs, the abolition of matrifocal and matrilineal culture, and the annihilation or co-optation of the Goddess religion.[2] Old European culture survived for nearly two millennia longer on the Aegean islands and nearby Malta. North of the Aegean, however, the Bronze Age cultures, such as the Mycenaean in Greece and the Celtic in the Rhineland, France, and the British Isles, were an amalgam of the Old European substrate and the elements that had been imposed on Europe by the patriarchal clans from the Russian steppes. The Indo-European tribes introduced a religious cult centered on warrior-gods (the light-of-the-sky god, the thunderbolt god, and the god of death and the underworld) and the glorification of death in battle, as the hero is touched by the spear of the god of death.[3]

Cultural records, such as legends and myths lasting even into the classical era, tell of the indigenous women's resistance to the invaders in Greece, refusing to eat or sleep with them, for example. If the indigenous men also resisted, their campaign does not seem to have been as long-lived. What, one wonders, was the reaction of the men of Old Europe at the time the first wave of invading horsemen swept across the plains from the east? Did they say, "Thank *God* you guys have arrived; we've been waiting thirty thousand years!" Or did they challenge the invaders: "Dump Gaia in order to revere a sword-wielding sky-god? Treat the women as chattel? Convince ourselves that their procreative powers are scary and require dominance? Blow off our sophisticated art and holistic worldview in exchange for a crude warrior cult? Drive ourselves half-nuts making sure that culture always has to stand in opposition to nature and females? You guys are really weird. Get outta here, you low-life boors!" Or was their response something else altogether, perhaps resignation laced with "pragmatism," the logic of collaborating survivors, who, after all, get to write history.

The earliest schools of Greek thought admitted into the canon of Western philosophy, the pre-Socratics (roughly 600–400 B.C.), reflect the cultural transition from the old to the new order. Most historians of Western philosophy pay little attention to any preceding body of collective thought, asserting authoritatively, for example, "Pre-Socratic philosophy differs from all other philosophy in that it had no predecessors."[4] No predecessors? An unbroken heritage of symbolic, mythic, and ritual artifacts unearthed in scores of Neolithic settlements dating at least as far back as 6500 B.C. relates the centrality of concepts that were of primary interest to the pre-Socratics: a primal state of unity (mythically interpreted as the womb of the Great Mother) from which all diversity came forth, the immanence of the divine in the physical world (Heraclitus), the universe as a *harmonia* (Pythagoras), the centrality to life of water (Thales), the functional appreciation of love over strife (Empedocles). Many of the pre-Socratic philosophers, especially those in the Milesian school, rejected the degraded remnants of myth—what Jung called "the hackneyed *chronique scandaleuse* of Olympus"—in order to seek universal principles that function without the intervention of anthropomorphized divine agency. Still, the organic ways in which the pre-Socratics viewed the natural world indeed had deeply rooted precedent in the long era of the Goddess.

Heraclitus of Ephesus was a particularly important transitional figure among the pre-Socratics. By the time he was born, Greek culture was well established: nature was being increasingly desacralized, humans were considered separate from nature, and patriarchal social structure was in place. Heraclitus functioned as something of a crochety preacher, railing at his fellow Ephesians to wake up and perceive the essential flux underlying the illusion of stasis and permanence and to grasp the Divine Law, or Universal Order, by which all differences and seeming opposites reside in unity. He regarded as the highest good that intellectual activity which fosters the greatest receptivity to the divine reason around us.[5] As such, he stood in opposition to self-involution and individual intensification, or egotism, the roots of imbalanced subjectivity in so much of Western philosophy.[6] Heraclitus's monism, an anachronistic burst of primal organicism, did not serve the psychological needs of the new patriarchal cultures built on separateness, reactive (male) autonomy, and control—even though he approved of strife and warfare as dynamics within the unitary flux of Divine Order. He was successfully countered by Socrates and then Plato, who established a dualism of universal and particular, noumenon and phenomenon, mind and body, and spirit and matter, which has subsequently dominated philosophy and religion.[7] Moreover, the succession of Socrates, Plato, and Aristotle refuted Heraclitic thought by asserting the doctrine of transcendent reason.[8] Although Heraclitus exhibited many attitudes characteristic of patriarchal Greek society, he paid homage to the old ways by depositing the one book of his recorded teachings, *On Nature*, in the great Ephesian temple of the goddess Artemis.

Another school of pre-Socratics, the Pythagoreans, formalized in a table of opposites the preference for separateness and distinct boundaries that had been present in Greek culture ever since the introduction of the warrior-hero cult. The Pythagoreans emphasized substance, viewing the world as a mixture of principles of determinate, fixed form, which were considered good, and others associated with formlessness (the unlimited, irregular, or disorderly), which were considered bad. Their patriarchal, dualistic scheme linked femaleness with the unbounded (the vague, the indeterminate) and maleness with the bounded (the precise and clearly determined).[9]

In the following century Plato made a sharp distinction between mind, the principle that understands the rational, and matter, which has no part in knowledge. The freedom of the soul was to be gained through the cultivation of rational thought, which for Plato meant the contemplation of abstract, eternal forms. Aristotle brought the forms down from the transcendent realm to become intelligible principles of changing, sensible things, grasped by the exercise of a purely intellectual faculty.[10] Aristotle avoided Plato's soul/body separation, but viewed male individuals as firmly independent substances and females as a passive deformity of that norm.

After Emperor Constantine merged the remaining infrastructure of the Roman Empire, which had certainly specialized in control, with the young Christian church, the worldview of the empire of Christendom was destined to have widespread influence. In its full bloom, medieval theology, owing especially to Saint Thomas Aquinas's "baptism" of the Aristotelian concepts that had been preserved by Muslim scholars, asserted a hierarchical universe whose lowest level is unformed (prime matter) and whose highest level is pure form without material entanglement, that is, God. In between, beings were ranked according to the perceived dignity of their existence. Men were categorized below angels but quite separate from and more highly valued than women, followed by animals (also in hierarchal ordering), plants, and the earth. Within the categories of humans, monarchs and nobles were ranked closer to God than were the common folk.

When the exploitative system of feudalism began to break up and peasants migrated into the cities, it was clearly a time of upheaval, transition, and the birthing of new economic relations.

There existed the possibility of developing an economic system that would have protected and nurtured the well-being of all: worker-owned enterprises in the crafts, trades, and mercantile ventures, all linked in self-defined webs of cooperatives and benevolent societies. Of course, that is not what happened. Separateness, fear, a culturally induced compulsion for control and autonomy, and an ethic of "every man for himself" among those who could grab economic power resulted in a new system in which, again, a relatively few people prospered at the expense of others. Except for those craftsmen who were able to attain membership in the guilds, security in the new reality was hard to come by. Since options for control and autonomy increase in such a system in proportion to one's wealth, gaining concentrations of capital became a "logical" goal within the patriarchal orientation for the owners of businesses, as decentralized early capitalism gave way over the centuries to more centralized, modern forms.

During the midfourteenth through sixteenth centuries, later labeled the Renaissance, the trend of the decreasing authority of the church and increasing authority of the newly centralized monarchies began. Humanism, which emphasized human-centered values, encouraged a focus on the classics and individual interpretation as opposed to the tradition of scholasticism and religious authority. The glorification of man became a common theme. (When the Renaissance humanists declared that man is the measure of all things, echoing Protagoras, they clearly had males in mind: while the era increased options for men, it tightened controls on women. Most convents that had allowed and encouraged scholarly pursuits for women had been closed by then, and those Renaissance laywomen who were educated in the classics studied a curriculum based on grammar rather than rhetoric and dialectic, skills of persuasion and argumentation that were reserved for men.)[11]

The Renaissance humanists, particularly those influenced by Neoplatonism, were scornful of natural science and the axiomatic logic derived from "first principles," turning away from nature to man as the vital concern of man. Yet the development of a new science that would eventually become the dominant ethos of the modern era had been slowly progressing from roots in two critical scientific schools in the late Middle Ages, the Ockhamites and the Averroistic Aristotelians. In time, the authority of the ancients was ignored in a quest to find an authoritative and infallible method by which to determine truth.

At this critical moment of transition, it would not have been impossible to move away from the assumptions of hierarchy in the medieval synthesis while maintaining, refining, and expanding the natural science in the various expressions of organicism—Christian, Neoplatonic, gnostic, and Hermetic, which drew from Plato, Aristotle, and the Stoics, who, in turn, had built on the organic foundation of the pre-Socratics. In the reactive swing from control-oriented hierarchy to the promise of a powerful new autonomy, however, all notions of living, organic unity, vitalism, naturalism, and animism eventually were mocked and discarded. The universe came to be viewed as dead matter moved by mechanical forces, a clockwork that God had set in motion. The Thomistic attention to ethics and to the purpose of life forms gave way to the study of their operative characteristics in order that such knowledge would yield control over nature. In knowledge lay the power to enlarge "the bounds of Human Empire," as Francis Bacon asserted in his utopian *New Atlantis*. The Baconian spirit, triumphantly declaring that nature must be "bound into service" and made a "slave," suited the new demands of commerce, industry, and imperial seafaring, but the very quest for such wealth, usually acquired exploitatively, was itself a response to the deep cultural pattern of craving autonomy and control. (The fifteenth through seventeenth centuries, a time of persecution of Jews and homosexuals, were also the era of the witch trials, burnings, and hangings, in which hundreds of thousands of women were tortured and killed.)

The Scientific Revolution located truth in quantitative data, mathematical formulation, and theoretical "laws" of physical forces. Descartes declared in his *Discourse on Method* that knowing the force and action of "bodies that environ us" would yield a practical philosophy by which we would "render ourselves the masters and possessors of nature." He reaffirmed the separation of mind and matter, which had long been established as a cultural presence, particularly by Plato and Augustine, by using the language of mathematics: he perceived the material world in terms of extension, divisibility, figure, and motion. Moreover, he considered human will and intellect quite separate from sensations and emotions, tending to view the latter as confused forms or stimulators of the former.[12] Just as virtue was available to one through force of will, Descartes believed, so possession of nature was available to society by the application of rationalist methodology. Hence the ideal Cartesian modern individual is a manipulative spectator in the natural world.

Building on the heady promise of objective, context-free truth that the new science had seemingly established,[13] a small number of *philosophes* in eighteenth-century Europe propagated the "Enlightenment." They viewed reason as a homogeneous formative power[14] that was corrupted in most humans by the influence of the Church (their primary target of contempt), despotic monarchs, economic and social class, ignorance, prejudice, folk customs, and community tradition. They sought the universal and uniform and believed that unbounded human progress could result from rationalist education in service to social engineering.

Enlightenment thinkers began with axioms that seemed "natural" and rational to them; that is, what they took to be reasonable, and socially useful to the middle class, seemed to them necessarily written into God's system of natural laws for the universe.[15] (Atheistic "skepticism" became popular among Enlightenment enthusiasts only in the later stages; most of the *philosophes* held onto belief in a noninterfering God via Deism or "natural religion.") From their faith in the God-given (Newtonian) laws of nature, (males') natural rights, the state of ("uncorrupted" human) nature, and the right of revolution came the great ideals of the Enlightenment: egalitarian humanitarianism (except in regard to equal rights for women), tolerance (except for Catholics and atheists, Locke urged), cosmopolitanism (the projection of European norms onto "exotic" Chinese and New World Indians), and the ideal of democratic government with internal checks and balances.

The development of theories of natural rights and social contract progressed via Locke and Rousseau beyond Hobbes's extreme expression of separateness (that human life in its natural state is "solitary, poor, nasty, brutish, and short," a perpetual drive for power in a war of all against all), which led Hobbes to advocate absolute monarchy. Even in its democratic forms, rights theory was premised on a view of humanity as fundamentally unconnected individuals who must be protected from each other. (The Age of Reason, by the way, included a wave of interest in sadistic pornography written by men about women, an expression of power and resentment that was not addressed in discussions of social contract and rights theory.)

The reaction against the rationalist mind-set began to appear even in the works of some Enlightenment proponents in the second half of the eighteenth century. In addition, the Romantics redefined the central ideas of reason, nature, and progress. What was reason to the *philosophe* was merely calculable comprehension, the kind of thinking a bookkeeper does; the higher, better reason (*Vernunft* to the German Romantics) had a component of depth, intuition, and transcendence, the kind of thinking a real philosopher does. The Age of Reason considered nature to be calm, uniform (once really understood), the Golden Mean revealed; the Romantics saw nature as wild, varied, unruly, and favoring the unique, the individual. Progress, which was basically a physical, almost mechanical process to eighteenth-century rationalists, was considered by Romantics to be a process of growth, an organic unfolding. The ideal of autonomy in the Enlightenment notion of *liberté* was celebrated by Romantics in a more radical form: heroic subjectivity, the unfettered "instinctive wisdom" of the individual. (Such bold rejection of constraint was, as usual, subject to the double standard for the sexes, as the romantic and marital behavior of Shelley and Byron exemplify.)[16]

The Victorian era in England was driven by a faith in expansive material progress that captivated nearly everyone, including Karl Marx. Combining the rationalist philosophy of enlightened self-interest (an expression of fundamental separateness on which classical economic liberalism had been founded) with the Hegelian concept of ineluctable development through conflict, Marx arrived at his theory of dialectical historical materialism, with its tendencies toward economic determinism.[17] Neither the "scientific" Marxists nor the liberals nor the conservatives doubted the rightness of humans' despoiling the earth. It was simply a logical development of control, following on the "obvious" facts of humanity's separateness and autonomy with regard to nature. In fact, the march of technological progress acquired a fascination that had mythic overtones of deliverance, especially in the United States during the years between the First and Second World Wars, where "machine aesthetics" dominated much of architecture, design, and photography.[18]

After the beginning of this century, however, the modernist movement began to manifest itself in artistic and intellectual circles. While many of the male modernist writers and painters were inspired by the macho aesthetics of industrialism (and were often determined to assert such values over expressions of feminism),[19] the "movement," loosely considered, challenged other cultural assumptions that had roots in the smug certainty of the Victorian era. They rejected historical narrative and universalist claims, favoring attention to the particular, especially via "direct analysis" (later called "close reading") of an object removed from historical sequence, which depended on assumptions of continuity.[20] They favored the fragmented, the discordant, the random. Modernism declared that life consists of far more separateness than society, for all its conceptual inventions, is willing to face. Where, after all, had the grand assumptions led but to massive suffering, carnage, and dehumanization? Following the Great War, modernist pessimism and cultural despair

were widespread in Europe. (The question of whether postmodernism breaks with or continues the projects of modernism is currently debated.[21] Clearly modernism was a revolt against the certainties assumed by the modernity of the Victorian era, which carried on the Cartesian paradigm, but deconstructive postmodernism undercuts a great deal more with its rejections; see Appendix A.)

In the 1930s a group of neo-Marxist social critics that came to be known as the Frankfurt school—principally Max Horkheimer, Theodor Adorno, and Herbert Marcuse—acknowledged the inadequacy of Marxism's obsessive focus on economism, which reduced culture to a mere superstructure reflecting the economic base and resulted in a narrow theory of history. They produced expressions of "critical theory" that sought to supplement Marx's account of the exploitation of human labor in the sphere of production, maintaining the Hegelian focus on dynamic conflict in civil society, coupled with a theory of the development of self-consciousness within the family. Unfortunately, a number of them turned to Freud for leadership in their undertaking, so they added even more assumptions of fundamental separateness to the Hegelian-Marxist framework, for example, the emphasis on thorough separating (by males) from the (female) Other as healthful, the resultant need to erect firm boundaries, a patriarchal theory of childhood development, and a focus on development of the male child. (Marcuse, however, clearly distanced himself from the Freudian orientation.)[22] Although one can find in critical theory the frequent decrying of the domination of women, a recent critique of the Frankfurt school concludes that the issue of women's desire has been largely written out of the modern emancipatory project of critical theory.[23] For all its stimulating observations and insights, there is another large problem with critical theory: its explorations are largely bounded by the humanist focus, so "the domination of nature" in their writings usually refers to human nature, or "first nature," a concept based on the Freudian notion of the nirvanic state of unity between infant and mother. "Second nature" means to the Frankfurt school the layering of internal repression that socialization adds. For Horkheimer and Adorno, the rest of the natural world has meaning insofar as it is instrumental to human purposes.[24] They expanded the scope of analysis of domination, but remained true to a patriarchal orientation: human relations are primarily power relations, or means of control.

The Existentialists rejected the Freudian and economic-determinist explanations of behavior offered by various neo-Marxists. Insisting on choice and authenticity as "projects" of the individual, they drew on the works of Nietzsche and Kierkegaard to grapple with painful paradoxes of self-determination in what they (especially Sartre and Camus) perceived as a meaningless and indifferent universe. Heidegger believed man's "generalized sense of dread" to be an ontological constituent of the universe (rather than a result of the patriarchal worldview!). Although Heidegger and Jaspers were considered central to this school of thought in Europe, it was the Sartrean branch that became best known in this country. In his work the theme of patriarchal dread of nature and the female is undisguised in the expressions of radical separateness and reactive autonomy. Sartre, a good Cartesian, divides being into two types. Being-in-itself means the self-contained being of a thing, the natural, the "immanent," the pointless. For him this vast realm is associated with images of softness, stickiness, viscosity, sliminess, corpulence, flabbiness, excessive fruitfulness, and woman as the archetype of nature. (His protagonist in *Nausea* becomes disgusted and nauseated in looking at the tangled roots of a large chestnut tree!) Being-for-itself, in contrast, partakes of the realm of consciousness, of transcendence, which extends perpetually beyond itself. In Sartre's existential psychology, For-itself is the masculine capability by which man forms himself in radical freedom, makes projects, and fends off any expectations or interference from the Other, thereby giving his life whatever strictly human meaning it has.[25]

For anyone whose identity is entwined with the patriarchal project of separateness and reactive autonomy—which is a personal choice, not a matter of biological determinism—the cultural history of the West could indeed be viewed as a triumphant progression toward the unencumbered strutting of the existential Lone Cowboy. He is the proud heir of an energetic dynamic that has stomped on the encompassing organicism of Gaia, degraded any soft boundaries of interdependence, delivered a sucker punch to religion, pumped up the haunting war against nature with an aggressive scientism, and through it all held the female at arm's length by denying education or other access to the playing fields of culture. By the mid-1960s the thoroughly modern, secular intellectual imbued with this heritage could enjoy self-congratulations on many fronts.

Yet a problematic construct had emerged: Lévi-Strauss had introduced structuralism, the theory that an objective, universal cultural system, or code, structures our mental processes, language, and social institutions. Here began the "death of the subject," or the "fading" of man from the humanist role of glorious freewheeler at the center of everything. Being both provocative and subversive, even if fanciful, structuralism attracted and engendered several renowned adherents, but the philosophical idealism of that belief system eventually was found too confining to suit the deeply rooted cravings for autonomy.

In time most of the men championing structuralism moved into various forms of poststructuralism. Of these, Derrida's deconstructionism achieved the greatest leap on behalf of the existential Lone Cowboy, although Foucault's conclusion that all relationships are power-laden and "dangerous" to the theoretically autonomous self also played a central role. Derrida ostensibly sought to dismantle the conditions for philosophical dualism that had developed since the early Greek philosophers, but he delegitimized far more than that. He smashed the "anxiety of influence," once and for all.[26] He liberated himself from the "humiliating fact" that one's interior monologue, one's entire repertoire of possibilities for thought, is limited by language, which was invented by—*horrors*—other people! He declared that one's entire mental array of received "signifiers" (words, concepts, metaphors, symbolic associations) need not have constraining effects because they actually have no fixed referential meaning, only indeterminate participation in endless chains of shifting, context-bound signifiers! For many deconstructionists any spoken, written, or even thought expressions of bonding, responsibility, or love are all merely relative—and extremely tangential. *Free at last.*

Obsessive subjectivity has finally folded in on itself until it has devoured the (language-based) sense of self and destroyed the logic of subjectivity altogether. But, of course, there *is* a subject acting here. It is Man the Autonomous Destroyer, a painfully distorted and alienated caricature of the human embedded in the unfolding universe. The contemporary forms of subjective idealism that assure the individual that nothing outside one's constructing mind has any claim on him or her are initially experienced as liberating for anyone who has suffered domination. Such idealism and hypersubjectivity are particularly alluring to those most severely damaged by patriarchal socialization: they who experience *all* relationship as as oppressive. The aggressive surge of denial called for by deconstructionism, however, leads to a flattened valuelessness in which nothing is left but the will to power. The preferences of an individual or a group can then carry the day only through political manipulations and displays of power, control, and forceful domination. Hence some observers conclude that the extreme relativism of deconstructive postmodernism leads to a societal model of ruthless power plays and perhaps even fascism. The causal dynamics underlying such behavior were not invented only twenty-some years ago in Paris. Their long history has its origins in patriarchal culture's brutal and self-destructive divorce from the body—the Earthbody, the female body, the body of the mother. Inculcated perceptions of profound separateness yield alienation, deep-seated rage, and reactive cravings for autonomy and control. In every era their presence seeks lofty philosophical justification.

Denial, even systemically elaborated, cannot lessen our existential dependence on the complex ways of the Earthbody. Now even those elemental processes are besieged, degraded, and unreliable. Tragically, the nihilism implicit in deconstructive postmodernism is *simpatico* with the larger dynamics of disintegration and loss of meaning in our time: the death of the planetary Grand Subject, the ruin of the majestic ecosphere that gives us life and is our greater body. What is needed is not a lockstep ecocentric "foundationalism," so feared by deconstructionists, but a creative orientation of *attentive and respectful engagement* with the natural world, from our own body to the unfolding presence of the entire cosmos. After all, what is human culture but an extension of the dynamic physicality of the planet?

Notes

Chapter 1 • Saving Grace

1. Robert Wright, "The Information Age," *The Sciences*, vol. 25, no. 3 (1985): 7–9, cited approvingly by Myrdene Anderson in "Projection of Organicism and Mechanism in the Shadow of Gaia" (a paper presented at the conference titled "Is the Earth a Living Organism?" sponsored by the National Audubon Expedition Institute, Amherst, MA, 1–6 August 1985).
2. The "Ten Key Values" of the American Green politics movement are ecological wisdom, grassroots democracy, personal and social responsibility, nonviolence, decentralization, community-based economics, postpatriarchal values, respect for diversity, global responsibility, and future focus. Information about this grassroots movement is available from the Green Committees of Correspondence, National Clearinghouse, P.O. Box 30208, Kansas City, MO 64112.
3. The State Univ. of New York Press publishes a "Series in Constructive Postmodern Thought," edited by David Ray Griffin. Titles include *The Reenchantment of Science: Postmodern Proposals; Spirituality and Society: Postmodern Visions; Varieties of Postmodern Theology;* and *Sacred Interconnections: Postmodern Spirituality, Political Economy, and Art.* Authors who have contributed to these anthologies include John Cobb, Herman Daly, Richard Falk, Frederick Ferré, Matthew Fox, David Griffin, Joe Holland, Catherine Keller, Joanna Macy, Brian Swimme, and myself. Griffin also directs the Center for a Postmodern World (3463 State Street, Suite 252, Santa Barbara, CA 93105), which has sponsored several conferences and symposia on constructive, or ecological, postmodernism.

   The art critic Suzi Gablik also discusses the two types of postmodernism, which she labels "deconstructive" and "reconstructive," in her book titled *The Reenchantment of Art* (New York: Thames and Hudson, 1991).

4. See, for example, Ashis Nandy, ed., *Science, Hegemony, and Violence: A Requiem for Modernity* (Tokyo: United Nations Univ.; Delhi: Oxford Univ. Press, 1988).
5. See James A. Carpenter, "Irenaeus and the East," in *Nature and Grace* (New York: Crossroad, 1988), 18–36.
6. Paul Tillich, *Systematic Theology*, vol. 3 (Chicago: Univ. of Chicago Press, 1963), 274.
7. Karl Rahner, "Concerning the Relationship between Nature and Grace," in *Theological Investigations*, vol. 1 (New York: Seabury Press, 1966), 302; also see "Nature and Grace," in *Theological Investigations*, vol. 4, 178.
8. Expanding the sense of grace beyond denominational boundaries is not as eccentric as it might seem. For several decades numerous returning Christian missionaries have urged church officials to recognize the presence of grace in other spiritual traditions, but to little avail.
9. See Arianna Stassinopoulos Huffington, *Picasso: Creator and Destroyer* (New York: Simon and Schuster, 1988), 338.
10. Paul R. Ehrlich, quoted by Philip Shabecoff in "Scientists Urgently Ask Action to Save Species," *New York Times*, 28 Sept. 1986.
11. Barry Lopez, "The Passing Wisdom of Birds," in *Crossing Open Ground* (New York: Vintage Books, 1989), 204.
12. Richard A. Falk, "In Pursuit of the Postmodern," in *Spirituality and Society: Postmodern Visions*, ed. David Ray Griffin (Albany: State Univ. of New York Press, 1988), 83.
13. See Thomas Berry, "The Ecological Age," in *The Dream of the Earth* (San Francisco: Sierra Club Books, 1988), 36–49.
14. This passage was written by Brian Swimme for an early draft of the forthcoming book tentatively titled *The Universe Story,* which is coauthored with Thomas Berry.
15. For example, Francis Fukuyama attracted a good deal of attention, mostly admiring responses initially, with his recent assertion in *The National Interest* (Summer 1989) that a liberal, consumerist, modern society is the omega point of history and that now that such a model is spreading worldwide, we have achieved our destiny. He regretted that we can look forward only to boredom, emptiness, and lack of philosophical challenge in the comfy "post-historical period" before us! The destruction of nature, native cultures, the Third World, and other victims of industrialization are not minor problems to be fine-tuned, but inherent costs of the modern, globalized, technocratic, consumerist project.
16. By the pejorative adjectives "objectivist," "mechanistic," and "rationalist" I do not mean the endeavor to observe phenomena as clearly as possible, the study of mechanisms of animate and inanimate action, and the practice of logical modes of thought. Rather, these terms refer to an arrogant insistence that (1) an objective, "outer" reality exists, separate from the individual, about which one can gather objective data that is inherently free of biases of perspective and subjective choices concerning which aspects of a phenomenon to investigate and how to do so, (2) that which cannot be

quantified and observed as mechanistic processes does not exist, and (3) the "rational" selection of which aspects of a situation to consider and how to do so are never influenced by fear, desire, or other emotions.

Chapter 2 • The Center Holds

1. *Majjhima Nikaya* (Collection of Long Discourses), PTS Edition, 36, I, 246. The scene Gotama recalled was a ritual plowing, part of his father's duty as the local ruler. Here is the passage, with the translation used in *Buddhism* by Hans Wolfgang Schumann (Wheaton, IL: Theosophical Publishing House, 1974):

   > I remember(ed) how, sitting recollected in the shadow of a jambu tree while my father Sakka worked the furrows, I have rested from desires, free from unwholesome emotions, after I had reached the joyful-happy first (stage of) trance connected with thinking and pondering, resulting from seclusion. (I asked myself:) Should this be the path to enlightenment?

2. Nearly all meditation practices throughout the Buddhist nations of south Asia are based on interpretations of the Buddha's *Mahasatipatthana Sutta* and on particular traditions of instruction. Rather than present all the variations and interpretations, I have selected a sample, the teachings received by a Burmese monk, the Venerable Ledi Sayadaw (1846–1923), who transmitted them to lay teachers, notably Saya Thet Gyi, who taught U Ba Khin, who taught S. N. Goenka and several Western teachers of *vipassana*. Another lineage of teachers of *vipassana* meditation in the West received similar teachings from the Venerable Mahasi Sayadaw (1904–1982). Both of these streams of teaching relay the emphasis the Buddha placed on *vedana* (the physical and mental aspects of sensations). For an essay on this central aspect of Dhamma and for relevant passages from the Buddha's *suttas*, see Appendixes A and B in *The Art of Living: Vipassana Meditation as Taught by S. N. Goenka* by William Hart (San Francisco: Harper & Row, 1987).

   There are many other practices and interpretations, which vary in particulars, but all share the basic concepts of Dhamma. I have tried to present the teachings of a living tradition as it exists today in Buddhist communities, which is often different and richer than what has been captured in books by Western scholars.

3. Perhaps this sequence of events, particularly the last one, is the phenomenon observed by Dr. Benjamin Libet, of the University of California at San Francisco, in his studies of the role of the brain in volition. He has concluded, "The conscious mind doesn't initiate voluntary actions. The unconscious mind initiates actions, while the conscious selects among and controls these urges, either permitting or vetoing them" (*U.C. Clip Sheet*, Univ. of California, 25 March 1986; interview about Dr. Libet's research findings that were published in *The Behavioral and Brain Sciences*). Dr. Libet found consistently that brain activity began approximately 550 msec before an action, while conscious awareness of the intention occurred only 200 msec before

an action. The Buddha would agree that it is the deep levels of the mind (the unconscious) that react, but would add that the unconscious initiates reactions in response to subtle bodily sensations resulting from the conscious mind's evaluating of a perceived stimulus.

4. Dr. Candace Pert, a neuropharmacologist who has conducted research into the nature of endorphins and other neurochemicals, explains, "When human beings engage in various activities, it seems that neuro juices are released that are associated with either pain or pleasure" (*San Francisco Chronicle*, 14 December 1987). On a rather horrifying note elsewhere in that article, the journalist cheerily reported, "Scientists are already exploring ways to enhance aesthetic and spiritual capacities by injecting biochemicals directly into the brain."
5. Clearly the experience of *nibbana* lies beyond the descriptive boundaries of discourse. The Buddha taught that no positive statement could be made about it except that it is the end of suffering. In order to refute mistaken views about it, however, he sometimes had to speak about what *nibbana* is not:

> There is, monks, something which is neither earth, nor fire, nor air, neither boundless space nor boundless consciousness, nor nothingness, nor the state of neither-perception-nor-non-perception; neither this world nor another world, neither sun nor moon. That, monks, I call neither coming nor going, nor remaining, neither dying nor being born. It is without support, development or foundation. That is the end of suffering.

(*Samyutta Nikaya* [Collection of Kindred Sayings] 22.59, translation used in *Tranquility and Insight* by Amadeo Solé-Leris [Boston: Shambhala Books, 1987]).

Elsewhere the Buddha spoke of *nibbana* as "something that is not born, not originated, not made, not compound" (*Udana* 8.3, *Kuddaka Nikaya* [Smaller Collection], translation source as above).

6. Walpola Rahula, *What the Buddha Taught*, 2d ed. (New York: Grove Press, 1974), 1.
7. Rahula, *What the Buddha Taught*, 81–89.
8. Rahula, *What the Buddha Taught*, 85.
9. Nanavasa Thera, translation ed., *Mahaparinibbana Sutta, Digna Nikaya* II (Colombo, Sri Lanka, 1929).

   The Buddhist scholar Walpola Rahula, drawing on the *Digha Nikaya Commentary* (Colombo edition), notes that "*dipa* here does not mean "lamp," but "island," as in a support or resting place. Hence the well-known translation by Rhys Davids ("Be ye lamps unto yourselves") is incorrect.
10. A lecture given by Thich Nhat Hahn, First Congregational Church, Berkeley, CA, 20 April 1987.
11. The theory called "Neural Darwinism," put forth by Gerald Edelman, who received the Nobel Prize in Physiology or Medicine in 1972, posits that strong reactions in the brain to certain stimuli result in the nerve cells

involved with such reactions forming groups, neuronal groups that become organized into sheets or "maps," which interact with each other. (See Israel Rosenfeld, *The Invention of Memory: A New View of the Brain* [New York: Basic Books, 1988].) Dr. Edelman believes that "every experience in a person's life alters and shapes that individual's brain" (David Hellerstein, "Plotting a Theory of the Brain," *New York Times Magazine* [22 May 1988]).

The psychobiologists Richard Thompson of USC and William Greenough of the Univ. of Illinois conducted studies with fifteen rabbits over a two-year period and isolated the first case in which brain cells involved in the performance of a task clearly participated in structural change of intercellular connections, or "anatomical circuitry," as they put it. They reported their findings at the Nov. 1989 meeting of the Society for Neuroscience, held in Phoenix.

Regarding the structural plasticity of the nervous system, Humberto Maturana and Francisco Varela, researchers and theorists in the biology of cognition, note that structural changes occur not in the broad lines of connectivity that unite groups of neurons, which are generally the same in all individuals in a species, but in the local characteristics of those connections. "There [in the 'final' ramifications and the synapses] molecular changes result in changes in the efficiency of the synaptic interactions that can modify drastically how the entire neuronal network functions" (*The Tree of Knowledge* [Boston: Shambhala Books, 1988], 167).

Also see Sandra Blakeslee, "Memory Repair," *New York Times "Good Health" Magazine*, 8 October 1989.

12. This Buddhist insight—that Descartes mistook the penultimate step for the ultimate in what he viewed as the uncompromisingly rational dissection of mental experience—was presented by Tyrone Cashman at a conference titled "Is the Earth a Living Organism?," Univ. of Massachusetts, Amherst, 1–6 August 1985; later published as "The Living Earth and the Cybernetics of Self," *ReVision*, vol. 9, no. 2 (Winter/Spring 1987): 25–32.
13. David Loy, "The Cloture of Deconstruction: A Mahayana Critique of Derrida," *International Philosophical Quarterly*, vol. XXVI, no. 1, issue 105 (March 1987). Also see David Loy, *Nonduality: A Study in Comparative Philosophy* (New Haven, CT: Yale Univ. Press, 1988). Loy argues that Derrida, although aware that each term of a duality is the *differance* of the other, does not fully realize how deconstructing one term (transcendental signified, self-presence, reference, etc.) must also transform the other (*differance*, temporization, supplementation, etc.). Derrida's single deconstruction of "commonsense" dualities leads to the "temporary" reversal of their hierarchy and/or to a discontinuous, irruptive "liberation" from reference grounded of a free-floating meaning beyond any conceptual "closure." Deconstructionists then advocate playful "change of style," but, maintains Loy, end up only with self-conscious "reinscription" of the dualities, unlike the Buddha's teachings, which lead one to a mode of existence that is not governed by dualism.

14. See Thomas McEvilley, "Early Greek Philosophy and Madhyamika," *Philosophy East and West* 31 (April 1981).
15. Mervyn Sprung, trans., *Lucid Exposition of the Middle Way: The Essential Chapters from the Prasannapada of Candrakirti* (Boulder: Prajna Press, 1979). The passage is from Candrakirti's commentary on Nagarjuna's *Mulamadhyamikakarika*, XXV, 24, as it is cited in Loy's article (see note 13).
16. Buddhist meditation teachers generally warn that taking up meditation in order to cure a physical ailment is likely to be fruitless because one tends to focus attention on the state of the ailment rather than on the exercises in developing mindfulness. On the other hand, the cases in which physical ailments have decreased in strength or disappeared after one has become established in *vipassana* are legion. For an account of reducing high blood pressure, for example, see Daniel Goleman, "Hypertension? Relax," *New York Times Magazine*, 11 December 1988. The *vipassana* teacher S. N. Goenka first attended a meditation retreat only because he suffered from severe migraine headaches that doctors in Asia, Europe, and the United States had been unable to cure; the migraines subsequently disappeared, but he looks back laughingly at how narrow his focus was when he first encountered Dhamma.

    Medical researchers have determined that depression impairs our immune system (*U.C. Clip Sheet*, Univ. of California, 28 April 1987) and that habitual mindstates of anger and cynicism may actually shorten one's life (*San Francisco Chronicle*, 17 Jan. 1989). Diminishing the occurrence of negative and unwholesome mindstates seems to free the body of degenerative patterns.
17. Historic accounts vary on the end of Asoka's reign and the dissolution of his empire. According to Buddhist sources, Asoka's grandson was murdered by Pushametra (Pushyamitra) Sung, who then imposed Vedic rule and established a dynasty of Brahmanic ministers. Buddhists and Jains were persecuted, and Sung even offered a bounty for the head of any Jain or Buddhist monk. The practice of Dhamma became corrupted, as some of the survivors yielded to pressures from the new regime, and was eventually destroyed in India.

    According to Hindu sources, there is no evidence for anything more than the abrupt cessation of royal patronage for the Buddhist monasteries after Asoka's death and the inexplicable migration of Buddhists and Jains from Pataliputra and most of the lands of the crumbling Asokan empire. The Hindu sources agree, however, that Pushyamitra Sung was a staunch supporter of Brahmanic orthodoxy.
18. Joanna Macy, *Dharma and Development: Religion as Resource in the Sarvodaya Self-Help Movement*, rev. ed. (West Hartford, CT: Kumarian Press, 1985), 33.
19. E. F. Schumacher, *Small Is Beautiful: Economics as if People Mattered* (New York: Harper & Row Perennial Library, 1973), 57.
20. Schumacher, *Small Is Beautiful*, 54–55.

21. See Fred Eppsteiner, ed., *The Path of Compassion: Writings on Socially Engaged Buddhism* (Berkeley: Buddhist Peace Fellowship/Parallax Press, 1988). Also see Ken Jones, *The Social Face of Buddhism* (London and Boston: Wisdom Publications, 1989). Also see Allan Hunt Badiner, *Dharma Gaia: A Harvest of Essays in Buddhism and Ecology* (Berkeley: Parallax Press, 1990).
22. Hannah Arendt, *On Violence* (New York: Harcourt Brace & World, 1970), 56.
23. For numerous other examples of successful nonviolent resistance in recent history, see *The Politics of Nonviolent Action, Part One: Power and Struggle*, 3 vols. (Boston: Porter Sargent Publishers, 1973). For a detailed presentation of scores of tactics of "political jiu-jitsu," see *Part Two: The Methods of Nonviolent Action.*

    For an account of the nonviolent resistance against the Pinochet regime in Chile, see Phil McManus, "Nonviolence on the Front Lines," *Fellowship*, Fellowship of Reconciliation, November 1987, 13.
24. Coretta Scott King, ed., *The Words of Martin Luther King, Jr.* (New York: Newmarket Press, 1983), 73.
25. King, *Martin Luther King, Jr.*, 71.
26. Dhirendra Mohan Datta, *The Philosophy of Mahatma Gandhi* (Madison: Univ. of Wisconsin Press, 1953), 42.
27. M. K. Gandhi, *My Autobiography* (Boston: Beacon Press, 1957), 504.
28. M. K. Gandhi, *Satyagraha* (Ahmedabad, India: Navajivan Publishing House, 1951), 109.
29. See, for example, Gene Sharp, *Gandhi as a Political Strategist* (Boston: Porter Sargent Publishers, 1979); Joan Bondurant, *Conquest of Violence: The Gandhian Philosophy of Conflict*, rev. ed. (Princeton: Princeton Univ. Press, 1988); and *Fighting Fair: A Non-Violent Strategy for Resolving Everyday Conflicts* (San Francisco: Harper & Row, 1986).
30. Datta, *Philosophy of Mahatma Gandhi*, 29.
31. M. K. Gandhi, *Satyagraha in South Africa* (New York: Tanam Press, 1983), 109–10.
32. M. K. Gandhi, *The Supreme Power* (Bombay: Bharatiya Vidya Bhavan, 1966), 3 (reprinted from *Young India*, 21 Jan. 1926).
33. N. A. Nikam, *Gandhi's Discovery of Religion* (Bombay: Bharatiya Vidya Bhavan, 1965), 22.
34. Margaret Chatterjee, *Gandhi's Religious Thought* (London: Macmillan Press, 1983), 51.
35. Chatterjee, *Gandhi's Religious Thought*, 21.
36. Chatterjee, *Gandhi's Religious Thought*, 11, 74; Gandhi, *Supreme Power*, 55 (reprinted from *Harijan*, 22 Feb. 1942).
37. D. K. Bedekar, *Towards Understanding Gandhi* (Bombay: Popular Prakashan, 1975), 79; citing from Gandhi's introduction to the biography of Raichand, a Jain sage.
38. M. K. Gandhi, *Hindu Dharma* (Ahmedabad, India: Navajivan Publishing House, 1950), 13.

39. Datta, *Philosophy of Mahatma Gandhi*, 94.
40. Gandhi, *Satyagraha*, 384.
41. M. K. Gandhi, *Towards Non-Violent Politics and the Relation of Constructive Work to Ahimsa* (Thanjavur, Tamilnad, India: Sarvodaya Prachuralaya, 1969), 3.
42. M. K. Gandhi, *All Religions Are True* (Bombay: Bharatiya Vidya Bhavan, 1962), 10.
43. Gandhi, *All Religions Are True*, 10.
44. Gandhi, *All Religions Are True*, 3.
45. Gandhi, *Supreme Power*, 27.
46. Bondurant, *Conquest of Violence*, 24; citing from Gandhi's *From Yeravda Mandir: Ashram Observances*, 3rd ed. (Ahmedabad, India: Navajivan Publishing House, 1945).
47. Chatterjee, 90; citing from a letter Gandhi published in *Modern Review*, Oct. 1916.
48. Geoffrey Ashe, *Gandhi: A Study in Revolution* (London: William Heinemann, 1968), 182.
49. Chatterjee, 151.
50. Chatterjee, 84.
51. Michael W. Sonnleitner, *Gandhian Nonviolence: Levels of Satyagraha* (New Delhi: Abhinav Publications, 1985), 14; citing from *Young India*, 1 Oct. 1931.
52. Mark Juergensmeyer, *Fighting Fair: A Non-Violent Strategy for Resolving Everyday Conflicts* (San Francisco: Harper & Row, 1986), 106.
53. Bondurant, *Conquest of Violence*, 139.
54. Arne Naess, *Gandhi and the Nuclear Age* (Totowa, NJ: The Bedminster Press, 1965), 22.
55. M. K. Gandhi, "Axioms of Non-Violence," in *My Religion* (Lahore: Dewan's Publications), 37.
56. Thomas Merton, ed., *Gandhi on Non-Violence* (New York: New Directions, 1965), 75.
57. Merton, *Gandhi on Non-Violence*, 74.
58. Merton, *Gandhi on Non-Violence*, 74.
59. Kanti Shah, ed., *Vinoba on Gandhi* (Varanasi, India: Sarva Seva Sangh Prakashan, 1973), 86.
60. Sharp, *Gandhi as a Political Strategist*, 289.
61. Naess, *Gandhi and the Nuclear Age*, 37; citing from *Young India*, 26 Dec. 1924.
62. Gandhi, *Satyagraha*, 109.
63. Chatterjee, 12.
64. M. K. Gandhi, *My Non-Violence* (Ahmedabad, India: Navajivan Publishing House, 1960), 89.
65. Chatterjee, 73; citing from *Modern Review*, October 1921.
66. Francisco Claver, *Fellowship*, June 1985; cited in "The Nonviolent Revolution That Surprised the World" by Richard Deats, *Fellowship*, Fellowship of Reconciliation, March 1987, 5.

67. "Culture of Violence Infects Life in the U.S.," *San Francisco Examiner and Chronicle*, 5 Feb. 1989.
68. "Culture of Violence."
69. "Shelters with Comforts of Home," *U.C. Clip Sheet*, Univ. of California, 22 March 1988.
70. "Firearm Suicides Increase," *U.C. Clip Sheet*, Univ. of California, 7 March 1989.
71. See Richard Hammersley and John Cregan, "Drug Addiction and Vipassana Meditation," *Vipassana Newsletter* (P.O. Box 51, Shelburne Falls, MA 01370), vol. 14, no. 2, June 1987.
72. See Mimi Silbert and Ayala Pines, "Sexual Abuse as an Antecedent to Prostitution," *Child Abuse and Neglect*, vol. 5, no. 4, 1981, 407–11. Also see Silbert and Pines, "Early Sexual Exploitation as an Influence in Prostitution," *Social Work*, vol. 28, no. 4 (July/Aug. 1983): 285–89.
73. "Culture of Violence."

    Speaking specifically of violence in films, the critic Vincent Canby observed recently that "mass-market movies are getting rougher all the time, at least in part because each succeeding movie attempts to top all those that have gone before." He added, "The percentage of permissible mayhem in any conventional movie keeps increasing." (*New York Times*, 13 May 1990).
74. "Culture of Violence."
75. "Culture of Violence."
76. See Neil Malamuth and Edward Donnerstein, *Pornography and Sexual Aggression* (New York: Academic Press, 1984).

    Also, a study presented by Larry Barron and Murray A. Straus at the 1985 meeting of the American Association for the Advancement of Science found that circulation of pornographic magazines in the states with the highest incidence of rape is more than double the circulation in states that rank among the lowest in rape.
77. "Culture of Violence."
78. An international group of biologists, psychologists, geneticists, anthropologists, ethologists, neurophysiologists, and other scientists issued "The Seville Statement on Violence" in 1986 to halt the "misuse of scientific theories and data to justify violence and war." They stated that it is "scientifically incorrect" to say that we have inherited a tendency to make war from our animal ancestors, that war or any other violent behavior is genetically programmed into our human nature, that in the course of human evolution there has been a selection for aggressive behavior more than for other kinds of behavior, that humans have a "violent brain," or that war is caused by "instinct" or any single motivation.
79. Roger Ailes, *Advertising Age*; cited in the *San Francisco Chronicle*, 17 Nov. 1988.
80. A journalist in Washington, D.C., for a major news magazine was full of praise for my work in *Green Politics: The Global Promise* (New York: Dutton, 1984) until I mentioned that I checked the accuracy of all the quotes

I had decided to use from my interviewing trip to West Germany by sending the relevant quote from my transcripts to each interviewee. He then became very agitated and declared that the book was worthless. Didn't I understand that the point is to get interviewees to say something that they don't really want to have in print? The fact that not one of my interviewees changed her or his quote, many of which were filled with self-criticism of the German Greens, did not faze the journalist.

81. "America Gets Nasty," *San Francisco Chronicle*, 6 Jan. 1989.
82. "Liberal Bait for Morton Downey Jr.," *San Francisco Examiner and Chronicle, This World* magazine, 12 Feb. 1989.
83. "Liberal Bait."
84. "Taking Nonviolence into Prisons," *Fellowship*, Fellowship of Reconciliation, March 1988, 29.
85. See Alice Miller, *For Your Own Good* (New York: Farrar Straus Giroux, 1984); also see Susan Griffin, "The Child and the Shape of History," *Creation*, vol. 4, no. 6 (Jan./Feb. 1989): 22.
86. See Samuel P. Oliner and Pearl M. Oliner, *The Altruistic Personality: Rescuers of Jews in Nazi Europe* (New York: The Free Press, 1988).
87. "Amnesty Reports More Death Squads," *San Francisco Chronicle*, 5 Oct. 1988. The membership address of Amnesty International is 322 Eighth Avenue, New York, NY 10017-0389.
88. The core teachings of Dhamma are nonsectarian, and the practice of Dhamma does not require anyone to consider him- or herself a Buddhist. Many Christians, Jews, Moslems, Hindus, Jains, Marxists, and others have attended courses in *vipassana* meditation, for example, reporting afterward that their own spiritual life had been strengthened. The following is a letter to the staff of the Vipassana International Academy, near Igatpuri in the Indian state of Maharashtra, from a Catholic priest after having attended two ten-day retreats:

> [Mr. Goenka's] Dhamma talks are words of wisdom. There is nothing that I cannot accept as Catholic. On the contrary, they helped me to deepen my appreciation of Christian attitudes. They foster a genuine and universal religious spirit of love and compassion. The practice of meditation helps me to become more unattached and spiritually free. It actualizes the Principle and Foundation of the Spiritual Exercises of Ignatius. I feel a greater sense of tranquility and inward stillness and trust in Providence, in whatever is joy. The sharpened sense of awareness will be most useful in my traditional practice of examination of conscience.

(cited in *Vipassana Journal*, published in 1983 by the Vipassana International Academy)

The late Father Anthony DeMello, an Indian Jesuit who studied at the same *vipassana* meditation center, combined many aspects of Dhamma and Christian practice, which he presented in *Sadhana, A Way to God: Christian Exercises in Eastern Form* (St. Louis: The Institute of Jesuit Sources, 1978). The book and his lectures proved extremely popular with Catholic audiences in the United

States.

Many forms of Buddhist meditation are taught in the United States today. See Donald Morreale, *Buddhist America: Centers, Retreats, Practices* (Santa Fe, NM: John Muir Publications, 1988).

Speaking only from my own experience, I can highly recommend the ten-day *vipassana* courses taught by S. N. Goenka or his assistant teachers (nearly half of whom worldwide are female, by the way). The courses are free of charge (people leave donations afterward for the next group's food, maintenance of the facility, and so forth; the teachers accept no pay) and require ten days' residence (one is free to leave at any time). An introductory pamphlet and schedule of course dates and locations worldwide are available from the Vipassana Meditation Center, Box 24, Shelburne Falls, MA 01370.

I also feel deep gratitude toward Joseph Goldstein, the *vipassana* teacher who first invited me onto the path of Dhamma and taught me the initial mental exercise, *anapana*, for concentrating attention. Joseph and his equally esteemed colleague Sharon Salzburg teach *vipassana* courses at the Insight Meditation Society, Barre, MA 01005, and elsewhere. A schedule is available on request.

Chapter 3 • Participation in the Mystery

1. James Lovelock postulated the Gaia Hypothesis in 1972 as an explanation of the constancy of life-supporting conditions amid the disequilibrium in Earth's atmosphere: the Earth is alive, in that it is self-organizing, self-regulating, and demonstrates the capacity to control its life-supporting chemical composition and maintain homeostasis through responses of marine algae and other living organisms. These dynamics of self-regulation can be understood as cybernetic feedback loops. Later joined in this work by the biologist Lynn Margulis, Lovelock asserts that Gaian homeostasis starts from the local activity of individual organisms; species and their physical environment comprise a single system. See James Lovelock, *Gaia: A New Look at Life on Earth* (Oxford: Oxford Univ. Press, 1979) and *The Ages of Gaia: A Biography of Our Living Earth* (New York: Norton, 1988).
2. Some ecological Christian theologians have recently suggested moving beyond both dominion and stewardship to "a theology of relationship"; see, for example, Wesley Granberg-Michaelson, "Renewing the Whole Creation," *Sojourners*, Feb./March 1990. Others, such as Matthew Fox, locate their Christianity in the tradition of creation-centered spirituality; see Matthew Fox, *Original Blessing* (Santa Fe: Bear & Co., 1983) and *The Coming of the Cosmic Christ* (San Francisco: Harper & Row, 1988). Also see John B. Cobb, Jr., *Is It Too Late? A Theology of Ecology* (Beverly Hills, CA: Bruce, 1972), and two books by Jay B. McDaniel: *Of God and Pelicans: A Theology of Reverence for Life* (Philadelphia: Westminster/John Knox, 1989) and *Earth, Sky, Gods and Mortals: Developing an Ecological Spirituality* (Mystic, CT: Twenty-third Publications, 1990).
3. See, for example, Irene Diamond and Gloria Orenstein, eds., *Reweaving the World: The Emergence of Ecofeminism* (San Francisco: Sierra Club Books,

1990) and Judith Plant, ed., *Healing the Wounds: The Promise of Ecofeminism* (Philadelphia and Santa Cruz: New Society Publishers, 1989).

4. See, for example, Arne Naess, *Ecology, Community, and Lifestyle: Outline of an Ecosophy* (Cambridge: Cambridge Univ. Press, 1989); Bill Devall and George Sessions, eds., *Deep Ecology* (Salt Lake City: Peregrine Smith Books, 1985); Bill Devall, *Simple in Means, Rich in Ends* (Salt Lake City: Peregrine Smith Books, 1988); Warwick Fox, *Toward a Transpersonal Ecology* (Boston: Shambhala, 1990); and *The Trumpeter: Journal of Ecosophy*, ed. Alan R. Drengson (Lightstar, P.O. Box 5853, Stn. B, Victoria, B.C. Canada V8R 6S8). A journal drawing upon both deep ecology and the cosmology articulated by Thomas Berry, among other orientations, is *Ecospirit*, ed. Don St. John (Institute for Ecosophical Studies, Moravian College, Bethlehem, PA 18018).

5. See, for example, Van Andruss, Christopher Plant, Judith Plant, and Eleanor Wright, eds., *Home! A Bioregional Reader* (Philadelphia and Santa Cruz: New Society Publishers, 1990); Kirkpatrick Sale, *Dwellers in the Land: The Bioregional Vision* (San Francisco: Sierra Club Books, 1985); Stephanie Mills, *What Ever Happened to Ecology?* (San Francisco: Sierra Club Books, 1989); Peter Berg, Beryl Magilavy, and Seth Zuckerman, *A Green City Program* (San Francisco: Planet Drum Foundation, 1989); and *Proceedings* from the biennial North American Bioregional Congress.

   Also see the bioregional journals *Katuah Journal*, ed. Marnie Muller et al. (Box 638, Leicester, NC, Katuah Province 28748); *Raise the Stakes*, ed. Peter Berg et al. (Planet Drum Foundation, Box 31251, San Francisco, Shasta Province, CA 94131); and *New Catalyst*, ed. Judith Plant et al. (P.O. Box 189, Gabriola Island, B.C., VOR 1XO, Canada).

6. "Endgames," Notebook Column, *Harper's Magazine*, Nov. 1989.

   Recently a backlash of denial has been expressed regarding the evidence of global warming, but even the conservative journal *The Economist* advocates making changes necessary to slow the perceived warming because they are the same changes that need to be made for other environmental reasons (16 Dec. 1989, 14).

7. Herman E. Daly, "Economics, Environment, and Community," *Earth Ethics*, Public Resource Foundation (Fall 1989): 10.

8. See Herman E. Daly and John B. Cobb, Jr., *For the Common Good: Redirecting the Economy toward Community, the Environment, and a Sustainable Future* (Boston: Beacon Press, 1989); Hazel Henderson, *The Politics of the Solar Age* (Indianapolis: Knowledge Systems, 1988); and James Robertson, *Future Wealth* (London: Cassell, 1989).

9. See Amory Lovins, "Abating Global Warming—at a Profit," *Rocky Mountain Institute Newsletter*, vol. 5, no. 3 (Fall 1989): 1–3; also 4, 6.

10. A meat-based diet causes far more harm to the environment than a vegetarian one in terms of water consumption, water pollution, land erosion, soil depletion, land-use required, wildlife habitat destroyed, and so forth. See John Robbins, *Diet for a New America* (Walpole, NH: Stillpoint, 1987).

11. Bear & Company, Paulist Press, and New Directions all publish series on the Western mystics. The selection from Bear & Company, in particular, focuses on creation-centered mystics. In addition to textual works, they have published *Illuminations of Hildegard of Bingen*, ed. Matthew Fox, 1985.
12. An admirable example is the ten-page pastoral letter on ecology composed by the Catholic bishops of the Philippines, *What Is Happening to Our Beautiful Land?* (1988). For a copy, write to *Lingkod Tao Kalikasan*, c/o Sr. Ma. Aida Velasquez, P.O. Box 2734, Manila, 1099, The Philippines. (I suggest enclosing a donation via an international postal money order to cover copying and mailing.)
13. Shomrei Adamah, under the direction of Ellen Bernstein, is a project of the Federation of Reconstructionist Congregations and Havurot, Church Road and Greenwood Avenue, Wyncote, PA 19095.
14. Excerpts from Assisi Declarations were published in *Creation*, Sept./Oct. 1988 (P.O. Box 19216, Oakland, CA 94619). Also see the analysis of the Declarations by Joseph W. Meeker, "Assisi and the Steward," in *Minding the Earth* (Alameda, CA: The Latham Foundation, 1988).
15. John Collier, *On the Gleaming Way* (Chicago: Sage Books, 1962), 37.
16. Joseph Epes Brown, *The Spiritual Legacy of the American Indian* (New York: Crossroad, 1982), 39.
17. In conversation with Vera Jane He Did It Half, Bozeman, MT, 21 July 1986.
18. G. Reichel-Dolmatoff, "Cosmology as Ecological Analysis: A View from the Rain Forest," *The Ecologist*, vol. 7, no. 1, 1977, 4–11.
19. Peggy V. Beck and Anna L. Walters, *The Sacred: Ways of Knowledge, Sources of Life* (Tsaile [Navajo Nation], AZ: Navajo Community College Press, 1977), 11.
20. Anita Parlow, *Cry, Sacred Ground* (Washington, DC: The Christic Institute, 1988), 52.
21. Bell's theorem states that reality must be nonlocal, at least partially. "Local reality" refers to events (or microevents) occurring as the result of local causes, but it has been demonstrated that some effects occurring in one location correlate with events (or microevents) occurring elsewhere at the same moment.
22. Heisenberg's Uncertainty Principle states that the results of a precise measurement of a particle's position or its velocity are affected by the intention of the person measuring. Position and velocity cannot be measured simultaneously with precision; if one decides to measure a particle's position, it will not exhibit a well-defined momentum, and vice versa. The physicist John Wheeler felt that the most important feature of quantum physics was the realization that the "observer" is really a "participator" (cited in Fritjof Capra, *The Tao of Physics* [Boston: Shambhala Publications, 1975], 140–41).
23. For an excellent study of a native community's sense of spiritual power in animals, see Richard K. Nelson, *Make Prayers to the Raven: A Koyukon View of the Northern Forest* (Chicago: Univ. of Chicago Press, 1983).

24. Steven Charleston, "Public Proclamation, Not Private Conversation: Toward a Native American Theology," *Jubilee: Social Concerns of the Episcopal Church*, New York, NY, Episcopal Church, U.S.A., vol. 2, no. 2 (Spring 1985): 25.
25. See Nelson, *Make Prayers to the Raven*, 44, 53, 91, 98, 105, 124, 142, 158. Nelson notes that several of these riddles were recorded by Julius Jetté in 1913.
26. Cited in Annie Dillard, *A Pilgrim at Tinker's Creek* (New York: Harper & Row, 1974), 122.
27. John B. Carroll, ed., *Language, Thought, and Reality: Selected Writings of Benjamin Lee Whorf* (Cambridge: The M.I.T. Press, 1956), 61–62.
28. Carroll, *Language, Thought*, 62.
29. Dorothy Lee, *Freedom and Culture* (Englewood Cliffs, NJ: Prentice-Hall, 1959), 121.
30. Lee, *Freedom and Culture*, 129.
31. Lee, *Freedom and Culture*, 128.
32. Hyemeyohsts Storm, *Seven Arrows* (New York: Ballantine Books, 1972), 10.
33. Beck and Walters, *The Sacred*, 60.
34. Brown, *Spiritual Legacy*, 43.
35. Brown, *Spiritual Legacy*, 72.
36. Jamake Highwater, *The Primal Mind: Vision and Reality in Indian America* (New York: New American Library, 1981), 76.
37. Charleston, "Public Proclamation."
38. Beck and Walters, *The Sacred*, 75.
39. Lee, *Freedom and Culture*, 79.
40. Joseph Epes Brown, "Contemplation through Actions: North American Indians," in *Contemplation and Action in World Religions*, ed. Yusuf Ibish and Ileana Marculescu (Seattle: Rothko Chapel Books, Univ. of Washington, 1979), 248.
41. Brown, "Contemplation through Actions."
42. Brown, "Contemplation through Actions," 249.
43. Parlow, *Cry, Sacred Ground*, 49.
44. Parlow, *Cry, Sacred Ground*, 48.
45. Beck and Walters, *The Sacred*, 199.
46. Beck and Walters, *The Sacred*, 51.
47. Beck and Walters, *The Sacred*, 51.
48. Brown, *Spiritual Legacy*, 60.
49. Jamake Highwater, *Ritual of the Wind* (New York: Alfred Van Der Marck Editions, 1984), 67.
50. Beck and Walters, *The Sacred*, 226, includes a photo from 1908 of a Luiseño sand painting of the universe used in menarche rituals.
51. Parlow, *Cry, Sacred Ground*, 161–62.
52. Storm, *Seven Arrows*, 5.
53. Brown, *Spiritual Legacy*, 17, 44–45, 53–54.

54. Frank R. LaPena, "My World Is a Gift of My Teachers," in *Contemporary Northern California Native American Art in Cultural Perspective* (Sacramento, CA: Crocker Art Museum, 1985), 13.
55. John Mohawk, "Indigenous Creation-centered Spirituality" (John Mohawk interviewed by Charlene Spretnak), *Creation* (Sept./Oct. 1988): 17.
56. The anthropologist and naturalist Loren Eisley felt that we humans have violated our nature by our exploitative response to the universe. He pointed out that we are ontologically linked with all of nature because of the evolutionary stages we have shared. See *The Immense Journey* (New York: Vintage Books, 1957) and *The Invisible Pyramid* (New York: Macmillan, 1985).
57. All-species parades are community celebrations of the animal citizens in the bioregion. Generally they feature children in costumes of local animals. Further information is available from the All-Species Project, 804 Apodaca Hill, Santa Fe, NM 85701.
58. For example, a tree-planting ceremony at home or on public land needing more vegetation could be part of rites of baptism, First Communion, marriage, and funerals. The liturgical language used in all of those ceremonies could be enriched by including awareness and appreciation of the creation.

    An example of moving in the other direction, that is, bringing rituals of blessing and thanksgiving to events of the natural world, is offered by Gertrude Mueller Nelson in "Blessing for First Fruits and Herbs," using Psalm 65 and derived from "the old ones found in the Roman Ritual" in her inspiring book *To Dance with God: Family Ritual and Community Celebration* (Mahwah, NJ: Paulist Press, 1986), 211.
59. People who observe all eight of the old "Earth holy days" usually consider themselves part of the neo-Pagan movement. "Pagan" means "country person."
60. The spring garland for the Earth in that ritual was the idea of the late Leslie Mahler, a creative and inspiring ritualist whose presence is deeply missed. Some of the other elements, including the songs, traveled from other ritual groups. A cassette tape of several widely used Earth-ritual songs, *Reclaiming Chants*, is available from the Reclaiming Collective, P.O. Box 14404, San Francisco, CA 94114.
61. George Santayana, *Reason in Religion* (New York: Dover Books, 1982 [1905]), 191.
62. Cited from *The New Settler* in *The Progressive*, Sept. 1987, 10.
63. A good textbook on ecology is *Living in the Environment* by G. Tyler Miller, Jr. (Belmont, CA: Wadsworth Publishing, 1982).
64. John Seed, "Beyond Anthropocentrism," in John Seed, Joanna Macy, Pat Fleming, and Arne Naess, *Thinking Like a Mountain: Towards a Council of All Beings* (Philadelphia and Santa Cruz: New Society Publishers, 1988), 36.

Chapter 4 • Embracing the Body

1. See Elisabeth Sahtouris, *Gaia: The Human Journey from Chaos to Cosmos* (New York: Pocket Books, 1989), 105.

2. Peggy Reeves Sanday, *Female Power and Male Dominance: On the Origins of Sexual Inequality* (Cambridge: Cambridge Univ. Press, 1981).
3. See Peggy Reeves Sanday, "The Socio-Cultural Context of Rape: A Cross-cultural Study," *The Journal of Social Issues*, vol. 37, no. 4, 1981, 5–27.
4. Sanday, *Female Power and Male Dominance*, 35.
5. "The Shocking Rape Facts," *San Francisco Chronicle*, 14 May 1990; citations, using FBI figures, from Karen Johnson and Tom Ferguson, *Trusting Ourselves, the Sourcebook on Psychology for Women* (Boston: Atlantic Monthly Press, 1990). The number of reported rapes, that is, the FBI figures, is thought to be much smaller than the number of actual rapes.

   Also see Diana E. H. Russell, *Sexual Exploitation* (Beverly Hills, CA: Sage Publications, 1984). According to Russell's probability sample survey of 930 women in San Francisco, 44 percent had been victims of rape or attempted rape at least once in their lifetime. Of those who had been raped, 50 percent had been raped more than once.

   A survey of 1,292 women, conducted by *Glamour* magazine in 1989, found that only 4 percent of those women who had been sexually abused before age eighteen had been abused by a stranger. For 28 percent the abuser was their father; for 31 percent it was another blood relative; for 23 percent it was an unrelated man they knew; and for 13 percent it was a stepfather or boyfriend of their mother.
6. "Shelters with Comforts of Home," *U.C. Clip Sheet*, Univ. of California, 7 March 1989.
7. "Child Sexual Abuse Study Says Race Has No Bearing on Risk," *U.C. Clip Sheet*, Univ. of California, 6 May 1986.
8. "Teenage Mothers' History of Abuse," *San Francisco Chronicle*, 15 Sept. 1987.
9. See Kathleen Hirsch, *Songs from the Alley* (Boston: Ticknor and Fields, 1989).
10. See Lori Heise, "Crimes of Gender," *WorldWatch*, vol. 2, no. 2 (March/April 1989) 12–21.

    Also see Jane Caputi and Diana E. H. Russell, "'Femicide': Speaking the Unspeakable," *Ms.*, vol. 1, no. 2 (Sept./Oct. 1990): 34–37. The authors suggest *femicide* to name the category of murders of women by men who were motivated by hatred, contempt, pleasure, or a sense of ownership of women. "Murder is simply the most extreme form of sexist terrorism. . . . Femicide includes mutilation murder, rape murder, battery that escalates into murder; historical immolation of witches in Europe; historical and contemporary immolation of brides and widows in India; and 'honor crimes' in some Latin and Middle Eastern countries, where women believed to have lost their virginity sometimes are killed by male relatives."
11. See "Progress for Half the World's People: The United Nations Decade for Women," in *Issues of the Eighties* (U. N. Association of the United States, 1980).

    According to the findings presented at the 34th session of the U.N. Commission on the Status of Women, which ended in March 1990, there has been no tangible progress in achieving real equality for women throughout the world. (See "No Real Progress in Achieving Women's Equality," *Fellowship*, Fellowship of Reconciliation, June 1990, 25.)

12. See Bruno Bettelheim, *Symbolic Wounds: Puberty Rites and the Envious Male* (New York: Collier Books, 1962).
13. See Charlene Spretnak, "Naming the Cultural Forces that Push Us toward War," in *Exposing Nuclear Phallacies*, ed. Diana E. H. Russell (New York: Pergamon Press, 1989).
14. See Bettina Birch, *Radical by Design* (New York: E. P. Dutton, 1988), a biography of the British fashion designer Elizabeth Hawes. Birch describes an evening in 1938 when Hawes's husband, the film director Joseph Losey, invited Hemingway over to dinner. When Hemingway arrived and saw Hawes's protruding abdomen, he asked Losey if they really had to dine with her at the table because he could not stand the sight of pregnant women.
15. Klaus Theweleit, *Male Fantasies*, vol. 1, *Women, Floods, Bodies, History* (Minneapolis: Univ. of Minnesota Press, 1987).
16. See Sandra M. Gilbert and Susan Gubar, *No Man's Land: The Place of the Woman Writer in the Twentieth Century*, vol. 1, *The War of the Words* (New Haven: Yale Univ. Press, 1988).

    Also see Susan Rubin Suleiman, *Subversive Intent: Gender, Politics, and the Avant-Garde* (Cambridge, MA: Harvard Univ. Press, 1990).

    Also see Arianna Stassinopoulos Huffington, *Picasso: Creator and Destroyer* (New York: Simon and Schuster, 1988).

    Steven Connor concludes in *Postmodernist Culture* (London: Basil Blackwell, 1989), 110, that the postmodern literary critic Ihab Hassan asserts "the heroic maleness of modernist/postmodernist denial against the disgusting 'female' acquiescence of matter, of the world, history, tradition."
17. Structuralism is a mode of analysis based on the central tenet that all societies and cultures possess a common and invariant structure. Based on the anthropological writings of Claude Lévi-Strauss, structuralists perceive "deep" structures composed of interacting, complementary "opposites," such as men and women, in all cultural expressions.
18. Michel Foucault, "Preface to *The History of Sexuality*, Volume Two," in *The Foucault Reader*, ed. Paul Rabinow (New York: Pantheon Books, 1984), 335.
19. It is apparent to those who will admit that personal desires have some influence on "pure scholarship" that Foucault, as a homosexual in a society that oppresses homosexuals because such behavior is taken to be "obviously" depraved, had something of a personal stake in proving that a society's responses to sexual acts are entirely culturally constructed. If the act of sodomy were to be decriminalized and neutralized, the same would have to be done with rape, as specifically sexual assault.
20. "What Is Enlightenment?," in *The Foucault Reader*, ed. Paul Rabinow (New York: Pantheon Books, 1984), 49.
21. Arthur and Marilouise Kroker, "Theses on the Disappearing Body in the Hyper-Modern Condition," in *Body Invaders*, ed. Arthur and Marilouise Kroker (New York: St. Martin's Press, 1987), 31.

22. The following are examples of works that explore themes of cultural feminism. *Chrysalis* magazine, published in the late 1970s and early 1980s, was a forum of cultural feminism. Among the articles it published were "The Freudian Cover-Up: The Sexual Abuse of Children" by Florence Rush, "Psychoanalysis, Patriarchy, and Power" by Jean Baker Miller, "'Disloyal to Civilization': Feminism, Racism, and Gynephobia" by Adrienne Rich, "The Erotic as Power" by Audre Lorde, and "Nuclear Madness: An Interview with Helen Caldicott." *Woman and Nature* by Susan Griffin (New York: Harper & Row, 1978), plus scores of books on the history and relevance of Goddess spirituality (see "Related Reading" at the end of this book) explore cultural history from a feminist perspective. Two other expressions of cultural feminism are my "Naming the Cultural Forces that Push Us toward War" in *Exposing Nuclear Phallacies*, ed. Diana E. H. Russell (New York: Pergamon Press, 1989) and my introduction to *The Politics of Women's Spirituality* (Garden City, NY: Doubleday, 1982), which proposes, among other things, that cultural power hoarded by males is a compensatory response to a fearful perception of the elemental power of the female, and that Jungian notions of the "eternal feminine" and the passive receptivity it entails are cultural constructions of patriarchy rather than universal truths about females.
23. See Mary Daly, *The Church and the Second Sex* (New York: Harper & Row, 1968) and Elizabeth Cady Stanton and the Revising Committee, *The Woman's Bible* (1985), republished as *The Original Feminist Attack on the Bible* (New York: Arno Press, 1974). Also available by then was Mary Daly's *Beyond God the Father: Toward a Philosophy of Women's Liberation* (Boston: Beacon Press, 1973), which she refers to in the introduction as a sequel to *The Church and the Second Sex* and which advocated women's charting a postpatriarchal path.

    It is important to note that Canaan was one of the last, not first, areas in the eastern Mediterranean region and southeastern Europe to "go patriarchal." The Yahwehists who migrated into Canaan definitely were not the sole cause of the destruction of all Goddess religion.
24. See Charlene Spretnak, *Lost Goddesses of Early Greece: A Collection of Pre-Hellenic Myths* (Boston: Beacon Press, 1981).
25. See, for example, Peggy Reeves Sanday, "The Decline of the Women's World: The Effect of Colonialism," chapter seven, in *Female Power and Male Dominance: On the Origins of Sexual Inequality* (Cambridge: Cambridge Univ. Press, 1981).
26. David Anthony of Hartwick College, Oneonta, NY, presented this finding at the International Conference on Archaeozoology in Washington, DC, in May 1990.
27. Marija Gimbutas's pioneering archaeological work concerning Old Europe falls into two areas: (1) the nature of society in Old Europe and the transformation caused by the Indo-European migrations, and (2) archaeomythology, a field she invented in order to consider the religious significance of excavated artifacts. The nature of the Old European substratum and

the social shift she has documented with regard to the first area of research is widely accepted by archaeologists internationally; some of her interpretive work associated with the second area is controversial among certain archaeologists.

Concerning the first area, see Marija Gimbutas, *The Civilization of the Goddess: Neolithic Europe before the Patriarchy* (San Francisco: HarperCollins, 1991). In addition, see her article "The Collision of Two Ideologies," in *When World Collide: The Indo-Europeans and the Pre–Indo-Europeans,* ed. T. L. Markey and John A. C. Greppin (Ann Arbor, MI: Karoma Publishers, 1990). Professor Gimbutas also edited volume 8 of *The Journal of Indo-European Studies* on "The Transformation of European and Anatolian Culture c. 4500–2500 B.C. and Its Legacy, Part II," Fall/Winter 1980, which contains articles on the great transformation by archaeologists from the Soviet Union and numerous countries in Eastern Europe.

Concerning the second area, see Marija Gimbutas, *The Language of the Goddess: Unearthing the Hidden Symbols of Western Civilization* (San Francisco: Harper & Row, 1989) and *The Goddesses and Gods of Old Europe, Myths and Cult Images, 6500–3500 B.C.* (Berkeley: Univ. of California Press, 1974).

28. For a thoughtful exploration of this experience, see Adrienne Rich, "Prepatriarchal Female/Goddess Images," in *The Politics of Women's Spirituality* (Garden City, NY: Doubleday, 1982), excerpted from her *Of Woman Born: Motherhood as Experience and Institution* (New York: W. W. Norton, 1976).

29. See Gimbutas, *Language of the Goddess.*

Skeptics sometimes accuse feminist cultural historians of "prettifying" the pre-Indo-European goddesses by ignoring the bloodthirsty, devouring ones, which they are certain must have existed. Actually, those forms seem to arise with the advent of patriarchal culture. The prepatriarchal goddesses represented the entire cycle of being—birth, maturation, death, regeneration—but apparently not as demonic forces. Even Kali, the devouring Hindu goddess, is believed by many scholars to be a revised version of an indigenous Earth goddess who long predated the Aryan invasion; see the discussion by David R. Kinsley in chapter three of *The Sword and the Flute: Kali and Krsna* (Berkeley: Univ. of California Press, 1975).

30. See Elinor W. Gadon, *The Once and Future Goddess* (San Francisco: Harper & Row, 1989) and Gloria Feman Orenstein, *The Reflowering of the Goddess* (New York: Pergamon Press, 1990).

Also see Mary Beth Edelson, *Seven Cycles: Public Rituals; Seven Sites: Painting on Walls;* and *Shape Shifters: Seven Mediums* (all available from the artist: 110 Mercer St., New York, NY 10012).

Also see Janine Canan, ed., *She Rises Like the Sun; Invocations of the Goddess by Contemporary American Women Poets* (Freedom, CA: The Crossing Press, 1989).

31. Surely penis envy is not the universal response that Freud assumed it to be. The feminist author Elizabeth Dodson Gray relates a young mother's

account of the aftermath of a visit in which her pre-school-age daughter took a bath with a boy of the same age. After the boy and his mother had left, the girl said to her mother with earnest compassion, "Isn't it a blessing it didn't grow on his face?"

32. Luce Irigaray, "The Sex Which Is Not One," in *New French Feminism*, ed. Elaine Marks and Isabelle de Courtivron (New York: Schocken Books, 1981), 103.

 Also see Arleen B. Dallery, "The Politics of Writing (the) Body," in *Gender/Body/Knowledge: Feminist Reconstructions of Being and Knowing*, ed. Alison M. Jaggar and Susan R. Bordo (New Brunswick, NJ: Rutgers Univ. Press, 1989).

 Also see the special issue of *Signs: Journal of Women in Culture and Society*, 1981, vol. 7, no. 1, on French feminism, focusing on the works of Hélène Cixous, Luce Irigaray, Julia Kristeva, and Christine Fauré.

33. Although the focus of this chapter is the renewal of Goddess spirituality by women who left institutional patriarchal religion, I do not mean to imply that only those women who left were feminist. A strong feminist movement exists today within both Judaism and Christianity (see "Related Reading" for chapter 5). An example is the response issued in 1990 by Rosemary Radford Ruether and several Catholic women's organizations to the U.S. bishops' pastoral letter on women. Here is an excerpt from their open letter, which was published in *Christianity and Crisis*, vol. 50, no. 8 (28 May 1990):

 > In the new draft of the pastoral letter on women which your office has recently released you call on the world to repent of sexism and to give to women that full equality of personhood which is their God-given nature. Yet your pastoral reaffirms every aspect of the patriarchal system which is the basis of sexism. Dear Bishops, you embarrass us. You insult our intelligence. . . .
 >
 > What you want, Dear Bishops, is to seduce us into helping to rescue your patriarchal ecclesial system, while conceding nothing that is essential to that system itself. . . .
 >
 > Let me say clearly to you, Dear Bishops, we will not raise one cent for your patriarchal church. We will not lift one finger to rescue your patriarchal system. We will not bend one knee to worship the patriarchal idol that you blasphemously insist on calling "God." We are not fooled.
 >
 > We have heard the gospel of the authentic Jesus, the Christ: good news to the poor, release to the captives, the setting at liberty of those who are oppressed. We are raising money to promote the ministries of that authentic gospel. . . .
 >
 > But not one cent, not one finger lifted, not one knee bent for the church of patriarchy: the arrogant, blind, hypocritical, unrepentant Church of patriarchy. . . .

34. The internationally known postmodern semioticist Umberto Eco has noted, perhaps inadvertently, that this traditional motivation for men raised under

patriarchy indeed helped shape his life. At twenty-two he decided that intimacy itself held far less appeal than the desire to project his name (or "sign") beyond the death of the body via writing a book and making a son. For this budding semioticist, the abstract "sign" of his own being (his name) seemed to be the primary focus in life. (See Marshall Blonsky, "A Literary High-Wire Act," *New York Times Magazine*, 10 Dec. 1989, 79.)

For a related and quite lively article, see Christine Brooke-Rose, "Woman as a Semiotic Object," in *The Female Body in Western Culture*, ed. Susan Rubin Suleiman (Cambridge: Harvard Univ. Press, 1986), 305–16.

35. Excerpted, and slightly adapted, from Spretnak, *Lost Goddesses of Early Greece*, 77–81.
36. A spiral dance, developed by Starhawk and the Reclaiming Collective, has become a popular closing ceremony at conferences. During the course of the spiraling, one sees the face (and body) of each participant pass before him or her twice. For directions and a diagram, see Starhawk, *The Spiral Dance*, Tenth Anniversary Edition (San Francisco: Harper & Row, 1989), 246–47.
37. Apparently the label "mythopoetic" was attached to the "earthy masculinity" branch of the men's movement by Shepherd Bliss in the mid-1980s. Robert Bly is probably the best-known practitioner. For a feminist response to Bly's analyses about men's liberation that is both appreciative and critical, see Terry Allen Kupers, "Feminist Men," *Tikkun: a Bimonthly Jewish Critique of Politics, Culture, and Society*, July/Aug. 1990, 35–38.
38. A professor of religious studies told me of attending a conference on ecology and religion and hearing a male speaker insist that we must stop "the rape of Mother Earth" and stop "ripping into Her placenta." He repeated the latter phrase frequently, always with a passionate tone that sounded increasingly sadistic. Is that a common, if unspoken, response in patriarchal culture? I do not claim to know.
39. This objection was first raised, to my knowledge, by Elizabeth Dodson Gray.
40. Not all women's ritual groups, of course, locate themselves within the Goddess tradition. For an account of Christian-based rituals conducted with her women's group and with her family, see Gertrude Mueller Nelson's lovely *To Dance with God: Family Ritual and Community Celebration* (Mahwah, NJ: Paulist Press, 1986).
41. Spretnak, "The Myth of Aphrodite," in *Lost Goddesses of Early Greece*, 72.
42. See Robin May Schott, *Cognition and Eros: A Critique of the Kantian Paradigm* (Boston: Beacon Press, 1988).
43. See Jane Flax, "Political Philosophy and the Patriarchal Unconscious: A Psychoanalytic Perspective on Epistemology and Metaphysics," in *Discovering Reality*, ed. Sandra Harding and Merrill B. Hintikka (Dordrecht, Holland: D. Reidel Pub., 1983).
44. Flax, "Political Philosophy."

45. Sandra Harding, "Is Gender a Variable in Conceptions of Reality?," a paper delivered at the Fifth International Colloquium on Rationality, Vienna, 1981; cited by Susan Bordo in "The Cartesian Masculinization of Thought," *Signs: Journal of Women and Culture in Society*, vol. 11, no. 3, 441.
46. See Bordo, "Cartesian Masculinization," 439–56. Also see her *The Flight to Objectivity: Essays on Cartesianism and Culture* (Albany, NY: SUNY Press, 1987).
47. See Carolyn Merchant, *The Death of Nature: Women, Ecology, and the Scientific Revolution* (San Francisco: Harper & Row, 1980).
48. See H. A. Witkin et al., *Psychological Differentiation* (New York: Wiley, 1962); cited in Dale Spender, *Man Made Language* (London: Routledge & Kegan Paul, 1980), 164.

    Also see Carol Gilligan, *In a Different Voice: Psychological Theory and Women's Development* (Cambridge, MA: Harvard Univ. Press, 1982).
49. See Deborah Tannen, *You Just Don't Understand: Women and Men in Conversation* (New York: Morrow, 1990). Also see Dale Spender, *Man Made Language* (London: Routledge & Kegan Paul, 1980) and Robin Lakoff, *Language and Woman's Place* (New York: Harper & Row, 1975).
50. See Evelyn Fox Keller, *A Feeling for the Organism: The Life and Work of Barbara McClintock* (New York and San Francisco: W. H. Freeman, 1983).
51. See Linda Holler, "Thinking with the Weight of the Earth: Feminist Contributions to an Epistemology of Concreteness," *Hypatia: A Journal of Feminist Philosophy*, vol. 5, no. 1 (Spring 1990): 1–23. Holler's concept of "lateral transcendence" describes the act of knowing as "a mode of transcendence based on being-in-relation-to, which, by rendering the knower incarnate, lessens the temptation to abstract 'things' from concrete space and time." She explains that this concept builds on Merleau-Ponty's notion of the "lateral universal."

    I find her article altogether admirable, with the exception of a problem with terminology: she uses the unqualified term "postmodern" mostly to draw from postmodern physics so assumes the acceptance of the concept of a whole, a cosmos, as in ecological postmodernism. However, deconstructive postmodernists rooting their thinking in the works of Foucault, Derrida, and others dismiss such an assertion as merely "the narrative of holism," yet another cultural invention of scientists. They certainly would not call holism "postmodern."
52. Evelyn Fox Keller, "Dynamic Objectivity: Love, Power, and Knowledge," chapter six, in *Reflections on Gender and Science* (New Haven: Yale Univ. Press, 1985). "'Dynamic objectivity' is the pursuit of a form of knowledge that grants to the world around us independent integrity but does so in a way that remains cognizant of, indeed relies on, our connectivity with that world" (117).

Chapter 5 • Who Is the Other?

1. See Michael H. Brown, *The Search for Eve* (New York: Harper & Row, 1990).

2. Francine Klagsbrun, *Voices of Wisdom: Jewish Ideals and Ethics for Everyday Living* (Middle Village, NY: Jonathan David Publishers, 1980), 327.

   Also see Edith Wyschogrod, "Works that 'Faith': The Grammar of Ethics in Judaism," *CrossCurrents: Religion and Intellectual Life*, vol. 40, no. 2 (Summer 1990): 176–93. This article "makes the case for Judaism as ethics," with an understanding of ethics as "something far different from the meaning given to it by Enlightenment philosophy."
3. See Ronald J. Sider, ed., *Cry Justice: The Bible on Hunger and Poverty* (Downers Grove, IL: InterVarsity Press, 1980); John C. Cort, *Christian Socialism*, chapter 3 (Maryknoll, NY: Orbis Books, 1988) and Jim Wallis, ed., *The Rise of Christian Conscience* (San Francisco: Harper & Row, 1987).
4. Frederick M. Denny, *Islam* (San Francisco: Harper & Row, 1987), 41.
5. See Merlin Stone, *When God Was A Woman* (New York: Dial Press, 1976) and Savina J. Teubal, *Sarah the Priestess: The First Matriarch of Genesis* (Athens, OH: Swallow Press, 1984).
6. Although patriarchal bias is evident in all three of the Semitic traditions, feminist scholars and activists have drawn attention to egalitarian practices from the early eras that have been papered over by the institutionalized history of the faith. See, for example, Elisabeth Schüssler Fiorenza, *In Memory of Her* (New York: Crossroad, 1983) and *Bread Not Stone* (Boston: Beacon Press, 1984).

   In addition, as women in Islamic countries have attained literacy, they have discovered that many oppressive rules "of Islam" are not in the Qur'an, but were merely invented by various patriarchs.
7. See, for example, Judith Plaskow, *Standing Again at Sinai* (San Francisco: Harper & Row, 1990); Susannah Heschel, ed., *On Being a Jewish Feminist* (New York: Schocken, 1983); Rosemary Radford Ruether, *Sexism and God-Talk* (Boston: Beacon Press, 1983) and *Womanguides* (Boston: Beacon Press, 1985).
8. Plaskow, *Standing Again at Sinai*, 216–17.
9. See Bernard Nietschmann, "The Third World War," *Cultural Survival Quarterly*, vol. 11, no. 3, 1987, 1–15.
10. Vandana Shiva, *Staying Alive: Woman, Ecology and Development* (London: Zed Books, 1988).

    This book includes a description of the Chipko movement, in which rural Indian women hugged the forest trees in order to save them from "development" by bulldozers.

    Also see Bina Agarwal, ed., *Structures of Patriarchy: The State, the Community and the Household* (London: Zed Books, 1986). These essays challenge the assumption that state-directed development in Asia is gender-neutral.
11. "U.N.'s Dire Environmental Diagnosis," *San Francisco Chronicle*, 6 June 1990.
12. In conversation with Helena Norberg-Hodge, 2 February 1990.

13. "U.S. Businesses Loosen Link to Mother Country," *New York Times*, 21 May 1989.
14. "Superfirms' World of No Borders," *Washington Post*, reprinted in the *San Francisco Chronicle*, 5 April 1989.
15. The automotive industry is one example: Chrysler owns Italy's Lamborghini, 16 percent of Maserati, and 24 percent of De Tomaso, plus 12 percent of Mitsubishi and a joint venture with Renault, from which it bought American Motors. Ford owns England's Jaguar, 50 percent of Great Britain's AC Cars, 70 percent of Taiwan's Lio Ho, 25 percent of Mazda, and 10 percent of Kia; it has joint ventures with Fiat, Nissan in Australia, and Volkswagen in South America. General Motors owns Germany's Opel, Australia's Holden, England's Lotus and Vauxhall, 50 percent of Korea's Daewoo, 38 percent of Japan's Isuzu, and has joint ventures in California and Australia. Germany's Volkswagen owns Porsche, Audi, 76 percent of Spain's SEAT, and has joint ventures with Shanghai Tractor and Auto, with Ford in South America and Daimler-Benz at home. Italy's Fiat owns Alfa Romeo, Lancia, 90 percent of Ferrari, 15 percent of Zavodi Crvena Zastava (Yugo), and joint ventures with Ford and Maserati. In addition, there are the well-known joint ventures in North America such as the New United Motor Manufacturing plant (General Motors and Toyota), Diamond-Star Motors (Chrysler and Mitsubishi), and Canadian-American Manufacturing Inc. (GM of Canada and Suzuki). Source: "Buy an American Car—If You Can Find One," *San Francisco Examiner*, 1 April 1990.
16. This central motivation for our defense buildup is usually spoken of only obliquely, but former Secy. of Defense Caspar Weinberger was quite direct about it in his annual report for fiscal year 1984.
17. See Maurice Zeitlin, *The Large Corporation and Contemporary Classes* (New Brunswick, NJ: Rutgers Univ. Press, 1989).

    A report in August 1990 based on data from the Internal Revenue Service stated that the richest 1 percent own 28.5 percent of U.S. wealth, more than the entire G.N.P. (*San Francisco Chronicle*, 23 Aug. 1990).

    Robert Greenstein, director of the Center on Budget and Policy Priorities, has concluded, "During the 1950s and 1960s, the benefits of economic growth were widely shared. The gap between the rich and poor actually narrowed a bit. But during the 1980s, the gains of economic recovery overwhelmingly went to a small group at the top. . . . This was not typical of previous decades of growth" ("Study Says 80s Were Best to Wealthy," *San Francisco Chronicle*, 24 July 1990).
18. "Study Finds Steep Inequality in Wealth," excerpts from a report by Thomas Shapiro and Melvin Oliver that was published in the *American Journal of Economics and Sociology*, April 1990; cited in the *San Francisco Chronicle*, 30 March 1990.
19. Zeitlin, *Large Corporation*.
20. Shapiro and Oliver, "Steep Inequality in Wealth."
21. "Schools Join Self-Esteem Movement," sidebar titled "Highlights," *San Francisco Chronicle*, 9 April 1990.

22. "S.F. Fed Chief's Inflation Alert," *San Francisco Chronicle*, 21 April 1990.
23. Because of such situations, people of color have entered the environmental movement in significant ways. See *Race, Poverty and the Environment Newsletter*, ed. Carl Anthony and Luke Cole, Earth Island Institute, 300 Broadway, Suite 28, San Francisco, CA 94133-3312. Also see Holly Brough, "Minorities Redefine 'Environmentalism,'" *WorldWatch*, vol. 3, no. 5 (Sept./Oct. 1990): 5–7.
24. Michael Ferber, "Religious Revival on the Left," *The Nation*, 6–13 July 1985, 12.
25. Rosa Parks's refusal to go to the back of the bus on 1 December 1955, and her subsequent arrest, inspired Jo Ann Robinson and other African-American women of the Women's Political Council to stay up nearly all night composing and reproducing an open letter calling for a boycott. E. D. Nixon, another local activist, was also central in the growth and steering of the long boycott. See Taylor Branch, *Parting the Waters: America in the King Years, 1954–63* (New York: Simon and Schuster, 1988), 132.
26. See the transcript of *Bill Moyers' World of Ideas: Cornel West* (New York: Public Affairs Television, 1990), 7.

    Also see Cornel West, *Prophetic Fragments* (Grand Rapids, MI: Eerdmans Pub., 1988).

    Also see Vincent Harding, *Hope and History: Why We Must Share the Story of the Movement* (Maryknoll, NY: Orbis Books, 1990).
27. See Guy and Candi Carawan, eds., *Sing for Freedom: The Story of the Civil Rights Movement through Its Songs* (Philadelphia and Santa Cruz: New Society Publishers, 1990).
28. Pastor Will Herzfeld, lecture on the spiritual dimension of the civil-rights movement, Institute in Culture and Creation Spirituality, Holy Names College, Oakland, CA, 26 Feb. 1986.
29. See, for example, Susan Brooks Thistlethwaite and Mary Potter Engel, eds., *Lift Every Voice: Constructing Theologies from the Underside* (San Francisco: Harper & Row, 1990). Also see *The Road to Damascus: Kairos and Conversion*, the document issued by a conference of Third World Christians, published in *Sojourners*, vol. 19, no. 1, Jan. 1990.
30. Lilith Quinlan, cited in "Gandhian Strategy at Kings Bay Submarine Base," *Fellowship*, Fellowship of Reconciliation, Nyack, NY, Dec. 1989, 24.
31. Edward L. Cleary, *Crisis and Change; The Church in Latin America Today* (Maryknoll, NY: Orbis Books, 1985), 118.
32. Philip and Sally Scharper, eds., *The Gospel in Art by the Peasants of Solentiname* (Maryknoll, NY: Orbis Books, 1984), 20.
33. Brady Tyson, "Contagious Compassion: Base Communities in Brazil," in *Set My People Free: Liberation Theology in Practice* (Hyattsville, MD: Quixote Center, 1986), 9.
34. Arthur F. McGovern, *Liberation Theology and Its Critics: Toward an Assessment* (Maryknoll, NY: Orbis Books, 1989), 146.
35. McGovern, *Liberation Theology and Its Critics*, 146.
36. McGovern, *Liberation Theology and Its Critics*, 146.

37. McGovern, *Liberation Theology and Its Critics*, 146, 160.
38. Gustavo Gutierrez, "Expanding the View," *A Theology of Liberation*, Fifteenth Anniversary Edition (Maryknoll, NY: Orbis Books, 1988).
39. McGovern, *Liberation Theology and Its Critics*, 148.
40. McGovern, *Liberation Theology and Its Critics*, 164.
41. Kenneth Aman, "Marxism(s) in Liberation Theology," *Cross Currents* (Winter 1984–85): 427–38.
42. Niall O'Brien, "From the Island of Negros," *Fellowship*, Fellowship of Reconciliation, July/Aug. 1989, 7.
43. "Priest helped Philippine poor resist 'system of virtual serfdom,'" *Christian Science Monitor*, 21 March 1988.
44. *Quadragesimo anno, (Forty Years After,* or *On Restructuring the Social Order)*, was a commemoration and expansion of Pope Leo XIII's 1891 encyclical *Rerum Novarum*, or *On the Condition of Workers*.
45. Andrew M. Greeley, *No Bigger than Necessary: An Alternative to Socialism, Capitalism, and Anarchism* (New York: New American Library, 1977), 10–12. Another insightful commentary on Catholic social teaching is Maria Riley's *Transforming Feminism* (Kansas City, MO: Sheed & Ward, 1989).
46. New Economics Foundation, 88–94 Wentworth Street, London E1 7SE, U.K. Also see a well-edited anthology by one of its founders, Paul Ekins, *The Living Economy: A New Economics in the Making* (London and New York: Routledge & Kegan Paul, 1986). Another important work by a TOES affiliate, Herman E. Daly, is *For the Common Good: Redirecting the Economy toward Community, the Environment, and a Sustainable Future* (Boston: Beacon Press, 1989), which he wrote with the theologian John B. Cobb, Jr.

    Also see the *Oxford Declaration on Christian Faith and Economics* (available from Dr. Ronald J. Sider, 10 Lancaster Ave., Philadelphia, PA 19151). Also see *Grapevine*, newsletter of the Christian interdenominational Joint Strategy and Action Committee (475 Riverside Dr., Rm. 560, New York, NY 10115).
47. John Hellman, "John Paul II and the Personalist Movement," *Cross Currents* (Winter 1980–81): 412.
48. Hellman, "John Paul II," 416.
49. Bohdan Pilacinski, "Poland's Solidarity: A Personalist Revolution," *New Oxford Review*, March 1990, 14.
50. Unfortunately for the personalist "third way" (and probably for Poland), the possibility of putting that model into action was abandoned by the Solidarity government after Solidarity's Parliamentary Club heard a passionate speech in 1989 by Jeffrey Sachs, a young Harvard professor of economics. The Polish leaders decided that their country should undergo Sachs's high-speed "capitalist shock treatment," which not only eliminates all subsidies and controls but also forbids any third-way experiments with democratic controls, public ownership, cooperatives, or worker-ownership. During the first half of 1990, Poles suffered a 40 percent drop in real wages and a deep

recession under the Sachs free-market plan. Writing in *The Nation* ("Capitalist Shock Therapy," 25 June 1990), Jon Weiner noted that the big successes among capitalist economies since World War II are found in countries that have generally rejected the free market in favor of export subsidies, low-cost credit, and protection from foreign competition.

51. Elsa Tamez, ed., *Through Her Eyes: Women's Theology from Latin America* (Maryknoll, NY: Orbis Books, 1989), 152.
52. Alida Verhoeven, "The Concept of God: A Feminine Perspective," in *Through Her Eyes: Women's Theology from Latin America*, ed. Elsa Tamez (Maryknoll, NY: Orbis Books, 1989), 54–55.
53. Consuelo del Prado, "I Sense God in Another Way," in *Through Her Eyes: Women's Theology from Latin America*, ed. Elsa Tamez (Maryknoll, NY: Orbis Books, 1989), 141.
54. Ivone Gebara, "Women Doing Theology in Latin America," in *Through Her Eyes: Women's Theology from Latin America*, ed. Elsa Tamez (Maryknoll, NY: Orbis Books, 1989), 46.
55. Verhoeven, "Concept of God," 54–55.
56. See, for example, Robert Allan Warrior, "Canaanites, cowboys, and Indians: Deliverance, conquest, and liberation theology today," *Christianity and Crisis*, 11 Sept. 1989.
57. Jim Wallis, "The Second Reformation Has Begun," *Sojourners*, Jan. 1990, 15.
58. For some inspiring ideas on this subject, see Thomas Berry, "The American College in the Ecological Age," in *The Dream of the Earth* (San Francisco: Sierra Club Books, 1988), 89–108.
59. "Management professors note few changes in ethical values in past 25 years," *U.C. Clip Sheet*, Univ. of California, 10 Oct. 1989. A study by Professors Hal Kassarjian and Barbara Kahn, U.C.L.A., found that one change noticed in surveying business people in 1964 and 1989 was that the contemporary group "felt that, once an individual has met the requirements of the law, one has fulfilled one's ethical responsibilities and is free to conduct business as one pleases without acting unethically."
60. See Douglas Frantz, *Levine & Co.: Wall Street's Insider Trading Scandal* (New York: Henry Holt, 1987).
61. Mickey Kaus, "For a New Equality," *The New Republic*, 7 May 1990, 21. Kaus, however, regards high taxes for the very wealthy as ineffective since they always find tax shelters and loopholes.
62. "Lincoln Memo Listed Likely Bond 'Targets,'" Associated Press, *San Francisco Chronicle*, 31 March 1990.
63. This description comes from Gordon Cosby, an inner-city minister in Washington, D.C., in an interview conducted by Jim Wallis, "Spirituality and Community: Reflections on Evil and Grace," in *The Rise of Christian Conscience* (San Francisco: Harper & Row, 1987), 157.
64. Kristin Helmore, "Growing Food and Pride," *Christian Science Monitor*, 1 March 1989.

65. Jim Wallis, "Idols Closer to Home: Christian Substitutes for Grace," in *The Rise of Christian Conscience* (San Francisco: Harper & Row, 1987), 191.
66. Wallis, "Idols Closer to Home," 196.

Chapter 6 • The Recovery of Meaning

1. Stephen McKnight, *Sacralizing the Secular: The Renaissance Origins of Modernity* (Baton Rouge, LA: Louisiana Univ. Press, 1989). The author includes a bibliography of studies that "led the way in opening the new perspective on Renaissance thought and experience."
2. McKnight, *Sacralizing the Secular*, 21.
3. For a fuller discussion, see McKnight, *Sacralizing the Secular*, chapter 5.
4. See the catalogue of an exhibition titled *The Spiritual in Art: Abstract Painting, 1890–1985* (New York: Abbeville Press and the Los Angeles County Museum of Art, 1986). This exhibition was presented in Los Angeles, Chicago, and The Hague (the Netherlands) between Nov. 1986 and Nov. 1987. I assume copies of the extremely interesting catalogue are still available from the book store in the Los Angeles County Museum of Art.

   Another potential stream of spiritual content into twentieth-century art was the interest demonstrated by many famous painters during the first four decades in Paris in sculptures and masks from native cultures; many of the artists owned large collections. In fall 1984 the Museum of Modern Art in New York mounted a major exhibition called "'Primitivism' in 20th-Century Art," in which they juxtaposed pieces of native people's art (from Africa, North America, and Oceania) with art by modern Western artists. Much of the native art exhibited were the very pieces that had been owned by an artist or had been exhibited in a Parisian museum and widely known in artistic circles then. Although the modern borrowers often drew quite closely from the native people's work, it seems to me that this spiritual catalyst was only "potential" because the modern interpretations and creations appear to lack the holistic, organic worldview that informed the native works. It appears that a number of the modern artists missed, or ignored, the spiritual and cosmological content and simply took the form and played with it. For some of the modernist painters, the smashing of form into jaggedly protruding planes, as in Picasso's *Les demoiselles d'Avignon*, seems to shout of the "creative destruction" so central to the macho modernist project (see note 16 in chapter 4 of this book). In the MOMA exhibit, the description beneath Jackson Pollack's painting *Birth* read: "Pollack painted his violent image [*Birth*] in 1939, just after Picasso's *Les demoiselles d'Avignon* had gone on view at the Museum of Modern Art. Looking for a way to go even beyond the deformations of Picasso's masklike faces, Pollack turned to the whorllike forms of an Eskimo mask from the University Museum in Philadelphia."
5. Maurice Tuchman, "Hidden Meanings in Abstract Art," in *The Spiritual in Art: Abstract Painting, 1890–1985* (New York: Abbeville Press and the Los Angeles County Museum of Art, 1986), 38.

6. Tuchman, "Hidden Meanings," 49.

In between the metaphysical abstract expressionists and the earlier cosmological abstract painters had come the macho mood of the modernist painters, such as Picasso. That posture seems to have left traces in the ways the abstract expressionists framed their metaphysical interests. Note the verbs to "penetrate," "dig," and "wrest" in the following passage by Barnett Newman during the mid-1940s, opposing his intentions and those of Gottlieb, Rothko, Pollack, and others of the emerging New York School to the design-oriented abstraction of the 1930s:

> The present painter is concerned not with his own feelings or with the mystery of his own personality but with the penetration into the world mystery. His imagination is therefore attempting to dig into metaphysical secrets. To that extent his art is concerned with the sublime. It is a religious art which through symbols will catch the basic truth of life. . . . The artist tries to wrest truth from the void.

7. The historian Jaroslav Pelikan notes that the Enlightenment deposed the cosmic Christ and made the quest for the historical Christ inevitable (see *Jesus Through the Centuries* [New Haven, CT: Yale Univ. Press, 1985], 184).

For an exploration of the cosmic Christ, see Matthew Fox, *The Coming of the Cosmic Christ* (San Francisco: Harper & Row, 1988).

8. See Freny Mistry, *Nietzsche and Buddhism* (Berlin and New York: Walter de Gruyter, 1981), 6–7.
9. Mistry, *Nietzsche and Buddhism.*
10. Sigmund Freud, *The Future of an Illusion* (New York: Liveright Publishing, 1953).
11. Bruno Bettelheim, *Freud and Man's Soul* (New York: Alfred A. Knopf, 1983), 32.
12. Brian Swimme made this observation during a remarkable course on cosmology he taught at the Institute in Culture and Creation Spirituality at Holy Names College in Oakland in fall 1985. His vibrant lectures on this subject have been videotaped, and the series, titled *Canticle to the Cosmos*, is available from Tides/NewStory Project, 134 Coleen St., Livermore, CA 94550.
13. Alister Hardy, *The Spiritual Nature of Man: A Study of Contemporary Religious Experience* (Oxford: Oxford Univ. Press, 1979), 1.
14. See Caroline Franks Davis, *The Evidential Force of Religious Experience* (Oxford: Oxford Univ. Press, 1989), 177. Franks Davis identifies these four categories as "irreducible types of experience."

On page 167 Franks Davis cites five "very representative types of experience": (1) a numinous experience of "creature-consciousness" when one feels oneself to be in the presence of an awe-inspiring and supremely holy power; (2) a rapturous theistic mystical experience apparently of loving intimacy with a personal "Other"; (3) a monistic experience of seeming to transcend "all barriers, all sense of duality, differences, separateness," including the idea of a God with personal attributes, and arriving at the realization of "profound Silence or Profound Peace, wherein all thoughts cease and you become identical with the Supreme Self"; (4) a "natural mystical" experience of a fundamental unity behind but going no further than the things of this world, with "perceptions" such as R. M. Bucke's "that all men are immortal; that the cosmic order is such that. . . .all things work together for the good of each and all; that the foundation principle of the world . . . is what we call love . . ."; (5) a Buddhist experience going "beyond Yogin identity with the universe, beyond Christian union with God, to limitless expansion, to the unthinkable"—in its most extreme form, an experience in which the meditator sees that all suffers from "impermanence, imperfection, and non-self," and in which he "truly knows that he is no self, either bodily or spiritually, but only a series of processes and thoughts, that all other 'realities' are also thus empty and transient."

15. Steven T. Katz, "Language, Epistemology, and Mysticism," in *Mysticism and Philosophical Analysis*, ed. Steven T. Katz (Oxford and New York: Oxford Univ. Press, 1978), 26.

    Also see *Mysticism and Religious Traditions*, ed. Steven T. Katz (Oxford and New York: Oxford Univ. Press, 1983).

16. An example of the shock such moments sometimes bring was recorded by Don Johnson in *The Protean Body: A Rolfer's View of Human Flexibility* (New York: Harper & Row, 1977), 129–30. Johnson, a former Jesuit priest, describes an experience he once had immediately after receiving a bodywork session from Ida Rolf:

    > Once when Ida had done a session with me, spending most of the hour loosening and restructuring my sacrum, I walked out onto a dock in the Gulf of Mexico. *I* ceased to exist. I experienced being a part of the sea breeze, the movement of the water and the fish, the light rays cast by the sun, the colors of the palms and tropical flowers. I had no sense of past or future. It was not a particularly blissful experience: it was terrifying. It was the kind of ecstatic experience I'd invested a lot of energy in avoiding.
    >
    > I did not experience myself as the *same* as the water, the wind, and the light, but as participating with them in the *same system* of movement. We were all dancing together. To experience all boundaries as conventional is not to experience everything as the same, but everything as interrelated.
    >
    > The psychotic quality of this experience came from my fear, which itself was rooted deep in my flesh. Over the years, as my body has become more integrated, the same kind of experience is available without the terror.

17. See Donald Rothberg, "Contemporary Epistemology and the Study of Mysticism," in *The Problem of Pure Consciousness: Mysticism and Philosophy*, ed. Robert K. C. Forman (Oxford and New York: Oxford Univ. Press, 1990), 168, 183–87. That entire anthology challenges the deconstructionist (or constructivist) interpretation of mystical experience.

18. See Arthur J. Deikman, "Deautomatization and the Mystical Experience" and "Bimodal Consciousness and the Mystical Experience," in *Understanding Mysticism*, ed. Richard Woods (Garden City, NY: Doubleday/Image Books, 1980).
19. See, for example, David Ray Griffin, *God and Religion in the Postmodern World* (Albany: State Univ. of New York, 1989), 8.
20. Robert Cummings Neville, *The Recovery of the Measure: Interpretation and Nature* (Albany: State Univ. of New York, 1989), 324.
21. Neville, *Recovery of the Measure*, 325.
22. Gandhi, for one, insisted that rights are derivative of responsibilities. He was thinking mostly of the social realm, but Gary Snyder suggests the concept of a "natural contract" between a community and its "local natural system" as a parallel concept with "social contract" (see his *The Practice of the Wild* [San Francisco: North Point Press, 1990], 31). Regarding both areas, a former judge of the Supreme Court of Sri Lanka, C. Weeramanty, has suggested that law be expanded to include such guidelines as the Principle of Rights of the Environment, Principle of Pollution Control, Principle of Communal Ownership, Principle of Limited Ownership, and Principle of Trusteeship (see his *Slumbering Sentinels: Law and Human Rights in the Wake of Technology* [London and New York: Penguin Books, 1983]).
23. When I was in West Germany in 1983 interviewing dozens of members of the Green Party for the book *Green Politics*, a few pointed out that they use even such an innocent symbol as the sunflower with care because "Germans have trouble handling symbols." They were referring, of course, to the Nazi manipulations of people's deep love for their hometown and homeland. Anyone, however, can "handle symbols" if they are alert for the cultivation of nationalism and hatred of others.
24. A well-known article that addresses these problems in political groups is "Overcoming Masculine Oppression" by Bill Moyer, available from Movement for a New Society, 4722 Baltimore Avenue, Philadelphia, PA 19143.
25. During the civil-rights movement, the Fellowship of Reconciliation, at the request of Dr. Martin Luther King, Jr., put together guidelines for nonviolent political action that emphasize such points as listening well and avoiding self-righteousness. Those guidelines are published in *The Universe Bends toward Justice: A Reader on Christian Nonviolence in the U.S.*, ed. Angie O'Gorman (Philadelphia and Santa Cruz: New Society Publishers, 1990).
26. *Basic Call to Consciousness* (Mohawk Nation, via Rooseveltown, NY: *Akwesasne Notes*, 1978), 71.
27. In spite of their sincere efforts, deconstructive postmodernism has been criticized, and self-criticized, for replicating certain situations it deplores. First, deconstructive postmodernism is energetically contemptuous of "totalizing discourses," comprehensive systems of analysis and interpretation such as Marxism, Enlightenment humanism, or Christianity, which force a particular mode of perception on as many individuals as possible. Yet deconstructive postmodernism itself is generally championed as the one

correct mode of regarding everything in human experience; there is no room for other perceptions. Hence the claim of "renunciation" (of fixed beliefs and opinions) in order to hear "differences" is literally impossible: faithful deconstructive postmodernists cannot respect the perspectives of others as partial truths, since they "know" that there is no truth. They can respect only the various opinions of other true believers, who "know" that all perspectives are merely empty language games played out within "socially produced" systems of meaning.

Second, the macho intensity of the declarations of modernity's "totalizing" ideologies has been widely replicated in the declarations of deconstructive postmodernism.

Third, while deploring the "ahistorical," sheeplike acceptance of (constructed) values, deconstructive postmodernists have often seemed to revel in a hermetically sealed chamber of discovery, oblivious to related developments in philosophy, linguistics, psychology, and religion that preceded their movement. Most deconstructive postmodernists have expressed almost no curiosity about correspondent thinking outside their self-defined turf, since everyone else is understood to be hopelessly benighted.

Fourth, deconstructive postmodernists explain that every "totalizing discourse" creates its own internal logic so that opinions and actions follow from the core perceptions and interpretations of the particular system. One certainly sees this dynamic within deconstructive postmodernism: all human experience is believed to be composed entirely of "socially produced" constructs; therefore, everything in human experience is essentially relative (just someone's invention) and ultimately meaningless; therefore, cynicism and passivity are the savvy responses.

28. This view—that everything is added to a child's consciousness and nothing subtracted—is well represented by Richard Rorty in *Contingency, Irony, and Solidarity* (Cambridge: Cambridge Univ. Press, 1989). Distancing himself from "historicists" in whom the desire for self-creation dominates, such as Heidegger and Foucault, and who tend to see socialization as Nietzsche did, that is, as antithetical to something deep within us, Rorty proposes a utopia in which human solidarity would not be regarded as a fact to be recognized by clearing away prejudice or "burrowing down to previously hidden depths" but, rather, as a goal to be achieved solely by the imagination, by the imaginative ability to see strange people as fellow sufferers.
29. Robert Plomin, a developmental psychologist at Pennsylvania State Univ., quoted by Deborah Franklin in "What a Child Is Given," *New York Times Magazine*, 3 Sept. 1989, 38.
30. See Steven Connor, *Postmodernist Culture* (London and New York: Basil Blackwell, 1989), 34. The quotation is Connor's description of the "deliverance from the epochal delusions of metaphysical thinking" offered by the works of Lyotard, Deleuze, and Foucault.
31. Jean Baudrillard, *Mirror of Production* (St. Louis: Telos Press, 1975 [1973]), 82–83.

32. See Jacques Derrida, *Of Spirit: Heidegger and the Question* (Chicago: Univ. of Chicago Press, 1989). Also see an interesting review of this book by Mitchell Stephens, "Deconstruction Crew," *Tikkun: A Bimonthly Jewish Critique of Politics, Culture, and Society*, vol. 5, no. 5 (Sept./Oct. 1990): 80–83.
33. Ihab Hassan, "The New Gnosticism," in *Paracriticisms: Seven Speculations of the Times* (Urbana: Univ. of Illinois Press, 1975), 122–23; and *The Right Promethean Fire: Imagination, Science, and Cultural Change* (Urbana: Univ. of Illinois Press, 1980), 23.
34. The first two concerns are found in Fredric Jameson, "Postmodernism and the Logic of Late Capitalism," *New Left Review*, no. 146, 1984. The third appears in Fredric Jameson, "Postmodernism and Consumer Society," in *The Anti-Aesthetic: Essays on Postmodern Culture*, ed. Hal Foster (Seattle: Bay Press, 1983), 125.
35. See Chantal Mouffe, "Radical Democracy: Modern or Postmodern?" in *Universal Abandon? The Politics of Postmodernism*, ed. Andrew Ross (Minneapolis: Univ. of Minnesota Press, 1988).
36. Connor, *Postmodernist Culture*, 244.
37. See Dick Hebdige, "The Impossible Object: Toward a Sociology of the Sublime," *New Formations*, vol. 1, no. 1, 1987, 67.
38. Jean-François Lyotard, *The Postmodern Condition: A Report on Knowledge* (Minneapolis: Univ. of Minnesota Press, 1984), 81.
39. That particular transformation is an ironic mode of disempowerment, since seeing has long been the sense of choice in patriarchal, Eurocentric culture, from the Pythagoreans through the Scientific Revolution, to afford knowledge, judgment, and control of "the Other," whether human or nonhuman, without the "entanglement" involved with the other senses. The knowledge that resulted was decidedly limited, but sufficient for the desired ends. Now we witness vision (the sound being turned off by many viewers of sporting events and commercials) as the medium of participation in the mesmerizing presentation of a keenly pared version of reality that influences millions of lives.
40. Adam Michnik, "Notes on the Revolution," *New York Times Magazine*, 11 March 1990, 44.
41. In recent weeks I have read news items about county environmental-protection officials in northern California who declined to call attention to a local manufacturer of leaky septic tanks because such action might have slowed the county's growth rate; about Florida officials giving a developer permission to fill in twelve acres of supposedly protected wetland habitat so that his golf course and residential complex could achieve his desired level of profit; about the drain-off projects proposed along the once majestic Platte River, whose flow has been decreased by 70 percent since 1938, which require a total of more water than remains in the river! Such situations abound in our country.
42. At the time of this writing, the negotiations on revising the General Agreement on Tariffs and Trade (GATT) are leaning toward some hair-raising

changes. The U.S. GATT Amendments, proposed by the Bush administration to the "Uruguay Round" of negotiations, seek a more perfect realization of "free trade" by prohibiting national governments from enforcing any laws—concerning health standards, environmental protection, subsidies, patents, protection of local business, labor—that could be construed by the transnational corporations as a "restraint on trade." See Robert Schaeffer, "Trading Away the Planet," *Greenpeace*, vol. 15, no. 5 (Sept./Oct. 1990): 13–16.

43. Theodore Roszak, "The Third Way: The Individual, the Collective, the Personal," chapter 4, in *Person/Planet: The Creative Disintegration of Industrial Society* (Garden City, NY: Anchor Press/Doubleday, 1979).
44. Sister Miriam Therese MacGillis, director of Genesis Farm in New Jersey, is a gifted storyteller who focuses on the unfolding story of the universe, incorporating many insights from Thomas Berry's work. A four-cassette audio recording of Sister Miriam's presentation, *Education for a Small Planet*, and a single-cassette recording, *The Fate of the Earth*, are available from Global Perspectives, P.O. Box 925, Sonoma, CA 95476.
45. "Havel Urges U.S. Aid for the Soviets," *Los Angeles Times*, 22 February 1990; "Havel's Paradoxical Plea: Help Soviets," *New York Times*, 22 February 1990.

Appendix A • The Merely Relative: A Brief Survey of Deconstructive Postmodernism

1. Several of Derrida's books have been translated into English, among them *Dissemination* (Chicago: Univ. of Chicago Press, 1981), *Of Grammatology* (Baltimore: Johns Hopkins Univ., 1976), *Positions* (Chicago: Univ. of Chicago Press, 1981), and *Writing and Difference* (Chicago: Univ. of Chicago Press, 1978). Summaries of Derrida's positions are included in admiring books by Jonathan Culler, Geoffrey Hartman, Vincent Leitch, Stanley Fish, Christopher Norris, and others.
2. For a detailed critique of the weaknesses in linguistics and logic in Derrida's work, see John M. Ellis, *Against Deconstruction* (Princeton: Princeton Univ. Press, 1989). For critiques of deconstruction in literary theory, see Frederick Crews, *Skeptical Engagements* (New York: Oxford Univ. Press, 1986) and Robert Alter, *The Pleasures of Reading in an Ideological Age* (New York: Simon and Schuster, 1989).

   Recently some of the major proponents of literary deconstruction have softened their claims, professing that Derrida's work is not, after all, about indeterminacy of meaning but merely about amplifying our sense of the paradoxes inherent in a "languaged" life (see, for example, Stanley Fish, *Doing What Comes Naturally: Change, Rhetoric, and the Practice of Theory in Literary and Legal Studies* (Durham, NC: Duke Univ. Press, 1989).

   Also see Todd Gitlin, "Hip-Deep in Post-Modernism," *New York Times Book Review*, 6 Nov. 1988; also published in *Cultural Politics in Contemporary America*, ed. Ian Angus and Sut Jhally (New York and

London: Routledge, 1989). Also see Richard A. Shweder, "In Paris—Miniskirts of the Mind," *New York Times Book Review*, 8 Jan. 1989.

3. For a critique of deconstructionist presuppositions, see, for example, David Ray Griffin, "Postmodern Theology and A/theology: A Response to Mark C. Taylor," in *Varieties of Postmodern Theology* by David Ray Griffin, William A. Beardslee, and Joe Holland (Albany: State Univ. of New York Press, 1989), 29–61.
4. Several of Foucault's books have been translated into English, among them *Madness and Civilization* (New York: Random House, 1965), *The Order of Things: An Archaeology of the Human Sciences* (New York: Random House, 1970), *The Archaeology of Knowledge* (New York: Irvington Publications, 1972), *Discipline and Punish: The Birth of the Prison* (New York: Random House, 1979), *The History of Sexuality*, three volumes (New York: Random House, 1978, 1985, 1986), and *Power/Knowledge: Selected Interviews and Other Writings, 1972–1977* (New York: Pantheon Books, 1980). Also see Paul Rabinow, ed., *The Foucault Reader* (New York: Pantheon Books, 1984).
5. Gary Peller, "Reason and the Mob: The Politics of Representation," *Tikkun: A Bimonthly Jewish Critique of Politics, Culture, and Society*, vol. 2, no. 3 (July/Aug. 1987): 28–31, 92–95.
6. Objections to the deconstructive-postmodern "defense" of the "margin" have come from supposedly marginalized people themselves. See, for example, Barbara Christian, "The Race for Theory," *Feminist Studies*, vol. 14, no. 1 (Spring 1988): 67–79. Christian notes that "people of color have always theorized—but in forms quite different from the Western form of abstract logic." She is critical of the "academic hegemony" of deconstruction and of "its linguistic jargon, its emphasis on quoting its prophets; its tendency toward biblical exegesis; its refusal to even mention specific works of creative writers, far less contemporary ones; its preoccupation with mechanical analysis of language, graphs, algebraic equations; its gross generalizations about culture," all of which, she feels, has silenced many people.

   For a critique of gender-skepticism among postmodernists, see Susan Bordo, "Feminism, Postmodernism, and Gender-Scepticism," in *Feminism/Postmodernism*, ed. Linda J. Nicholson (New York: Routledge, 1990). Bordo critically examines the "recent academic marriage which has brought indigenous feminist concerns over the ethnocentrisms and unconscious racial biases of gender theory into a theoretical alliance with (a highly programmatic appropriation of) the more historicist, politically oriented wing of poststructuralist thought (e.g., Foucault, Lyotard)." Bordo identifies a new feminist "methodologism" emerging from this union that lays claim to an authoritative critical framework that "often implicitly (and mistakenly) supposes that the adoption of a 'correct' theoretical approach makes it possible to *avoid* ethnocentrism." She also discusses the result of certain feminist appropriations of deconstructionism that are animated by "fantasies" of replacing the "view from nowhare" but arrive only in a "dream of everywhere."

7. See Laura Kipnis, "Feminism: The Political Conscience of Postmodernism?" in *Universal Abandon? The Politics of Postmodernism*, ed. Andrew Ross (Minneapolis: Univ. of Minnesota Press, 1988), 159. Kipnis also notes, "Whereas 'American feminism' is a discourse whose political subject is biological women, 'continental feminism' is a political discourse whose subject is a structural position—variously occupied by the feminine, the body, the Other."

   Articles by several of the French postmodernist feminists have been gathered in *New French Feminisms*, ed. Elaine Marks and Isabelle de Courtivron (New York: Schocken Books, 1981) and *French Feminist Thought*, ed. Toril Moi (New York: Basil Blackwell, 1987). Also see the special issue on French feminism of *Signs: Journal of Women in Culture and Society*, vol. 7, no. 1, 1981.

8. See "Social Criticism without Philosophy: An Encounter between Feminism and Postmodernism" by Nancy Fraser and Linda Nicholson and "Feminism: The Political Conscience of Postmodernism?" by Laura Kipnis, in *Universal Abandon? The Politics of Postmodernism*, ed. Andrew Ross (Minneapolis: Univ. of Minnesota Press, 1988). Also see the essays in *Feminism and Foucault*, ed. Irene Diamond and Lee Quinby (Boston: Northeastern Univ. Press, 1988), as well as Linda Alcoff, "Feminist Politics and Foucault: The Limits to a Collaboration," in *Crises in Continental Philosophy*, eds. Arleen B. Dallery and Charles E. Scott with P. Holley Roberts (Albany: State Univ. of New York Press, 1990).

9. See Donna Haraway, "Situated Knowledges: The Science Question in Feminism and the Privilege of Partial Perspective," *Feminist Studies*, vol. 14, no. 3 (Fall 1988). Haraway's observation that what must pass for "objectivity" is partial *connection* between the two selves who are ever in process (p. 586) is *simpatico* not only with ecofeminist attention to connectedness but also with the ancient teachings of Dhamma on the ever-changing "self" (see chapter 2).

10. John Barth, "The Literature of Replenishment: Postmodern Fiction," *The Atlantic*, January 1980; Umberto Eco, "Postmodernism, Irony, the Enjoyable," in *Postscript to 'The Name of the Rose'* (New York: Harcourt Brace Jovanovich, 1984).

11. Tom Wolfe, quoted in "Age of the New Babbitt," by Jeffrey H. Brooks, *San Francisco Chronicle*, "Review" section, 7 July 1987.

12. Celia Tichi, "Video Novels," *Boston Review*, June 1987.

    In dissenting from Ms. Tichi's rave review of "video fiction," novelist Rosellen Brown spoke for many contemporary authors in insisting that writers have traditionally been refusers of the worst of their generation's compromises and limitations, of "current tendencies" that seek to simplify, or even nullify, "complexity of emotion and intellect, analysis, a celebration of historical memory" (Letters column, *Boston Review*, August 1987).

13. Frederick Barthelme, "Being Wrong: A Convicted Minimalist Spills the Bean," *New York Times Book Review*, 3 April 1988.
14. Charles Jencks, *What Is Postmodernism?* (New York: St. Martin's Press, 1986), 33–34.
15. Eugene Narrett, "Image Eaters," *Boston Review*, June 1987. Narrett's discussion of postmodern aesthetics uses the paintings of David Salle and the film *Blue Velvet*, directed by David Lynch, as examples.
16. Narrett, "The Image Eaters."
17. Adam Gopnik suggests in "Originals" (*The New Yorker*, 23 May 1988) that deconstructive-postmodern artists miss the point in proclaiming originality to be impossible now that one cannot break entirely free of the ubiquitous context of mass culture: "For 'originality' to exist, it is less important that artists be 'free' than we as an audience accept the instability of meaning as a convention in the game of art. . . . The real issue is not 'Is this work original?' but 'Does it reimagine tradition in a way that is an extension and illumination of our lives?'" Also see Suzi Gablik, *The Reenchantment of Art* (New York: Thames and Hudson, 1991), in which she discusses two types of postmodern art, which she labels "deconstructive" and "reconstructive."
18. See Humberto R. Maturana and Francisco J. Varela, *The Tree of Knowledge: The Biological Roots of Human Understanding* (Boston: Shambala Publications, 1987).
19. Humberto R. Maturana, "Ontology of Observing: Biological Foundations of Self Consciousness and the Physical Domain of Existence," in *Conference Workbook for "Texts in Cybernetic Theory,"* American Society for Cybernetics conference, Felton, CA, 18–23 October 1988, 51.
20. Maturana, "Ontology of Observing," 35.
21. Maturana, "Ontology of Observing," 36.
22. See Tyrone Cashman, "Epistemology and the Extinction of Species," in *ReVisioning Philosophy*, ed. Jay Ogilvy (Albany: State Univ. of New York Press, 1991).

    Also see Tyrone Cashman, "The Elysian Dialogs," *Continuing the Conversation: A Newsletter of Ideas in Cybernetics*, published by Hort-Ideas, Rt. 1, Box 302, Gravel Switch, KY 40328, Summer 1989.
23. See Ernst von Glasersfeld, "An Exposition of Radical Constructivism," in the *Conference Workbook for 'Texts in Cybernetic Theory'* cited in note 19. Also see Von Glasersfeld et al. in *The Invented Reality: How Do We Know What We Believe We Know? Contributions to Constructivism*, ed. Paul Watzlawick (New York: W. W. Norton, 1984).
24. See Morris Berman, "The Cybernetic Dream of the Twenty-first Century," *Journal of Humanistic Psychology*, vol. 26, no. 2 (Spring 1986): 24–51. Berman critiques the "cyberneticization" of the contemporary quest for holism for being just as "formal, abstract, 'value-free,' and disembodied" as the mechanistic paradigm it seeks to replace. He feels "the affective, concrete, and sensual experience of life" is ignored by "cybernetic mechanism" and its influence in such disciplines as psychology, ecology, and biology.

Berman advocates a "sensuous, situational, living approach to process" rather than an abstract "process mechanism."

25. Michele Bogard, "Family Systems Approaches to Wife Beating: A Feminist Critique," *American Journal of Orthopsychiatry*, vol. 54, no. 4 (Oct. 1984): 558–68; and Virginia Goldner, "Feminism and Family Therapy," *Family Process*, vol. 24 (March 1985): 33–47. Also see Paul F. Dell, "In Defense of Lineal Causality," *Family Process*, vol. 25 (Dec. 1986), plus two responses in the same issue: Evan Imber-Black, "Maybe 'Lineal Causality' Needs Another Defense Lawyer: A Feminist Response to Dell," and Paul F. Dell, "Toward a Foundation for Addressing Violence."
26. Naomi Scheman, "The Body Politic / The Body Impolitic / Bodily Politics," a paper submitted to the "Conference on Philosophy and Gender," Esalen Institute, CA, March 1989.
27. See Neil Postman, *Amusing Ourselves to Death* (New York: Viking, 1985). Also see Todd Gitlin, ed., *Watching Television* (New York: Pantheon Books, 1987). Also see Jerry Mander, *Four Arguments for the Elimination of Television* (New York: Morrow, 1978).
28. Frederic Jameson, "Postmodernism, or The Cultural Logic of Late Capitalism," *New Left Review*, no. 146, 1984.
29. Jenny Teichman, "Don't Be Cruel or Reasonable," a review of *Contingency, Irony, and Solidarity* by Richard Rorty, *New York Times Book Review*, 23 April 1989.
30. See Marshall Berman, "Why Modernism Still Matters," *Tikkun: A Bimonthly Jewish Critique of Politics, Culture and Society*, vol. 4, no. 1 (Jan./Feb. 1989): 11–14, 81–86.

    For another activist critique of deconstructive postmodernism, see Todd Gitlin, "Phoney Gardens with Real Toads in Them," *Tikkun: A Bimonthly Jewish Critique of Politics, Culture, and Society*, vol. 4, no. 2 (March/April 1989): 68–70.

    The citation from Derrida at the end of that section is from *Of Grammatology* (Baltimore: Johns Hopkins Univ. Press, 1976), 158.
31. Cited by Eugenio Donato, "The Two Languages of Criticism," in *The Structuralist Controversy: The Languages of Criticism and the Sciences of Man*, ed. Richard Macksey and Eugenio Donato (Baltimore and London: Johns Hopkins Univ., 1972), 96–97.

Appendix B • A Feminist Consideration of the Philosophical Roots and Attractions of Deconstructive Postmodernism

1. See "Proceedings of the International Conference on the Transformation of European Culture at 4500—2500 B.C.," Dubrovnik, 12–17 Sept. 1979, ed. Marija Gimbutas, *Journal of Indo-European Studies*, vol. 8 (three volumes). Also see J. P. Mallory, *In Search of the Indo-Europeans* (New York: W. W. Norton) and Marija Gimbutas, *The Goddesses and Gods of Old Europe, 6500–3500 B.C.* (Berkeley: Univ. of California Press, 1974), *The Language of the Goddess* (San Francisco: Harper & Row, 1989), and *The Civilization of the Goddess* (San Francisco: HarperCollins, 1991). Also see

Marija Gimbutas, in *When Worlds Collide: The Indo-Europeans and The Pre–Indo-Europeans,* ed. T. L. Markey and John A. C. Greppin (Ann Arbor, MI: Karoma Publishers, 1990).

2. Gimbutas—see note 1; also see Marija Gimbutas, "Women and Culture in Goddess-oriented Old Europe," in *The Politics of Women's Spirituality,* ed. Charlene Spretnak (Garden City, NY: Anchor Press/Doubleday, 1982).
3. Gimbutas—see notes 1 and 2.
4. W. K. C. Guthrie, "Pre-Socratic Philosophy," in *The Encyclopedia of Philosophy*, ed. Paul Edwards (New York: Macmillan Pub. & The Free Press, 1967), 441.
5. G. T. W. Patrick, "Introduction to *The Fragments of the Work of Heraclitus of Ephesus: On Nature,*" *Heraclitus of Ephesus* (Chicago: Argonaut, 1969), 70.
6. Patrick, *Heraclitus of Ephesus*, 71, 77.

   Patrick goes on to note, "Socrates was a professor of clear thinking. Clear thinking is in itself well, but two solid centuries of clear thinking from Descartes to Hegel have in modern times ended in failure. We long to know what *natural* thinking would have accomplished if it had been left an open field a while longer in Greece" (p. 77).
7. Patrick, *Heraclitus of Ephesus,* 80.
8. Patrick, *Heraclitus of Ephesus,* 79.

   Patrick briefly recounts "how this dualism fastened itself upon subsequent thought": ". . . how as realism and nominalism it divided the schoolmen; how as mind and matter it left Descartes in hopeless difficulty; how Spinoza founded a philosophy expressly to resolve it, but succeeded only by the artifice of terms; how Leibnitz solved the problem, though with too much violence, by use of the same boldness with which its founders established it; how Kant finally left the antithesis unexplained; how again as the material and immaterial it fixed itself in the psychology of Aristotle, who affirmed as the higher part of the human mind, the active Nous or principle of pure immateriality, cognizant of the highest things, identical with the divine Prime Mover, and immortal, thus constituting for man the highest glorification that he ever received from his own hand; how Thomas Aquinas, spokesman for a powerful church, adopted this psychology and fastened it upon the modern popular world; how finally, in the sphere of religion proper, the transcendentalism of Plato has grown into the belief in pure Spirit and spiritual existences, peopling heaven and earth, and holding communion with matter and body, though having absolutely nothing in common (if the paradox may be excused) with them. Such has been in part the wonderful expansion of the Platonic Idealism" (p. 80).
9. Genevieve Lloyd, *The Man of Reason: "Male" and "Female" in Western Philosophy* (Minneapolis: Univ. of Minnesota, 1984), 3.
10. Lloyd, *Man of Reason*, 4–9.
11. Joan Gibson, "Educating for Silence: Renaissance Women and the Language Arts," *Hypatia: A Journal of Feminist Philosophy*, vol. 4, no. 1 (Spring 1989): 9–27.

12. Bernard Williams, "René Descartes," in *The Encyclopedia of Philosophy* (New York: Macmillan Pub. & The Free Press, 1967), 354.
13. Carolyn Merchant, *The Death of Nature: Women, Ecology, and the Scientific Revolution* (San Francisco: Harper & Row, 1980), 228.

    Merchant notes that science since the seventeenth century has been widely considered to be objective, value-free, context-free knowledge of the external world, based on the following assumptions:

    1. Matter is composed of particles (the ontological assumption).
    2. The universe is a natural order (the principle of identity).
    3. Knowledge and information can be abstracted from the natural world (the assumption of context independence).
    4. Problems can be analyzed into parts that can be manipulated by mathematics (the methodological assumption).
    5. Sense data are discrete (the epistemological assumption).
14. Ernst Cassirer, *The Philosophy of the Enlightenment* (Princeton: Princeton Univ. Press, 1951), 5.
15. John Herman Randall, Jr., *The Making of the Modern Mind: A Survey of the Intellectual Background of the Present Age* (New York: Columbia Univ. Press, 1976 [1926]), 340.
16. See Emily W. Sunstein, *Mary Shelley: Romance and Reality* (Boston: Little, Brown, 1989).
17. Randall, *Making of the Modern Mind*, 465.
18. See Richard Guy Wilson, Dianne H. Pilgrim, Dickran Tashjian, *The Machine Age in America, 1918–1941* (New York: The Brooklyn Museum & Harry N. Abrams, Publishers, 1986).
19. See Sandra M. Gilbert and Susan Gubar, *No Man's Land: The Place of the Woman Writer in the Twentieth Century*, vol. 1, *The War of the Words* (New Haven, CT: Yale Univ. Press, 1988). Also see Susan Rubin Suleiman, *Subversive Intent: Gender, Politics, and the Avant-Garde* (Cambridge, MA: Harvard Univ. Press, 1990).
20. See Norman F. Cantor, *Twentieth Century Culture: Modernism to Deconstruction* (New York: Peter Lang Publishing, 1989).
21. See Andreas Huyssen, "Mapping the Postmodern," in *Feminism/Postmodernism*, ed. Linda J. Nicholson (New York: Routledge, 1990). Huyssen presents a strong case for regarding poststructuralism, the French-based critical theory that is usually considered in the United States to be a subset of the larger phenomenon of postmodernism, as primarily a theory of and about modernism. He asserts that the obsession of the poststructuralist critical discourse with "*écriture* and writing, allegory and rhetoric, and its displacement of revolution and politics to the aesthetic" is embedded in the very modernist tradition, which, "at least in American eyes," it presumably transcends. Huyssen notes that American poststructuralist writers and critics "emphatically privilege aesthetic innovation and experiement; that they call for self-reflexiveness, not, to be sure, of the author-subject, but of the text; that they purge life, reality, history, society from the work of art and its reception, and construct a new autonomy,

based on a pristine notion of textuality, a new art for art's sake which is presumably the only kind possible after the failure of all and any commitment." He further observes, "The insight that the subject is constituted in language and the notion that there is nothing outside the text have led to the privileging of the aesthetic and the linguistic which aestheticism has always prompted to justify its imperial claims. The list of 'no longer possibles' (realism, representation, subjectivity, history, etc., etc.) is as long in post-structuralism as it used to be in modernism, and it is very similar indeed." In contrast, Huyssen views postmodernity as a historical condition and a political sensibility following upon the erosion of "the triple dogma of modernism/modernity/avantgardism."

22. Herbert Marcuse, "The Obsolescence of the Freudian Concept of Man," in *Critical Theory and Society* (New York and London: Routledge, 1989), 233–46.
23. Patricia Jagentowicz Mills, "Part Three, Dialectical Development: Woman and Nature in Critical Theory," in *Woman, Nature, and Psyche* (New Haven, CT: Yale Univ. Press, 1987), esp. 200.
24. David Held, *Introduction to Critical Theory* (Berkeley: Univ. of California Press, 1980), 154.
25. William Barrett, *Irrational Man: A Study in Existential Philosophy* (Garden City, NY: Anchor Press/Doubleday, 1962), 245, 254.
26. Harold Bloom proposed the thesis that (male) poets suffer from competitive anxiety with regard to their (male) predecessors; see his *The Anxiety of Influence* (London and New York: Oxford Univ. Press, 1973).

Acknowledgments

My life has been graced with the presence of three wise elders who, directly or indirectly, nurtured the work presented in this book: Thomas Berry, cultural historian and "geologian"; Marija Gimbutas, archaeologist of Old Europe; and S. N. Goenka, teacher of *vipassana* meditation. I am grateful to have encountered not only their knowledge and enriching insights but also their personal integrity and generosity of spirit.

In 1985 I sat in on a stimulating course in cosmology taught by Brian Swimme, a physicist who is an extremely gifted lecturer. I am grateful for that rather amazing experience and for subsequent conversations. The thinking of Thomas Berry and Brian Swimme overlaps with my own in many respects, but the brief mentions of their work in this book do not begin to do justice to the breadth and depth of their explorations. For readers wishing further information, I recommend their forthcoming book, tentatively titled *The Universe Story*, as well as others they have written separately (see "Related Reading" in this book). Dr. Berry is director of the Riverdale Center for Religious Research, in New York; Dr. Swimme is director of the Center for the Story of the Universe, at the California Institute of Integral Studies in San Francisco.

I thank the following colleagues for reading all or parts of my manuscript and sharing their responses: Morris Berman, Victoria Bomberry, Tyrone Cashman, Frederick Crews, Marlene De Nardo, Marija Gimbutas, S. N. Goenka, David Ray Griffin, John Grim, Renate Holub, Mara Lynn Keller, Daniel Moses, F. David Peat, Carol Lee Sanchez, Brian Swimme, Mary Evelyn Tucker, and Michael Zimmerman.

For research assistance in various areas, I thank Paula Gunn Allen, Rachel Bagby, José Barreiro, Mike Becker, Clayborne Carson, Barbara Christian, Michael Closson, Marlene De Nardo, Pamela Eakins, Elinor Gadon, Harold Gilliam, Todd Gitlin, Vera Jane He Did It Half, James Hughes, P. S. Jaini, Daniel Matt, Helena Norberg-Hodge, Steve Prevette, Deborah Rhode, Diana E. H. Russell, Jim Ryan, Bert Schwartzchild, Yvonne Vowels, and Adrienne Zihlman. Regarding my research in Native American spirituality, I am grateful to have received encouragement from the late Bill Wapehpah.

I am also grateful for an overnight stay in Mary Beth Edelson's loft in New York in 1988; I found her latest art to be tremendously energizing for my work. I also thank Sheila Ballantyne and Ann Flanagan for moral support.

I thank Elena Fiant and her indefatigable staff of librarians, who tracked down even my most obscure book requests through far-flung computer search networks. Inge Sofer of Coastside Books and Don Gehre also helped with bibliographic requests.

I thank my computer gurus, Sypko Andreae and Carolyn Shafer, for their saintly patience and "house calls" via telephone during incidents of distress.

Against all odds (as a female author/thinker working outside academia), I received three modest but much appreciated grants during the six years I worked on this book. I wish to gratefully acknowledge research grants in 1986, 1987, and 1988, respectively, from the Institute in Culture and Creation Spirituality, at Holy Names College in Oakland; the L. J. Skaggs and Mary C. Skaggs Foundation, made possible by Laura J. Lederer; and the Max and Anna Levinson Foundation, made possible largely by

Charlotte J. Levinson and Lynda B. Levinson. I thank Fritjof Capra and my other friends at the Elmwood Institute, which acted as my fiscal sponsor in administering the last two grants. I also thank Irene Diamond, Jerry Mander, and Ira Shapiro for suggestions about funding.

I am grateful for all the encouragement, kindness, and understanding I received while working on the book, particularly during the last three and a half years, when I had to withdraw from nearly all other activities in order to concentrate on this work.

I enjoyed working with my editors, Marie Cantlon and Barbara Moulton, at HarperCollins Publishers. Thanks also to Barbara Archer, editorial assistant, for various support services.

My literary agent, Frances Goldin, and her associate, Sydelle Kramer, were most helpful, as usual.

I am grateful for the encouragement from my family: my mother, Donna Spretnak; my sister, Nicole Spretnak; and my daughter, Lissa Merkel. Most of all, I wish to express my deep gratitude to my husband, Daniel Moses, for his love, humor, and wisdom throughout the creation of this book.

Related Reading

(Books related to more than one chapter are listed only under the chapter to which they are most relevant.)

Chapter 1 • Saving Grace

Berry, Thomas. *The Dream of the Earth*. San Francisco: Sierra Club Books, 1988.

Birch, Charles, and John B. Cobb, Jr. *The Liberation of Life: From the Cell to the Community*. Cambridge: Cambridge University Press, 1981.

Boulding, Kenneth E. *The World as a Total System*. Beverly Hills, CA: Sage Publications, 1985.

Carpenter, James A. *Nature and Grace: Toward an Integral Perspective*. New York: Crossroad Press, 1988.

Gablik, Suzi. *The Reenchantment of Art*. New York: Thames and Hudson, 1991.

Griffin, David Ray. *God and Religion in the Postmodern World*. Albany: State University of New York Press, 1989.

———, ed. *The Reenchantment of Science: Postmodern Proposals*. Albany: State University of New York Press, 1989.

———, ed. *Sacred Interconnections: Postmodern Spirituality, Political Economy, and Art*. Albany: State University of New York Press, 1990.

———, ed. *Spirituality and Society; Postmodern Visions*. Albany: State University of New York Press, 1988.

Griffin, David Ray, William A. Beardslee, and Joe Holland. *Varieties of Postmodern Theology*. Albany: State University of New York, 1989.

Griffin, David Ray, and Huston Smith. *Primordial Truth and Postmodern Theology*. Albany: State University of New York Press, 1989.

Kassiola, Joel Jay. *The Death of Industrial Civilization: The Limits to Growth and the Repoliticization of Advanced Industrial Society*. Albany: State University of New York Press, 1990.

Nandy, Ashis, ed. *Science, Hegemony and Violence: A Requiem for Modernity*. Tokyo: United Nations University; Delhi, India: Oxford University Press, 1988.

Panikkar, Raimundo. *The Intrareligious Dialogue*. Mahwah, NJ: Paulist Press, 1978.

Spretnak, Charlene. *The Spiritual Dimension of Green Politics*. Santa Fe, NM: Bear & Co., 1986.

Spretnak, Charlene, and Fritjof Capra. *Green Politics: The Global Promise*. New York: E. P. Dutton, 1984; Santa Fe, NM: Bear & Co., 1986.

Swimme, Brian. *The Universe Is a Green Dragon*. Santa Fe, NM: Bear & Co., 1985.

Chapter 2 • The Center Holds

Aitken, Robert. *The Mind of Clover: Essays in Zen Buddhist Ethics*. San Francisco: North Point Press, 1984.

———. *Taking the Path of Zen*. San Francisco: North Point Press, 1982.

Aldridge, Bob and Janet. *Children and Nonviolence*. Pasadena, CA: Hope Publishing House, 1987.

Arendt, Hannah. *On Violence*. New York: Harcourt Brace & World, 1970.

Ashe, Geoffrey. *Gandhi: A Study in Revolution*. London: William Heinemann, 1968.

Bedekar, D. K. *Towards Understanding Gandhi*. Bombay: Popular Prakashan, 1975.

Berry, Thomas. *Buddhism*. New York: Thomas Y. Crowell Company, 1967.

Bondurant, Joan V. *Conquest of Violence: The Gandhian Philosophy of Conflict*, rev. ed. Princeton: Princeton University Press, 1988.

Brown, Robert McAfee. *Religion and Violence*. 2d ed. Philadelphia: Westminster Press, 1987.

Buddhadasa Bhikku. *Dhammic Socialism*. Bangkok: Thai Inter-Religious Commission for Development, 1986.

Capra, Fritjof. *The Tao of Physics*. Boston: Shambhala Publications, 1975.

Chatterjee, Margaret. *Gandhi's Religious Thought*. London: Macmillan Press, 1983.

Ch'en, Kenneth K. S. *The Chinese Transformation of Buddhism*. Princeton: Princeton University Press, 1973.

Chopra, P. N., and Tokan Sumi, eds. *Contribution of Buddhism to World Civilization and Culture*. New Delhi: S. Chand & Company, 1983.

Conze, Edward, ed. *Buddhist Scriptures*. Harmondsworth, England: Penguin Books, 1959.

———. *A Short History of Buddhism*. London: George Allen & Unwin, 1980.

Datta, Dhirendra Mohan. *The Philosophy of Mahatma Gandhi*. Madison: University of Wisconsin Press, 1953.

de Mello, Anthony, S. J. *Sadhana: A Way to God: Christian Exercises in Eastern Form*. St. Louis: The Institute of Jesuit Sources, 1978.

Easwaran, Eknath. *Gandhi the Man*. Petaluma, CA: Nilgiri Press, 1978.

———. *A Man to Match His Mountains: Badshah Khan, Nonviolent Soldier of Islam*. Petaluma, CA: Nilgiri Press, 1984.

Eppsteiner, Fred, ed. *The Path of Compassion: Writings on Socially Engaged Buddhism*. Berkeley: Parallax Press, 1988.

Fry, A. Ruth. *Victories without Violence*. Santa Fe, NM: Liberty Literary Works/Ocean Tree Books, 1986.

Gandhi, Mohandas Karamchand. *All Religions Are True*. Bombay: Bharatiya Vidya Bhavan, 1962.

———. *Discourses on the Gita*. Ahmedabad, India: Navajivan Publishing House, 1960.

———. *Gita the Mother*. Lahore: Indian Printing Works, 1946.

———. *Hindu Dharma*. Ahmedabad, India: Navajivan Publishing House, 1950.

———. *My Autobiography*. Boston: Beacon Press, 1957.

———. *My Non-Violence*. Ahmedabad, India: Navajivan Publishing House, 1960.

———. *My Religion*. Lahore: Dewan's Publications.

———. *Satyagraha*. Ahmedabad, India: Navajivan Publishing House, 1951.

———. *The Science of Satyagraha*. Bombay: Bharatiya Vidya Bhavan, 1962.

———. *The Supreme Power*. Bombay: Bharatiya Vidya Bhavan, 1963.

———. *Towards Non-Violent Politics and the Relation of Constructive Work to Ahimsa*. Thanjavur, India: Sarvodaya Prachuralaya, 1969.

———. *Towards Non-Violent Socialism*. Ahmedabad, India: Navajivan Publishing House, 1951.

———. *Unto This Last: Paraphrase of Ruskin*. Ahmedabad, India: Navajivan Publishing House, 1951.

Gokhale, B. G. *Buddhism and Asoka*. Baroda, India: Padmaja Publications, 1949.

Goldstein, Joseph. *The Experience of Insight: A Natural Unfolding*. Santa Cruz, CA: Unity Press, 1976.

Gyatso, Tenzin, the Fourteenth Dalai Lama. *A Human Approach to World Peace*. London: Wisdom Publications, 1984.

Hanh, Nhat, Thich. *Being Peace*. Berkeley: Parallax Press, 1987.

———. *The Miracle of Mindfulness*. Boston: Beacon Press, 1976.

Hart, William. *The Art of Living: Vipassana Meditation as Taught by S. N. Goenka*. San Francisco: Harper & Row, 1987.

Hixon, Les. *Coming Home: The Experience of Enlightenment in Sacred Traditions*. Garden City, NY: Doubleday/Anchor Press, 1978.

Ingram, Catherine. *In the Footsteps of Gandhi: Conversations with Spiritual Social Activists*. Berkeley: Parallax Press, 1990.

Jesudasan, Ignatius. *A Gandhian Theology of Liberation*. Maryknoll, NY: Orbis Books, 1984.

Jones, Ken. *The Social Face of Buddhism: An Approach to Social and Political Activism*. London: Wisdom Books, 1989.

Juergensmeyer, Mark. *Fighting Fair: A Non-Violent Strategy for Resolving Everyday Conflicts*. San Francisco: Harper & Row, 1986.

Kane, Pandurang Vaman. *History of Dharmasastra*. Vol. 1. Poona, India: Bhandarkar Oriental Research Institute, 1930.

Loy, David. *Nonduality: A Study in Comparative Philosophy*. New Haven, CT: Yale University Press, 1988.

Macy, Joanna. *Dharma and Development: Religion as Resource in the Sarvodaya Self-Help Movement*. West Hartford, CT: Kumarian Press, 1983.

———. *Mutual Causality in Buddhism and General Systems Theory: The Dharma of Natural Systems*. Albany: State University of New York Press, 1991.

Merton, Thomas, ed. *Gandhi on Non-Violence*. New York: New Directions Publishing Corp., 1965.

Mookerji, Radha Kumud. *Asoka*. New Delhi: Motilal Banarsidass, 1928; rev. ed., 1962.

Murthy, B. Srinivasa, ed. *Mahatma Gandhi and Leo Tolstoy Letters*. Long Beach, CA: Long Beach Publications, 1987.

Naess, Arne. *Gandhi and the Nuclear Age*. Totowa, NJ: Bedminster Press, 1965.

Nikam, N. A. *Gandhi's Discovery of Religion*. Bombay: Bharatiya Vidya Bhavan, 1963.

Nu, U. "What Is Buddhism?" Text of a lecture delivered under sponsorship of New York University, 6 July 1955.

Rahula, Walpola. *What the Buddha Taught*. New York: Grove Press, 1959.

Schumann, Hans Wolfgang. *Buddhism: An Outline of Its Teachings and Schools*. Translated by Georg Feuerstein. Wheaton, IL: Theosophical Publishing House, 1973.

Shah, Kanti, ed. *Vinoba on Gandhi*. Varanasi, India: Sarva Seva Sangh Prakashan, 1973.

Sharp, Gene. *Gandhi as a Political Strategist*. Boston: Porter Sargent Publishers, 1979.

———. *The Politics of Nonviolent Action*. 3 vols. Boston: Porter Sargent Publishers, 1973.

Sivaraksa, Sulak. *Religion and Development*. Bangkok: Thai Inter-Religious Commission for Development, 1987.

Smith, Huston. *The Religions of Man*. New York: Harper & Row, 1958.

Snyder, Gary. *Earth House Hold: Technical Notes and Queries to Fellow Dharma Revolutionaries*. New York: New Directions, 1969.

Solé-Leris, Amadeo. *Tranquillity and Insight: An Introduction to the Oldest Form of Buddhist Meditation*. Boston: Shambhala Publishers, 1986.

Soni, R. L. *The Only Way to Deliverance: The Buddhist Practice of Mindfulness*. Boulder, CO: Prajna Press, 1980.

Sonnleitner, Michael W. *Gandhian Nonviolence: Levels of Satyagraha*. New Delhi: Abhinav Publications, 1985.

Suzuki, Shunryu. *Zen Mind, Beginner's Mind*. New York and Tokyo: John Weatherhill, 1970.

Tolstoy, Leo. *The Law of Love and the Law of Violence*. New York: Holt, Rinehart and Winston, 1970.

Tsomo, Karma Lekshe. *Sakyahika: Daughters of the Buddha*. Ithaca, NY: Snow Lion Publications, 1988.

Walshe, Maurice, ed. and trans. *Thus Have I Heard: The Long Discourses of the Buddha*. London: Wisdom Publications, 1987.

Chapter 3 • Participation in the Mystery

Allen, Paula Gunn. *The Sacred Hoop: Recovering the Feminine in American Indian Traditions*. Boston: Beacon Press, 1986.

Anderson, William. *Green Man: The Archetype of Our Oneness with the Earth*. San Francisco: HarperCollins, 1990.

Andruss, Van, Christopher Plant, Judith Plant, and Eleanor Wright. *Home! A Bioregional Reader*. Philadelphia and Santa Cruz, CA: New Society Publishers, 1990.

Barreiro, José, ed. "Indian Corn of the Americas: Gift to the World." *Northeastern Indian Quarterly* 6, nos. 1 and 2 (1989).

Beck, Peggy V., and Anna L. Walters. *The Sacred: Ways of Knowledge, Sources of Life*. Tsaile (Navajo Nation), AZ: Navajo Community College Press, 1977.

Berg, Peter, Beryl Magilavy, and Seth Zuckerman. *A Green City Program*. San Francisco: Planet Drum Foundation, 1989.

Black Elk, Wallace, and William S. Lyon. *Black Elk: The Sacred Ways of a Lakota*. San Francisco: Harper & Row, 1990.

Brody, Hugh. *Maps and Dreams*. New York: Pantheon Books, 1982.

Brodzky, Anne Trueblood, Rose Danesewich, and Nick Johnson, eds. *Stones, Bones and Skin*. Toronto: The Society for Art Publications, 1977.

Brown, Joseph Epes. *The Spiritual Legacy of the American Indian*. New York: Crossroad Publishing Co., 1982.

Collier, John. *On the Gleaming Way: Navajos, Eastern Pueblos, Zunis, Hopis, Apaches and Their Land and Their Meanings to the World*. Chicago: Sage Books (The Swallow Press), 1962.

Courlander, Harold. *Hopi Voices: Recollections, Traditions, and Narratives of the Hopi Indians*. Albuquerque: University of New Mexico Press, 1982.

Deloria, Vine, Jr. *God Is Red*. New York: Dell, 1973.

DeMallie, Raymond J., ed. *The Sixth Grandfather: Black Elk's Teachings Given to John G. Neihardt*. Lincoln: University of Nebraska Press, 1984.

Ehrenfeld, David. *The Arrogance of Humanism*. Oxford: Oxford University Press, 1978.

Erdoes, Richard, and Alfonso Ortiz, eds. *American Indian Myths and Legends*. New York: Pantheon Books, 1984.

Ferrero, Pat, ed. *A Resource Handbook for "Hopi: Songs of the Fourth World."* San Francisco: Ferrero Films, 1986.

Fox, Warwick. *Toward a Transpersonal Ecology: Developing New Foundations for Environmentalism*. Boston: Shambhala Publishers, 1990.

Gribbin, John, and Martin Rees. *Cosmic Coincidences: Dark Matter, Mankind and Anthropic Cosmology*. New York: Bantam Books, 1989.

Grim, John A. *The Shaman: Patterns of Religious Healing among the Ojibway Indians*. Norman: University of Oklahoma Press, 1987.

Highwater, Jamake. *The Primal Mind: Vision and Reality in Indian America*. New York: New American Library, 1981.

———. *Ritual of the Wind: North American Indian Ceremonies, Music, and Dance*. Toronto: Methuen Publications, 1984.

Hultkrantz, Åke. *Native Religions of North America*. San Francisco: Harper & Row, 1987.

LaChapelle, Dolores. *Sacred Land, Sacred Sex, Rapture of the Deep: Concerning Deep Ecology and Celebrating Life*. Silverton, CO: Finn Hill Arts, 1988.

Lane, Belden C. *Landscapes of the Sacred: Geography and Narrative in American Spirituality*. Mahwah, NJ: Paulist Press, 1988.

Lee, Dorothy. *Freedom and Culture*. Englewood Cliffs, NJ: Prentice-Hall, 1959.

Lopez, Barry. *Crossing Open Ground*. New York: Vintage Books, 1989.

Lovelock, James. *The Ages of Gaia: A Biography of Our Living Earth*. New York: W. W. Norton, 1988.

———. *Gaia: A New Look at Life on Earth*. Oxford: Oxford University Press, 1979.

Macy, Joanna. *World as Lover, World as Self*. Berkeley: Parallax Press, 1991.

Marriott, Alice, and Carol K. Rachlin, eds. *American Indian Mythology*. New York: New American Library, 1968.

McGaa, Ed (Eagle Man). *Mother Earth Spirituality: Native American Paths to Healing Ourselves and Our World*. San Francisco: Harper & Row, 1990.

McKibben, Bill. *The End of Nature*. New York: Random House, 1989.

McLuhan, T. C., ed. *Touch the Earth: A Self-Portrait of Indian Existence*. New York: Pocket Books, 1972.

Meeker, Joseph. *Minding the Earth*. Alameda, CA: Latham Foundation, 1988.

Miller, Alan. *Gaia Connections: Ecology, Ecoethics, Economics*. Washington, DC: Rowman Littlefield, 1991.

Mills, Stephanie. *What Ever Happened to Ecology?* San Francisco: Sierra Club Books, 1989.

Munitz, Milton K. *Cosmic Understanding: Philosophy and Science of the Universe*. Princeton: Princeton University Press, 1986.

Nelson, Richard K. *Make Prayers to the Raven: A Koyukon View of the Northern Forest*. Chicago: University of Chicago Press, 1983.

Niethammer, Carolyn. *Daughters of the Earth: The Lives and Legends of American Indian Women.* New York: Collier Books, 1977.

Nollman, Jim. *Spiritual Ecology: A Guide to Reconnecting with Nature.* New York: Bantam Books, 1990.

Parlow, Anita. *Cry, Sacred Ground: Big Mountain, U.S.A.* Washington, DC: Christic Institute, 1988.

Peters, Ted, ed. *Cosmos as Creation: Theology and Science in Consonance.* Nashville: Abingdon Press, 1989.

Powers, Marla N. *Oglala Women: Myth, Ritual, and Reality.* Chicago: University of Chicago Press, 1986.

Robbins, John. *Diet for a New America.* Walpole, NH: Stillpoint, 1987.

Rothenberg, Jerome, ed. *Technicians of the Sacred.* Garden City, NY: Anchor Books/Doubleday, 1969.

Sahtouris, Elisabeth. *Gaia: The Human Journey from Chaos to Cosmos.* New York: Pocket Books, 1989.

Sale, Kirkpatrick. *The Conquest of Paradise: Christopher Columbus and the Columbian Legacy.* New York: Knopf, 1990.

———. *Dwellers in the Land: The Bioregional Vision.* San Francisco: Sierra Club Books, 1985.

Scully, Vincent. *Pueblo: Mountain, Village, Dance.* 2d ed. Chicago: University of Chicago Press, 1989.

Seed, John, Joanna Macy, Pat Fleming, and Arne Naess. *Thinking Like a Mountain: Towards a Council of All Beings.* Philadelphia and Santa Cruz, CA: New Society Publishers, 1988.

Snyder, Gary. *The Practice of the Wild.* San Francisco: North Point Press, 1990.

Swan, James A. *Sacred Places in Nature.* Santa Fe, NM: Bear & Co., 1990.

Tedlock, Dennis, and Barbara Tedlock. *Teachings from the American Earth: Indian Religion and Philosophy.* New York: Liveright Books, 1975.

Thompson, Robert Farris. *Flash of Spirit: African and Afro-American Art and Philosophy.* New York: Random House, 1983.

Tooker, Elisabeth, ed. *Native North American Spirituality of the Eastern Woodlands.* New York: Paulist Press, 1979.

Toulmin, Stephen. *The Return to Cosmology: Postmodern Science and the Theory of Nature.* Berkeley and Los Angeles: University of California Press, 1982.

Turner, Frederick. *Beyond Geography: The Western Spirit Against the Wilderness.* New York: Viking Press, 1980.

Vanderwerth, W. C., ed. *Indian Oratory: Famous Speeches by Noted Indian Chieftains*. Norman: University of Oklahoma Press, 1971.

Wildschut, William. *Crow Indian Medicine Bundles*. New York: Museum of the American Indian, 1975.

Williamson, Ray A. *Living the Sky: The Cosmos of the American Indian*. Boston: Houghton Mifflin, 1984.

Chapter 4 • Embracing the Body

Adler, Margot. *Drawing Down the Moon*. New York: Viking Press, 1979.

Agarwal, Bina, ed. *Structures of Patriarchy: The State, the Community and the Household*. London: Zed Books, 1986.

Austen, Hallie Iglehart. *The Heart of the Goddess: Art, Myth and Meditations of the World's Sacred Feminine*. Berkeley: Wingbow Press, 1990.

Berger, Pamela. *The Goddess Obscured: Transformation of the Grain Protectress from Goddess to Saint*. Boston: Beacon Press, 1985.

Berman, Morris. *Coming to Our Senses: Body and Spirit in the Hidden History of the West*. New York: Simon and Schuster, 1989.

Bettelheim, Bruno. *Symbolic Wounds: Puberty Rites and the Envious Male*. New York: Collier Books, 1962 (1954).

Bolen, Jean Shinoda. *The Goddesses in Everywoman*. San Francisco: Harper & Row, 1984.

Bordo, Susan. *The Flight to Objectivity: Essays on Cartesianism and Culture*. Albany: State University of New York Press, 1987.

Budapest, Zsuzsanna E. *The Grandmother of Time: A Woman's Book of Celebrations, Spells, and Sacred Objects*. San Francisco: Harper & Row, 1989.

Campanelli, Pauline. *Wheel of Life: Living the Magical Life*. St. Paul, MN: Llewellwyn Publications, 1990.

Canan, Jeanine, ed. *She Rises Like the Sun: Invocations of the Goddess by Contemporary American Women Poets*. Freedom, CA: Crossing Press, 1989.

Cashford, Jules, and Anne Baring. *The Myth of the Goddess: The Evolution of an Image*. London: Penguin Books, 1991.

Christ, Carol P. *Laughter of Aphrodite: Reflections on a Journey to the Goddess*. San Francisco: Harper & Row, 1987.

Christ, Carol P., and Judith Plaskow, eds. *Weaving the Visions: New Patterns in Feminist Spirituality*. San Francisco: Harper & Row, 1989.

———. *Womanspirit Rising: A Feminist Reader in Religion.* San Francisco: Harper & Row, 1979.

Condren, Mary. *The Serpent and the Goddess: Women, Religion, and Power in Celtic Ireland.* San Francisco: Harper & Row, 1989.

Daly, Mary. *Gyn/Ecology: The Metaethics of Radical Feminism.* Boston: Beacon Press, 1978.

Dexter, Miriam Robbins. *Whence the Goddesses: A Source Book.* New York: Pergamon Press, 1990.

Diamond, Irene, and Gloria Feman Orenstein, eds. *Reweaving the World: The Emergence of Ecofeminism.* San Francisco: Sierra Club Books, 1990.

Dundes, Alan, ed. *Sacred Narrative: Readings in the Theory of Myth.* Berkeley and Los Angeles: University of California Press, 1984.

Ecker, Gisela, ed. *Feminist Aesthetics.* Boston: Beacon Press, 1986.

Edelson, Mary Beth. *Seven Cycles: Public Rituals.* New York: Mary Beth Edelson (110 Mercer St., New York, NY 10012), 1980.

———. *Seven Sites: Painting on the Wall.* New York: Mary Beth Edelson (110 Mercer St., New York, NY 10012), 1988.

———. *Shape Shifter: Seven Mediums.* New York: Mary Beth Edelson (110 Mercer St., New York, NY 10012), 1990.

Eisler, Riane. *The Chalice and the Blade.* San Francisco: Harper & Row, 1987.

Farias, Helen G. *The College of Hera.* Clear Lake, WA: Juno's Peacock Press, 1988.

Gadon, Elinor W. *The Once and Future Goddess.* San Francisco: Harper & Row, 1989.

Getty, Adele. *Goddess: Mother of Living Nature.* New York: Thames and Hudson, 1990.

Gilligan, Carol. *In a Different Voice: Psychological Theory and Women's Development.* Cambridge: Harvard University Press, 1982.

Gimbutas, Marija. *The Civilization of the Goddess: Neolithic Europe Before the Patriarchy.* San Francisco: HarperCollins, 1991.

———. *The Goddesses and Gods of Old Europe: Myths and Cult Images, 6500–3500* B.C. Berkeley and Los Angeles: University of California Press, 1982 (1974).

———. *The Language of the Goddess: Unearthing the Hidden Symbols of Western Civilization.* San Francisco: Harper & Row, 1989.

Gray, Elizabeth Dodson. *Sacred Dimensions of Women's Experience.* Wellesley, MA: Roundtable Press, 1988.

Griffin, Susan. *Woman and Nature.* New York: Harper & Row, 1978.

Harding, Sandra. *Discovering Reality: Feminist Perspectives on Epistemology, Metaphysics, Methodology, and Philosophy of Science.* Boston: D. Reidel Pub. Co., 1983.

Heyward, Carter. *Touching Our Strength: The Erotic as Power and the Love of God.* San Francisco: Harper & Row, 1989.

Hurcombe, Linda. *Sex and God: Some Varieties of Women's Religious Experience.* London: Routledge & Kegan Paul, 1987.

Jaggar, Alison M., and Susan R. Bordo, eds. *Gender/Body/Knowledge: Feminist Reconstructions of Being and Knowing.* New Brunswick, NJ: Rutgers University Press, 1989.

Johnson, Buffie. *Lady of the Beasts: Ancient Images of the Goddess and Her Sacred Animals.* San Francisco: Harper & Row, 1988.

Johnson, Don. *Body.* Boston: Beacon Press, 1983.

Johnson, Sonia. *Wildfire.* Albuquerque: Wildfire Books, 1989.

Keller, Catherine. *From a Broken Web: Separation, Sexism, and Self.* Boston: Beacon Press, 1986.

Keller, Evelyn Fox. *A Feeling for the Organism: The Life and Work of Barbara McClintock.* New York: W. H. Freeman, 1983.

———. *Reflections on Science and Gender.* New Haven, CT: Yale University Press, 1985.

Kelly, Mary B. *Goddess Embroideries of Eastern Europe.* Winona, MN: Northland Press of Winona, 1989.

Lederer, Wolfgang. *The Fear of Women.* New York: Harcourt Brace Jovanovich, 1968.

Lippard, Lucy R. *Overlay: Contemporary Art and the Art of Prehistory.* New York: Pantheon Books, 1983.

Merchant, Carolyn. *The Death of Nature: Women, Ecology, and the Scientific Revolution.* San Francisco: Harper & Row, 1980.

Merleau-Ponty, Maurice. *The Phenomenology of Perception.* London: Routledge & Kegan Paul, 1962.

———. *Signs.* Evanston, IL: Northwestern University Press, 1964.

Mullins, Edwin. *The Painted Witch: Female Body/Male Art.* London: Secker & Warburg, 1985.

Neumann, Erich. *The Great Mother.* Princeton: Princeton University Press, 1955.

Orenstein, Gloria Feman. *The Reflowering of the Goddess.* New York: Pergamon Press, 1990.

Plant, Judith, ed. *Healing the Wounds: The Promise of Ecofeminism.* Philadelphia and Santa Cruz, CA: New Society Publishers, 1989.

Ruddick, Sara. *Maternal Thinking: Toward a Politics of Peace.* Boston: Beacon Press, 1989.

Rufus, Anneli S., and Kristan Lawson. *Goddess Sites: Europe.* San Francisco: HarperCollins, 1991.

Russell, Diana E. H., ed. *Exposing Nuclear Phallacies.* New York: Pergamon Press, 1989.

Sanday, Peggy Reeves. *Female Power and Male Dominance: On the Origins of Sexual Inequality.* Cambridge: Cambridge University Press, 1981.

Sanday, Peggy Reeves, and Ruth Gallagher Goodenough, eds. *Beyond the Second Sex: New Directions in the Anthropology of Gender.* Philadelphia: University of Pennsylvania Press, 1990.

Schott, Robin May. *Cognition and Eros; A Critique of the Kantian Paradigm.* Boston: Beacon Press, 1988.

Shuttle, Penelope, and Peter Redgrove. *The Wise Wound: Myths, Realities, and Meanings of Menstruation.* New York: Bantam Books, 1990 (1978).

Sjoo, Monica, and Barbara Mor. *The Great Cosmic Mother: Rediscovering the Religion of the Earth.* San Francisco: Harper & Row, 1987.

Spelman, Elizabeth V. *Inessential Woman: Problems of Exclusion in Feminist Thought.* Boston: Beacon Press, 1988.

Spender, Dale. *Man Made Language.* London: Routledge & Kegan Paul, 1980.

Spretnak, Charlene. *Lost Goddesses of Early Greece: A Collection of Pre-Hellenic Myths.* Boston: Beacon Press, 1981 (1978).

———, ed. *The Politics of Women's Spirituality: Essays on the Rise of Spiritual Power within the Feminist Movement.* Garden City, NY: Anchor Press/Doubleday, 1982.

Starhawk. *Dreaming the Dark: Magic, Sex and Politics.* Boston: Beacon Press, 1982.

———. *The Spiral Dance: A Rebirth of the Ancient Religion of the Great Goddess.* San Francisco: Harper & Row, 1989 (1979).

———. *Truth or Dare: Encounters with Power, Authority, and Mystery.* San Francisco: Harper & Row, 1987.

Stern, Karl. *The Flight from Woman.* New York: Paragon House, 1985 (1965).

Stone, Merlin. *Ancient Mirrors of Womanhood: Our Goddess and Heroine Heritage*. Boston: Beacon Press, 1984 (1979).

———. *When God Was A Woman*. New York: Harcourt Brace Jovanovich, 1976.

Suleiman, Susan Rubin, ed. *The Female Body in Western Culture*. Cambridge: Harvard University Press, 1986.

Teish, Luisah. *Jambalaya: The Natural Woman's Book*. San Francisco: Harper & Row, 1985.

Teubal, Savina J. *Sarah the Priestess: The First Matriarch of Genesis*. Athens, OH: Swallow Press, 1984.

Theweleit, Klaus. *Male Fantasies*. Vol. 1, *Women, Floods, Bodies, History*. Minneapolis: University of Minnesota Press, 1987.

Walker, Barbara G. *The Crone: Woman of Age, Wisdom, and Power*. San Francisco: Harper & Row, 1985.

———. *The Woman's Dictionary of Symbols and Sacred Objects*. San Francisco: Harper & Row, 1988.

———. *The Woman's Encyclopedia of Myths and Secrets*. San Francisco: Harper & Row, 1983.

———. *Women's Rituals: A Sourcebook*. San Francisco: Harper & Row, 1990.

Waugh, Patricia. *Feminine Fictions: Revisiting the Postmodern*. London and New York: Routledge, 1989.

Chapter 5 • Who Is the Other?

Berdyaev, Nikolai. *Slavery and Freedom*. New York: Scribner's, 1944.

Berryman, Phillip. *Liberation Theology*. New York: Pantheon Books, 1987.

Boff, Leonardo. *Faith on the Edge: Religion and Marginalized Existence*. San Francisco: Harper & Row, 1989.

Bowker, John. *Problems of Suffering in Religions of the World*. Cambridge: Cambridge University Press, 1970.

Branch, Taylor. *Parting the Waters: America in the King Years, 1954–63*. New York: Simon and Schuster, 1988.

Carawan, Guy and Candie. *Sing for Freedom: The Story of the Civil Rights Movement through Its Songs*. Philadelphia and Santa Cruz, CA: New Society Publishers, 1990.

Carr, Anne E. *Transforming Grace: Christian Tradition and Women's Experience*. San Francisco: Harper & Row, 1988.

Cleary, Edward L. *Crisis and Change: The Church in Latin America Today*. Maryknoll, NY: Orbis Books, 1985.

Cort, John C. *Christian Socialism*. Maryknoll, NY: Orbis Books, 1988.

Daly, Herman E., and John B. Cobb, Jr. *For the Common Good: Redirecting the Economy toward Community, the Environment, and a Sustainable Future*. Boston: Beacon Press, 1989.

Denny, Frederick M. *Islam and the Muslim Community*. San Francisco: Harper & Row, 1987.

Eagleson, John, and Philip Scharper. *Puebla and Beyond*. Maryknoll, NY: Orbis Books, 1979.

Ferguson, John. *The Politics of Love: The New Testament and Nonviolent Revolution*. Nyack, NY: Fellowship Publications, 1979.

Fiorenza, Elisabeth Schüssler. *Bread Not Stone: The Challenge of Feminist Biblical Interpretation*. Boston: Beacon Press, 1984.

———. *In Memory of Her: A Feminist Theological Reconstruction of Christian Origins*. New York: Crossroads, 1983.

Fox, Matthew. *Creation Spirituality: Liberating Gifts for the Peoples of the Earth*. San Francisco: HarperCollins, 1991.

Gilk, Paul. *Nature's Unruly Mob: Farming and the Crisis in Rural Culture*. Millville, MN: North Country Anvil, 1986.

Greeley, Andrew M. *No Bigger than Necessary: An Alternative to Socialism, Capitalism, and Anarchism*. New York: New American Library, 1977.

Gutierrez, Gustavo. *A Theology of Liberation*, Fifteenth Anniversary Edition. Maryknoll, NY: Orbis Books, 1988.

———. *The Truth Shall Make You Free*. Maryknoll, NY: Orbis Books, 1990.

———. *We Drink from Our Own Wells: The Spiritual Journey of a People*. Maryknoll, NY: Orbis Books, 1984.

Harding, Vincent. *Hope and History: Why We Must Share the Story of the Movement*. Maryknoll, NY: Orbis Books, 1990.

Heschel, Susannah, ed. *On Being a Jewish Feminist*. New York: Schocken Books, 1983.

Holland, Joe. *Creative Communion: Toward a Spirituality of Work*. Mahwah, NJ: Paulist Press, 1989.

Holland, Joe, and Peter Heriott. *Social Analysis: Linking Faith and Justice*. Maryknoll, NY: Orbis Books, 1983.

Keating, Thomas. *Open Mind, Open Heart: The Contemplative Dimension of the Gospel*. Warwick, NY: Amity House, 1986.

King, Coretta Scott, ed. *The Words of Martin Luther King, Jr.* New York: Newmarket Press, 1983.

Klagsbrun, Francine. *Voices of Wisdom: Jewish Ideals and Ethics for Everyday Living*. Middle Village, NY: Jonathan David Publishers, 1980.

Knudsen-Hoffman, Gene. *Forming Spiritual Base Communities in the U.S.A.* Madison, WI: InterHelp, 1988.

Lernoux, Penny. *Cry of the People*. Garden City, NY: Doubleday & Co., 1980.

———. *People of God: The Struggle for World Catholicism*. New York: Viking, 1989.

Lohfink, Gerhard. *Jesus and Community*. Philadelphia and New York: Fortress Press and Paulist Press, 1984.

Marshall, Joyce and Gene. *The Reign of Reality*. Dallas: Realistic Living Press, 1987.

McGovern, Arthur F. *Liberation Theology and Its Critics*. Maryknoll, NY: Orbis Books, 1989.

Morris, Aldon D. *The Origins of the Civil Rights Movement: Black Communities Organizing for Change*. New York: Free Press, 1984.

Mott, Stephen Charles. *Biblical Ethics and Social Change*. New York and Oxford: Oxford University Press, 1982.

National Council of Catholic Bishops. *Economic Justice for All: Pastoral Letter on Catholic Social Teaching and the U.S. Economy*. Washington, DC: United States Catholic Conference, 1986.

O'Gorman, Angie, ed. *The Universe Bends toward Justice: A Reader on Christian Nonviolence in the U.S.* Philadelphia and Santa Cruz, CA: New Society Publishers, 1990.

Plaskow, Judith. *Standing Again at Sinai: Judaism from a Feminist Perspective*. San Francisco: Harper & Row, 1990.

Ruether, Rosemary Radford. *Sexism and God-Talk*. Boston: Beacon Press, 1983.

———. *Womanguides*. Boston: Beacon Press, 1985.

Riley, Maria. *Transforming Feminism*. Kansas City, MO: Sheed & Ward, 1989.

Scharper, Philip and Sally, eds. *The Gospel in Art by the Peasants of Solentiname*. Maryknoll, NY: Orbis Books, 1984.

Shiva, Vandana. *Staying Alive: Women, Ecology and Development*. London: Zed Books, 1988.

Sider, Ronald J., ed. *Cry Justice: The Bible on Hunger and Poverty*. Downers Grove, IL: InterVarsity Press, 1980.

Sobrino, Jon, S. J. *Christology at the Crossroads*. Maryknoll, NY: Orbis Books, 1978 (1976).

———. *Spirituality of Liberation: Toward Political Holiness*. Maryknoll, NY: Orbis Books, 1988 (1985).

———. *The True Church and the Poor*. Maryknoll, NY: Orbis Books, 1984 (1981).

Soelle, Dorothee, and Shirley A. Cloyes. *To Work and To Love: A Theology of Creation*. Philadelphia: Fortress Press, 1984.

Tamez, Elsa, ed. *Through Her Eyes: Women's Theology from Latin America*. Maryknoll, NY: Orbis Books, 1989.

Thistlethwaite, Susan Brooks, and Mary Potter Engel, eds. *Lift Every Voice: Constructing Christian Theologies from the Underside*. San Francisco: Harper & Row, 1990.

Wallis, Jim. *Agenda for Biblical People*. San Francisco: Harper & Row, 1984 (1976).

———. *The Rise of Christian Conscience: The Emergence of a Dramatic Renewal Movement in Today's Church*. San Francisco: Harper & Row, 1987.

Washington, James M., ed. *A Testament of Hope: The Essential Writings of Martin Luther King, Jr*. San Francisco: Harper & Row, 1986.

Waskow, Arthur I. *God-Wrestling*. New York: Schocken Books, 1978.

———. *These Holy Sparks: The Rebirth of the Jewish People*. San Francisco: Harper & Row, 1983.

West, Cornel. *Prophetic Fragments*. Grand Rapids, MI: Wm. B. Eerdmans Pub. Co., 1988.

Whyte, William and Kathleen. *Making Mondragon: the Growth and Dynamics of the Worker Cooperative Complex*. Ithaca, NY: Cornell University ILR Press, 1988.

Wink, Walter. *Violence and Nonviolence in South Africa: Jesus' Third Way*. Philadelphia and Santa Cruz, CA: New Society Publishers, 1987.

Chapter 6 • The Recovery of Meaning

Abraham, William J., and Steven W. Holtzer, eds. *The Rationality of Religious Belief: Essays in Honour of Basil Mitchell*. Oxford: Oxford University Press, 1987.

Barreiro, Jose, ed. *Indian Roots of American Democracy. Northeast Indian Quarterly* 4, no. 4, and 5, no. 1. (1988).

Barrett, William. *Death of the Soul: From Descartes to the Computer*. Garden City, NY: Anchor Books/Doubleday, 1986.

———. *The Illusion of Technique: A Search for Meaning in a Technological Civilization*. Garden City, NY: Anchor Books/ Doubleday, 1978.

Batson, C. Daniel, and W. Larry Ventis. *The Religious Experience: A Social-Psychological Perspective*. New York: Oxford University Press, 1982.

Berman, Morris. *The Reenchantment of the World*. Ithaca, NY: Cornell University Press, 1981.

Capra, Fritjof. *The Turning Point: Science, Society, and the Rising Culture*. New York: Simon and Schuster, 1982.

Daly, Mary. *Beyond God the Father*. Boston: Beacon Press, 1973.

Eck, Diane L., and Devaki Jain, eds. *Speaking of Faith: Global Perspectives on Women, Religion, and Social Change*. Philadelphia and Santa Cruz, CA: New Society Publishers, 1987.

Eliade, Mircea. *The Sacred and the Profane: The Nature of Religion*. New York: Harcourt Brace Jovanovich, 1959.

Forman, Robert K. C., ed. *The Problem of Pure Consciousness: Mysticism and Philosophy*. Oxford and New York: Oxford University Press, 1990.

Fox, Matthew. *The Coming of the Cosmic Christ*. San Francisco: Harper & Row, 1988.

Fuller, Andrew R. *Insight into Value: An Exploration of the Premises of a Phenomenological Psychology*. Albany: State University of New York Press, 1990.

Goleman, Daniel. *The Varieties of the Meditative Experience*. New York: E. P. Dutton, 1977.

Hardy, Alister. *The Spiritual Nature of Man: A Study of Contemporary Religious Experience*. Oxford: Oxford University Press, 1979.

James, William. *The Varieties of Religious Experience: A Study of Human Nature*. New York: Collier Books, 1961 (1902).

Katz, Steven T., ed. *Mysticism and Philosophical Analysis*. Oxford and New York: Oxford University Press, 1978.

Levin, David Michael. *The Body's Recollection of Being: Phenomenological Psychology and the Deconstruction of Nihilism*. London: Routledge & Kegan Paul, 1985.

Lipsey, Roger. *An Art of Our Own: The Spiritual in Twentieth-Century Art*. Boston: Shambhala Publications, 1988.

McKnight, Stephen A. *Sacralizing the Secular: The Renaissance Origins of Modernity*. Baton Rouge: Louisiana University Press, 1989.

Mistry, Freny. *Nietzsche and Buddhism.* Berlin and New York: De Gruyter, 1981.

Nasr, Seyyed Hossein. *Knowledge and the Sacred.* New York: Crossroad, 1981.

Needleman, Jacob. *A Sense of the Cosmos: The Encounter of Modern Science and Ancient Truth.* Garden City, NY: Doubleday & Co., 1975.

Neville, Robert Cummings. *Recovery of the Measure: Interpretation and Nature.* Albany: State University of New York Press, 1989.

Oliver, Donald W., with Kathleen Waldron Gershman. *Education, Modernity, and Fractured Meaning.* Albany: State University of New York Press, 1989.

Smith, Huston. *Beyond the Post-Modern Mind.* Wheaton, IL: Theosophical Publishing House, 1989.

Soskice, Janet Martin. *Metaphor and Religious Language.* Oxford: Oxford University Press, 1985.

Swidler, Leonard, ed. *Toward a Universal Theology of Religion.* Maryknoll, NY: Orbis Books, 1987.

Tuchman, Maurice, et al. *The Spiritual in Art: Abstract Painting, 1890–1985.* Los Angeles and New York: Los Angeles County Museum of Art and Abbeville Press, 1986.

Whitehead, Alfred North. *Process and Reality,* corr. ed. Edited by David Ray Griffin and Donald W. Sherburne. New York: Free Press, 1978 (1929).

Wiber, Ken, ed., with Ann Niehaus. *Quantum Questions: Mystical Writings of the World's Great Physicists.* Boulder, CO: Shambhala Publications, 1984.

Woods, Richard. *Understanding Mysticism.* Garden City, NY: Image Books/Doubleday, 1980.

Zaehner, R. C. *Mysticism, Sacred and Profane.* Oxford: Oxford University Press, 1957.

Appendix A • The Merely Relative: A Brief Survey of Deconstructive Postmodernism

Alter, Robert. *The Pleasures of Reading in an Ideological Age.* New York: Simon & Schuster, 1989.

Anderson, Walter Truett. *Reality Isn't What It Used to Be.* San Francisco: Harper & Row, 1990.

Baudrillard, Jean. *For a Critique of the Political Economy of the Sign.* St. Louis: Telos Press, 1981.

———. *The Mirror of Production.* St. Louis: Telos Press, 1975.

Benjamin, Andrew, ed. *The Lyotard Reader*. Oxford and Cambridge, MA: Basil Blackwell, 1989.

Connor, Steve. *Postmodern Culture: An Introduction to Theories of the Contemporary*. Oxford and New York: Basil Blackwell, 1989.

Crews, Frederick. *Skeptical Engagements*. New York: Oxford University Press, 1986.

Derrida, Jacques. *Disseminations*. Chicago: University of Chicago Press, 1981.

———. *Of Grammatology*. Baltimore: Johns Hopkins University Press, 1976.

———. *On Spirit: Heidegger and the Question*. Chicago: University of Chicago Press, 1989.

———. *Positions*. Chicago: University of Chicago Press, 1981.

———. *Writing and Difference*. Chicago: University of Chicago Press, 1978.

Diamond, Irene, and Lee Quinby, eds. *Feminism and Foucault: Reflections on Resistance*. Boston: Northeastern University Press, 1988.

Ellis, John M. *Against Deconstruction*. Princeton: Princeton University Press, 1989.

Foucault, Michel. *The Archaeology of Knowledge*. New York: Irvington Publications, 1972.

———. *The History of Sex*. 3 vols. New York: Random House, 1978, 1985, 1986.

———. *The Order of Things: An Archaeology of the Human Sciences*. New York: Random House, 1970.

Fuss, Diana. *Essentially Speaking: Feminism, Nature, and Difference*. New York: Routledge, 1989.

Gordon, Colin, ed. *Power/Knowledge: Selected Interviews and Other Writings by Michel Foucault, 1972–1977*. New York: Pantheon, 1980.

Harvey, David. *The Condition of Postmodernity*. Oxford and Cambridge, MA: Basil Blackwell, 1989.

Hassan, Ihab. *The Dismemberment of Orpheus: Toward a Postmodern Literature*. New York: Oxford University Press, 1971.

Huyssen, Andreas. *After the Great Divide: Modernism, Mass Culture, Postmodernism*. Bloomington, IN: Indiana University Press, 1986.

Jencks, Charles. *What Is Postmodernism?* New York: St. Martin's Press, 1986.

Kroker, Arthur and Marilouise. *Body Invaders: Panic Sex in America.* New York: St. Martin's Press, 1987.

Lyotard, Jean-François. *The Postmodern Condition: A Report on Knowledge.* Minneapolis: University of Minnesota Press, 1984.

Maturana, Humberto R., and Francisco J. Varela. *The Tree of Knowledge: The Biological Roots of Human Understanding.* Boston: Shambhala Publications, 1987.

Nicholson, Linda J., ed. *Feminism/Postmodernism.* New York: Routledge, 1990.

Poster, Mark, ed. *Jean Baudrillard: Selected Writings.* Stanford, CA: Stanford University Press, 1988.

Rabinow, Paul, ed. *The Foucault Reader.* New York: Pantheon Books, 1984.

Rorty, Richard. *Contingency, Irony, and Solidarity.* Cambridge: Cambridge University Press, 1989.

Ross, Andrew, ed. *Universal Abandon? The Politics of Postmodernism.* Minneapolis: University of Minnesota Press, 1988.

Watzlawick, Paul, ed. *The Invented Reality: How Do We Know What We Believe We Know? (Contributions to Constructivism).* New York: W. W. Norton, 1984.

Wyschogrod, Edith, David Crownfield, and Carl A. Raschke. *Lacan and Theological Discourse.* Albany: State University of New York Press, 1989.

Appendix B • A Feminist Consideration of the Philosophical Roots and Attractions of Deconstructive Postmodernism

Arato, Andrew, and Eike Gebhardt, eds. *The Essential Frankfurt School Reader.* New York: Continuum, 1982.

Barrett, William. *Irrational Man: A Study in Existential Philosophy.* Garden City, NY: Anchor/Doubleday, 1958.

Bronner, Stephen E., and Douglas M. Kellner, eds. *Critical Theory and Society.* New York and London: Routledge, 1989.

Cantor, Norman F. *Twentieth Century Culture: Modernism to Deconstruction.* New York: Peter Lang Publishers, 1989.

Cassirer, Ernst. *The Philosophy of the Enlightenment.* Princeton: Princeton University Press, 1951.

Cassirer, Ernst, Paul O. Kristeller, and John H. Randall, Jr., eds. *The Renaissance Philosophy of Man.* Chicago: University of Chicago Press, 1948.

Horkheimer, Max, and Theodor T. Adorno. *Dialectic of Enlightenment.* New York: Seabury, 1972.

Lloyd, Genevieve. *The Man of Reason: "Male" and "Female" in Western Philosophy*. Minneapolis: University of Minnesota Press, 1984.

Mills, Patricia Jagentowicz. *Woman, Nature, and Psyche*. New Haven, CT: Yale University Press, 1987.

Patrick, G. T. W. *Heraclitus of Ephesus*. Chicago: Argonaut, 1969.

Randall, John Herman, Jr. *The Making of the Modern Mind: A Survey of the Intellectual Background of the Present Age*. New York: Columbia University Press, 1976 (1926).

Index

About the Author

Charlene Spretnak was born in Pittsburgh and raised in Columbus, Ohio. She holds degrees from St. Louis University and the University of California at Berkeley. Her work has contributed to the framing of the women's spirituality, ecofeminist, and Green politics movements. She is author of *Lost Goddesses of Early Greece* and *The Spiritual Dimension of Green Politics*, coauthor of *Green Politics*, and editor of an anthology, *The Politics of Women's Spirituality*.